OXFORD INTERNATIONAL ARBITRATION SERIES

Series Editor: LOUKAS MISTELIS
*Professor of Transnational Commercial Law and Arbitration,
Queen Mary, University of London*

The Concept of Investment in ICSID Arbitration

OXFORD INTERNATIONAL ARBITRATION SERIES

Series Editor: LOUKAS MISTELIS

The aim of this series is to publish works of quality and originality on specific issues in international commercial and investment arbitration. The series aims to provide a forum for the exploration of important emerging issues and those issues not adequately dealt with in leading works. It should be of interest to both practitioners and scholarly lawyers.

Editorial Board

PROFESSOR ANDREA K. BJORKLUND
L. Yves Fortier Chair in International Arbitration and International Commercial Law, McGill University

PROFESSOR LAWRENCE BOO
Resident, The Arbitration Chambers, Singapore

TERESA CHENG
Des Voeux Chambers, Hong Kong

LAWRENCE COLLINS, LORD COLLINS OF MAPESBURY
Professor, University College London
Honorary and Emeritus Fellow, Wolfson College, Cambridge

PAUL FRIEDLAND
Global Head, International Arbitration Practice Group, White & Case LLP, New York

PROFESSOR HANS VAN HOUTTE
Director of the Institute for International Trade Law, University of Louvain (KU Leuven)

PROFESSOR CATHERINE KESSEDJIAN
Professor of European Business Law and International Dispute Resolution, University of Panthéon-Assas, Paris II

PROFESSOR VAUGHAN LOWE
Essex Court Chambers, London, and Emeritus Fellow of All Souls College, Oxford

PROFESSOR FRANCISCO ORREGO VICUÑA
Professor of Law, Heidelberg University Center for Latin America, Santiago

PROFESSOR WILLIAM W. PARK
Professor of Law, Boston University

The Concept of Investment in ICSID Arbitration

MARKUS PETSCHE

Great Clarendon Street, Oxford, OX2 6DP,
United Kingdom

Oxford University Press is a department of the University of Oxford.
It furthers the University's objective of excellence in research, scholarship,
and education by publishing worldwide. Oxford is a registered trade mark of
Oxford University Press in the UK and in certain other countries

© Markus Petsche 2024

The moral rights of the author have been asserted

First Edition published in 2024

All rights reserved. No part of this publication may be reproduced, stored in
a retrieval system, or transmitted, in any form or by any means, without the
prior permission in writing of Oxford University Press, or as expressly permitted
by law, by licence or under terms agreed with the appropriate reprographics
rights organization. Enquiries concerning reproduction outside the scope of the
above should be sent to the Rights Department, Oxford University Press, at the
address above

You must not circulate this work in any other form
and you must impose this same condition on any acquirer

Public sector information reproduced under Open Government Licence v3.0
(http://www.nationalarchives.gov.uk/doc/open-government-licence/open-government-licence.htm)

Published in the United States of America by Oxford University Press
198 Madison Avenue, New York, NY 10016, United States of America

British Library Cataloguing in Publication Data

Data available

Library of Congress Control Number: 2023946870

ISBN 978–0–19–887760–8

DOI: 10.1093/law-iic/9780198877608.001.0001

Printed and bound by
CPI Group (UK) Ltd, Croydon, CR0 4YY

Links to third party websites are provided by Oxford in good faith and
for information only. Oxford disclaims any responsibility for the materials
contained in any third party website referenced in this work.

General Editor's Preface

This series of monographs is dedicated to specific issues in international arbitration law and practice and gives authors the opportunity and the challenge of a more in-depth treatment than is possible in leading generalist works. It also provides an international forum for the profound exploration of important practical and theoretical matters and will further the development of arbitration as a self-luminous academic discipline and major international legal practice area.

This twenty-fifth title in the series is a monograph by an experienced academic and practitioner which provides a comprehensive analysis of the scholarship and the case law of investment treaty arbitral tribunals on the concept of investment in ICSID arbitration. This is a challenging and pervasive topic given that the drafters of the ICSID Convention decided not to define the concept of investment, notwithstanding the fact that it is one of the pillars of jurisdiction pursuant to Article 25 of the ICSID Convention. Inevitably, this lacuna has been addressed by many international investment agreements which contain their own definition of investment. At the same time there has been a larger debate about an autonomous notion of investment in the ICSID Convention. Hence, investment arbitration tribunals and commentators have extensively discussed the topic over the years. It appears that the broader consensus is that there is a duality in this notion: investors will have to prove that they have a covered investment under both the ICSID convention and the other applicable international investment agreement. There are, however, many variations and nuances in these approaches.

Professor Markus Petsche offers, in this monograph, 'a comprehensive and holistic examination of all legal issues arising in connection with the jurisdictional threshold of the existence of an investment in ICSID arbitration, covering all ... categories of legal instruments'. He consistently examines treaties, national laws, and arbitral case law and provides both a historical and current state of affairs perspective.

The book is organized into nine substantive chapters, with Chapter 1 being introduction and Chapter 9, conclusion. Chapter 2 provides the context (via a series of preliminary matters) in which the question of the existence of an investment arises in ICSID arbitration. Chapters 3 and 4 explore Article 25 of the ICSID Convention focusing on the autonomous nature of the notion.

Chapters 5 and 6 address definitions of investment contained in international investment agreements, discussing traditional asset-based definitions, common features found in treaty definitions, and recent developments in treaty and arbitral practice.

Chapter 7 discusses definitions in investment laws and contrasts them with definitions in international investment agreements.

Chapter 8 discusses categories of assets and transactions typically classified as investment and looks at controversial cases.

In the concluding chapter, Chapter 9, Professor Markus Petsche sets the agenda for future discussions and explores the contours of uniformity.

This is a detailed analysis of the concept of investment and focuses not only on case law but also on treaties, national law, and scholarly writings. It is focused in its scope and thorough in its research and analysis. Most importantly, it is also accessible and authoritative and hence it is a very useful text for arbitration practitioners and scholars alike.

LM
Virginia Water, 29 September 2023

Contents

Table of Cases xi
Table of Legislation xvii

1. Introduction 1
    I. Importance of the Concept of Investment 1.01
    II. Complexity of the Concept of Investment 1.04
    III. Existing Literature 1.10
    IV. Object and Purpose of this Book 1.16
    V. Scope of this Book 1.18

2. Preliminary Matters 9
    I. Introduction 2.01
    II. Practical Relevance of the Concept of Investment 2.02
        A. Relevance for the jurisdiction of ICSID tribunals 2.02
        B. Relevance for the assessment of damages 2.10
    III. Procedural Settings in Which the Question of the Existence of an Investment Arises 2.13
        A. Jurisdictional objections 2.14
        B. *Ex officio* examination of jurisdiction 2.17
        C. Screening of requests for arbitration by ICSID's Secretary General 2.19
    IV. Applicable Law 2.21
    V. The Concept of Investment as an Interpretive Issue 2.26
    VI. Ordinary Meaning of the Term 'Investment' 2.33
    VII. Meaning of the Economic Concept of Investment 2.39
    VIII. The Nature of Investment 2.45
    IX. Interests Involved in Defining the Concept of Investment 2.54
        A. Investor and host State interests 2.54
        B. Systemic interests 2.59

3. The Question of Whether Art 25 ICSID Convention Lays Down Independent Requirements for the Existence of an Investment 28
    I. Introduction 3.01
    II. Conceptual Framework 3.02
        A. Prevailing conceptualization 3.02
        B. Critical analysis of the prevailing conceptualization 3.06
        C. Reframing the question: does the term 'investment' under Art 25 ICSID Convention have an 'implied' or 'independent' meaning? 3.14
        D. Terminology used in this book 3.16
    III. Arbitral Case Law 3.18
        A. Silent and inconclusive decisions 3.18
        B. Decisions holding that Art 25 ICSID Convention lays down independent requirements for the existence of an investment 3.21

	C. Decisions holding that Art 25 ICSID Convention does not lay down independent requirements for the existence of an investment	3.44
	D. Decisions adopting the ambivalent typical-characteristics approach	3.55
IV.	Scholarly Opinions	3.63
	A. Broad support for the existence of independent requirements under Art 25 ICSID Convention	3.63
	B. Limited support for the absence of independent requirements under Art 25 ICSID Convention	3.71
V.	Assessment	3.77
	A. Objective approach	3.77
	B. Subjective approach	3.84

4. The Meaning of Investment Under Art 25 ICSID Convention — 56

I.	Introduction	4.01
II.	The *Salini* Test	4.02
	A. History, evolution, and nature of the *Salini* test	4.02
	B. The three core *Salini* criteria: contribution, duration, and risk	4.14
	C. The controversial criterion of a contribution to the economic development of the host State	4.39
	D. Other criteria	4.50
	E. Critical assessment	4.59
III.	The Permissibility Test	4.65
	A. Meaning and recognition	4.65
	B. Assessment	4.72
IV.	The Commercial-Transaction Test	4.78
	A. Meaning and recognition	4.78
	B. Assessment	4.88
V.	Principal Scholarly Debates and Viewpoints	4.93
	A. Nature of the *Salini* test	4.93
	B. Core *Salini* criteria	4.96
	C. Requirement of a contribution to the host State's economic development	4.102

5. The Concept of Investment in Investment Treaties: Traditional Definitions and Typical Requirements — 90

I.	Introduction	5.01
II.	The Traditional Model: Broad, Asset-Based Definitions	5.03
	A. Asset-based definitions	5.03
	B. Broad definitions	5.12
III.	Ownership or Control of the Investment	5.18
	A. Overview	5.18
	B. Direct ownership	5.22
	C. Indirect ownership	5.29
	D. Control	5.34
IV.	Localization of the Investment in the Territory of the Host State (Territoriality)	5.38
	A. Treaty practice	5.38
	B. Localization of different categories of assets	5.45
	C. Case law	5.50
V.	Legality of the Investment	5.67
	A. Legality provisions in investment treaties	5.67
	B. Meaning of legality	5.72
	C. Legality beyond investment treaties	5.82

VI. Requirement that the Investment be 'Actively' Made by the Investor		5.86
A. Overview		5.86
B. Textual foundations of the requirement		5.88
C. Recognition and meaning of the requirement		5.92
D. Assessment of the requirement		5.96
E. Requirement of an active investment under Art 25 ICSID Convention?		5.100

6. Recent Developments in Treaty and Arbitral Practice — 121

- I. Introduction — 6.01
- II. Enterprise-Based Definitions of Investment — 6.04
- III. Requirement that an Investment must Present Certain 'Characteristics' — 6.12
  - A. Meaning and trend — 6.12
  - B. Comparison with the *Salini* criteria — 6.16
  - C. Assessment — 6.20
- IV. Exclusions — 6.25
  - A. Commercial transactions — 6.25
  - B. Portfolio investments — 6.30
  - C. Assets not connected to any economic or business activity — 6.36
  - D. Sovereign debt instruments — 6.39
- V. Arbitral Recognition of an 'Objective' or 'Implied' Meaning of the Concept of Investment under Investment Treaties — 6.42
  - A. Overview — 6.42
  - B. Decisions rendered by non-ICSID tribunals — 6.44
  - C. Decisions rendered by ICSID tribunals — 6.54
  - D. Assessment — 6.66

7. Definitions of Investment in Investment Laws — 142

- I. Introduction — 7.01
- II. Asset-Based Definitions — 7.07
- III. Enterprise-Based Definitions — 7.11
  - A. Types of definitions — 7.11
  - B. Meaning of 'enterprise' — 7.16
  - C. Conclusions — 7.21
- IV. Activity- and Project-Based Definitions — 7.24
  - A. Definitions — 7.24
  - B. Conclusions — 7.29
- V. Requirement of a Capital Investment — 7.32
- VI. Requirement of a Contribution to the Host State's Economic Development — 7.36
- VII. Case Law — 7.43

8. Investment Status of Specific Categories of Assets and Operations — 158

- I. Introduction — 8.01
- II. Construction and Service Contracts Concluded with the Host State or a Host State Entity — 8.04
  - A. Overview — 8.04
  - B. Construction contracts — 8.07
  - C. Contracts for the provision of services — 8.13
  - D. Critical assessment — 8.16
- III. Debt Instruments — 8.23
  - A. Preliminary observations — 8.23
  - B. Sovereign bonds — 8.27
  - C. Loans — 8.38

IV. Arbitral Awards and Court Judgments	8.50
A. The terms of the problem	8.50
B. Case law	8.56
V. Funds 'Invested'	8.65
9. Conclusion	**182**
I. Summary of Principal Findings	9.01
II. The Way Forward	9.12
Index	189

Table of Cases

INTERNATIONAL CENTRE FOR SETTLEMENT OF INVESTMENT DISPUTES (ICSID)

Abaclat and others v Argentine Republic, ICSID Case No ARB/07/5, Decision on
  Jurisdiction and Admissibility (4 August 2011) 2.28, 5.25, 5.62–5.65, 6.41, 8.29,
                                                                                    8.33–8.35
ACP Axos Capital GmbH v Republic of Kosovo, ICSID Case No ARB/15/22,
  Award (3 May 2018).. 3.19, 5.47
Adel A Hamadi Al Tamimi v Sultanate of Oman, ICSID Case No ARB/11/33,
  Award (3 November 2015) 3.18, 3.46
Alcoa Minerals of Jamaica Inc. v Jamaica, ICSID Case No ARB/74/2,
  Decision on Jurisdiction and Competence (6 July 1975) 3.37
Álvarez y Marín Corporación S.A. v Republic of Panama, ICSID Case
  No ARB/15/14, Award (12 October 2018) 5.71
Ambiente Ufficio S.P.A. and others v Argentine Republic, ICSID Case No ARB/08/9,
  Decision on Jurisdiction and Admissibility (8 February 2013) 6.41, 8.29, 8.34–8.35, 8.37
Anglo-Adriatic Group Ltd v Republic of Albania, ICSID Case No ARB/17/6,
  Award (7 February 2019) 3.18, 5.23, 7.51, 7.54
ATA Construction, Industrial and Trading Co v Hashemite Kingdom of Jordan,
  ICSID Case No ARB/08/2, Award (18 May 2010) 3.44, 3.53

Bayindir Insaat Turizm Ticaret Ve Sanayi A.Ş. v Islamic Republic of Pakistan,
  ICSID Case No ARB/03/29, Decision on Jurisdiction (14 November 2005) 4.23, 4.44,
                                                                                  8.07–8.12, 8.71
Bear Creek Mining Corporation v Republic of Peru, ICSID Case No ARB/14/21,
  Award (30 November 2017) 5.71
Biwater Gauff (Tanzania) Ltd v United Republic of Tanzania, ICSID Case
  No ARB/05/22, Award (24 July 2008) 3.58, 3.60–3.61
Bureau Veritas, Inspection, Valuation, Assessment and Control, BIVAC B.V. v
  Republic of Paraguay, ICSID Case No ARB/07/9, Decision of the Tribunal
  on Objections to Jurisdiction (29 May 2009) 4.68–4.70, 4.73, 8.35

Caratube Interntional Oil Co LLP v Republic of Kazakhstan, ICSID Case
  No ARB/08/12, Award (5 June 2012)... 5.100
Ceskoslovenska Obchodni Banka, A.S. v Slovak Republic, ICSID Case No ARB/97/4,
  Decision of the Tribunal on Objections to Jurisdiction (24 May 1999)...... 3.21, 3.41, 3.56, 8.45
CMC Muratori Cementisti CMC Di Ravenna Soc. Coop. and others v Mozambique,
  ICSID Case No ARB/17/23, Award (24 October 2019)................... 3.21, 3.37, 4.71, 4.73
CMS Gas Transmission Co v Argentine Republic, ICSID Case No ARB/01/8,
  Decision of the Tribunal on Objections to Jurisdiction (17 July 2003) 3.52
CMS Gas Transmission Co v Argentine Republic, ICSID Case No ARB/01/8,
  Decision of the Ad Hoc Committee on the Application for Annulment of the
  Argentine Republic (25 September 2007).. 3.44, 3.54
Consorzio Groupement L.E.S.I.—DIPENTA v Democratic and Popular
  Republic of Algeria, ICSID Case No ARB/03/08, Award
  (10 January 2005)............. 3.21, 3.37, 4.21–4.22, 4.33, 4.46, 4.48–4.49, 8.07, 8.09–8.10, 8.12

TABLE OF CASES

Cortec Mining Kenya Ltd and others v Republic of Kenya, ICSID Case No ARB/15/29,
　　Award (22 October 2018) 3.21, 3.37, 4.38, 4.40

Dan Cake (Portugal) S.A. v Hungary, ICSID Case No ARB/12/9,
　　Decision on Jurisdiction and Liability (24 August 2015) 2.17–2.18, 5.22
Deutsche Bank AG v Democratic Socialist Republic of Sri Lanka, ICSID
　　Case No ARB/09/02, Award (31 October 2012)...... 4.14, 4.16, 4.22, 4.30, 4.32, 4.45–4.48, 4.53,
　　　　　　　　　　　　　　　　　　　　　　　　　　　　　　　　　　5.63–5.65, 8.14
Enron Corporation and Ponderosa Assets, L.P. v Argentine Republic,
　　ICSID Case No ARB/01/3, Decision on Jurisdiction (14 January 2004) 5.33

Fedax N.V. v Republic of Venezuela, ICSID Case No ARB/96/3, Decision of the
　　Tribunal on Objections to Jurisdiction (11 July 1997)..... 3.38, 3.49, 4.02–4.03, 4.08, 4.10, 4.14,
　　　　　　　　　　　　　　　　　　　　　　4.23–4.24, 4.39, 4.44, 4.50–4.51, 5.22,
　　　　　　　　　　　　　　　　　　　　　　5.59, 5.61–5.62, 5.64–5.66, 6.16, 9.03
Fraport AG Frankfurt Services Worldwide v Republic of the Philippines (II),
　　ICSID Case No ARB/11/12, Award (10 December 2014) 5.71

Garanti Koza LLP v Turkmenistan, ICSID Case No ARB/11/20, Award
　　(19 December 2016) 3.21, 3.30, 3.46, 4.70–4.71, 4.73, 4.76, 8.07–8.09
GEA Group Aktiengesellschaft v Ukraine, ICSID Case No ARB/08/16,
　　Award (31 March 2011) 1.03, 3.19, 6.54, 6.57–6.59, 6.61, 6.65–6.67, 6.69–6.70, 8.56
Generation Ukraine, Inc. v Ukraine, ICSID Case No ARB/00/9,
　　Award (16 September 2003) 3.44
Giovanni Alemanni and others v Argentine Republic, ICSID Case No ARB/07/8,
　　Decision on Jurisdiction and Admissibility (17 November 2014) 8.29, 8.35
Global Trading Resource Corp. and others v Ukraine, ICSID Case No ARB/09/11,
　　Award (1 December 2010) 1.03, 2.16, 2.26, 3.21, 3.37, 3.43, 4.79, 4.86, 6.61

Hassan Awdi and others v Romania, ICSID Case No ARB/10/13,
　　Award (2 March 2015)... 5.36

Inceysa Vallisoletana, S.L. v Republic of El Salvador, ICSID Case No ARB/03/26,
　　Award (2 August 2006) 2.06, 5.73, 5.75, 5.82
Inmaris Perestroika Sailing Maritime Services GmbH and others v Ukraine,
　　ICSID Case No ARB/08/8, Decision on Jurisdiction (8 March 2010) 3.44–3.45, 5.43
Interocean Oil Development Co and Interocean Oil Exploration Co v Federal
　　Republic of Nigeria, ICSID Case No ARB/13/20, Award (6 October 2020) 7.43
Ioannis Kardassopoulos v Georgia, ICSID Case No ARB/05/18, Decision on
　　Jurisdiction (6 July 2007) 5.81
Italba Corporation v Oriental Republic of Uruguay, ICSID Case No ARB/16/9,
　　Award (22 March 2019)... 3.18, 5.23, 5.47

Jan de Nul N.V. and Dredging International N.V. v Arab Republic of Egypt,
　　ICSID Case No. ARB/04/13, Decision on Jurisdiction (16 June 2006) 4.23
Joy Mining Machinery Ltd v Arab Republic of Egypt, ICSID Case No ARB/03/11,
　　Award on Jurisdiction (6 August 2004)................ 1.03, 3.03, 3.21, 3.27, 3.36, 3.42–3.43,
　　　　　　　　　　　　　　　　　　　　　　　　　　　　4.44, 4.50, 4.79, 4.82, 4.86

KT Asia Investment Group B.V. v Republic of Kazakhstan, ICSID Case No ARB/09/8,
　　Award (17 October 2013) 5.100

Lighthouse Corporation Pty Ltd and Lighthouse Corporation Ltd, Ibc v Democratic
　　Republic of Timor-Leste, ICSID Case No ARB/15/2, Award (22 December 2017).......... 7.43

TABLE OF CASES   xiii

Magyar Farming Co Ltd and others v Hungary, ICSID Case No ARB/17/27,
    Award (13 November 2019) 2.17–2.18
Makae Europe Sarl v Kingdom of Saudi Arabia, ICSID Case No ARB/17/42,
    Award (30 August 2021) 3.18
Malaysian Historical Salvors Sdn, Bhd v Government of Malaysia,
    ICSID Case No ARB/05/10, Award on Jurisdiction (17 May 2007)............. 1.03, 3.21, 3.31,
                                                                        3.37–3.38, 3.57, 4.13, 4.23,
                                                                        4.28–4.29, 4.34, 4.44,
                                                                        4.50, 4.79, 4.103, 8.15
Malaysian Historical Salvors Sdn, Bhd v Government of Malaysia, ICSID Case
    No ARB/05/10, Decision on the Application for Annulment
    (16 April 2009).............................3.03, 3.21, 3.31–3.32, 3.34, 3.44, 4.80, 4.86, 8.15
Marco Gavazzi and Stefano Gavazzi v Romania, ICSID Case No ARB/12/25,
    Decision on Jurisdiction, Admissibility and Liability (21 April 2015) 8.55, 8.62
M.C.I. Power Group, L.C. and New Turbine, Inc., v Republic of Ecuador,
    ICSID Case No ARB/03/6, Award (31 July 2007)...................................3.44, 3.50
Menzies Middle East and Africa S.A. and Aviation Handling Services International Ltd v
    Republic of Senegal, ICSID Case No ARB/15/21, Award (5 August 2016).................7.43
MNSS B.V. and Recupero Credito Acciaio N.V. v Montenegro,
    ICSID Case No ARB(AF)/12/8, Award (4 May 2016) 4.19, 4.22, 4.25–4.26, 4.43,
                                                                        7.43, 8.40, 8.44
Mr. Patrick H. Mitchell v Democratic Republic of Congo,
    ICSID Case No ARB/99/7, Award (9 February 2004) 2.52, 3.03, 3.20, 6.57
Mr. Patrick Mitchell v Democratic Republic of Congo, ICSID Case No ARB/99/7,
    Decision on the Application for Annulment of the Award
    (1 November 2006) 1.03, 4.40–4.42, 4.44, 4.66, 4.74
Mr. Saba Fakes v Republic of Turkey, ICSID Case No ARB/07/20, Award
    (14 July 2010) 3.03, 3.21, 3.29, 3.36, 4.16, 4.22, 4.46–4.47, 4.53, 4.56, 5.23, 5.26, 5.28, 5.47

Nova Scotia Power Incorporated (Canada) v Bolivarian Republic of Venezuela,
    ICSID Case No ARB(AF)/11/1, Award (30 April 2014) 1.03, 6.48–6.49, 6.52

Occidental Petroleum Corporation and Occidental Exploration and Production Co v
    Republic of Ecuador, ICSID Case No ARB/06/11, Decision on Annulment of the
    Award (2 November 2015) 5.24–5.25, 5.27
Oded Besserglik v Republic of Mozambique, ICSID Case No ARB(AF)/14/2,
    Award (28 October 2019) 7.43
Orascom TMT Investments S.à.r.l. v People's Democratic Republic of Algeria,
    ICSID Case No ARB/12/35, Award (31 May 2017) 5.95

Pac Rim Cayman LLC v Republic of El Salvador, ICSID Case No ARB/09/12,
    Decision on the Respondent's Jurisdictional Objections (1 June 2012) 7.43
Parkerings-Compagniet AS v Republic of Lithuania, ICSID Case No ARB/05/8,
    Award (11 September 2007)..3.44–3.45
Pawlowski AG and Projekt Sever s.r.o. v Czech Republic, ICSID Case No ARB/17/11,
    Award (1 November 2021) 4.89
Philippe Gruslin v Malaysia, ICSID Case No ARB/99/3, Award (27 November 2000) 3.44, 3.54
Phoenix Action, Ltd v Czech Republic, ICSID Case No ARB/06/5,
    Award (15 April 2009)......................... 4.26, 4.32, 4.40, 4.43, 4.55–4.56, 5.84, 6.57
Poštová banka, a.s. and Istrokapital SE v Hellenic Republic, ICSID Case No ARB/13/8,
    Award (9 April 2015)................. 1.03, 3.19, 4.18–4.19, 4.22, 4.25, 4.37–4.38, 4.87, 6.41,
                                                                        8.30–8.31, 8.36, 8.39–8.40, 8.48
PSEG Global Inc. and others v Turkey, ICSID Case No ARB/02/5,
    Decision on Jurisdiction (4 June 2004) 1.03, 3.18

xiv   TABLE OF CASES

Quiborax S.A. and others v Plurinational State of Bolivia, ICSID Case No ARB/06/2,
    Decision on Jurisdiction (27 September 2012). 3.15, 4.46, 6.59, 6.62, 6.65

Raymond Charles Eyre and others v Democratic Socialist Republic of Sri Lanka,
    ICSID Case No ARB/16/25, Award (5 March 2020) 1.03, 4.19, 4.22, 4.25, 4.37, 4.45, 5.47,
                                                                                    6.63, 6.65, 8.40

Saipem S.p.A. v People's Republic of Bangladesh, ICSID Case No ARB/05/07, Decision on
    Jurisdiction and Recommendation on Provisional Measures (21 March 2007). 8.59, 8.61
Salini Costruttori S.P.A. and Italstrade S.P.A. v Kingdom of Morocco,
    ICSID Case No ARB/00/4, Decision on Jurisdiction (23 July 2001) 1.09–1.10, 1.13–1.15,
            2.25, 2.28, 2.50, 2.58, 2.60, 3.21, 3.24, 3.30, 3.37–3.38, 3.46, 3.55, 3.58–3.59, 3.62–3.63,
                3.72, 3.75, 4.01–4.02, 4.07–4.18, 4.20, 4.22–4.23, 4.25–4.26, 4.28–4.29, 4.31–4.33,
                4.35, 4.38–4.41, 4.44–4.45, 4.49–4.50, 4.53–4.56, 4.59–4.64, 4.66–4.67, 4.70–4.73,
                4.78, 4.80–4.88, 4.92–4.96, 4.98, 4.100–4.101, 4.103, 4.105, 5.04, 5.22, 5.49, 5.56,
                    5.100, 6.02–6.03, 6.16–6.24, 6.28–6.29, 6.41, 6.53, 6.64, 6.66–6.67, 7.33, 8.02,
                        8.04, 8.07–8.14, 8.17, 8.19, 8.22, 8.24–8.25, 8.32–8.34, 8.40, 8.44, 8.49,
                            8.51, 8.58, 8.61, 8.69, 8.72, 9.01, 9.03–9.08, 9.11, 9.13
SGS Société Générale de Surveillance S.A. v Islamic Republic of Pakistan,
    ICSID Case No ARB/01/13, Decision of the Tribunal on Objections to
    Jurisdiction (6 August 2003). 3.44, 3.53, 8.13, 8.18
SGS Société Générale de Surveillance S.A. v Republic of Paraguay,
    ICSID Case No ARB/07/29, Decision on Jurisdiction
    (12 February 2010) 5.55–5.56, 4.69–4.70, 4.73, 8.13, 8.18
SGS Société Générale de Surveillance S.A. v Republic of the Philippines,
    ICSID Case No ARB/02/6, Decision of the Tribunal on Objections
    to Jurisdiction (29 January 2004). 3.44–3.45, 5.52, 5.54–5.56, 5.66, 8.18
Société Resort Company Invest Abidjan and others v Republic of Côte d'Ivoire,
    ICSID Case No ARB/16/11, Decision on Respondent's Preliminary Objection to
    Jurisdiction (1 August 2017). 7.43
Standard Chartered Bank v United Republic of Tanzania, ICSID
    Case No ARB/10/12, Award (2 November 2012). 1.03, 5.92–5.93, 5.96–5.98, 8.43
Standard Chartered Bank (Hong Kong) Ltd v United Republic of Tanzania,
    ICSID Case No ARB/15/41, Award (11 October 2019). 3.59, 8.07

Tethyan Copper Co Pty Ltd v Islamic Republic of Pakistan, ICSID Case
    No ARB/12/1, Decision on Jurisdiction and Liability (10 November 2017). 3.18, 3.46
Theodoros Adamakopoulos and others v Republic of Cyprus, ICSID
    Case No ARB/15/49, Decision on Jurisdiction (7 February 2020). 5.25
Tokios Tokelės v Ukraine, ICSID Case No ARB/02/18, Decision on
    Jurisdiction (29 April 2004) 3.44, 3.52, 5.77, 5.79
Tradex Hellas S.A. (Greece) v Republic of Albania, ICSID Case No ARB/94/2,
    Decision on Jurisdiction (24 December 1996). 7.44
Tradex Hellas S.A. (Greece) v Republic of Albania, ICSID Case No ARB/94/2,
    Award (29 April 1999). 7.44–7.45, 7.47, 7.54

Vestey Group Ltd v Bolivarian Republic of Venezuela, ICSID Case No ARB/06/4,
    Award (15 April 2016). 2.02, 3.15, 7.43
Victor Pey Casado and Foundation 'Presidente Allende' v Republic of Chile,
    ICSID Case No ARB/98/2, Award (8 May 2008) 3.21, 3.28, 3.36, 3.61, 4.46, 4.49
Vladislav Kim and others v Republic of Uzbekistan, ICSID Case No ARB/13/6,
    Decision on Jurisdiction (8 March 2017) 5.25, 5.95

Waguih Elie George Siag and Clorinda Vecchi v Arab Republic of Egypt,
    ICSID Case No ARB/05/15, Decision on Jurisdiction (11 April 2007) 3.44, 3.52
Wintershall Aktiengesellschaft v Argentine Republic, ICSID Case No ARB/04/14,
    Award (8 December 2008) 2.31
World Duty Free Co Ltd v Republic of Kenya, ICSID Case No ARB/00/7,
    Award (25 September 2006) 5.83

Zhinvali Development Ltd v Republic of Georgia, ICSID Case No ARB/00/1,
    Award (24 January 2003). 7.48, 7.54

INTERNATIONAL COURT OF JUSTICE (ICJ)

Case concerning the Barcelona Traction, Light and Power Company, Ltd
    (Belgium v Spain) [1970] ICJ Rep 3. . . . . 5.31, 5.35

PERMANENT COURT OF ARBITRATION (PCA)

Clorox Spain S.L. v Bolivarian Republic of Venezuela, PCA Case No 2015-30,
    Award (20 May 2019) 1.03, 5.94, 5.96–5.97, 5.99
Professor Christian Doutremepuich (France) and Antoine Doutremepuich
    (France) v Republic of Mauritius, PCA Case No 2018-37, Award on
    Jurisdiction (23 August 2019). 2.28, 6.51, 6.66, 6.70
Romak S.A. (Switzerland) v Republic of Uzbekistan, PCA Case No AA280,
    Award (26 November 2009) . . . 1.03, 2.28, 3.74–3.75, 4.30, 4.35–4.38, 4.45, 4.52, 4.54, 4.79, 4.84,
                                     6.44, 6.46, 6.49–6.50, 6.54, 6.57–6.58, 6.61, 6.66–6.70, 8.63, 9.14

AD HOC ARBITRATION

Alps Finance and Trade AG v Slovak Republic, Investment Ad Hoc Arbitration,
    Award (5 March 2011). 4.79, 4.85

Table of Legislation

CONVENTIONS AND RULES

Convention on the Settlement of Investment Disputes between States and Nationals of Other States (adopted 18 March 1965, entered into force 14 October 1966) (ICSID Convention) 1.01, 1.03–1.04, 1.07–1.08, 1.10–1.11, 1.14, 1.16, 2.02, 2.16–2.18, 2.22, 2.27–2.30, 2.33, 2.50, 2.53–2.54, 2.57, 2.60–2.61, 3.04, 3.08–3.09, 3.14, 3.18–3.20, 3.28–3.30, 3.32–3.33, 3.36, 3.39, 3.41, 3.43, 3.45, 3.47–3.54, 3.56–3.57, 3.60, 3.64–3.65, 3.67–3.70, 3.72–3.74, 3.76–3.81, 3.83–3.84, 3.88. 4.03–4.04, 4.16, 4.24, 4.30, 4.42, 4.46, 4.55–4.57, 4.63, 4.67–4.72, 4.74–4.76, 4.79–4.80, 4.85, 4.88, 4.94, 4.96–4.97, 4.103, 5.26, 5.84–5.85, 5.100, 6.23, 6.41–6.43, 6.53–6.57, 6.60–6.62, 6.65, 7.43, 7.49, 8.02, 8.04, 8.07, 8.15, 8.33, 8.35–8.36, 8.44, 8.46–8.47, 8.57–8.58, 8.62, 9.02, 9.04
Preamble 4.09, 4.41–4.42, 4.46, 4.60, 4.104, 7.36
Art 25...... 1.03–1.04, 1.06–1.10, 1.12–1.15, 1.17, 1.19, 2.09, 2.16, 2.19, 2.26, 2.30–2.31, 2.51–2.52, 2.58, 2.60, 3.01–3.05, 3.08, 3.10, 3.14–3.15, 3.17–3.29, 3.31, 3.33–3.35, 3.37–3.47, 3.50–3.52, 3.54–3.56, 3.59, 3.62–3.69, 3.71–3.75, 3.78–3.80, 3.82–3.83, 3.85–3.88, 4.01, 4.23, 4.42, 4.44, 4.47, 4.55, 4.57–4.59, 4.64–4.70, 4.72–4.74, 4.76, 4.78–4.80, 4.83–4.87, 4.93, 4.95, 5.04, 5.22, 5.84–5.85, 5.100, 6.02–6.03, 6.16, 6.21–6.23, 6.28–6.29, 6.41–6.42, 6.50, 6.57–6.61, 6.63–6.65, 6.67–6.68, 7.33, 7.36, 8.07, 8.09, 8.13–8.15, 8.32–8.35, 8.40, 8.49, 8.57, 8.61–8.62, 8.69, 8.72. 9.01–9.03, 9.06, 9.08, 9.11–9.14, 9.16
Art 25(1) 1.02, 1.04, 2.03, 2.07, 3.15, 3.22, 3.26, 3.37, 3.64, 3.72, 4.46, 4.56, 4.70, 4.98, 5.84–5.85, 5.100
Art 25(4) 2.57
Art 36(3) 2.19
Art 54(1) 1.18
Art 66 .... 2.61
ICSID Rules of Procedure for Arbitration Proceedings
  Rule 41(1) 2.14–2.15
  Rule 41(2) 2.17
  Rule 41(3) 2.14
  Rule 41(5) 2.15–2.16
UNCITRAL Rules 2.04
United Nations Charter 4.104
Vienna Convention on the Law of Treaties (adopted 23 May 1969, entered into force 27 January 1980) 2.27, 2.30–2.32, 3.68–3.69, 5.85
Arts 31–33 .... 2.22, 3.32
Art 31 .... 2.28–2.29, 2.33, 3.32, 3.68, 6.46
Art 31(1) 2.28
Art 31(3) 3.69
Art 31(3)(a) 2.29
Art 31(3)(b) 2.29
Art 32 .... 2.30, 3.32, 3.68. 3.81
Art 32(b) 6.46
Art 41 .... 3.70
Art 41(1) 3.70
Art 41(1)(b)(i) 3.70
Washington Convention, *See* Convention on the Settlement of Investment Disputes between States and Nationals of Other States (ICSID Convention)

BILATERAL INVESTMENT TREATIES

Agreement between Australia and the Islamic Republic of Pakistan on the Promotion and Protection of Investments (adopted 7 February 1998, entered into force 14 October 1998) 3.18
Art 1(3) 5.34
Agreement between Canada and Mongolia for the Promotion and Protection of Investments (adopted 8 September 2016, entered into force 24 February 2017) 6.11
Art 1 .... 6.08, 6.11

xviii   TABLE OF LEGISLATION

Agreement Between Canada and the Republic of Peru for the Promotion and Protection of Investments (adopted 14 November 2006, entered into force 20 June 2007)
Art 1 ....5.14
Agreement between Japan and Georgia for the Liberalisation, Promotion and Protection of Investment (adopted 29 January 2021, entered into force 23 July 2021)
Art 1(a) 5.05, 6.13
Agreement between the Federal Republic of Germany and the Argentine Republic Concerning the Promotion and Reciprocal Protection of Investments (adopted 9 April 1991, entered into force 8 November 1993)
Art 2(2) 5.21
Agreement Between the Government of Australia and the Government of the Republic of India on the Promotion and Protection of Investments (adopted 26 February 1999, entered into force 4 May 2000)
Art 1(h) 5.34
Agreement between the Government of Hungary and the Government of the United Arab Emirates for the Promotion and Reciprocal Protection of Investments (adopted 15 July 2021, entered into force 10 April 2022) 6.36
Art 1(1) 6.36
Agreement between the Government of the Czech and Slovak Federal Republic and the Government of the Hellenic Republic for the Promotion and Reciprocal Protection of Investments (adopted 3 June 1991, entered into force 31 December 1992) 8.30–8.31
Art 1(1) 8.30
Art 1(1)(c) 8.30, 8.39
Agreement between the Government of the Federal Democratic Republic of Ethiopia and the Government of the Russian Federation on the Promotion and Reciprocal Protection of Investments (adopted 10 February 2000, not in force)
Art 2(1) 5.68, 5.72, 5.74
Agreement between the Government of the Hellenic Republic and the Government of the Republic of Georgia on the Promotion and Reciprocal Protection of Investments (adopted 9 November 1994, entered into force 3 August 1996)
Art 9(1) 2.07
Art 9(3) 2.04
Art 12.............................5.81
Agreement between the Government of the Italian Republic and the Government of the Republic of Mozambique on the Promotion and Reciprocal Protection of Investments (adopted 14 December 1998, entered into force 17 November 2003)
Art 1(c) 4.71
Agreement between the Government of the Republic of Finland and the Government of the Republic of Albania on the Promotion and Protection of Investments (adopted 24 June 1997, entered into force 20 February 1999)
Art 1(1) 5.67, 5.72, 5.74
Agreement between the Government of the Republic of Kazakhstan and the Government of the Republic of Uzbekistan on the promotion and protection of investments (adopted 2 June 1997, entered into force 8 September 1997) 5.95
Art 1(2) 5.21, 5.39, 5.89
Agreement between the Government of the Republic of Lithuania and the Government of Ukraine for the promotion and reciprocal protection of investments (adopted 8 February 1994, entered into force 6 March 1995)
Art 1(1) 5.67, 5.72, 5.74
Agreement between the Government of the Republic of Turkey and the Government of the Kingdom of Cambodia on the Reciprocal Promotion and Protection of Investments (adopted 21 October 2018, not in force)................ 6.31, 6.35, 6.37
Art 1(1) 6.31, 6.33, 6.35, 6.37
Art 1(1)(c).........................6.35
Agreement between the Government of the State of Israel and the Government of the United Arab Emirates on Promotion and Protection of Investments (adopted 20 October 2020, not in force)
s A................................5.88
Agreement between the Government of the Sultanate of Oman and the Government of Hungary for the Promotion and Reciprocal Protection of Investments (adopted 2 February 2022, not in force)
Art 1(1) 6.13, 6.36

Agreement between the Government of
  the United Kingdom of Great
  Britain and Northern Ireland and
  the Government of Malaysia for
  the Promotion and Protection of
  Investments (adopted 21 May 1981,
  entered into force 21 October 1988)
Art 1(1)(a)(iii)..........................6.27
Agreement between the Government of the
  United Kingdom of Great Britain and
  Northern Ireland and the Government of
  the United Republic of Tanzania for the
  Promotion and Protection of Investments
  (adopted 7 January 1994, entered into
  force 2 August 1996) 1.03, 5.90,
                                   5.92–5.93, 8.43
Art 8(1) 5.90
Art 11...............................5.90
Agreement Between the Government of
  the United Mexican States and the
  Government of the State of Kuwait on the
  Promotion and Reciprocal Protection of
  Investments (adopted 22 February 2013,
  entered into force 28 April 2016)
Art 1(5) 5.14
Agreement between the Kingdom of Spain
  and the Republic of Venezuela on
  the Promotion and Reciprocal
  Protection of Investments (adopted
  2 November 1995, entered into force
  10 September 1997)............ 1.03, 5.94
Art 1(2) 1.03, 5.89
Agreement between the Republic of Hungary
  and the People's Republic of China
  Concerning the Encouragement and
  Reciprocal Protection of Investments
  (adopted 29 May 1991, entered into
  force 1 April 1993)
Art 10...............................2.07
Agreement between the Republic of
  the Philippines and the Swiss
  Confederation on the Promotion and
  Reciprocal Protection of Investments
  (adopted 31 March 1997, entered into
  force 23 April 1999)................3.45
Art II 1.03, 5.88
Agreement for the Promotion and Protection
  of Investment between the Government
  of the Republic of Austria and the
  Government of the Kyrgyz Republic
  (adopted 22 April 2016, entered into
  force 1 October 2017)
Art 1(2) 5.06, 6.07
Art 1(2)(a)......................5.06, 6.07
Art 1(2)(b)......................5.06, 6.07
Art 1(2)(c)–(f) 6.07
Art 1(3) 6.08
Agreement for the Promotion and Reciprocal
  Protection of Investments between
  Canada and the Republic of Guinea
  (adopted 27 May 2015, entered into
  force 27 March 2017)................6.26
Art 1............................6.25–6.26
Agreement on encouragement and reciprocal
  protection of investments between the
  Kingdom of the Netherlands and the
  Argentine Republic (adopted 20 October
  1992, entered into force 1 October 1994)
Art 2..................... 5.68, 5.72, 5.74
Agreement on Reciprocal Encouragement
  and Protection of Investments
  between the Kingdom of the
  Netherlands and the Republic of Turkey
  (adopted 27 March 1986, entered into
  force 1 November 1989)............ 5.26
Art 1(b) 5.20
Art 2(2) 5.20, 5.41, 5.69, 5.72, 5.74
Bilateral Agreement for the Promotion and
  Protection of Investments between the
  Government of the United Kingdom of
  Great Britain and Northern Ireland and
  the Republic of Colombia (adopted
  17 March 2010, entered into force
  10 October 2014) 8.28
Art I(2)(a) 5.19, 5.30, 5.39
Art I(2)(b)(i).............. 6.39, 8.28, 8.48
Art I(2)(b)(ii) 6.25
Cooperation and Facilitation Investment
  Agreement between the Federative
  Republic of Brazil and the United Arab
  Emirates (adopted 15 March 2019, not
  in force)
Art 3(1)(3)...........................6.33
French Model BIT 2006
Art 1(1) 2.56
German Model BIT 2008................5.16
Art 1(1) 2.56, 5.12, 5.39
Investment Cooperation and Facilitation
  Treaty between the Federative Republic of
  Brazil and the Republic of India (adopted
  25 January 2020, not in force) 6.32
Art 2(4) 6.35
Art 2(4)(1)......................6.31–6.32
Reciprocal Investment Promotion and
  Protection Agreement between the
  Government of the Kingdom of
  Morocco and the Government of
  the Federal Republic of Nigeria
  (adopted 3 December 2016,
  not in force) 6.09–6.10, 6.31–6.32, 8.28

Art 1 . . . . 5.05, 6.06, 6.31–6.32,
6.35, 6.39, 8.28, 8.48
Treaty between the Federal Republic
of Germany and Ukraine on the
Promotion and Mutual Protection
of Capital Investments (adopted
15 February 1993, entered into force
29 June 1996) 1.03, 5.43–5.44,
6.54, 8.56–8.58
Art 1 . . . . .8.57
Art 1(1) 5.42, 8.58
Art 4(1) 5.42
Treaty between the Government of the
United States and the Government of
the Republic of Rwanda Concerning the
Encouragement and Reciprocal Protection
of Investments (adopted 19 February 2008,
entered into force 1 January 2012)
Art 1 . . . . .6.13
Treaty between the United States of America
and the Argentine Republic Concerning
the Reciprocal Encouragement and
Protection of Investment (adopted
14 November 1991, entered into force
20 October 1994)
Art I(1)(a) 5.19, 5.30, 5.39
Treaty between the United States of America
and the Oriental Republic of Uruguay
Concerning the Encouragement and
Reciprocal Protection of Investment
(adopted 4 November 2005, entered
into force 31 October 2006) 6.14
Art 1 . . . . .6.13
Treaty between the United States of
America and the Republic of Ecuador
concerning the Encouragement and
Reciprocal Protection of Investments
(adopted 27 August 1993, entered
into force 11 May 1997)
Art I(1)(a) 5.30
United Kingdom Model BIT 2008 . . . . .5.16
Art 1(a) 2.56, 5.12–5.14, 5.19
Art 1(a)(ii). 8.48
Art 1(a)(iii) 5.51
United States Model BIT 1994
Art 1(d) 6.20
United States Model BIT 2004
Art 1 . . . . .6.20
United States Model BIT 2012. . . . . . . 4.14, 6.19,
6.21, 8.06
Art 1 . . . . 2.56, 4.14, 5.17, 5.40,
6.12, 6.16, 8.06
Art 24. . . . . .1.02

MULTILATERAL INVESTMENT TREATIES

ASEAN Comprehensive Investment
Agreement (adopted 26 February 2009,
entered into force 24 February 2012)
Art 3(1) 5.41

FREE TRADE AGREEMENTS

Free Trade Agreement between the United
Kingdom of Great Britain and Northern
Ireland and New Zealand (adopted 28
February 2022, not in force)
Art 14(2) 6.13

NATIONAL LEGISLATION

Albania
Foreign Investment Act (1990)
Art 1. . . . . .7.08
Law No 7764 on Foreign Investments
(1993) 7.44–7.46, 7.51, 7.53
Art 1. . . . . .3.18
Art 1(3)(b). 7.47
Art 1(3)(c) 7.53, 8.39
Art 1(3)(e). 7.46

Angola
Private Investment Law (2018)
Art 3. . . . . .7.24

Azerbaijan Republic
Law on Investment Activity (1995)
Art 1. . . . . 7.27, 7.30

Bolivia
Investment Promotion Law (2014). 7.40
Art 4. . . . . .7.38

Bolivarian Republic of Venezuela
Constitutional Law on Productive Foreign
Investment (2017)
Art 7(1) 7.09
Law on the Promotion and Protection of
Investments 7.43

Cameroon
Investment Charter (2002)
Art 4. . . . . .7.08

Cape Verde
Investment Law (2013)
  Art 4(c) 7.26, 7.30, 8.68

Egypt
Investment Law (2017)
  Art 1 .... 7.24, 7.38, 7.40–7.41

El Salvador
Investment Law (1999)................... 2.06
  Art 2(a) 7.09

Ethiopia
Proclamation No 1180/2020 (2020)
  s 2(1) 7.14

Georgia
Investment Law.................... 7.49–7.50

Haiti
Investment Code (1989)
  Art 5(f)............................ 7.09

Indonesia
Law Concerning Investment (2007)
  Art 1(1) 7.25, 7.30

Iraq
Investment Law (2006)............. 7.40–7.41
  Art 1............................. 7.39

Kazakhstan
Law on Investments (2003)
  Art 1(3) 7.09

Kenya
Investment Promotion Act (2004)
  s 2................................ 7.14

Kingdom of Saudi Arabia
Foreign Investment Law (2000)
  Art 1.............................. 7.28

Kosovo
Law No 04/L-220 on Foreign Investment (2014)
  Art 2(1)(4).......................... 7.09
  Art 16(1) 2.07
  Art 16(2) 2.04

Kyrgyzstan
Law on Investments (2003)
  Art 1(1) 7.08

Lao People's Democratic Republic
Law on Investment Promotion (2016)
  Art 3............................. 7.09

Madagascar
Law No 2007-036 relating to investment
  law in Madagascar (2008)
  Art 1.............................. 7.09

Mali
Law No 2012-016 on an Investment
  Code (2012) 7.32
  Art 2.............................. 7.10

Moldova
Law on Investments
  Art 3......................... 7.09, 7.27

Mongolia
Law on Investment (2013)...... 7.17, 7.19, 7.22
  Art 3(1) 7.10, 7.15
  Art 3(5) 7.03, 7.17,
                                    7.19, 7.22

Montenegro
Foreign Investment Law 7.43

Myanmar
Investment Law (2016)
  Art 2(q) 7.08

Namibia
Investment Promotion
  Act (2016).................... 7.17, 7.22
  s 1 .... 7.03, 7.12, 7.17, 7.22

Nigeria
Investment Promotion Commission
  Act (1995)........................ 7.18
  s 31 .... 7.13, 7.18

Palau
Foreign Investment Act (2014)
  s 102(j)............................ 7.14

Papua New Guinea

Investment Promotion Act (1992) 7.08
    s 3(1) 7.08

People's Republic of China

Foreign Investment Law (2019)
    Art 2..........................7.25, 7.30

Philippines

Foreign Investment Act (1991)............7.20
    s 3(b) 7.12
    s 3(e)..............................7.20
    s 3(f)..............................7.20

Republic of Benin

Law No 2020-02 on the Investment Code in
    the Republic of Benin (2020)
    Art 1..............................7.38

Republic of Guinea-Bissau

Investment Code, Law No 3/2011 (6 July 2011)
    Art 1..............................7.09

Republic of Moldova

Law on Investments in Entrepreneurial
    Activity (2004)
    Preamble 7.02

Republic of Uzbekistan

Law on Investments and Investment
    Activity (2019)
    Art 3..................... 7.09, 7.27, 7.30
    Art 63.............................1.02

Russian Federation

Federal Law on Foreign Investments (1999)
    Art 2..................... 7.26, 7.30, 8.68

Sierra Leone

Investment Promotion Act (2004)
    s 1...........................7.14, 7.20

South Africa

Protection of Investment Act (2015)
    s 2(1) 7.12

State of Palestine

Law on the Encouragement of
    Investment in Palestine (1998)........7.17
    Art 1.........................7.14, 7.17

Swaziland

Investment Promotion Act (1998)
    s 2................................7.14

Syrian Arab Republic

Investment Promotion Law (2007)
    Art 1(d) 7.13
    Art 1(f)............................7.18

Turkmenistan

Law on Investment Activities (1992)
    Art 1.........................7.09, 7.39

Vanuatu

Foreign Promotion Act No 15
    of 1998 (1998)
    Art 1(a) 7.02
    Art 1(c) 7.02
    Art 2(1) 7.28

Zambia

Development Agency
    Act (2006)
    Art 3..............................7.14

1
Introduction

I. Importance of the Concept of Investment	1.01	III. Existing Literature		1.10
II. Complexity of the Concept of Investment	1.04	IV. Object and Purpose of this Book		1.16
		V. Scope of this Book		1.18

I. Importance of the Concept of Investment

The concept of investment is undoubtedly the single most important term in the field of international investment law, including the Convention on the Settlement of Investment Disputes between States and Nationals of Other States[1] and investor-state arbitration proceedings brought under this treaty. In fact, the notion of investment defines the very object of this area of law (and practice) and delineates its scope. It is to the field of international investment law what the term 'contract' is to contract law or the word 'constitution' to constitutional law. **1.01**

In more practical terms, the notion of investment is primarily—though not exclusively[2]—relevant as a factor determining the jurisdiction of ICSID and other investor-state arbitral tribunals. The existence of an investment (and frequently also various connected requirements pertaining to the relationship between investment and investor) is, indeed, a prerequisite for the jurisdiction of such tribunals. This requirement is contained in Art 25(1) ICSID Convention[3] and virtually all investment treaties and laws granting investors access to investor-state arbitration.[4] **1.02**

---

[1] Convention on the Settlement of Investment Disputes between States and Nationals of Other States (adopted 18 March 1965, entered into force 14 October 1966) (hereafter ICSID Convention).

[2] See Chapter 2 Section II.B.

[3] ICSID Convention (n 1) Art 25(1) (providing that the Centre—and ICSID arbitral tribunals established under the Convention—has/have jurisdiction over 'any legal dispute arising directly out of an investment, between a Contracting State ... and a national of another Contracting State').

[4] Virtually all investor-state dispute settlement provisions contained in investment treaties and laws define the scope of jurisdiction of investor-state tribunals by reference to the notion of investment or investment dispute. See, for example, United States Model BIT 2012 Art 24 (providing for arbitration of 'investment dispute[s]'); Law of the Republic of Uzbekistan on Investments and Investment Activity (2019) Art 63 (providing for the referral to arbitration of 'investment disputes', which it defines as 'dispute[s] related to foreign investment and arising from the investment activity of a foreign investor ... in the Republic of Uzbekistan').

1.03 The jurisdictional relevance of the concept of investment is far from being a theoretical matter. There are, indeed, numerous decisions, rendered both in ICSID and non-ICSID proceedings, in which tribunals have declined jurisdiction on the grounds that there was no investment under the ICSID Convention, the applicable investment treaty, or both.[5] There are also decisions in which tribunals have not declined jurisdiction, but have held that certain assets owned, or operations conducted, by the investor did not constitute investments, thus excluding the relevant assets or operations from the scope of their jurisdiction.[6] Finally, there are also cases where tribunals have found that they lacked jurisdiction because certain requirements pertaining to the relationship between the investor and the alleged investment were not met.[7] Depending on the wording of the relevant provisions, non-compliance with such requirements either

---

[5] For ICSID decisions, see, for example, *PSEG Global Inc. and others v Turkey*, ICSID Case No ARB/02/5, Decision on Jurisdiction (4 June 2004) para 189 (holding that the option held by the second Claimant, NACC, to acquire an ownership interest in the project company owned by the first Claimant, PSEG, did not constitute an investment under the BIT between the United States and Turkey); *Joy Mining Machinery Limited v The Arab Republic of Egypt*, ICSID Case No ARB/03/11, Award on Jurisdiction (6 August 2004) paras 41–63 (holding that a contract for the provision of mining systems and supporting equipment concluded between the presumed investor and an Egyptian state entity, as well as the bank guarantees provided by the former, did not constitute an investment under either the ICSID Convention or the BIT between the United Kingdom and Egypt); *Mr Patrick Mitchell v The Democratic Republic of Congo*, ICSID Case No ARB/99/7, Decision on the Application for Annulment of the Award (9 February 2004) paras 34–48 (annulling the Tribunal's jurisdictional holding that a law firm operated by the Claimant in the Congo constituted an investment under the ICSID Convention and the BIT between the United States and the Republic of Zaïre—which suggests that the ad hoc Committee would most probably have declined jurisdiction, if it had heard the case); *Malaysian Historical Salvors Sdn, Bhd v The Government of Malaysia*, ICSID Case No ARB/05/10, Award on Jurisdiction (17 May 2007) para 146 (concluding that a contract for the salvage of a shipwreck concluded between the Claimant and Malaysia did not qualify as an investment under Art 25 ICSID Convention); *Global Trading Resource Corp and others v Ukraine*, ICSID Case No ARB/09/11, Award (1 December 2010) para 57 (ruling that contracts under which the Claimant sold poultry to a private company nominated by a Ukrainian state enterprise were 'pure commercial transactions that [could not] on any interpretation be considered to constitute "investments" within the meaning of Article 25 of the ICSID Convention'); *Poštová banka A.S. and others v The Hellenic Republic*, ICSID Case No ARB/13/8, Award (9 April 2015) para 359 (holding that 'the definition of investment in the BIT at issue does not extend to Poštová banka's GGBs [Greek Government Bonds]'); *Raymond Charles Eyre and others v Democratic Socialist Republic of Sri Lanka*, ICSID Case No ARB/16/25, Award (5 March 2020) para 303 (holding that a plot of land owned by the Claimants did not constitute an investment under either the ICSID Convention or the BIT between the United Kingdom and Sri Lanka).

For non-ICSID decisions, see, for example, *Romak S.A. v The Republic of Uzbekistan*, PCA Case No AA280, Award (26 November 2009) paras 213–32 (holding that various contracts under which Romak agreed to deliver specified quantities of wheat to several Uzbek state entities (or the rights arising under such contracts) did not constitute an investment under the BIT between Switzerland and Uzbekistan); *Nova Scotia Power Incorporated (Canada) v The Bolivarian Republic of Venezuela*, ICSID Case No ARB(AF)/11/1, Award (30 April 2014) para 113 (deciding that a contract under which a company controlled by Venezuelan state-owned entities agreed to supply certain quantities of coal to the Claimant (or the rights arising under such contract) did not qualify as an investment under the BIT between Canada and Venezuela).

[6] See, for example, *GEA Group Aktiengesellschaft v Ukraine*, ICSID Case No ARB/08/16, Award (31 March 2011) paras 150–51, 157, 161. In this case, the Tribunal decided that the conversion contract binding the parties (a contract under which the Claimant's predecessor agreed to provide Oriana, a Ukrainian state-owned entity, with certain quantities of naphtha fuel for conversion) constituted an investment under the BIT between Germany and Ukraine and the ICSID Convention. The Claimant argued that the settlement and repayment agreements concluded by the parties to settle their dispute, as well as the ICC arbitral award obtained by the Claimant, also had to be regarded as investments. The Tribunal disagreed.

[7] See, for example, *Standard Chartered Bank v United Republic of Tanzania*, ICSID Case No ARB/10/12, Award (2 November 2012) paras 257–66 (holding that rights under a loan agreement were not a protected investment because the investment was not actively made by the Claimant, as required under the BIT between the United Kingdom and Tanzania); *Clorox Spain S.L. v The Bolivarian Republic of Venezuela*, PCA Case No 2015-30, Award (20 May 2019) para 834 (concluding that the company shares acquired by the Claimant (and/or the acquisition of those shares) did not qualify as an investment under the BIT between Spain and Venezuela because this acquisition did not involve any real 'action of investing', as required under the treaty).

affects the investment status of the relevant assets or operations[8] or causes them not to be 'covered' or 'protected' under a given treaty, without affecting such status.[9]

II. Complexity of the Concept of Investment

The concept of investment is not only of great practical relevance for ICSID arbitration; **1.04** it is also highly complex. This complexity stems from the fact that ICSID arbitration proceedings have two distinct legal bases. One such basis is—evidently—the ICSID Convention which establishes the institutional and procedural framework of ICSID arbitration and defines, in Art 25(1), the Centre's scope of jurisdiction as covering 'any legal dispute arising directly out of an investment, between a Contracting State ... and a national of another Contracting State ...'. However, and this is a source of major controversy, neither Art 25 nor any other provision contained in the Convention defines the concept of investment.

The second legal basis of ICSID arbitration proceedings consists of an instrument con- **1.05** taining the parties' consent to refer a given dispute to ICSID arbitration (or sometimes multiple such instruments), commonly referred to as 'instrument of consent' or 'consent instrument'. There are three types of such instruments: (1) investment treaties, (2) investment laws, and (3) direct agreements between the parties to the dispute, typically ICSID arbitration clauses contained in investment contracts. While such clauses are per se constitutive of consent, investor-state dispute settlement provisions found in investment treaties and laws merely constitute 'offers of consent' which must be accepted by the investor (this generally happens when the investor initiates ICSID proceedings based on the relevant provision).

Like Art 25 ICSID Convention, investor-state dispute settlement clauses in investment **1.06** treaties and laws define the scope of jurisdiction of investor-state tribunals. While this scope may vary, an almost universally recognized requirement is the existence of an investment owned, controlled, made, etc., by a qualifying investor. A significant majority of investment treaties and laws define the term 'investment',[10] and compliance with these definitions constitutes a jurisdictional threshold under the relevant instrument.

---

[8] See, for example, Agreement between the Kingdom of Spain and the Republic of Venezuela on the Promotion and Reciprocal Protection of Investments (adopted 2 November 1995, entered into force 10 September 1997) Art 1(2) which defines 'investment' as 'any type of asset *invested* by investors of one Contracting Party in the territory of the other Contracting Party' (emphasis added, translation of the Spanish original by the author). Although one may wonder what it means that an asset must be 'invested', this provision suggests that an asset that has not been (actively) invested does not constitute an investment.

[9] See, for example, Agreement between the Republic of the Philippines and the Swiss Confederation on the Promotion and Reciprocal Protection of Investments (adopted 31 March 1997, entered into force 23 April 1999) Art II which specifies that the Treaty only applies to 'investments in the territory of one Contracting Party *made* ... by investors of the other Contracting Party' (emphasis added). In other words, investments that do not meet the requirement of having been 'made' by an investor are still investments; however, they do not fall within the Treaty's sphere of application.

[10] See Chapter 2 Section II.A.2.

1.07 The systematic presence of definitions of 'investment' in investment treaties and laws and the absence of such a definition under the Convention have given rise to a question that would otherwise be perplexing, namely, whether the term 'investment' in Art 25 ICSID Convention has a meaning or, put differently, whether it has a meaning that is independent of the definition contained in the applicable consent instrument. One may, in fact, wonder whether the silence of Art 25 could be construed as entailing an implicit incorporation of, or referral to, the definition featured in the applicable treaty or law. If this question is answered in the affirmative, ie if one considers that the concept of investment under the Convention does have an independent meaning, another question arises: the question of what that meaning is (or should be).

1.08 Although contrary decisions are not exceptional,[11] and although one rather common arbitral approach is inherently ambiguous,[12] it is fair to say that a majority of tribunals have considered that the concept of investment under Art 25 ICSID Convention does indeed have an independent meaning.[13] These tribunals have frequently referred to this meaning as being an 'objective' one and have similarly qualified their approach as 'objective' (in contrast to the 'subjective' approach under which the Convention's concept of investment does not have an independent meaning). The implication of this approach is that the existence of an investment must be assessed both under the ICSID Convention and under the applicable consent instrument. This twofold or two-stage inquiry is commonly referred to as the 'double-keyhole' or 'double-barrelled' test.[14]

1.09 As far as the second question is concerned (ie the question of the meaning of 'investment' under Art 25), most tribunals have applied, and continue to apply, the so-called *Salini* test derived from the ruling of the Tribunal in *Salini v Morocco*.[15] Although this test is not applied in a uniform manner, its three core elements, namely, contributions, a minimum duration, and risk, are rarely disputed. However, as will be seen, there is substantial controversy as to whether these criteria are binding or not, ie as to whether they constitute jurisdictional requirements or merely 'typical characteristics' of an investment.[16]

---

[11] See Chapter 3 Section III.C.
[12] See Chapter 3 Section III.D.
[13] See Chapter 3 Section III.B.
[14] See, for example, Stephan W Schill, Christoph W Schreuer and Anthony Sinclair, 'Article 25' in Loretta Malintoppi, August Reinisch, Christoph W Schreuer and Anthony Sinclair (eds), *Schreuer's Commentary on the ICSID Convention: A Commentary on the Convention on the Settlement of Investment Disputes between States and Nationals of Other States* (Cambridge University Press 2022) para 186 (hereafter Schill, Schreuer and Sinclair, 'Article 25').
[15] *Salini Costruttori S.P.A. and Italstrade S.P.A. v Kingdom of Morocco*, ICSID Case No ARB/00/4, Decision on Jurisdiction (23 July 2001) para 52.
[16] See Chapter 3 Section III.D; Chapter 4 Section II.A.

III. Existing Literature

Most scholars exploring the concept of investment in ICSID arbitration (and international investment law more generally) have focused on Art 25 ICSID Convention and, more particularly, on the second question this provision raises, namely, the question of the meaning of 'investment'.[17] Many of these contributions discuss—often critically—the prevailing arbitral approach, ie the *Salini* test. There is some analysis of the basic question of whether 'investment' under the Convention has any (independent) meaning at all.[18] However, given the growing and widespread acceptance of the objective approach (which answers this question in the affirmative), this discussion is generally rather limited.[19]

1.10

In contrast, engagement with the concept of investment under investment treaties and laws, and the definitions contained in such instruments, has been more sporadic. While there are a few studies dealing with investment treaty definitions of 'investment'[20] and the meaning of individual requirements set forth in such definitions,[21] there is virtually

1.11

---

[17] See, for example, Noah Rubins, 'The Notion of "Investment" in International Investment Arbitration' in Norbert Horn and Stefan Kröll (eds), *Arbitrating Foreign Investment Disputes: Procedural and Substantive Legal Aspects* (Kluwer Law International 2004) 283; Farouk Yala, 'The Notion of "Investment" in ICSID Case Law: A Drifting Jurisdictional Requirement?' (2005) 22 J Int'l Arb 105; Michael Waibel, 'Opening Pandora's Box: Sovereign Bonds in International Arbitration' (2007) 101 AJIL 711; Sébastien Manciaux, 'The Notion of Investment: New Controversies' (2008) 9 JWIT 443; Emmanuel Gaillard, 'Identify or Define? Reflections on the Evolution of the Concept of Investment in ICSID Practice' in Christina Binder, Ursula Kriebaum, August Reinisch and Stephan Wittich (eds), *International Investment Law for the 21st Century: Essays in Honour of Christoph Schreuer* (Oxford University Press 2009) 403; Michael Hwang and Jennifer Lee Cheng Fong, 'Definition of "Investment"—A Voice from the Eye of the Storm' (2011) 1 Asian J Int Law 99; Helena Jung Engfeldt, 'Should ICSID Go Gangnam Style in Light of Non-Traditional Foreign Investments Including Those Spurred on by Social Media—Applying an Industry-Specific Lens to the Salini Test to Determine Article 25 Jurisdiction' (2014) 32 Berkeley J Int'l L 44; Michael Waibel, 'Investment Arbitration: Jurisdiction and Admissibility' (2014) Legal Studies Research Paper Series, University of Cambridge Faculty of Law, Paper No 9/2014, February 2014 (hereafter Waibel, 'Jurisdiction and Admissibility'); Alex Grabowski, 'The Definition of Investment under the ICSID Convention: A Defense of Salini' (2014) 15 Chi J Int'l L 287; Jeremy Marc Exelbert, 'Consistently Inconsistent: What Is a Qualifying Investment Under Article 25 of the ICSID Convention and Why the Debate Must End' (2016) 85 Fordham L Rev 1243; Stratos Pahis, 'Investment Misconceived: The Investment-Commerce Distinction in International Investment Law' (2020) 45 Yale J Int'l L 69 (hereafter Pahis, 'Investment Misconceived'); Michael Waibel, 'Subject Matter Jurisdiction: The Notion of Investment' (2021) 19 ICSID Reports 25 (hereafter Waibel, 'Subject Matter Jurisdiction').

[18] Jean Ho, 'The Meaning of "Investment" in ICSID Arbitrations' (2010) 26 Arb Int'l 633 (hereafter Ho, 'The Meaning of "Investment"'); Joshua Fellenbaum, 'GEA v. Ukraine and the Battle of Treaty Interpretation Principles Over the Salini Test' (2011) 27 Arb Int'l 249 (hereafter Fellenbaum, 'GEA v. Ukraine'); Waibel, 'Jurisdiction and Admissibility' (n 17); Pahis, 'Investment Misconceived' (n 17); Waibel, 'Subject Matter Jurisdiction' (n 17).

[19] Two exceptions are: Ho, 'The Meaning of "Investment"' (n 18) (offering a detailed argumentation in favour of the subjective approach); Fellenbaum, 'GEA v. Ukraine' (n 18) (expressing dissatisfaction with the fact that the decision examined in his contribution failed to take a position on whether the objective or subjective approach was preferable or correct).

[20] Existing studies include, for example, Manaz Malik, 'Definition of Investment in International Investment Agreements' (2009) International Institute for Sustainable Development, Best Practices Series, Bulletin No 1; Jeswald Salacuse, *The Law of Investment Treaties* (3rd edn, Oxford University Press 2021) 207–45. There are also a few contributions that touch upon this issue in the specific context of the United States bilateral investment treaty program. See, for example, Kenneth J Vandevelde, 'A Comparison of the 2004 and 1994 U.S. Model BITs—Rebalancing Investor and Host Country Interests' in Karl P Sauvant (ed) *Yearbook of International Investment Law and Policy* (2009) 283; Lee M Caplan and Jeremy K Sharpe, 'United States' in Chester Brown (ed) *Commentaries on Selected Model Investment Treaties* (Oxford University Press 2013) 755.

[21] See Chapter 5 Sections III–VI.

no discussion of definitions contained in investment laws.[22] The more limited attention to these questions is, of course, understandable considering that these definitions have not given rise to controversy that would be comparable to the one resulting from the ICSID Convention's silence on the meaning of 'investment'. Also, given that only a relatively small number of cases are based on investment laws,[23] the practical relevance of definitions found in such laws is comparatively limited.

1.12 The existing literature is characterized by several gaps or omissions. One such gap flows from the above-mentioned focus on Art 25 ICSID Convention. In fact, this focus implies that scholarly analysis of definitions contained in investment treaties and laws is limited. For instance, few authors have examined the various definitional requirements commonly found in investment treaties (such as the requirements of territoriality, ownership or control, and legality). These requirements are, however, of significant practical relevance, given that their application has proven to be decisive in a number of cases.[24]

1.13 For the same reason, there is little to no discussion of two significant recent developments affecting the drafting and interpretation of investment treaty definitions of 'investment'. The first such development consists of the incorporation into treaty definitions of the requirement that investments must possess certain specified 'characteristics', generally bearing a striking resemblance to the *Salini* criteria.[25] The second development relates to a series of decisions in which both non-ICSID and ICSID tribunals have held that treaty concepts of investment, like 'investment' under Art 25 ICSID Convention, have an objective meaning.[26] Despite their profound impact, these developments have generally been neglected by scholarly writers.

1.14 A further shortcoming of existing writings is the quasi-total absence of studies providing a holistic or global analysis of the various legal issues and, more particularly, of the two branches of the double-keyhole test. In fact, virtually all studies examine either Art 25 ICSID Convention or, less frequently, definitions found in investment treaties and/or laws, but not both. However, given that these two questions form part of a single jurisdictional inquiry, they are evidently interrelated. The way in which the applicable treaty defines the concept of investment, for example, may have an impact on how an arbitral tribunal construes Art 25. If the Tribunal perceives the definition to be unduly broad—which may be a not uncommon assessment of traditional asset-based definitions—this may prompt the Tribunal to apply a set of allegedly objective requirements under the ICSID Convention. Also, any development affecting one branch of the

---

[22] The leading commentary on the ICSID Convention devotes a few pages to these definitions and to how they have been applied in a handful of cases. See Schill, Schreuer and Sinclair, 'Article 25' (n 14) paras 201–12. General studies on investment laws typically fail to analyse the definitions of the term 'investment'. See, for example, Jarrod Hepburn, 'Domestic Investment Statutes in International Law' (2018) 112 AJIL 658.
[23] See Chapter 2 Section II.A.2.
[24] See Chapter 5 Sections III–VI.
[25] See Chapter 6 Section III.
[26] See Chapter 6 Section V.

analysis is likely to have repercussions on the other. The incorporation of *Salini*-type criteria into treaty definitions of 'investment', for example, may cause some tribunals to deny the applicability of these criteria under Art 25 ICSID Convention. In the existing literature, this interrelatedness has been almost entirely neglected, ie the two stages of the double-keyhole test are almost always examined separately and in isolation.

Finally, the academic discourse has also failed to explore the fundamental question of the 'nature' of investment. This is, however, a subject worthy of scholarly attention given the absence of a clear or unanimous answer and the significant practical implications of answering this question one way or another. The uncertainty surrounding the nature of investment stems, in part, from the lack of a unanimous approach in investment treaties and laws. In fact, while a significant majority of treaty definitions are asset-based, ie view investments as assets, one also finds, both in investment treaties and laws, enterprise-based and activity-based definitions under which investments are regarded not as assets, but as enterprises or activities. What is more, the prevailing Art 25 case law (ie the *Salini* test) also implicitly rejects the asset-nature of investments, arguably assimilating investments to activities or operations. 1.15

IV. Object and Purpose of this Book

This book seeks to contribute to the existing literature by filling the various gaps identified above. It offers a comprehensive and holistic examination of all legal issues arising in connection with the jurisdictional threshold of the existence of an investment in ICSID arbitration, covering all relevant categories of legal instruments, ie the ICSID Convention, investment treaties, and investment laws. Particular emphasis is placed on recent developments in treaty and legislative practice, as well as arbitral case law, with a special focus on the two trends referred to in Section III. Throughout this study, attention will be paid to the implications of both definitions of 'investment' and arbitral case law for the question of the nature of 'investment'. 1.16

This book is organized as follows. Chapter 2 examines a range of preliminary matters that are vital for a proper understanding of the general context in which the question of the existence of an investment arises in ICSID arbitration. Chapters 3 and 4 explore Art 25 ICSID Convention, with the first of these chapters examining whether the term 'investment' under this provision has an independent meaning and the second one discussing what that meaning is (it assumes, in line with the prevailing view, that the answer to the first question is in the affirmative). Chapters 5 and 6 deal with definitions of investment contained in investment treaties. Chapter 5 presents the main features of traditional, asset-based definitions and analyses the most common requirements found in treaty definitions. Chapter 6 examines recent developments in treaty and arbitral practice. Chapter 7 is devoted to definitions found in investment laws and notably highlights similarities with, and differences from, treaty definitions. Chapter 8 1.17

discusses the investment status of several specific categories of assets and transactions, focusing on controversial cases.

V. Scope of this Book

1.18 This book examines the notion of investment in the specific context of ICSID arbitration proceedings. This focus is justified in light of the overwhelming importance of ICSID and ICSID arbitration for the resolution of investor-state disputes. In fact, despite the unavailability of statistical data, it is safe to assume that a significant majority of investor-state disputes are referred to ICSID. Among other things, this can be inferred from the fact that a majority of investment treaties and laws offer investors the possibility to submit disputes to ICSID arbitration (typically as one of several options) and that, for a variety of reasons,[27] investors generally prefer ICSID arbitration over other dispute settlement options and forms of arbitration.

1.19 Although this book focuses on the concept of investment in ICSID arbitration, many of the issues covered are also relevant for non-ICSID contexts. In fact, Chapters 5, 6, and 7, which explore treaty and investment law definitions of investment, are of relevance for any dispute arising under a treaty or investment law, regardless of the forum in which it is heard (or the type of arbitration). Chapter 8 is relevant to the extent that it deals with the investment status of certain assets and transactions under investment treaties and laws. As for the two chapters dedicated to Art 25 ICSID Convention (Chapters 3 and 4), they are also of relevance beyond the sphere of ICSID arbitration given that Art 25 case law has arguably had a significant impact on treaty practice and arbitral interpretation of treaty definitions.[28] Decisions rendered under Art 25 ICSID Convention may thus be indirectly applicable under investment treaty definitions.

---

[27] The probably most significant such reason is that ICSID awards are 'automatically' enforceable in all ICSID contracting States, without any review by local courts. See ICSID Convention (n 1) Art 54(1): 'Each Contracting State shall recognize an award rendered pursuant to this Convention as binding and enforce the pecuniary obligations imposed by that award within its territories as if it were a final judgment of a court in that State.'

[28] See Chapter 6 Section V.

2
Preliminary Matters

I.	Introduction	2.01	IV.	Applicable Law	2.21
II.	Practical Relevance of the Concept of Investment	2.02	V.	The Concept of Investment as an Interpretive Issue	2.26
	A. Relevance for the jurisdiction of ICSID tribunals	2.02	VI.	Ordinary Meaning of the Term 'Investment'	2.33
	B. Relevance for the assessment of damages	2.10	VII.	Meaning of the Economic Concept of Investment	2.39
III.	Procedural Settings in Which the Question of the Existence of an Investment Arises	2.13	VIII.	The Nature of Investment	2.45
	A. Jurisdictional objections	2.14	IX.	Interests Involved in Defining the Concept of Investment	2.54
	B. *Ex officio* examination of jurisdiction	2.17		A. Investor and host State interests	2.54
	C. Screening of requests for arbitration by ICSID's Secretary General	2.19		B. Systemic interests	2.59

I. Introduction

This chapter examines several general matters that are vital for a better understanding of the issues discussed in this book, providing useful background information and illuminating the legal—and to some extent, economic—context in which those issues arise. These preliminary matters include (1) the practical relevance of the concept of investment, (2) the procedural settings in which the question of the existence of an investment arises, (3) the law or laws governing this question, (4) its interpretive nature, (5) the ordinary meaning of the term 'investment', (6) the meaning of 'investment' in the field of economics, (7) the question of the nature of investment, and (8) the interests involved in the definition of the concept of 'investment'.

2.01

II. Practical Relevance of the Concept of Investment

A. Relevance for the jurisdiction of ICSID tribunals

As has already been observed in Chapter 1 (Introduction), the primary relevance of the concept of investment stems from the fact that, in International Centre for Settlement of Investment Disputes (ICSID) arbitration, the existence of an investment

2.02

is a jurisdictional requirement. Although the relevant norms typically spell out this requirement in more specific ways (they may, for example, require that an investment be 'made' by a qualifying investor), the common denominator is that there must be an investment. References to this overarching requirement of the 'existence' of an investment can be found in various cases. In *Vestey v Venezuela*, for example, a case which arose under the bilateral investment treaty (BIT) between the United Kingdom and Venezuela, the Tribunal observed that its jurisdiction had to 'be established under both the ICSID Convention and the [United Kingdom–Venezuela] BIT' and that '[b]oth instruments ma[de] jurisdiction conditional upon the *existence of an investment*'.[1]

1. ICSID Convention

2.03 The existence of an investment is required under Art 25(1) ICSID Convention.[2] This provision, which defines the scope of jurisdiction of the Centre, establishes various criteria for the jurisdiction of ICSID tribunals. One such criterion is that the dispute must be between a Contracting State (or a designated subdivision or agency) and a national of another Contracting State. Another requirement pertains to consent, ie the need for the parties to have agreed to submit the dispute to ICSID. Lastly, and most importantly for present purposes, the dispute must be related to an investment (it must 'aris[e] directly out of an investment').

2. Instruments of consent

2.04 There are, as has been explained, three types of instruments of consent: investment treaties, investment laws, and investment contracts. While ICSID arbitration clauses contained in investment contracts are per se constitutive of consent, Investor–State Dispute Settlement (ISDS) provisions in investment treaties or laws which grant investors access to ICSID arbitration constitute 'offers of consent' (which investors can notably accept by commencing proceedings in reliance on such offers). Such ISDS provisions typically offer investors a choice between several options, ICSID arbitration generally being one of them.[3]

---

[1] *Vestey Group Limited v Bolivarian Republic of Venezuela*, ICSID Case No ARB/06/4, Award (15 April 2016) para 181 (emphasis added).
[2] Convention on the Settlement of Investment Disputes between States and Nationals of Other States (adopted 18 March 1965, entered into force 14 October 1966) Art 25(1) (providing that '[t]he jurisdiction of the Centre shall extend to any legal dispute arising directly out of an investment, between a Contracting State … and a national of another Contracting State, which the parties to the dispute consent in writing to submit to the Centre') (hereafter ICSID Convention).
[3] As far as investment treaties are concerned, see, for example, Agreement between the Government of the Hellenic Republic and the Government of the Republic of Georgia on the Promotion and Reciprocal Protection of Investments (adopted 9 November 1994, entered into force 3 August 1996) Art 9(3) (offering the investor a choice between ICSID arbitration and ad hoc arbitration under the United Nations Commission on International Trade Law (UNCITRAL) Rules) (hereafter Greece–Georgia BIT). As for investment laws, see, for example, Kosovo Law No 04/L-220 on Foreign Investment (2014) Art 16(2) (hereafter Kosovo Foreign Investment Law). This provision entitles the foreign investor to choose between litigation and four different types of arbitration: ICSID arbitration, ICSID Additional Facility Arbitration, ad hoc arbitration under the UNCITRAL Rules, and International Chamber of Commerce (ICC) arbitration.

2.05 In practice, a significant majority of ICSID cases are brought under investment treaties, most often BITs. In fact, between the creation of ICSID in 1966 and 2022, 78 per cent of the cases referred to the Centre were based on a treaty, 15 per cent on an investment contract, and 7 per cent on an investment law.[4] The relative importance of investment treaties as a source of consent appears to have grown over the years. In 2022, for instance, their 'share' was 86 per cent, while the proportion of cases brought under investment contracts and laws amounted to 12 per cent and 2 per cent, respectively.[5]

2.06 It should be noted that the ICSID statistics appear to assume that every case is based on one instrument of consent only. There are, however, a number of cases in which the Claimants relied on two (or several) such instruments. In *Inceysa v El Salvador*, for example, the Claimant invoked not only the BIT between El Salvador and Spain, but also the Investment Law of El Salvador.[6] Since such cases have apparently not been taken into account, the official statistics may not be entirely accurate. However, considering that cases brought under multiple consent instruments are rather uncommon, the central importance of investment treaties cannot be questioned.

2.07 Like Art 25(1) ICSID Convention, investment treaties and laws also condition the jurisdiction of investor–state tribunals upon the existence of an investment. Some ISDS provisions contained in such instruments provide that investor–state tribunals have jurisdiction over any dispute related to an investment.[7] Others define the scope of jurisdiction of these tribunals more narrowly, for example, by confining it to claims alleging violations of the rights granted under the relevant law or treaty[8] or to a more narrowly defined set of claims.[9] The common minimum requirement of all these provisions, however, is that an investment must exist (or have existed).

2.08 Since the concept of investment is thus of crucial importance for ISDS provisions contained in investment treaties and laws, it is not surprising that a significant majority of these instruments define the term 'investment'. While there does not seem to be any statistical data on how many investment *laws* contain (or do not contain) such definitions, the United Nations Conference on Trade and Development (UNCTAD) investment treaty database indicates that approximately 98 per cent of the existing *treaties* define the concept of 'investment'.[10]

---

[4] International Centre for Settlement of Investment Disputes, 'The ICSID Caseload—Statistics', Issue 2023-1 (2023) 11.
[5] ibid 23.
[6] See *Inceysa Vallisoletana, S.L. v Republic of El Salvador*, ICSID Case No ARB/03/26, Award (2 August 2006).
[7] See, for example, Kosovo Foreign Investment Law (n 3) Art 16(1) (referring to the broad concept 'investment dispute', without any further specification).
[8] See, for example, Greece–Georgia BIT (n 3) Art 9(1).
[9] See, for example, Agreement between the Republic of Hungary and the People's Republic of China Concerning the Encouragement and Reciprocal Protection of Investments (adopted 29 May 1991, entered into force 1 April 1993) Art 10 (offering access to investor–state arbitration in connection with disputes 'concerning the amount of compensation for expropriation').
[10] See UNCTAD, 'International Investment Agreements Navigator' <https://investmentpolicy.unctad.org/international-investment-agreements/iia-mapping> accessed 18 March 2023. According to the available data, only 50 out of 2,584 mapped treaties (roughly 2 per cent) do not contain any definition of the term 'investment'.

2.09 Under investment contracts providing for ICSID arbitration, there is no (separate) requirement pertaining to the existence of an investment. This is because by agreeing to refer disputes arising in connection with their contract to ICSID arbitration, the parties implicitly agree that their contract constitutes, or relates to, an investment. There is thus no need to stipulate any investment-related requirement and, therefore, also no need to define this concept. In contract-based cases, the requirements of Art 25 ICSID Convention therefore constitute the only applicable threshold.

B. Relevance for the assessment of damages

2.10 While the notion of investment is primarily relevant because of its jurisdictional implications (which is the focus of this book), its significance is not limited to the issue of jurisdiction. In fact, the concept of investment may also be relevant in connection with the determination of the amount of damages awarded to an investor. In this context, the question is not *whether* an investment *exists* (or whether the investor owns or has made an investment), but *what* the investment *consists of*.

2.11 Where the Respondent State is found to have breached an obligation (whether arising under a treaty, law, or contract), the question arises as to whether such breach has caused a loss to the investor and, if so, what the amount of such loss is. In some cases, it may not be necessary to determine what specific operations or assets an investment consists of in order to answer this question. For example, if the host State breaches a tax stabilization clause, the compensation awarded to the investor will in principle consist of the difference between the tax the investor effectively paid and the tax he or she would have paid if the host State had honoured the clause.

2.12 In other cases, however, the determination of the specific substance of the investor's investment may be crucial. This will be the case whenever it is necessary to determine the value of the investment, for example, where a tribunal finds that the investor has been expropriated. In such a scenario, it is necessary precisely to determine the specific assets and/or activities that qualify as investments under the relevant legal instruments.

III. Procedural Settings in Which the Question of the Existence of an Investment Arises

2.13 Most frequently, the question of the existence of an investment arises in connection with a jurisdictional objection alleging the absence of a qualifying investment. This is by far the most common scenario and virtually all decisions analysed in this book are decisions dealing with such objections. Yet, it is worth mentioning that there are two additional settings in which the existence of an investment may be (or may become) relevant. These include (a) *ex officio* examination by arbitral tribunals of the existence of an investment and (b) the screening of requests for arbitration by ICSID's Secretary General.

A. Jurisdictional objections

The existence of an investment may, first of all, be challenged via an 'ordinary' jurisdictional objection under Arbitration Rule 41(1).[11] Such an objection must in principle be filed 'no later than the expiration of the time limit fixed for the filing of the counter-memorial'.[12] Tribunals hearing such objections 'may decide to suspend the proceedings on the merits',[13] ie they may decide to deal with jurisdictional and merits-related issues in two separate stages of the proceedings.

2.14

Alternatively, the Respondent may raise the alleged absence of an investment by filing a preliminary 'objection that a claim is manifestly without legal merit'.[14] Such an objection must be filed within thirty days from the constitution of the arbitral tribunal and is heard summarily.[15] Given that the threshold for sustaining such objections is high, the rejection of a preliminary objection does not deprive the Respondent of the right to file a further objection under Arbitration Rule 41(1).[16]

2.15

Preliminary objections are raised relatively rarely and are seldom successful.[17] One of the few cases in which the Respondent's preliminary objection was successful and which involved the issue of the existence of an investment is *Global Trading v Ukraine*.[18] This case involved several contracts under which the Claimants sold poultry to a state-owned (or state-controlled) Ukrainian entity.[19] The Respondent argued that these contracts did not constitute investments under either the applicable BIT (the BIT between the United States and Ukraine) or the ICSID Convention.[20] While the Tribunal did not make any finding under the BIT,[21] it found that the contracts entered into by the Claimants were 'pure commercial transactions' and that they could not therefore qualify as investments under Art 25 ICSID Convention.[22]

2.16

---

[11] ICSID Rules of Procedure for Arbitration Proceedings Rule 41(1) (hereafter Arbitration Rules).
[12] ibid.
[13] Arbitration Rule 41(3).
[14] Arbitration Rule 41(5).
[15] ibid.
[16] ibid.
[17] Lars Markert, 'Summary Dismissal of ICSID Proceedings' (2016) 31 ICSID Review 690, 692.
[18] *Global Trading Resource Corp. and others v Ukraine*, ICSID Case No ARB/09/11, Award (1 December 2010) (hereafter *Global Trading v Ukraine*).
[19] ibid paras 36–38.
[20] ibid para 41.
[21] ibid para 53. The Tribunal noted that the treaty definition of 'investment' could be construed in several ways and that that issue was therefore not suitable for a summary decision under Rule 41(5).
[22] ibid para 56.

B. *Ex officio* examination of jurisdiction

2.17 It is possible for a tribunal to raise (and examine) jurisdictional matters, including the question of the existence of an investment, *ex officio*.[23] In *Dan Cake v Hungary*, for example, the Respondent did not raise any jurisdictional objections.[24] This did not, however, prevent the Tribunal from dealing with—and affirming—its jurisdiction.[25] In another case brought against Hungary, *Magyar Farming v Hungary*, the existence of an investment was similarly undisputed.[26] Yet, the Tribunal (briefly) addressed the issue, seemingly expressing agreement with the parties' common understanding that the Claimant's farming business constituted an investment under the applicable BIT and the ICSID Convention.[27]

2.18 As *Dan Cake* and *Magyar Farming* suggest, *ex officio* examination of jurisdictional questions is typically extremely limited, especially where the Tribunal does not identify any potential obstacles. In neither of these two cases did the Tribunals actually *analyse* the issue, ie neither of them provided any reasons for their conclusions. In *Dan Cake*, the Tribunal simply observed that 'the dispute relate[d] to an investment',[28] without further elaboration under either the applicable treaty or the Convention. In *Magyar Farming*, the Tribunal noted that the investment status of the Claimant's enterprise was 'common ground',[29] similarly failing to offer any substantiation.

C. Screening of requests for arbitration by ICSID's Secretary General

2.19 Requests for arbitration undergo a preliminary screening by ICSID's Secretary General.[30] If, in the context of such screening, the Secretary General 'finds, on the basis of the information contained in the request, that the dispute is manifestly outside the jurisdiction of the Centre', he or she may refuse to register the request.[31] As Schreuer has highlighted, one of the reasons for a dispute to be 'manifestly outside the jurisdiction of the Centre' may be the apparent absence of an investment in the sense of Art 25 ICSID Convention.[32]

---

[23] Arbitration Rule 41(2).
[24] *Dan Cake (Portugal) S.A. v Hungary*, ICSID Case No ARB/12/9, Decision on Jurisdiction and Liability (24 August 2015) para 67 (hereafter *Dan Cake v Hungary*).
[25] ibid paras 67–79.
[26] *Magyar Farming Company Ltd and others v Hungary*, ICSID Case No ARB/17/27, Award (13 November 2019) para 249 (hereafter *Magyar Farming v Hungary*).
[27] ibid.
[28] *Dan Cake v Hungary* (n 24) para 79.
[29] *Magyar Farming v Hungary* (n 26) para 249.
[30] ICSID Convention (n 2) Art 36(3).
[31] ibid.
[32] Christoph Schreuer, 'Article 36' in Loretta Malintoppi, August Reinisch, Christoph W Schreuer and Anthony Sinclair (eds), *Schreuer's Commentary on the ICSID Convention: A Commentary on the Convention on the Settlement of Investment Disputes between States and Nationals of Other States* (3rd edn, Cambridge University Press 2022) para 55.

Since decisions denying the registration of a request are not published or otherwise publicly available, it is not clear how often such denials occur, nor what prompts them. However, given that the applicable threshold is high (the dispute must be 'manifestly' outside the jurisdiction of the Centre) and that a summary dismissal procedure is available to deal with cases that are 'manifestly without legal merit', it can be assumed that the Secretary General only very exceptionally refuses to register a request. **2.20**

IV. Applicable Law

The determination of the meaning of 'investment' under a given legal instrument will generally not, or at least not ostensibly, involve any choice-of-law issue. Where the question arises under an investment treaty, for example, it will generally suffice to apply the definition contained in the relevant treaty. In most cases, it will not be necessary to refer to definitions found in other legal texts, whether of domestic or international nature. **2.21**

This does not mean, however, that the question of the governing law is entirely irrelevant. In fact, where interpretive issues arise, it is necessary to determine the law that governs interpretation. If a question of interpretation arises under the ICSID Convention or an investment treaty, the applicable rules of treaty interpretation, in principle those set forth under the Vienna Convention on the Law of Treaties (VCLT),[33] apply. In contrast, where an interpretive issue arises in connection with a definition contained in an investment law, the relevant domestic interpretive rules are in principle applicable. **2.22**

It would of course be possible for a legislator, or for States concluding an investment treaty, expressly to subject the meaning of 'investment' to a law other than the one that governs the relevant instrument. For example, nothing prevents State parties to a BIT from agreeing that the term 'investment' should be given the meaning that this concept has under the host State's domestic law. In practice, however, such provisions are largely unheard of, presumably because they entail the risk of dissimilar treatment of the investors of the two contracting States and/or because they would allow a contracting State to unilaterally alter the meaning of 'investment' and, thus, the treaty's scope of application. **2.23**

Respondent States have sometimes argued that treaty concepts of investment must be construed in conformity with the host State's domestic law, rather than in accordance with the applicable treaty or international law. In support of such contentions, they have generally relied on the applicable treaty's 'legality' clause which denies treaty protection (or investment status) to 'investments' made in violation of host State law. They have argued that such clauses should be read as governing not only the issue of an **2.24**

---

[33] Vienna Convention on the Law of Treaties (adopted 23 May 1969, entered into force 27 January 1980) Art 31–33 (hereafter VCLT).

investment's legality, but more generally the question of the meaning of 'investment'. Arbitral tribunals have invariably rejected such arguments.

2.25 In *Salini v Morocco*, for example, Morocco claimed that the reference to compliance with host State law found in the definition of 'investment' of the applicable BIT (the BIT between Italy and Morocco) implied that 'Moroccan law should define the notion of investment'.[34] According to the Respondent, a characterization based on Moroccan law would lead to the conclusion that the contract concluded between the Italian Claimants and the Société Nationale des Autoroutes du Maroc, the Moroccan state entity in charge of building, maintaining, and operating highways and various roadworks, was not an investment, but a contract for services.[35] The Tribunal rejected this line of reasoning, holding that the legality requirement pertained to 'the validity of the investment and not to its definition'.[36]

V. The Concept of Investment as an Interpretive Issue

2.26 In the context of investor–state arbitration proceedings, the meaning of the term 'investment' is, in essence, an interpretive issue. Under Art 25 ICSID Convention, for instance, the principal interpretive question is what meaning, if any, the undefined notion of investment should be given. Under definitions contained in investment treaties and laws, interpretive issues may arise in connection with the application of the various definitional components or requirements. A question may arise, for example, in relation to the meaning of a specific category of assets listed as an example of a qualifying investment.[37] Requirements pertaining to the relationship between investor and investment may also give rise to questions of interpretation.

2.27 Interpretive issues arising under the ICSID Convention and investment treaties must be resolved in accordance with the applicable rules of treaty interpretation. Investor–state tribunals have generally not hesitated to consider that the rules of the VCLT apply.[38] As tribunals habitually observe, those rules reflect principles of customary international law of general application, making it unnecessary to examine whether the investor's home State and the Respondent State are parties to the VCLT.[39]

---

[34] *Salini Costruttori S.P.A. and Italstrade S.P.A. v Kingdom of Morocco*, ICSID Case No ARB/00/4, Decision on Jurisdiction (23 July 2001) para 38.
[35] ibid.
[36] ibid para 46.
[37] See, for example, *Global Trading v Ukraine* (n 18) para 53. The Tribunal raised the question of whether the expression 'rights conferred by law or by contract' should be construed 'literally, to include any right of any kind deriving from any form of contract' or rather 'contextually, as restricted to rights capable of constituting investments in themselves'.
[38] See Tarcisio Gazzini, *Interpretation of International Investment Treaties* (Hart Publishing 2016) 56 (noting that '[a] large majority of investment arbitral tribunals have expressly referred to the VCLT rules on interpretation and most of them have also stressed its mandatory application') (hereafter Gazzini, *Interpretation of International Investment Treaties*).
[39] ibid 56–60.

Under the general rule of interpretation of Art 31 VCLT, a treaty must be interpreted 'in good faith in accordance with the ordinary meaning to be given to the terms of the treaty in their context and in the light of its object and purpose'.[40] With the exception of good faith, these different elements (or interpretive approaches) have regularly been referred to by tribunals examining the existence of an investment. The Tribunal in *Doutremepuich v Mauritius*, for example, considered that the three core *Salini* criteria[41] (contribution, duration, and risk) reflected the 'ordinary meaning' of the term 'investment'.[42] In *Romak v Uzbekistan*, the Tribunal relied on the context in which the applicable BIT had been concluded and, more particularly, on the concomitant conclusion between the State parties of a treaty dealing with trade matters.[43] The ICSID Convention's object and purpose has notably been invoked in *Abaclat v Argentina* where the Tribunal held that the *Salini* test (understood as a set of jurisdictional requirements) was incompatible with the Convention's aim 'to encourage private investment while giving the Parties the tools to further define what kind of investment they want to promote'.[44]

2.28

The general rule of interpretation set forth in Art 31 VCLT also allows the interpreter to take into account 'subsequent agreement[s] between the parties regarding the interpretation of the treaty or [its] application',[45] as well as 'subsequent practice in the application of the treaty'.[46] Commentators have raised the question of whether one might consider that BITs constitute such subsequent agreements or practice in relation to the ICSID Convention, ie whether one may argue that the term 'investment' under the Convention should be interpreted in light of the definitions contained in such treaties.[47] As will be shown in Chapter 3, such an approach is rather problematic, and it is thus not surprising that it has not been endorsed in arbitral practice.[48]

2.29

In addition to laying down a general rule of interpretation, the VCLT provides for recourse to 'supplementary means of interpretation', which include 'the preparatory work of the treaty [ie the legislative or drafting history] and the circumstances of its conclusion'.[49] Under the VCLT, these supplementary means may only be resorted to where the

2.30

---

[40] VCLT (n 33) Art 31(1).
[41] See Chapter 1 Section II. For a detailed analysis of the *Salini* test and criteria, see Chapter 4 Section II.
[42] *Professor Christian Doutremepuich (France) and Antoine Doutremepuich (France) v The Republic of Mauritius*, PCA Case No 2018-37, Award on Jurisdiction (23 August 2019) paras 117–18 (holding that the term 'investment' under the BIT between France and Mauritius had to be interpreted in accordance with its 'objective and ordinary meaning' and that such meaning consisted of the *Salini* test and, more specifically, the requirements of a contribution, duration, and risk).
[43] *Romak S.A. (Switzerland) v The Republic of Uzbekistan*, PCA Case No AA280, Award (26 November 2009) para 182. The Tribunal considered that this was evidence of the fact that the contracting States distinguished between trade and investment and that the term 'investment' did therefore not cover trade-related transactions.
[44] *Abaclat and others v The Argentine Republic*, ICSID Case No ARB/07/5, Decision on Jurisdiction and Admissibility (4 August 2011) para 364.
[45] VCLT (n 33) Art 31(3)(a).
[46] VCLT (n 33) Art 31(3)(b).
[47] See, for example, Roberto Castro de Figueiredo, 'The Investment Requirement of the ICSID Convention and the Role of Investment Treaties' (2015) 26 Am Rev Int'l Arb 453, 459–76 (examining whether bilateral investment treaties may be viewed as 'subsequent practice' under Art 31(3)(b) VCLT.
[48] See Chapter 3 Section IV.A.
[49] VCLT (n 33) Art 32.

general rule of interpretation 'leaves the meaning ambiguous or obscure' or 'leads to a result which is manifestly absurd or unreasonable'.[50] In practice, many tribunals have resorted to this interpretive method, in particular in connection with Art 25 ICSID Convention.[51] Interestingly, they have generally done so without examining whether the prerequisites for resort to the Convention's *travaux* were met.[52]

2.31 While investor–state tribunals have primarily applied the interpretive canons of the VCLT, they have sometimes also applied other rules. The probably most significant of these is the principle of effectiveness of treaty interpretation or *effet utile*. Under this rule, a treaty provision must be construed in a manner that ensures that it is not deprived of its meaning or usefulness.[53] As will be explained in more detail in Chapter 3, this approach has notably been relied upon in support of the idea that the term 'investment' under Art 25 ICSID Convention, though not defined, nevertheless has some specific meaning.[54]

2.32 A number of commentators have questioned the quality of the interpretive rulings of investor–state tribunals.[55] They have noted that while most tribunals refer to the VCLT's rules of interpretation, many ultimately fail to apply those rules, do not apply them correctly, or fail to explain how they arrive at a particular interpretive conclusion.[56] It has also been observed that arbitral decisions are characterized by excessive reliance on case law and scholarly writings, neglecting the interpretive analysis.[57]

VI. Ordinary Meaning of the Term 'Investment'

2.33 A useful starting point for any reflection on the meaning of investment under the ICSID Convention, investment treaties, or investment laws is the 'ordinary' meaning of this term. This is not only because rules of interpretation (such as the general rule of interpretation of Art 31 VCLT) generally mandate an interpretation in accordance with such ordinary meaning, but also because the ordinary (or everyday) meaning of the concept of investment inevitably influences the way in which tribunals construe this notion, irrespectively of any legal prescription to this effect.

---

[50] ibid.
[51] See Chapter 3 Sections III.B.2.b and III.C.2.a.
[52] ibid.
[53] For an arbitral ruling defining the principle of *effet utile*, see, for example, *Wintershall Aktiengesellschaft v Argentine Republic*, ICSID Case No ARB/04/14, Award (8 December 2008) para 165 (holding that the principle of effectiveness requires that 'a clause must be so interpreted as to give it a meaning rather than so as to deprive it of meaning') (internal footnote omitted).
[54] See Chapter 3 Section III.B.2.a.
[55] See, for example, Hai Yen Trinh, *The Interpretation of Investment Treaties* (Brill 2014) 75–79 (hereafter Trinh, *The Interpretation of Investment Treaties*). See also Gazzini, *Interpretation of International Investment Treaties* (n 38) 58 (noting that '[a]rbitral tribunals have not always displayed great accuracy in dealing with the applicability of the [rules of interpretation contained in] the VCLT').
[56] Trinh, *The Interpretation of Investment Treaties* (n 55) 76–83, 91–97.
[57] ibid 83–91.

PRELIMINARY MATTERS 19

According to the *Oxford English Dictionary*, there are two categories of senses in which the word 'investment' is used: (a) '[s]enses related to clothing, surrounding, installing, and endowing' and (b) '[s]enses relating to the investing of money or capital'.[58] For rather obvious reasons, only the second type of senses is relevant for present purposes. Within this category, there are two definitions (definitions 8.a and 8.b) pertaining to the meaning of 'investment' in the specific field of 'finance'. These are of particular relevance and will be the focus of this section.

2.34

Definition 8.a defines 'investment' as '[t]he use of money or capital to purchase an asset or assets (such as property, stocks, bonds, etc.) in the expectation of earning income or profit over time'.[59] Under definition 8.b., an investment consists of '[a]n act or instance of investing money or capital in property, stocks, bonds, etc.; an amount of money so invested' and, additionally, as 'a (form or type of) property, stock, bond, etc., in which money or capital has been or may be invested'.[60]

2.35

These two definitions provide a twofold insight. They highlight, first of all, the basic characteristic features or elements of an investment. These include (a) the purchase of an asset or assets (such as property, stocks, and bonds), (b) the pursuit of profit (the purchase is made 'in the expectation of earning income or profit'), and (c) the idea that such profit will materialize at some point in the future (the expectation is to earn income or profit 'over time').

2.36

The more interesting insight is that these definitions underline the complex nature of the concept of investment. In fact, the term 'investment' may refer to three different 'things' or 'realities'. It may, first of all, refer to a process or activity, ie to the act of investing. Understood in this sense, an investment consists of the act of purchasing certain assets with the aim of making a profit. Alternatively, the term 'investment' may be understood as the funds (money or capital) used to purchase the asset or assets concerned. Indeed, the *Oxford English Dictionary* expressly mentions that one meaning of 'investment' is 'an amount of money ... invested'.[61] From yet another perspective, an investment may be considered not as the process of investing or the funds used to invest, but as the assets purchased. In fact, the *Oxford English Dictionary* expressly states that 'investment' may also refer to 'a (form or type of) property, stock, bond, etc., in which money or capital has been or may be invested'.[62]

2.37

An example will be helpful to illustrate the complex (or uncertain) nature of 'investment'. Where an investor purchases land in order to build and operate a hotel, his or her investment could be viewed as referring to either of three 'things'. Under one view, the investment would consist of the act or process of purchasing the land. Under a second view, one would consider that the investment refers to the funds used to purchase the

2.38

---

[58] See https://www.oed.com/view/Entry/99052?redirectedFrom=investment#eid.
[59] ibid.
[60] ibid.
[61] ibid.
[62] ibid.

land. A third approach would be to equate the investment with the land purchased by the investor.

VII. Meaning of the Economic Concept of Investment

2.39 There is no single, uniform notion of investment in the field of economics. In fact, the meaning of this term may vary depending on the particular branch of study. In the area of finance, for example, the notion of 'investment' does not seem to be a term possessing a specific, universally acknowledged, meaning. It is telling in this respect that the index of one standard finance textbook does not feature any entry for the term 'investment', but merely entries for 'investment banker', 'investment banking', and 'investment value'.[63]

2.40 In the field of macroeconomics, on the other hand, the concept of investment appears to have an established meaning. As Pahis has explained, two forms of economic 'output' are typically distinguished under macroeconomic principles: consumption, on the one hand, and investment and savings, on the other hand.[64] As this author has rightly observed, no distinction is drawn at the macroeconomic level between trade and investment[65] and there is thus no basis for arguing that a trade-related transaction such as a sale of goods does not, or cannot, amount to an investment. Where, for example, a buyer purchases goods for resale, rather than for consumption, this transaction would, from the point of view of the buyer, qualify as an investment.[66]

2.41 As far as writings on the subject of international business are concerned, they generally approach the concept of investment from a microeconomic perspective, ie from the viewpoint of potential investors, generally multinational enterprises (MNEs). Among other things, this literature seeks to shed light on the process of 'internationalization' of business, ie on why and how businesses sell their services and goods in foreign markets.[67] The various ways in which such internationalization occurs are generally referred to as different modes of entry.[68]

2.42 It is generally recognized that there are two main types of entry modes.[69] The first category comprises non-equity modes, ie modes of entry that do not involve any acquisition of assets in the market of entry. These notably include direct and indirect exports, licensing and franchising agreements, and other similar contractual arrangements. The

---

[63] Ehsan Nikbakht and Angelico Groppelli, *Finance* (7th edn, Barron's 2018).
[64] Stratos Pahis, 'Investment Misconceived: The Investment-Commerce Distinction in International Investment Law' (2020) 45 Yale J Int'l L 69, 105.
[65] ibid (noting that '[e]conomic principles do not distinguish between commercial and investment activities').
[66] ibid 106.
[67] See, for example, Stuart Wall, Bronwen Rees, and Sonal Minocha, *International Business* (3rd edn, Pearson 2010) 38–78.
[68] See, for example, Simon Collinson, Rajneesh Narula, and Alan Rugman, *International Business* (8th edn, Pearson 2020) 61–65 (hereafter Collinson, Narula, and Rugman, *International Business*).
[69] Collinson, Narula, and Rugman, *International Business* (n 68) 61–62.

second category consists of equity modes of entry, ie modes of entry involving the acquisition of assets in the foreign market. These modes are generically referred to as foreign direct investment (FDI).

2.43 FDI has been defined as investment that 'provide[s] the owners with not just ownership, but through that ownership, strategic and managerial control of an ongoing enterprise'.[70] The key criterion of FDI is therefore the investor's ability to exercise control over the management of an enterprise. According to the Organisation for Economic Cooperation and Development benchmark definition, such control exists where the investor 'owns at least 10% of the voting power of the direct investment enterprise'.[71] Where an investor's interest in an enterprise falls below this threshold, the investment is deemed to be a 'portfolio' investment.

2.44 According to the literature, FDI may consist of either shared or full ownership of an enterprise. While joint ventures with local entities are generally provided as the sole example of shared ownership, in reality, any acquisition of an interest in a company's voting shares meeting the applicable threshold of control will also qualify. As far as full ownership, ie the setting up of a wholly owned subsidiary, is concerned, writers generally distinguish between greenfield investment, which 'involves the establishment of a completely new business unit in a foreign market', and the acquisition of an existing firm.[72]

VIII. The Nature of Investment

2.45 As the examination of the ordinary meaning of 'investment' has shown, this term can be conceptualized in three ways: (1) as the *funds* an investor uses to purchase an asset that he or she expects to be profit-bearing, (2) as the *asset* so purchased, and (3) as the *act* or *process* of purchasing the asset concerned.

2.46 The concept of FDI explored in the preceding section adds another possible dimension to the meaning of 'investment'. FDI, as has been explained, consists of a controlling interest in a foreign enterprise. An enterprise is, by definition, engaged in specific business activities (or operations) and the conduct of such activities can thus be regarded as a characteristic element of FDI. Accordingly, a fourth possible approach to the question of the nature of 'investment' is to assimilate an investment to certain economic activities. Where an investor purchases a plot of land in order to build and operate a hotel,

---

[70] ibid 37.
[71] Organisation for Economic Cooperation and Development, *OECD Benchmark Definition of Foreign Direct Investment* (4th edn, OECD 2008) 17 (observing that '[d]irect investment is a category of cross-border investment made by a resident in one economy (the direct investor) with the objective of establishing a lasting interest in an enterprise (the direct investment enterprise) that is resident in an economy other than that of the direct investor' and that '[t]he "lasting interest" is evidenced when the direct investor owns at least 10% of the voting power of the direct investment enterprise').
[72] Collinson, Narula, and Rugman, *International Business* (n 68) 62.

for example, the investment can be considered to consist not only of the funds used, the land purchased, or the act of purchasing the land, but also of the investor's business operations, ie the running of the hotel.

2.47 The fact that the term 'investment' may refer to four different 'realities' inevitably raises a number of questions. How does one know or decide which particular nature of investment is relevant in a given case? Will it simply depend on how the concept of 'investment' is defined in the applicable legal instrument? Is it at all necessary to determine what the 'nature' of a particular investment is, given that the various elements (in particular the funds used, the asset purchased, and the act of purchasing the asset) are interrelated and cannot in principle exist independently of each other?

2.48 Thus far, these questions have received very little attention from academic writers. While a few commentators have stressed the ambiguity surrounding the basic nature of 'investment', they have generally refrained from examining its implications or possible remedies to the existing uncertainty. Rubins, for example, has very aptly pointed out the absence of 'agreement [as to] whether "investment" is a thing or an activity',[73] highlighting the differences between investment treaties, on the one hand, and the views expressed by economists and legal scholars, on the other hand.[74] However, focusing on different issues, the author did not further analyse the causes, nature, or consequences of this disagreement.

2.49 In other writings, one finds an acknowledgement of the fact that different types of definitions coexist, both in investment treaties and in investment laws. These contributions typically refer to the commonly accepted view that 'asset-based' definitions of 'investment', ie definitions that view investments as assets, coexist with 'enterprise-based' definitions under which investments are considered as enterprises.[75] However, they do not further investigate the implications of each of these conflicting approaches, or the consequences of their coexistence.[76]

2.50 The question of the nature of 'investment' is particularly delicate under the ICSID Convention given that, as has been explained, the Convention does not contain any

---

[73] Noah Rubins, 'The Notion of "Investment" in International Investment Arbitration' in Norbert Horn and Stefan Michael Kröll (eds), *Arbitrating Foreign Investment Disputes: Procedural and Substantive Legal Aspects*, Studies in Transnational Economic Law, vol 19 (Kluwer Law International 2004) 283, 284.

[74] ibid (noting that '[w]hile investment treaties tend to view investment as a subset of assets, economists and legal commentators more often describe it as a phenomenon, a process, or an action') (internal footnotes omitted).

[75] As far as treaty definitions are concerned, see, for example, Stephan W Schill, Christoph W Schreuer, and Anthony Sinclair, 'Article 25' in Loretta Malintoppi, August Reinisch, Christoph W Schreuer, and Anthony Sinclair (eds), *Schreuer's Commentary on the ICSID Convention: A Commentary on the Convention on the Settlement of Investment Disputes between States and Nationals of Other States* (3rd edn, Cambridge University Press 2022) paras 214–21 (discussing various types of asset-based definitions), 222 (presenting enterprise-based definitions) (hereafter Schill, Schreuer, and Sinclair, 'Article 25'). As regards definitions of 'investment' found in investment laws, see, for example, UNCTAD, Investment Policy Monitor, *Investment Laws—A Widespread Tool for the Promotion and Regulation of Foreign Investment* (UNCTAD 2016) 4 (explaining that while some treaties 'apply a broad asset-based approach', others follow 'a limited enterprise-based approach').

[76] See, for example, Schill, Schreuer, and Sinclair, 'Article 25' (n 75) paras 214–22. While the authors acknowledge the coexistence of asset-based and enterprise-based treaty definitions, they do not discuss the resulting conceptual uncertainty.

definition of this concept. Under the *Salini* test (the prevailing arbitral approach), however, investments are arguably viewed as activities or operations. In fact, as will be shown in Chapter 4, the three core *Salini* criteria, ie contributions, duration, and risk, are only meaningful when applied to such activities or operations.[77] They are ill-suited as factors describing assets since it means very little to speak of contributions to, the duration of, or the risk associated with an asset.

In practice, this means that arbitral tribunals applying the double-keyhole test will often perform two inquiries based on different understandings of the nature of investment. Under the applicable investment treaty or law, the question is frequently going to be whether there is a qualifying asset, while the Art 25 inquiry will generally pertain to whether the investor is conducting (or has conducted) certain activities or operations. **2.51**

As *Mitchell v Congo* exemplifies, this state of affairs has led to some degree of confusion. In this case, the Claimant's presumed investment consisted of a legal counselling firm in the Democratic Republic of the Congo. In its analysis of the existence of an investment, the Tribunal focused on the BIT between the United States and the Congolese Republic, holding that the objective criteria that may apply under Art 25 ICSID Convention did not constitute 'formal requirement[s]', but merely 'elements [that were] frequently present in investment projects'.[78] It held that the Claimant owned both tangible (movable property) and intangible assets (various types of rights) that qualified as investments under the BIT.[79] **2.52**

The ad hoc Committee found this reasoning to be inadequate.[80] One aspect of its critique is particularly interesting. In fact, the Committee held that the Tribunal had confused 'the economic operation or project—which, if it fulfills certain characteristics, becomes the investment within the meaning of the Convention and the Treaty' with 'the rights and assets protected by the Treaty because they are part of the operation or project'.[81] According to the Committee, the Claimant's possible investment in this case did not, therefore, consist of the various assets it owned, but of the legal consulting services it provided. Clearly, the Tribunal and the ad hoc Committee took different views with regard to the nature of 'investment' in ICSID arbitration and the award's annulment is at least in part attributable to this difference of view. **2.53**

---

[77] See Chapter 4 Section II.B.
[78] *Patrick H. Mitchell v The Democratic Republic of the Congo*, ICSID Case No ARB/99/7, Award (9 February 2004) para 56.
[79] ibid para 48.
[80] *Mr Patrick Mitchell v the Democratic Republic of the Congo*, ICSID Case No ARB/99/7, Decision on the Application for Annulment of the Award (1 November 2006) paras 34–41.
[81] ibid para 38.

IX. Interests Involved in Defining the Concept of Investment

A. Investor and host State interests

2.54 The way in which the term 'investment' is defined in a particular legal instrument, or construed by an arbitral tribunal, evidently affects the interests of the parties to investment disputes, ie of investors and host States. This is because the concept of investment defines the sphere of the rights enjoyed by investors, as well as the scope of the obligations owed by host States under the ICSID Convention, investment treaties, and domestic investment laws.

2.55 To a large extent, investor interests and host State interests are conflicting. In fact, investors understandably have an interest in broad definitions of 'investment', ie definitions that cover a wide (or the widest possible) spectrum of assets or operations. The interests of host States, on the other hand, are generally best served by narrow definitions, ie definitions that allow them to minimize the scope of possible liability vis-à-vis foreign investors and ensure that legal protection is only granted to 'investments' that benefit the host State's economy.

2.56 The conflict between investor and host State interests plays out at two levels. It occurs, first of all, in the context of the negotiation, drafting, and conclusion of investment treaties. Many of these treaties are concluded between developed countries, on the one hand, and developing countries, on the other hand. In these cases, the investment flows between the States concerned are largely one-directional, ie investors from the developed country will invest in the developing country. As a consequence, the interests of the developed country will generally align with those of investors, while those of the developing country will be the usual host State interests described above. It is perhaps unrealistic to assume that the negotiators of investment treaties are fully aware of the possible implications of defining the term 'investment' broadly or narrowly. However, the fact that most Model BITs adopted by major capital-exporting nations such as the United States, Germany, the UK, or France contain broad definitions[82] could be viewed as indicating that some level of awareness exists.

2.57 The clash between the interests of developing and developed States (and their investors) became apparent during the negotiation and drafting of the ICSID Convention. In fact, the former generally preferred a narrowly defined scope of jurisdiction, repeatedly insisting on the need to define the concept of 'investment'.[83] In contrast, most developed

---

[82] US Model BIT 2012 Art 1; German Model BIT 2008 Art 1(1); UK Model BIT 2008 Art 1(a); French Model BIT 2006 Art 1(1). These provisions all contain broad, asset-based definitions of 'investment'. It should be noted, however, that the US Model BIT requires that an investment must have certain 'characteristics'. For a detailed analysis of this requirement and its significance for contemporary treaty practice, see Chapter 6 Section III.

[83] Julian Davis Mortenson, 'The Meaning of "Investment": ICSID's *Travaux* and the Domain of International Investment Law' (2010) 51 Harv Int'l LJ 257, 284. Commenting on the four 'Consultative Meetings of Legal Experts' which took place between December 1963 and May 1964, Mortenson notes that '[s]ome delegates, especially those from developing countries, called for a precise definition of the scope of jurisdiction of the Center', while '[o]thers, primarily from capital-exporting countries, found even the loose reference to "dispute of a legal character" too restrictive' (internal footnotes and quotation marks omitted).

States favoured a more extensive scope of jurisdiction[84] and took the view that it was not necessary to define the term 'investment' in the Convention, given that the State parties to the Convention (a) would have the possibility of specifying the categories of disputes that they wish or do not wish to submit to the Centre[85] and (b) would be able to restrict the notion of investment through definitions contained in investment treaties and laws.

2.58 The second level at which the opposing interests of developing and developed nations collide is the dispute resolution stage. Given the quasi-systematic presence of detailed definitions of investment in investment treaties and laws, the primary battleground has been the interpretation of Art 25 ICSID Convention. The different existing approaches are all more or less investor- or host State–friendly (it being understood that investor–friendly definitions favour developed States, while host State–friendly definitions favour developing States). On one end of the spectrum, the traditional *Salini* approach, which views the objective *Salini* criteria as jurisdictional requirements, is the least investor- and most host State–friendly. On the other end, the subjective approach, which entirely denies the existence of objective criteria under Art 25 ICSID Convention, is the most investor- and least host State–friendly.

B. Systemic interests

2.59 The way in which the concept of 'investment' is defined in legal instruments and/or construed by arbitral tribunals does not only involve the individual interests of investors, home States, and host States, but also systemic interests, ie the more general interests of the ISDS system as such. A fundamental interest in this respect is predictability. In fact, investors have an interest in being able to predict what types of operations and/or assets will be protected under a given legal instrument. Host States have an interest in being able to foresee the scope of the obligations they undertake under investment treaties or laws.

2.60 As far as Art 25 ICSID Convention is concerned, predictability seems to be largely compromised. In fact, the Convention's silence on the meaning of investment has generated a considerable variety of approaches in arbitral practice (the 'traditional' *Salini* test, the typical-characteristics approach, the permissibility test, the commercial-transaction test, and the subjective approach). Superficially, it would appear as though there is growing consensus on the applicability of the *Salini* test. However, the controversy surrounding the applicable criteria is still very much alive,[86] and there is considerable

---

[84] ibid.
[85] Such a possibility exists under the final text of the Convention. See ICSID Convention (n 2) Art 25(4): 'Any Contracting State may, at the time of ratification, acceptance or approval of this Convention or at any time thereafter, notify the Centre of the class or classes of disputes which it would or would not consider submitting to the jurisdiction of the Centre.'
[86] While there is, at least among arbitral tribunals, general consensus on the three 'core' *Salini* criteria of contributions, a minimum duration, and risk, the relevance of several other possible factors continues to be controversial. See Chapter 4 Sections II.C and II.D. See also Michael Waibel, 'Subject Matter Jurisdiction: The Notion of

support for the typical-characteristics approach[87] which, in reality, rejects the basic foundation of the *Salini* test, namely, the existence of objective requirements.[88]

2.61 There is very little that individual ICSID contracting States and investor–state tribunals can do to improve predictability. The former are evidently unable to amend the Convention and adopt a definition of the term 'investment' that would be binding on other contracting States. Such an amendment would require the consensus of all contracting States,[89] and it is virtually excluded that such consensus can be reached (in addition, it is rather unlikely that there is any real desire to amend the Convention). Tribunals generally opt for one of the existing approaches but have evidently no control over how other tribunals interpret the concept of investment in subsequent cases.

2.62 Unpredictability (and inconsistency of decisions) has been identified as a more general shortcoming of international investment law and the existing ISDS system,[90] well beyond the definition and interpretation of the concept of 'investment'. Several reform proposals are currently being discussed under the auspices of United Nations Commission on International Trade Law (UNCITRAL). These include, for example, the issuance of joint interpretative declarations by State parties to investment treaties[91] and the introduction of appellate mechanisms[92]. The most ambitious reform option consists of the establishment of a permanent multilateral investment court having appellate jurisdiction.[93]

2.63 Predictability as a systemic interest is closely linked to uniformity. If a uniform concept of investment is applied in all ICSID arbitration cases or in all investor–state disputes more generally, this would obviously benefit the achievement of predictability. The

Investment' (2021) 19 ICSID Reports 25, paras 129–30 (concluding that 'the notion of investment—which is the cornerstone of the subject matter jurisdiction of (ICSID) investment tribunals—remains in flux' and that 'a consensus among tribunals remains elusive').

[87] See Chapter 3 Section III.D.
[88] ibid.
[89] ICSID Convention (n 2) Art 66 (providing that amendments 'enter into force 30 days after dispatch by the depositary of this Convention of a notification to Contracting States that *all Contracting States* have ratified, accepted or approved the amendment', emphasis added).
[90] United Nations Commission on International Trade Law Working Group III (Investor–State Dispute Settlement Reform) Thirty-fourth session, Vienna, 27 November–1 December 2017, Possible reform of Investor–State Dispute Settlement (ISDS), Note by the Secretariat, A/CN.9/WG.III/WP.142, paras 31–41.
[91] United Nations Commission on International Trade Law Working Group III (Investor–State Dispute Settlement Reform) Thirty-ninth session, New York, 30 March–3 April 2020, Possible reform of ISDS Interpretation of investment treaties by treaty parties, A/CN.9/WG.III/WP.191.
[92] United Nations Commission on International Trade Law Working Group III (Investor–State Dispute Settlement Reform) Forty-fourth session, Vienna, 23–27 January 2023, Possible reform of ISDS Appellate mechanism, A/CN.9/WG.III/WP.224.
[93] United Nations Commission on International Trade Law Working Group III (Investor–State Dispute Settlement Reform) Thirty-eighth session (resumed), Vienna, 20–24 January 2020, Possible reform of ISDS Appellate and multilateral court mechanisms, A/CN.9/WG.III/WP.185.

question is whether such uniformity is at all desirable. As is well known, the current system rests on a very large number of BITs, giving the State parties to these treaties the opportunity to define the concept of 'investment' in a manner which best accommodates their individual preferences. It is difficult to assess whether this advantage would be outweighed by the existence of a uniform concept of investment.

3

The Question of Whether Art 25 ICSID Convention Lays Down Independent Requirements for the Existence of an Investment

I. Introduction	3.01	C. Decisions holding that Art 25 ICSID Convention does not lay down independent requirements for the existence of an investment	3.44
II. Conceptual Framework	3.02		
A. Prevailing conceptualization	3.02		
B. Critical analysis of the prevailing conceptualization	3.06	D. Decisions adopting the ambivalent typical-characteristics approach	3.55
C. Reframing the question: does the term 'investment' under Art 25 ICSID Convention have an 'implied' or 'independent' meaning?	3.14	IV. Scholarly Opinions	3.63
		A. Broad support for the existence of independent requirements under Art 25 ICSID Convention	3.63
D. Terminology used in this book	3.16	B. Limited support for the absence of independent requirements under Art 25 ICSID Convention	3.71
III. Arbitral Case Law	3.18		
A. Silent and inconclusive decisions	3.18		
B. Decisions holding that Art 25 ICSID Convention lays down independent requirements for the existence of an investment	3.21	V. Assessment	3.77
		A. Objective approach	3.77
		B. Subjective approach	3.84

I. Introduction

3.01 This chapter examines the question of whether Art 25 ICSID Convention lays down independent requirements for the existence of an investment. Section II discusses the terminological framework of this question, critically analyses the prevailing conceptualization, and suggests ways to reframe the issue. Section III reviews arbitral case law, distinguishing three categories of decisions: decisions following the prevailing objective approach (which considers that the term 'investment' under Art 25 ICSID Convention has an independent meaning), decisions adopting the subjective approach (which denies the existence of such a meaning), and decisions following the rather ambiguous 'typical-characteristics' approach which could be viewed as belonging to either of the first two categories. Section IV provides a brief overview of scholarly opinions, showing that a significant majority of writers favour the objective approach. Section V assesses the arguments put forward in support of, and against, the two competing viewpoints and argues that the objective approach is more compelling.

II. Conceptual Framework

A. Prevailing conceptualization

1. The question of whether the term 'investment' under Art 25 ICSID Convention possesses an 'objective' meaning

The question examined in this chapter is, in simple terms, whether the term 'investment' in Art 25 ICSID Convention, despite not being defined, nevertheless has some meaning. Taken out of context, this question may seem puzzling: why would the concept of 'investment' *not* have a meaning? As has already been explained,[1] the reason why this question has arisen is that unlike Art 25 ICSID Convention, most legal instruments containing the parties' consent to ICSID arbitration do define the concept of 'investment'. One may, therefore, wonder whether the definitions contained in these instruments should be solely relevant to determine the existence of an investment (which would be simpler) or whether, to the contrary, the term 'investment' in Art 25 should be considered as having a meaning of its own.

3.02

This issue is commonly conceptualized as the question of whether the term 'investment' in Art 25 ICSID Convention has an 'objective' meaning[2] or, to use other formulations found in arbitral case law, whether Art 25 lays down 'objective requirements' for the existence of an investment,[3] whether it sets forth an 'objective definition' of this term,[4] or whether 'investment' under Art 25 has an 'objective content'.[5] Tribunals do not explain, however, what exactly is meant by 'objective' meaning. What is fairly certain, though, is that the expression 'objective meaning' is employed to contrast the meaning of 'investment' under Art 25 ICSID Convention with the 'subjective' meaning that this concept (arguably) has under instruments of consent.[6]

3.03

There are, unsurprisingly, two possible answers to the question of whether the concept of 'investment' in Art 25 ICSID Convention has an 'objective' meaning. Under the so-called 'subjective' approach, the term 'investment' lacks such a meaning, and the definition contained in the applicable consent instrument, if any, constitutes the only relevant threshold.[7] According to the 'objective' approach, on the other hand, the concept of

3.04

---

[1] See Chapter 1 Section II.
[2] See, for example, Michael Waibel, 'Subject Matter Jurisdiction: The Notion of Investment' (2021) 19 ICSID Reports 25, para 1 (noting that Art 25 ICSID Convention raises two legal issues: first, whether the term 'investment' 'has an objective meaning' and, in the affirmative, 'which elements ought to be used to objectively determine investments') (hereafter Waibel, 'Subject Matter Jurisdiction').
[3] *Patrick H. Mitchell v The Democratic Republic of the Congo*, ICSID Case No ARB/99/7, Award (9 February 2004) para 56 (hereafter *Mitchell v Congo*); *Joy Mining Machinery Limited v The Arab Republic of Egypt*, ICSID Case No ARB/03/11, Award on Jurisdiction (6 August 2004) para 50 (hereafter *Joy Mining v Egypt*).
[4] *Mr. Saba Fakes v Republic of Turkey*, ICSID Case No ARB/07/20, Award (14 July 2010) para 108 (hereafter *Fakes v Turkey*).
[5] *Malaysian Historical Salvors Sdn Bhd v The Government of Malaysia*, ICSID Case No ARB/05/10, Decision on the Application for Annulment (16 April 2009) para 72 (hereafter *Malaysian Historical Salvors v Malaysia*).
[6] See Waibel, 'Subject Matter Jurisdiction' (n 2) para 6.
[7] See Mahnaz Malik, 'Definition of Investment in International Investment Agreements' (2009) International Institute for Sustainable Development, Best Practices Series 9 (noting that '[t]he subjective approach focuses on the state parties' definition of investment in the IIA [international investment agreement], and does not enforce

'investment' in Art 25 ICSID Convention does possess an objective meaning.[8] Under this approach, a transaction or asset must therefore meet the requirements of both the applicable consent instrument and Art 25 ICSID Convention in order to qualify as an investment.

2. The double-keyhole or double-barrelled test

3.05 The question of whether the term 'investment' in Art 25 ICSID Convention has an objective meaning is frequently associated with the question of whether arbitral tribunals should apply the so-called 'double-keyhole' or 'double-barrelled' test. These terms capture the idea, inherent in the objective approach, that the determination of the existence of an investment involves a twofold inquiry: one under the applicable consent instrument and another one under Art 25 ICSID Convention.[9] Scholars typically equate the existence of an objective meaning of investment with the double-keyhole approach.[10]

B. Critical analysis of the prevailing conceptualization

1. Distinction between the subjective and the objective meaning of investment

3.06 The widely accepted distinction between the subjective and the objective meaning of investment is, at least potentially, misleading. In fact, in the field of interpretation (in particular, contract interpretation), the subjective meaning of a provision refers to the actual intent of the parties, while its objective meaning denotes the parties' hypothetical intent, ie the meaning that reasonable third parties would attribute to a particular term or clause. Applying this distinction, one might therefore assume that the subjective and objective meaning of the concept of 'investment' reflect the parties' actual intent, on the one hand, and their hypothetical intent, on the other hand.

3.07 Both propositions, however, are at least partly inaccurate. To begin with, the subjective meaning of investment, ie the meaning that this term has under consent instruments,

---

an independent requirement to be met for the purposes of the ICSID Convention') (hereafter Malik, 'Definition of Investment'); Jeremy Marc Exelbert, 'Consistently Inconsistent: What is a Qualifying Investment Under Article 25 of the ICSID Convention and Why the Debate Must End' (2016) 85 Fordham L Rev 143, 1257 (observing that the subjective approach is 'deferential to the language chosen by the parties to a dispute') (hereafter Exelbert, 'Consistently Inconsistent'); Stratos Pahis, 'Investment Misconceived: The Investment-Commerce Distinction in International Investment Law' (2020) 45 Yale J Int'l L 77–79 (hereafter Pahis, 'Investment Misconceived').

[8] See Malik, 'Definition of Investment' (n 7) 5 (explaining that '[t]he so-called objective test states that the ICSID Convention entails objective requirements to define an investment').
[9] See Waibel, 'Subject Matter Jurisdiction' (n 2) para 7 (noting that, under this test, 'tribunals assess, over and above the applicable investment treaty, whether the transaction qualifies as an investment under Article 25 ICSID Convention'); Stephan W Schill, Christoph W Schreuer and Anthony Sinclair, 'Article 25' in Loretta Malintoppi, August Reinisch, Christoph W Schreuer and Anthony Sinclair (eds), *Schreuer's Commentary on the ICSID Convention: A Commentary on the Convention on the Settlement of Investment Disputes between States and Nationals of Other States* (3rd edn, Cambridge University Press 2022) para 186 (explaining that, under the double-keyhole approach, tribunals examine 'whether the activity in question is covered by the parties' consent and whether it meets the Convention's independent requirement') (hereafter Schill, Schreuer and Sinclair, 'Article 25').
[10] See, for example, Waibel, 'Subject Matter Jurisdiction' (n 2) para 7 (stating that '[t]his approach [the objective approach] is also known as the "outer limits" test, or a "double-barrelled test"') (internal footnotes omitted).

does not—despite statements to the contrary[11]—reflect the actual intent of parties to disputes arising under such instruments. In fact, investment treaty definitions of 'investment' and definitions of 'investment' contained in domestic investment laws reflect the will of the State or States concerned, not the intent of investors relying on such treaties or laws.

The idea of an 'objective' meaning of the term 'investment' under Art 25 ICSID Convention is similarly deceptive. In fact, while it is undeniable that the meaning of 'investment' under Art 25 does not correspond to the actual intent of investors initiating ICSID proceedings, it does however reflect the intent of the Respondent State, necessarily a party to the ICSID Convention. As will be seen below, many tribunals interpreting Art 25 ICSID Convention, in particular those that draw on the Convention's drafting history, seek to determine the actual intent of the Convention's drafters.[12] Their interpretations therefore reveal the subjective meaning of Art 25's notion of investment, not its objective meaning. **3.08**

In reality, the distinction drawn between the objective and the subjective meaning of 'investment' is not a distinction between two different types of meaning, but a distinction between two types of legal instruments: instruments of consent, on the one hand, and the ICSID Convention, on the other hand. However, as has been explained, there is no compelling reason why one should consider that 'investment' is a 'subjective' term under the former and an 'objective' term under the latter. In fact, under both instruments of consent and the ICSID Convention, the concept of 'investment' has both a subjective meaning reflecting the actual or 'subjective' will of the State parties to the applicable instrument and an objective meaning based on the understanding of reasonable third parties. **3.09**

2. Double-keyhole approach

The second common conceptualization, which consists of asking whether Art 25 ICSID Convention calls for a double-keyhole test to determine the existence of an investment, is also potentially misleading. In fact, this terminology assumes that there always is a first keyhole, ie that instruments of consent always contain a definition of the concept of 'investment'. This assumption, however, is not accurate. **3.10**

As far as investment treaties are concerned, it is certainly true that a significant majority of them define the term 'investment'. However, the data provided by the United Nations Conference on Trade and Development (UNCTAD) investment treaty database suggests that approximately 2 per cent of existing treaties (50 out of 2,584 mapped treaties) lack such a definition.[13] As one commentator has rightly pointed out in this **3.11**

---

[11] Exelbert, 'Consistently Inconsistent' (n 7) 1257 (affirming that investment treaty definitions of 'investment' represent 'the language chosen by the parties to a dispute').
[12] See Sections III.B.2.b and III.C.2.a below.
[13] UNCTAD, 'International Investment Agreements Navigator' <https://investmentpolicy.unctad.org/international-investment-agreements/iia-mapping> accessed 24 January 2023.

connection, treaties 'that do not contain any definition of "investment" do exist',[14] even though they may be rare.

3.12 There appears to be an even larger proportion of investment *laws* that fail to define the concept of 'investment'. According to UNCTAD's investment law database, 79 out of 136 mapped domestic investment laws feature definitions of 'investment', and 61 of these 136 laws contain definitions of the more specific notion of 'foreign investment'.[15] Although the database does not provide information on the number of laws that define both or neither of these terms, it can be assumed that a number of them specify the meaning of both concepts and that, therefore, a number of investment laws define neither.

3.13 Lastly, it is important to highlight that the third category of consent instruments, namely, investment contracts, (virtually) never contain any definitions of the concept of 'investment'. In fact, while investment treaties and laws need to determine their respective spheres of application, notably by defining the notion of investment, no such need arises in connection with investment contracts. The conclusion of an ICSID arbitration clause indicates that the parties to the contract view the transaction as constituting, or being related to, an investment,[16] and it would therefore be illogical for them to establish a jurisdictional requirement in the form of a definition of 'investment'.

C. Reframing the question: does the term 'investment' under Art 25 ICSID Convention have an 'implied' or 'independent' meaning?

3.14 Two arguably superior alternatives exist to the currently prevailing terminology. The first one is to ask whether the term 'investment' in Art 25 ICSID Convention has an 'implied' meaning. In fact, given that the Convention does not define the concept of 'investment', it follows that this term lacks an 'express' meaning. However, the Convention's silence does not mean that the term 'investment' cannot or does not have an 'implied' meaning. In fact, if it has any meaning at all, such meaning is, absent an express definition, necessarily an implied one.

3.15 The other option is to pose the question in terms of whether the concept of 'investment' under Art 25 ICSID Convention has an 'independent' meaning, ie a meaning that is independent of the meaning that this concept has, or may have, under the applicable consent instrument. This terminology can occasionally be found in arbitral case law. In *Quiborax v Bolivia*,[17] for example, the Tribunal noted that Bolivia did not dispute that

---

[14] See Jean Ho, 'The Meaning of "Investment" in ICSID Arbitrations' (2010) 26 Arb Int'l 644, n 69 (hereafter Ho, 'The Meaning of "Investment"').
[15] UNCTAD, 'Investment Laws Navigator' <https://investmentpolicy.unctad.org/investment-laws> accessed 24 January 2023.
[16] While investment contracts occasionally contain language confirming the investment status of the contract or the rights arising under it, they virtually never define the term 'investment'.
[17] *Quiborax S.A. and others v Plurinational State of Bolivia*, ICSID Case No ARB/06/2, Decision on Jurisdiction (27 September 2012).

the Claimant had made an investment within the meaning of the applicable bilateral investment treaty (BIT) and that the question to resolve was, therefore, 'whether Art. 25(1) of the ICSID Convention includ[ed] an investment test *independent* from, and thus additional to, the investment test of the BIT'.[18] The Tribunal in *Vestey v Venezuela* framed the issue in similar terms, explaining that a 'majority of ICSID tribunals hold that the term "investment" in Article 25 of the ICSID Convention has an *independent* meaning'.[19]

D. Terminology used in this book

As has been shown, it is somewhat confusing to frame the issue examined in this chapter as the question of whether the term 'investment' has an 'objective' meaning. However, since the distinction between the objective and the subjective meaning of investment and the related distinction between the objective and the subjective approach are widely recognized, and since many decisions discussed in this book refer to these distinctions and concepts, it would be inappropriate to reject this terminology. **3.16**

For the reasons indicated above, the present issue is more appropriately described as pertaining to whether the term 'investment' under Art 25 ICSID Convention has an 'independent' or 'implied' meaning. This book will therefore use the expressions 'independent meaning' and 'implied meaning' synonymously for 'objective meaning'. The adjectives 'objective', 'implied', and 'independent' will not only be used in connection with the 'meaning' of investment under Art 25, but also to qualify the corresponding definitional 'requirements', 'criteria', 'elements', or 'factors'. **3.17**

III. Arbitral Case Law

A. Silent and inconclusive decisions

Although many—if not most—ICSID cases involve objections alleging the absence of a qualifying investment, not all decisions rendered in these cases necessarily address the specific question of whether Art 25 ICSID Convention lays down independent requirements for the existence of an investment. There are, first of all, a number of cases where the Respondents only challenged the existence of an investment under the applicable investment treaty or law, not under the Convention. Examples of such cases notably **3.18**

---

[18] ibid para 210 (emphasis added).
[19] *Vestey Group Limited v Bolivarian Republic of Venezuela*, ICSID Case No ARB/06/4, Award (15 April 2016) para 187 (emphasis added, internal footnote omitted).

include *PSEG v Turkey*,[20] *Al Tamimi v Oman*,[21] *Tethyan Copper v Pakistan*,[22] *Italba v Uruguay*,[23] *Anglo-Adriatic v Albania*,[24] and *Makae v Saudi Arabia*.[25]

3.19 There are also cases in which the issue of the existence of independent requirements under Art 25 ICSID Convention arose, but where the tribunals failed to decide this issue, holding that it was not necessary to do so. In *GEA v Ukraine*,[26] for example, the Tribunal explained the conflicting subjective and objective approaches,[27] but decided that it was not necessary to opt for one or the other approach, given that the outcome would in any event be the same.[28] In *Poštová banka v Greece*,[29] the Tribunal also held that it was not necessary to decide whether the term 'investment' in Art 25 ICSID Convention had an independent meaning, given that there was no qualifying investment under the applicable treaty,[30] the BIT between Slovakia and Greece. Another example is *ACP v Kosovo* where the Tribunal similarly concluded that, absent an investment in the sense of the applicable investment treaty, there was no need to decide whether separate requirements were applicable under Art 25 ICSID Convention.[31]

3.20 Lastly, there are also decisions where tribunals did address the question of whether Art 25 ICSID Convention lays down implied requirements for the existence of an investment but provided unclear or inconsistent answers. In *Mitchell v Congo*, for instance, the Tribunal apparently endorsed the double-keyhole approach under which an asset

---

[20] *PSEG Global Inc. and others v Republic of Turkey*, ICSID Case No ARB/02/5, Decision on Jurisdiction (4 June 2004) paras 66–73 (the Respondent only objected to the existence of an investment under the applicable treaty, the BIT between the United States and Turkey).

[21] *Adel A Hamadi Al Tamimi v Sultanate of Oman*, ICSID Case No ARB/11/33, Award (3 November 2015) paras 91–92 (hereafter *Al Tamimi v Oman*). In this case, the Respondent argued that the Claimant's alleged investment did not exist on or after the date at which the applicable treaty, the Free Trade Agreement between the United States and Oman, entered into force. The Respondent's objection was therefore based on the treaty's rules governing its temporal scope of application, not on Art 25 ICSID Convention.

[22] *Tethyan Copper Company Pty Limited v Islamic Republic of Pakistan*, ICSID Case No ARB 12/1, Decision on Jurisdiction and Liability (10 November 2017) paras 599–600 (hereafter *Tethyan Copper v Pakistan*). The Respondent's arguments challenging the existence of an investment focused exclusively on the definition of 'investment' contained in the applicable treaty, the BIT between Australia and Pakistan.

[23] *Italba Corporation v Oriental Republic of Uruguay*, ICSID Case No ARB/16/9, Award (22 March 2019) paras 62, 191–93. The Respondent's objections related exclusively to the treaty requirement of ownership of, or control over, the investment.

[24] *Anglo-Adriatic Group Limited v Republic of Albania*, ICSID Case No ARB/17/6, Award (7 February 2019) para 122. Albania argued that the Claimant had failed to make a protected investment under Art 1 of the Albanian Law on Foreign Investment; it did not raise any objection under Art 25 ICSID Convention.

[25] *Makae Europe Sarl v Kingdom of Saudi Arabia*, ICSID Case No ARB/17/42, Award (30 August 2021) paras 65, 79. Saudi Arabia's objections all arose under the applicable treaty, the BIT between France and Saudi Arabia. Saudi Arabia argued that the Claimant's alleged investments failed to meet the BIT's requirement of ownership or control and that the Claimant did not 'actively' make an investment as required under the BIT.

[26] *GEA Group Aktiengesellschaft v Ukraine*, ICSID Case No ARB/08/16, Award (31 March 2011).

[27] ibid paras 139–42.

[28] ibid para 143.

[29] *Poštová banka, a.s. v The Hellenic Republic*, ICSID Case No ARB/13/8, Award (9 April 2015).

[30] ibid para 359 ('Given the Tribunal's conclusion that the definition of 'investment' in the BIT at issue does not extend to Poštová banka's GGBs [Greek Government Bonds], [the question of whether the term "investment" in Art 25 ICSID Convention has an independent meaning] is a controversy that this Tribunal does not need to resolve').

[31] *ACP Axos Capital GmbH v Republic of Kosovo*, ICSID Case No ARB/15/22, Award (3 May 2018) para 256 ('Because the Tribunal concludes that there is no investment under the BIT, there is no need for the Tribunal to address the issue [of] whether there is an investment for the purpose of the ICSID Convention (on the assumption that this is a separate requirement, an issue that the Tribunal needs not address here) . . .').

or operation must meet the requirements of both Art 25 ICSID Convention and the applicable consent instrument,[32] thus recognizing that the former lays down independent requirements. When addressing the Respondent's argument that the Claimant's alleged investment failed to satisfy the relevant 'objective requirements' under Art 25 ICSID Convention, however, the Tribunal observed that these 'elements' were '*not a formal requirement* for the finding that a particular activity or transaction constitutes an investment',[33] thus implicitly rejecting the applicability of independent requirements under this provision.

B. Decisions holding that Art 25 ICSID Convention lays down independent requirements for the existence of an investment

1. Overview

There is a substantial body of decisions in which arbitral tribunals have recognized that the term 'investment' under Art 25 ICSID Convention possesses an objective meaning. These decisions include not only numerous well-known and frequently cited cases,[34] but also various more recent or less well-known rulings.[35] As will be shown below, contrary decisions, ie decisions denying the existence of implied requirements, are much less frequent.[36] It is thus uncontroversial that the objective approach is prevalent in arbitral practice.

Scholarly writers generally acknowledge that a (significant) majority of ICSID tribunals follow the objective approach. Gaillard, for instance, has observed that 'most decisions recognize that the purely subjective approach ... is difficult to reconcile with

---

[32] *Mitchell v Congo* (n 3) para 43 ('Even if, in a particular case, a dispute arises out of an investment within the meaning of the Convention, one must further examine, however, whether such a dispute relates to an investment as defined in the Parties' consent to ICSID arbitration').

[33] ibid para 56 (emphasis added).

[34] See, for example, *Ceskoslovenska Obchodni Banka, A.S. v The Slovak Republic*, ICSID Case No ARB/97/4, Decision of the Tribunal on Objections to Jurisdiction (24 May 1999) paras 66–68 (hereafter *CSOB v Slovakia*); *Salini Costruttori S.P.A. and Italstrade S.P.A. v Kingdom of Morocco*, ICSID Case No ARB/00/4, Decision on Jurisdiction (23 July 2001) para 52 (hereafter *Salini v Morocco*); *Joy Mining Machinery Limited v The Arab Republic of Egypt*, ICSID Case No ARB/03/11, Award on Jurisdiction (6 August 2004) para 50 (hereafter *Joy Mining v Egypt*); *Consorzio Groupement L.E.S.I.—DIPENTA v Democratic and Popular Republic of Algeria*, ICSID Case No ARB/03/08, Award (10 January 2005) para 13(ii) of the legal analysis ('En Droit') (hereafter *LESI v Algeria*); *Malaysian Historical Salvors Sdn, Bhd v The Government of Malaysia*, ICSID Case No ARB/05/10, Award on Jurisdiction (17 May 2007) paras 65–106 (hereafter *Malaysian Historical Salvors v Malaysia*); *Victor Pey Casado and Foundation 'Presidente Allende' v Republic of Chile*, ICSID Case No ARB/98/2, Award (8 May 2008) paras 231–32 (hereafter *Pey Casado v Chile*); *Malaysian Historical Salvors Sdn Bhd v The Government of Malaysia*, ICSID Case No ARB/05/10, Decision on the Application for Annulment (16 April 2009) paras 57–62 (hereafter *Malaysian Historical Salvors v Malaysia*); *Mr. Saba Fakes v Republic of Turkey*, ICSID Case No ARB/07/20, Award (14 July 2010) para 108 (hereafter *Fakes v Turkey*); *Global Trading Resource Corp and others v Ukraine*, ICSID Case No ARB/09/11, Award (1 December 2010) para 43 (hereafter *Global Trading v Ukraine*).

[35] See, for example, *Garanti Koza LLP v Turkmenistan*, ICSID Case No ARB/11/20, Award (19 December 2016) paras 239–40 (hereafter *Garanti Koza v Turkmenistan*); *Cortec Mining Kenya Limited and others v Republic of Kenya*, ICSID Case No ARB/15/29, Award (22 October 2018) para 291 (hereafter *Cortec v Kenya*); *CMC Muratori Cementisti CMC Di Ravenna SOC. Coop. and others v Mozambique*, ICSID Case No ARB/17/23, Award (14 October 2019) para 193 (hereafter *CMC v Mozambique*).

[36] See Section II.C.

the specific language of Article 25(1) of the Convention'.[37] Fellenbaum has similarly remarked that '[a]rbitral tribunals have usually applied the "double-barrelled test" ... in determining whether a particular economic activity constitutes ... an "investment"'.[38] Engfeldt has pointed out that '[m]ost ... arbitration awards ... suggest that there is an objective definition of "investment" under Article 25'.[39]

3.23 Not only is the objective approach generally prevalent, but it has also enjoyed steadily growing recognition over the past ten to fifteen years. As Waibel has pointed out in his recent study of arbitral rulings under Art 25 ICSID Convention, 'an increasing line of decisions finds that Article 25 ICSID Convention contains an "objective" meaning of investment',[40] while only 'a few tribunals continue to adhere to the "subjective" meaning' of this concept.[41]

3.24 There is, however, one question mark over the prevalence of the objective approach. This has to do with the existence of the so-called 'typical-characteristics approach' under which the objective definitional requirements of Art 25 ICSID Convention are not viewed as 'requirements' properly speaking, but merely as 'typical characteristics' of investments. As will be shown below,[42] this approach—though formally a variation of the *Salini* test[43] (the predominant objective approach)—could be considered as a rejection of the existence of independent definitional requirements under Art 25.

2. Justifications
(a) The effectiveness principle: the term 'investment' in Art 25 ICSID Convention must have some meaning

3.25 A seemingly compelling legal argument in support of the existence of independent requirements under Art 25 ICSID Convention is based on the interpretive principle of effectiveness or *effet utile*, relied upon by a number of tribunals. Under this principle, a treaty or treaty provision must be construed in such manner as to ensure that it is meaningful, ie that it produces some effect.[44] The effectiveness principle thus aims to avoid interpretations that would deprive a treaty (or some of its provisions) of its (their) usefulness.

---

[37] Emmanuel Gaillard, 'Identify or Define? Reflections on the Evolution of the Concept of Investment in ICSID Practice' in Christina Binder, Ursula Kriebaum, August Reinisch, and Stephan Wittich (eds), *International Investment Law for the 21st Century: Essays in Honour of Christoph Schreuer* (Oxford University Press 2009) 403, 411.

[38] Joshua Fellenbaum, '*GEA v. Ukraine* and the Battle of Treaty Interpretation Principles Over the *Salini* Test' (2011) 27 Arb Int'l 249, 253.

[39] Helena Jung Engfeldt, 'Should ICSID Go Gangnam Style in Light of Non-Traditional Foreign Investments Including Those Spurred on by Social Media—Applying an Industry-Specific Lens to the Salini Test to Determine Article 25 Jurisdiction' (2014) 32 Berkeley J Int'l L 44, 45.

[40] Waibel, 'Subject Matter Jurisdiction' (n 2) para 6.

[41] ibid.

[42] See Section III. D.

[43] See Chapter 4 Section II.

[44] See Tarcisio Gazzini, *Interpretation of International Investment Treaties* (Hart Publishing 2016) 170 (explaining that effectiveness means that 'any provision is supposed to have intended to have some significance and to achieve some end').

Applied to Art 25 ICSID Convention and the notion of investment contained in this provision, the principle of effectiveness arguably requires that the term 'investment' be given some substantive meaning. Such a meaning necessarily comprises—implied—definitional components. Any other interpretation would deprive the term 'investment' of its usefulness because it would entirely negate the existence of Art 25's jurisdictional requirement that a dispute must arise 'directly out of an investment'.[45]

3.26

One of the first decisions to have relied on the effectiveness principle is the ruling of the Tribunal in *Joy Mining*. In this decision, the Tribunal observed that the parties to a dispute could not 'by contract or treaty, define as "investment", for the purpose of ICSID jurisdiction, something which does not satisfy the objective requirements of Article 25 of the Convention'.[46] It explained that, '[o]therwise, Article 25 and its reliance on the concept of investment, even if not specifically defined, would be turned into a meaningless provision'.[47]

3.27

Another case in which the Tribunal invoked the *effet utile* principle is *Pey Casado*. In this case, the Tribunal noted that there were two competing approaches concerning the meaning of investment under Art 25 ICSID Convention: an approach requiring the presence of some (not all) 'habitual characteristics' of an investment and a more demanding approach that considers that there is a 'genuine definition of investment' laying down specific requirements all of which have to be met.[48] The Tribunal found that the latter approach was the correct one because the application of the former 'would deprive certain terms of the ICSID Convention of their meaning, an outcome that would be incompatible with the need to ensure the Convention's *effet utile*'.[49]

3.28

The Tribunal in *Fakes* also based its analysis on the principle of effectiveness. It held that the concept of 'investment' '[could] not be defined simply through a reference to the parties' consent',[50] adding that it believed that 'an objective definition of the notion of investment [had been] contemplated within the framework of the ICSID Convention, since certain terms of Article 25 would otherwise be devoid of any meaning'.[51]

3.29

More recently, the Tribunal in *Garanti Koza* adopted a similar reasoning. It held that, 'even if the Convention itself does not define it', 'the term "investment" ... must have some meaning',[52] thus implicitly relying on the *effet utile* principle. Although it rejected the application of the *Salini* test,[53] the Tribunal acknowledged that there were limits to

3.30

---

[45] Convention on the Settlement of Investment Disputes between States and Nationals of Other States (adopted 18 March 1965, entered into force 14 October 1966) Art 25(1) (hereafter ICSID Convention).
[46] *Joy Mining v Egypt* (n 34) para 50.
[47] ibid.
[48] *Pey Casado v Chile* (n 34) para 231 (translation by the author).
[49] ibid para 232 (translation by the author).
[50] *Fakes v Turkey* (n 34) para 108.
[51] ibid.
[52] *Garanti Koza v Turkmenistan* (n 35) para 239.
[53] ibid.

the parties' ability to decide whether certain assets or activities constituted investments in the sense of this provision.[54]

(b) Drafting history of the ICSID Convention

3.31 A few tribunals have derived the existence of implied requirements under Art 25 ICSID Convention from the Convention's drafting history. An illustrative example is the decision of the ad hoc Committee in *Malaysian Historical Salvors*. In this case, the sole Arbitrator declined jurisdiction on the grounds that the Claimant's operations—which consisted of salvaging a shipwreck—did not constitute, or relate to, an investment under Art 25 ICSID Convention.[55] In the annulment proceedings brought by the Claimant, the ad hoc Committee was asked to examine whether the Arbitrator's jurisdictional ruling was tainted by a manifest excess of powers.[56]

3.32 Under the rules of interpretation set forth in the Vienna Convention on the Law of Treaties[57]—which virtually all ICSID tribunals apply—a treaty's drafting history constitutes a supplementary means of interpretation that can only be resorted to (1) to confirm the meaning resulting from the application of the general rule of interpretation[58] or (2) when the general rule of interpretation 'leaves the meaning ambiguous or obscure' or 'leads to a result which is manifestly absurd or unreasonable'.[59] The ad hoc Committee, therefore, first explained why it was appropriate, in the case at hand, to resort to the ICSID Convention's *travaux préparatoires*. It pointed out that there had been 'marked differences among ICSID tribunals and among commentators'[60] on the meaning of investment and that this concept was therefore ambiguous.[61]

3.33 Performing a detailed analysis of the ICSID Convention's drafting history,[62] the ad hoc Committee noted, first of all, that several unsuccessful attempts had been made to define the concept of 'investment' and to establish a minimum monetary threshold.[63] It also explained that the delegates' inability to agree on a suitable definition of 'investment' was considered to be a minor issue given the crucial role of the contracting parties' consent and their ability to determine the cases, or categories of cases, which

---

[54] ibid para 240.
[55] *Malaysian Historical Salvors v Malaysia*, Award on Jurisdiction (n 34) paras 65–106 (containing the Tribunal's analysis of the meaning of investment under Art 25 ICSID Convention, including a discussion of the different definitional elements or 'hallmarks' of an investment), 107–46 (containing the Tribunal's application of those hallmarks to the facts of the case).
[56] *Malaysian Historical Salvors v Malaysia*, Decision on Annulment (n 34) para 1.
[57] Vienna Convention on the Law of Treaties (adopted 23 May 1969, entered into force 27 January 1980) Art 31–33 (hereafter VCLT).
[58] ibid Art 31.
[59] ibid Art 32.
[60] *Malaysian Historical Salvors v Malaysia*, Decision on Annulment (n 34) para 57.
[61] ibid. It should be mentioned, however, that the Tribunal ultimately questioned the subsidiary interpretive role of a treaty's preparatory work, holding that it was possible to consider the ICSID Convention's drafting history even in the absence of any ambiguity or obscurity. It observed that 'courts and tribunals interpreting treaties regularly review the *travaux préparatoires* whenever they are brought to their attention; it is mythological to pretend that they do so only when they first conclude that the term requiring interpretation is ambiguous or obscure'.
[62] ibid paras 63–73.
[63] ibid paras 64–66.

they intended to submit to the Centre.[64] The ad hoc Committee quoted Broches, the Chairman of the Legal Committee tasked with the preparation of a draft Convention, who had on several occasions expressed the view that Art 25 ICSID Convention and the term 'investment' used in this provision merely established the 'outer limits' of ICSID jurisdiction, ie the limits beyond which 'no use could be made of the facilities of the Centre even with such consent [the consent of the parties to the dispute]'.[65]

The ad hoc Committee also drew on the Report of the Executive Directors which noted that 'the jurisdiction of the Centre [was] ... limited by reference to the nature of the dispute' and that, as a consequence, 'consent alone [would] not suffice to bring a dispute within its jurisdiction'.[66] It concluded that the term 'investment' in Art 25 ICSID Convention had an 'objective content',[67] even if such content was less demanding than the test applied by the sole Arbitrator.[68] In the ad hoc Committee's view, the only transactions that would not qualify as investments under the Convention were 'a simple sale and like transient commercial transactions'.[69]

3.34

(c) Case law and scholarship

Like most domestic legal orders, the investor–state dispute resolution system heavily relies on legal precedents.[70] In fact, references to arbitral case law are a standard feature of the submissions filed by parties to investor–state disputes and arbitral decisions. Rulings on the issue of whether Art 25 ICSID Convention lays down independent requirements for the existence of an investment are no exception.

3.35

In some cases, tribunals have referred to earlier decisions to provide (further) support for a specific substantive argument or line of reasoning. The *Fakes* Tribunal, for instance, cited the decision of the Tribunal in *Joy Mining* because it expressly endorsed that Tribunal's views on the relevance and impact of the *effet utile* principle.[71] The decision of the Tribunal in *Pey Casado* contains a similar express endorsement of the analysis performed in *Joy Mining*.[72]

3.36

More often than not, however, tribunals referring to case law to justify the existence of independent requirements under Art 25 ICSID Convention do not expressly approve

3.37

---

[64] ibid paras 67–70.
[65] ibid para 68.
[66] International Bank for Reconstruction and Development, *Report of the Executive Directors on the Convention on the Settlement of Investment Disputes between States and Nationals of Other States*, 18 March 1965, para 25.
[67] *Malaysian Historical Salvors v Malaysia*, Decision on Annulment (n 34) para 72.
[68] ibid para 69 (holding that 'it is important to note that the *travaux préparatoires* do not support the imposition of "outer limits" such as those imposed by the Sole Arbitrator in this case').
[69] ibid.
[70] On this issue, see, for example, Yas Banifatemi (ed), *Precedent in International Arbitration* (Juris Publishing 2007); René Urueña, 'Of Precedents and Ideology: Lawmaking by Investment Arbitration Tribunals' in Prabhakar Singh and Benoît Mayer (eds), *Critical International Law: Postrealism, Postcolonialism and Transnationalism* (Oxford University Press 2014) 276.
[71] *Fakes v Turkey* (n 34) paras 108–09 ('The Tribunal believes that an objective definition of the notion of investment was contemplated within the framework of the ICSID Convention... In this respect, the Tribunal agrees with the Tribunal in the *Joy Mining v. Egypt* case...').
[72] *Pey Casado v Chile* (n 34) para 232.

the underlying substantive reasons of the relevant decisions (if any). The many illustrative arbitral decisions notably include *Salini*,[73] *LESI*,[74] *Malaysian Historical Salvors*,[75] *Global Trading*,[76] *Cortec*,[77] and *CMC*.[78]

3.38 On occasion, ICSID tribunals have also relied on scholarly writings to justify the existence of objective definitional criteria under Art 25 ICSID Convention. An illustrative example is the decision of the Tribunal in *Salini*. In this case, the Tribunal appears to have attributed great weight to Gaillard's case note on *Fedax v Venezuela*.[79] The *Salini* tribunal's reliance on Gaillard's contribution was subsequently endorsed in *Malaysian Historical Salvors*.[80]

3. Implications

3.39 The principal implication of the objective approach is that the concept of 'investment' in Art 25 ICSID Convention limits the parties' freedom to decide what constitutes an investment for the purposes of ICSID arbitration proceedings. Under this approach, the parties are prevented from broadening the scope of the Convention's notion of investment, ie they cannot decide that a transaction or asset that does not present the characteristics required under Art 25 qualifies as an investment. They can, however, restrict Art 25's concept of 'investment' by adding further criteria or requirements.

3.40 This limitation applies across all categories of consent instruments. It affects (1) ICSID contracting States enacting domestic investment laws, (2) ICSID contracting States concluding bi- or multilateral investment treaties with other contracting States, and (3) parties to investment contracts providing for the referral of investor–state disputes to ICSID. None of these three types of legal instruments can widen the scope of the concept of 'investment' under Art 25 ICSID Convention.

---

[73] *Salini v Morocco* (n 34) para 52. The Tribunal noted that 'ICSID case law and legal authors agree that the investment requirement must be respected as an objective condition of the jurisdiction of the Centre', citing scholarship referring to *Alcoa Minerals v Jamaica*, without any further explanation of this decision.
[74] *LESI v Algeria* (n 34) para 13(ii) of the legal analysis ('En Droit'). The Tribunal referred to several decisions that it considered to support the approach adopted by the tribunal in *Salini*, without however discussing any of these cases or the underlying reasons.
[75] *Malaysian Historical Salvors v Malaysia*, Award on Jurisdiction (n 34) para 54. The Tribunal simply stated that '[i]t ha[d] been considered in *Salini* that the consensus of legal authors and ICSID case law [was] that the investment requirement under Article 25(1) [ICSID Convention] is an objective condition of the jurisdiction of the Centre'. The Tribunal did not elaborate on either the analysis of the *Salini* Tribunal or the authorities relied upon in *Salini*.
[76] *Global Trading v Ukraine* (n 34) para 43. The Tribunal referred to 'a long line of previous decisions' in which ICSID tribunals have held that 'the notion of "investment" … cannot be defined simply by reference to the parties' consent' but must be regarded 'as having an objective definition'. The Tribunal did, however, not mention, let alone examine, the substantive reasons relied upon in these decisions.
[77] *Cortec v Kenya* (n 35) para 291. The Tribunal noted that the meaning of the undefined term 'investment' in Art 25 ICSID Convention—including the question of whether this concept does at all have an independent meaning—had to be determined based on the *Salini* decision. No further explanations were provided by the Tribunal.
[78] *CMC v Mozambique* (n 35) para 193 (basing its rejection of the subjective approach on several cases, without however explaining the reasoning adopted in these decisions).
[79] *Salini v Morocco* (n 34) para 52.
[80] *Malaysian Historical Salvors v Malaysia*, Award on Jurisdiction (n 34) para 54 (mentioning the 'consensus of legal authors and ICSID case law' referred to in *Salini*).

Several tribunals have expressly acknowledged that the existence of an independent notion of investment under the Convention limits the effectiveness of consent instruments defining the term 'investment' more broadly. In *CSOB*, for example, the Tribunal observed that the definition contained in the applicable consent instrument constituted 'an important element in determining whether a dispute (sic!) qualifies as an investment under the Convention in any given case'.[81] However, it also added that 'an agreement of the parties describing their transaction as an investment is not, as such, conclusive',[82] that the term 'investment' had an objective meaning,[83] and that the parties could only restrict, but not broaden, such meaning.[84]

3.41

Another decision recognizing the limiting effect of the objective notion of investment of Art 25 ICSID Convention is the decision of the Tribunal in *Joy Mining*. In this case, as has already been explained, the Tribunal held that, under the principle of *effet utile*, Art 25 ICSID Convention had to be regarded as setting forth an objective notion of investment.[85] It concluded that there was, therefore, 'a limit to the freedom with which the parties may define an 'investment' if they wish to engage the jurisdiction of ICSID tribunals'.[86]

3.42

In *Global Trading*, the Tribunal similarly emphasized that '[t]he weight of authority [was] ... in favour of viewing the term "investment" as having an objective definition within the framework of the ICSID Convention'.[87] Endorsing the conclusion reached in *Joy Mining*, the Tribunal found that the 'parties to the dispute cannot by contract or a treaty define as 'investment', for the purposes of ICSID jurisdiction, something which does not satisfy the objective requirements of Article 25 of the Convention'.[88]

3.43

C. Decisions holding that Art 25 ICSID Convention does not lay down independent requirements for the existence of an investment

1. Overview

There are considerably fewer decisions denying the applicability of independent criteria under Art 25 ICSID Convention than decisions affirming the existence of such criteria. It would be exaggerated, however, to claim that such decisions are, or have been, exceptional. In fact, in an article published in 2010, Ho listed a total of twelve rulings in which ICSID tribunals arguably followed the subjective approach,[89] rejecting

3.44

---

[81] *CSOB v Slovakia* (n 34) para 66.
[82] ibid para 68.
[83] ibid (observing that '[t]he concept of an investment as spelled out in that provision [Art. 25 ICSID Convention] is objective in nature').
[84] ibid (noting that 'the parties may agree on a more precise or restrictive definition of their acceptance of the Centre's jurisdiction, but they may not choose to submit disputes to the Centre that are not related to an investment').
[85] *Joy Mining v Egypt* (n 34) para 50.
[86] ibid para 49.
[87] *Global Trading v Ukraine* (n 34) para 43.
[88] ibid.
[89] See Ho, 'The Meaning of "Investment"' (n 14) 634–35. The cases cited by this author include: *Philippe Gruslin v Malaysia*, ICSID Case No ARB/99/3, Award (27 November 2000) (hereafter *Gruslin v Malaysia*); *SGS Société*

the idea that Art 25 ICSID Convention lays down implied requirements for the existence of an investment.

3.45 Upon closer scrutiny, however, it appears that several of those decisions did not actually reject the objective approach. In two of these cases (*SGS v Philippines* and *Inmaris v Ukraine*), the Respondent's objection was based exclusively on the definition of 'investment' contained in the applicable investment treaty, not on Art 25 ICSID Convention.[90] The fact that these rulings only address the treaty objections raised by the Respondents, without examining whether requirements that may have been applicable under the ICSID Convention were met, cannot be considered as an implied rejection of the existence of such requirements. In another case referred to by Ho (*Parkerings v Lithuania*), the Respondent did not actually deny that the Claimant had made an investment;[91] the Tribunal appears to have examined this issue *ex officio*, and it would be exaggerated to construe the rather succinct analysis the Tribunal performed under the applicable BIT[92] as a rejection of the idea that Art 25 lays down independent definitional requirements.

3.46 Decisions denying the existence of independent requirements under Art 25 ICSID Convention have become even more rare, if not entirely inexistent, post-2010. Writing in 2022, Schill, Schreuer, and Sinclair mention three more recent decisions in which arbitral tribunals have supposedly followed the subjective approach: *Al Tamimi v Oman*, *Garanti Koza v Turkmenistan*, and *Tethyan Copper v Pakistan*. In reality, however, none of these decisions involve a rejection, whether express or implicit, of the existence of objective criteria under Art 25 ICSID Convention. In *Al Tamimi*, the Respondent did not object to the *existence* of an investment, but merely to its falling within the temporal scope of application of the relevant treaty, the Free Trade Agreement (FTA) between

---

Générale de Surveillance S.A. v Islamic Republic of Pakistan, ICSID Case No ARB/01/13, Decision of the Tribunal on Objections to Jurisdiction (6 August 2003) (hereafter *SGS v Pakistan*); *Generation Ukraine, Inc. v Ukraine*, ICSID Case No ARB/00/9, Award (16 September 2003); *SGS Société Générale de Surveillance S.A. v Republic of the Philippines*, ICSID Case No ARB/02/6, Decision of the Tribunal on Objections to Jurisdiction (29 January 2004) (hereafter *SGS v Philippines*); *Tokios Tokelės v Ukraine*, ICSID Case No ARB/02/18, Decision on Jurisdiction (29 April 2004); *Waguih Elie George Siag and Clorinda Vecchi v The Arab Republic of Egypt*, ICSID Case No ARB/05/15, Decision on Jurisdiction (11 April 2007) (hereafter *Waguih v Egypt*); *M.C.I. Power Group, L.C. and New Turbine, Inc., v Republic of Ecuador*, ICSID Case No ARB/03/6, Award (31 July 2007) (hereafter *MCI v Ecuador*); *Parkerings-Compagniet AS v Republic of Lithuania*, ICSID Case No ARB/05/8, Award (11 September 2007) (hereafter *Parkerings v Lithuania*); *CMS Gas Transmission Company v Argentine Republic*, ICSID Case No ARB/01/8, Decision of the Ad Hoc Committee on the Application for Annulment of the Argentine Republic (25 September 2007) (hereafter *CMS v Argentine Republic*); *Malaysian Historical Salvors v Malaysia*, Decision on Annulment (n 34); *Inmaris Perestroika Sailing Maritime Services GmbH and others v Ukraine*, ICSID Case No ARB/08/8, Decision on Jurisdiction (8 March 2010) (hereafter *Inmaris v Ukraine*); *ATA Construction, Industrial and Trading Company v The Hashemite Kingdom of Jordan*, ICSID Case No ARB/08/2, Award (18 May 2010) (hereafter *ATA Construction v Jordan*).

[90] *SGS v Philippines* (n 89) para 51(d) (the Respondent's only investment-related argument was that the Claimant's alleged investments did not meet the territoriality requirement applicable under the BIT between Switzerland and the Philippines); *Inmaris v Ukraine* (n 89) paras 60–61 (Ukraine asserted that the 'Claimants' contracts [did] not qualify as investments under the BIT', without raising any argument based on Art 25 ICSID Convention).

[91] *Parkerings v Lithuania* (n 89) para 243 (containing the Tribunal's summary of Lithuania's jurisdictional objections).

[92] ibid paras 249–54.

the United States and Oman.[93] In *Garanti Koza*, the Tribunal held that the *Salini* test was not applicable under Art 25 ICSID Convention,[94] without however discarding the more general idea that the concept of 'investment' contained in this provision had an independent meaning. On the contrary, it acknowledged that there were limits to the parties' freedom to decide what constituted an investment,[95] thus recognizing the existence of implied requirements under the Convention. In *Tethyan Copper*, Pakistan's allegation that the Claimant had not made a qualifying investment relied exclusively on the applicable BIT;[96] the meaning of investment under Art 25 ICSID Convention was not at issue.

2. Justifications
(a) The Convention's drafting history
As has been explained above, the ICSID Convention's drafting history has been relied upon by several tribunals adopting the objective approach. Those tribunals have emphasized the fact that various attempts had been made to define the term 'investment' (which suggests that the drafters intended this concept to have some meaning), the idea that Art 25 ICSID Convention establishes the 'outer limits' of the Centre's jurisdiction, and the related viewpoint according to which the parties' consent, though fundamental, is not sufficient to establish ICSID jurisdiction.

3.47

Interestingly, the Convention's negotiating history has also been invoked by several tribunals that have followed the opposite approach. Their reading of the Convention's drafting history is that consent is not only of crucial importance for the Centre's jurisdiction, but the only jurisdictional requirement. They consider that the absence of a definition of 'investment' in the Convention was deliberate because such a definition was expected to be agreed upon or established in the relevant instruments of consent. In other words, the requirement of consent and the prerequisite of the existence of an 'investment' are merged into a single, broadly framed, consent requirement.

3.48

A perhaps surprising example of a decision holding that the subjective approach can be derived from the Convention's drafting history is *Fedax v Venezuela*.[97] It is surprising because *Fedax* is one of the first decisions to hold that an investment is characterized by certain implied or objective 'features'.[98] In apparent contradiction to this holding, however, the Tribunal elsewhere endorsed the subjective approach, relying primarily on the Convention's negotiating history. Referring to the Report of the Executive Directors, the Tribunal observed that 'it was finally decided to leave any definition of the [term] "investment" to the consent of the parties'.[99] It drew additional support from Broches'

3.49

---

[93] *Al Tamimi v Oman* (n 21) paras 91–92.
[94] *Garanti Koza v Turkmenistan* (n 35) para 239.
[95] ibid para 240.
[96] *Tethyan Copper v Pakistan* (n 22) para 599–600.
[97] *Fedax N.V. v The Republic of Venezuela*, ICSID Case No ARB/96/3, Decision of the Tribunal on Objections to Jurisdiction (11 July 1997).
[98] ibid para 43.
[99] ibid para 21 (internal footnote omitted).

assessment that the deliberate omission of a definition of 'investment' 'indicates that the requirement that the dispute must have arisen out of an "investment" may be merged into the requirement of consent to jurisdiction'.[100] The Tribunal concluded that, 'as contemplated by the Convention, the definition of "investment" is controlled by consent of the Contracting Parties'.[101]

3.50 Another example of a decision in which the subjective approach was based on the Convention's drafting history is *MCI v Ecuador*. In this case, the Respondent argued that MCI did not make an investment within the meaning of the ICSID Convention,[102] claiming that certain implied criteria had to be present under Art 25.[103] The Tribunal rejected this allegation, relying *inter alia* on the statement contained in the Report of the Executive Directors according to which 'the Convention does not define the term "investments" (sic!) because it wants to leave the parties free to decide what class of disputes they would submit to the ICSID'.[104] As to Respondent's allegation that Art 25 ICSID Convention lays down a number of implied requirements, the Tribunal held that those were not strictly speaking requirements, but merely 'examples' (presumably, of typical characteristics of investments).[105]

(b) A necessary implication of the absence of a definition under the ICSID Convention

3.51 Other decisions adopting the subjective approach do not rely on any specific interpretive rule, but seem to consider that the only possible, or sensible, interpretation of Art 25's (and the Convention's) silence on the meaning of investment is that this provision does *not* lay down any definitional requirements and that it must be understood to refer to, and endorse, the definition contained in the applicable consent instrument.

3.52 A number of tribunals have held that the Convention's failure to define 'investment' precludes the existence of specific requirements under Art 25. In *Waguih*, for example, the Tribunal observed that '[t]he Convention require[d] an "investment" but d[id] not limit the term in any manner'.[106] In *CMS v Argentina*,[107] the Tribunal noted that, '[p]recisely because the Convention does not define "investment", it does not purport to define the requirements that an investment should meet to qualify for ICSID jurisdiction',[108] a holding that has been expressly endorsed by the Tribunal in *Tokios Tokelés*.[109]

3.53 Several tribunals have stressed the related idea that the Convention's silence on the meaning of 'investment' implies that ICSID contracting States are free to decide what

---

[100] ibid.
[101] ibid para 31.
[102] *MCI v Ecuador* (n 89) para 137.
[103] ibid para 138.
[104] ibid para 159 (internal footnote omitted).
[105] ibid para 165.
[106] *Waguih v Egypt* (n 89) para 207.
[107] *CMS Gas Transmission Company v The Republic of Argentina*, ICSID Case No ARB/01/8, Decision of the Tribunal on Objections to Jurisdiction (17 July 2003) (hereafter *CMS v Argentina*).
[108] ibid para 51.
[109] *Tokios Tokelés v Ukraine* (n 89) para 73.

constitutes an investment. In *SGS v Pakistan*, for instance, the Tribunal held that the absence of a definition of 'investment' 'leav[es] to the Contracting Parties a large measure of freedom to define that term'.[110] In *ATA Construction*, the Tribunal similarly stated that '[t]he ICSID Convention leaves the definition of the term investment open to the parties, allowing them to determine its scope and application pursuant to mutual agreement in the relevant BIT'.[111]

3.54 In a similar vein, various tribunals have emphasized that, absent a definition of 'investment' in Art 25 ICSID Convention, the definition enshrined in the applicable treaty is the sole relevant threshold. In *Gruslin v Malaysia*, for example, the Tribunal noted that Art 25 ICSID Convention did not 'operate to define [the term] ... investment' and that this was a matter 'to be determined by the terms of the IGA [the treaty between Malaysia and the Belgo-Luxembourg Economic Union]'.[112] In *CMS v Argentina*, the ad hoc Committee considered that the Convention failed to define the concept of 'investment' because 'this task was left largely to the terms of bilateral investment treaties or other instruments on which jurisdiction is based'.[113]

D. Decisions adopting the ambivalent typical-characteristics approach

3.55 Not all decisions provide a clear answer to the question of whether Art 25 ICSID Convention lays down independent definitional requirements of the term 'investment'. In fact, there is one rather common arbitral approach, the so-called 'typical-characteristics approach', which is inherently ambiguous. On the one hand, it endorses the *Salini* test under which an asset or transaction must satisfy certain specific requirements in order to qualify as an investment under Art 25 ICSID Convention. On the other hand, it considers that the *Salini* criteria are merely typical characteristics, rather than jurisdictional requirements, thus denying the mandatory nature of these criteria and, ultimately, the existence of any legally binding test.

3.56 An early case adopting this approach is the decision of the Tribunal in *CSOB*. In this case, as has already been explained, the Tribunal held that the concept of 'investment' under Art 25 ICSID Convention had an objective meaning. In its decision affirming jurisdiction, it attached particular weight to the contribution the Claimant's activity made to the economic development of Slovakia.[114] It also applied—without however expressly acknowledging its correctness—the test advocated by the Respondent under which an investment required a purchase of assets, the pursuit of profit, and the

---

[110] *SGS v Pakistan* (n 89) para 133.
[111] *ATA Construction v Jordan* (n 89) para 111.
[112] *Gruslin v Malaysia* (n 89) para 13.6.
[113] *CMS v Argentine Republic* (n 89) para 72.
[114] *CSOB v Slovakia* (n 34) para 88.

existence of risk.[115] The Tribunal recognized that these 'elements ... tend[ed] as a rule to be present in most investments'.[116] However, it also added that they did not constitute a 'formal prerequisite for the finding that a transaction constitutes an investment ... under the Convention'.[117]

3.57 The sole Arbitrator's decision in *Malaysian Historical Salvors* contains an illuminating discussion of the typical-characteristics approach. In his ruling, the Arbitrator examined the coexistence of the competing jurisdictional and typical-characteristics approaches.[118] Under the former, an asset or transaction only qualifies as an investment if all relevant criteria (the Arbitrator referred to them as 'hallmarks') are present.[119] Under the latter approach, on the other hand, an investment could exist 'even if one or more of the established hallmarks of "investment" were missing'.[120] According to the sole Arbitrator, the difference between the two approaches is, however, more formal than real,[121] given that tribunals adopting a jurisdictional approach frequently acknowledge the interrelatedness of the different hallmarks and take into account the specific circumstances of the case.[122]

3.58 The typical-characteristics approach was also adopted by the Tribunal in *Biwater Gauff v Tanzania*.[123] In this case, it was not disputed that the term 'investment' under the ICSID Convention had an implied meaning and that this meaning was appropriately captured by the *Salini* test.[124] Applying this test, the Tribunal held that the relevant criteria were 'not mandatory as a matter of law'.[125] It observed that 'there [was] [therefore] no basis for a rote, or overly strict, application of the five *Salini* criteria'[126] and that it was preferable to follow 'a more flexible and pragmatic approach'[127] instead. Such an approach should take into account not only the relevant criteria, but also the individual

---

[115] ibid para 78 (noting that the Slovak Republic defines an investment as 'the acquisition of property or assets through the expenditure of resources by one party (the "investor") in the territory of a foreign country (the "host State"), which is expected to produce a benefit on both sides and to offer a return in the future, subject to the uncertainties of the risk involved').
[116] ibid para 90.
[117] ibid.
[118] *Malaysian Historical Salvors v Malaysia*, Award on Jurisdiction (n 34) paras 70–72.
[119] ibid para 70.
[120] ibid. This is implicit in the sole Arbitrator's explanation that 'the Typical Characteristics Approach does not necessarily mean that a tribunal would find that there is an "investment", even if one or more of the established hallmarks of "investment" were missing'.
[121] ibid para 105 ('In any event, the differences between the two approaches are likely to be academic. In practice, it is unlikely that any difference in juristic analysis would make any significant difference to the ultimate finding of the tribunal. The existence of two possible approaches may be the result of the different emphases placed by the tribunal on each of the factors because the facts (or Counsel's submissions) in one case may require (or encourage) the tribunal to place a stronger emphasis on a particular factor than in another case. This will happen where, although the requisite hallmarks of "investment" under the ICSID Convention appear to exist, the presence of one or more hallmarks may appear weak, and the tribunal may need to look at the strength of the other hallmarks in arriving at its decision.')
[122] ibid para 72.
[123] *Biwater Gauff (Tanzania) Ltd. v United Republic of Tanzania*, ICSID Case No ARB/05/22, Award (24 July 2008) (hereafter *Biwater Gauff v Tanzania*).
[124] ibid paras 310–11.
[125] ibid para 312.
[126] ibid.
[127] ibid para 316.

circumstances of each case.[128] The Tribunal concluded that, 'even if the Republic could demonstrate that any, or all, of the *Salini* criteria are not satisfied in this case, this would not necessarily be sufficient—in and of itself—to deny jurisdiction.'[129]

A more recent decision adopting the typical-characteristics approach is the ruling of the Tribunal in *Standard Chartered v Tanzania*.[130] In this case, the Tribunal reviewed ICSID case law, noting that some decisions supported the application of the *Salini* test,[131] while others rejected either the test as such or its inflexible application.[132] The Tribunal ultimately sided with the latter approach, holding that the *Salini* criteria '[were] not to be taken as prescriptive or dispositive but merely as indicative of typical elements that the Tribunal could consider' in determining the presence of an investment under Art 25 ICSID Convention.[133]

3.59

The principal justification for the typical-characteristics approach appears to be the understandable desire to prevent 'arbitrary exclusion[s] of certain types of transaction',[134] ie decisions denying investment status to transactions or assets that should 'normally' qualify as investments under the Convention. Several tribunals have pointed out that in the absence of a definition of 'investment' in the ICSID Convention, a rigid application of definitional requirements established by ICSID tribunals risks undermining the drafters' intent to grant broad discretion to contracting States in determining the categories of disputes they wish to submit to the Centre.[135]

3.60

The specific practical implications of the typical-characteristics approach depend on how one construes its exact meaning. In fact, under a more 'moderate' construction, this approach could be viewed as implying that an investment can be found to exist if some of the relevant criteria are met.[136] According to a more 'radical' interpretation (expressly supported by the *Biwater Gauff* Tribunal), even the absence of *all* applicable criteria would not prevent a tribunal from characterizing a transaction or asset as an investment in a given case.

3.61

Either way, the typical-characteristics approach is highly problematic. In fact, it generates a high degree of legal uncertainty, given that it is not clear which, if any, of the *Salini* criteria are mandatory. In its radical form, the typical-characteristics approach

3.62

---

[128] ibid.
[129] ibid para 318.
[130] *Standard Chartered Bank (Hong Kong) Limited v United Republic of Tanzania*, ICSID Case No ARB/15/41, Award (11 October 2019).
[131] ibid para 198.
[132] ibid para 199.
[133] ibid para 200.
[134] *Biwater Gauff v Tanzania* (n 123) para 314.
[135] See, for example, *Biwater Gauff v Tanzania* (n 123) para 313 ('Given that the Convention was not drafted with a strict, objective, definition of "investment", it is doubtful that arbitral tribunals sitting in individual cases should impose one such definition which would be applicable in all cases and for all purposes.')
[136] See, for example, *Pey Casado v Chile* (n 34) para 231 ('It would suffice, according to this view, that some, but not all, of the habitual "characteristics" of an investment are present in order to conclude that an investment exists in a particular case') (translation by the author).

amounts to a complete rejection of the existence of independent definitional requirements under Art 25 ICSID Convention, ie of the objective approach.

IV. Scholarly Opinions

A. Broad support for the existence of independent requirements under Art 25 ICSID Convention

3.63 A significant majority of authors support the existence of independent requirements under Art 25 ICSID Convention. In some writings, this support is not stated expressly, but rather implicit in the positions advocated by the relevant writers. Scholars such as Grabowski and Exelbert, for example, have advocated the application of the 'traditional' four-prong *Salini* test, criticizing decisions denying the applicability of the requirement of a contribution to the economic development of the host State.[137] These authors thus implicitly support the view that Art 25 ICSID Convention lays down independent requirements for the existence of an investment.

3.64 Other scholarly writers have expressly advocated the idea that the term 'investment' in Art 25 ICSID Convention has an independent meaning. A central argument in support of this view consists of the alleged necessity to distinguish the requirement of the existence of an investment from the requirement of consent. Schill, Schreuer, and Sinclair, for instance, argue that '[t]he drafting history of the Convention leaves no doubt that the Centre's services would not be available for just any dispute that the parties may wish to submit' to it,[138] given that 'the term "investment" in Art 25(1) has an objective meaning that is independent of the parties' disposition'.[139]

3.65 Other commentators advocating this position notably include Waibel and Rubins. Relying on contributions authored by Broches and Parra, Waibel has observed that '[s]ubject matter jurisdiction under Article 25 is distinct from consent in the BIT' and that, in order to qualify as an investment, 'the transaction needs to fall within Article 25's "objective core"'.[140] Rubins has similarly argued that '[t]he drafters of the Convention consciously established the objective limitations of ICSID jurisdiction as distinct from the issue of consent' and that 'there is an objective boundary to the definition of investment for purposes of ICSID jurisdiction'.[141]

---

[137] Alex Grabowski, 'The Definition of Investment under the ICSID Convention: A Defense of Salini' (2014) 15 Chi J Int'l L 287; Exelbert, 'Consistently Inconsistent' (n 7) 1272–78.
[138] Schill, Schreuer and Sinclair, 'Article 25' (n 9) para 178.
[139] ibid para 179.
[140] Michael Waibel, 'Opening Pandora's Box: Sovereign Bonds in International Arbitration' (2007) 101 AJIL 711, 718.
[141] Noah Rubins, 'The Notion of "Investment" in International Investment Arbitration' in Norbert Horn and Stefan Michael Kröll (eds), *Arbitrating Foreign Investment Disputes: Procedural and Substantive Legal Aspects*, Studies in Transnational Economic Law, vol 19 (Kluwer Law International 2004) 283, 289.

3.66 A further argument relied upon by scholars advocating the existence of an independent concept of 'investment' under Art 25 ICSID Convention rests on the interpretive principle of *effet utile* under which, as has already been explained, the interpretation of the terms of a treaty must not deprive those terms of their meaning or usefulness. Pahis, for example, has observed that '[c]omplete deference to definitions of "investment" in Contracting States' consent documents would destroy the effect of [Art. 25's jurisdictional requirement that the dispute must arise out of an investment]',[142] concluding that the term 'investment' must be accorded an objective meaning.

3.67 A related argument has been raised by Manciaux.[143] According to this author, the existence of an independent notion of investment under Art 25 ICSID Convention is necessary to define the Convention's scope of application and, ultimately, the boundaries of international investment law more generally.[144] Absent a clearly defined concept of 'investment' under Art 25 ICSID Convention, the scope of ICSID jurisdiction would vary depending on the specific definitions contained in the applicable consent instruments, an outcome that, according to Manciaux, would substantially undermine legal certainty for both investors and capital-importing countries.[145]

3.68 Lastly, some scholars supporting the existence of implied requirements under Art 25 ICSID Convention have done so by highlighting the flaws of the competing subjective approach. One critique they have raised is that the ICSID Convention's drafting history, allegedly the primary legal basis of the subjective approach, is only of subsidiary relevance under the Vienna Convention on the Law of Treaties (VCLT) rules of interpretation,[146] given that, in principle, it may only be taken into account when the general rule of interpretation 'leaves the meaning ambiguous or obscure' or 'leads to a result which is manifestly absurd or unreasonable'.[147] These authors argue that, even though the term 'investment' is not defined in the Convention itself, it nonetheless possesses an ordinary meaning that is neither ambiguous, nor obscure. Recourse to the Convention's drafting history would therefore not be justified.

3.69 Another alleged defect of the subjective approach is that the rules of interpretation of the VCLT provide no basis for the role it ascribes to definitions of investment contained in consent instruments and, more particularly, investment treaties. In fact, one way of making sense of the subjective approach is to consider that it views definitions contained in such treaties as 'subsequent agreements' between the parties or 'subsequent practice' within the meaning of Art 31(3) VCLT,[148] which would allow those definitions

---

[142] Pahis, 'Investment Misconceived' (n 7) 81.
[143] Sebastien Manciaux, 'The Notion of Investment: New Controversies' (2008) 9 JWIT 443.
[144] ibid 448.
[145] ibid.
[146] Pahis, 'Investment Misconceived' (n 7) 79–80 (noting that '[a]ccording to Article 32 of the Vienna Convention, recourse to [the] negotiating history is optional ("may be had") "as a supplementary means of interpretation"' and that 'Article 31 of the Vienna Convention—and specifically its requirement that treaty terms be given their "ordinary meaning in their context and in light of [the treaty's] object and purpose"—remains the mandatory starting point for all treaty interpretation') (internal footnotes omitted).
[147] VCLT (n 57) Art 32.
[148] ibid Art 31(3) provides: 'There shall be taken into account, together with the context:

to be relied upon to interpret the term 'investment' under Art 25 ICSID Convention. The problem with this analysis is that the parties to investment treaties are obviously not identical with the parties to the ICSID Convention[149] and that it would be unreasonable to allow two ICSID contracting States concluding a BIT to bilaterally establish the meaning of the term 'investment' in the ICSID Convention.

3.70 According to another possible understanding of the subjective approach, investment treaty definitions of 'investment' are considered as *modifications* of the ICSID Convention under Art 41 VCLT. It is indeed possible for two or more parties to a multilateral treaty to conclude an agreement modifying that treaty as between themselves alone.[150] However, in order for such a modification to be valid, it must 'not affect the enjoyment by the other parties of their rights under the treaty or the performance of their obligations'.[151] According to Castro de Figueiredo, this requirement would not be met because the subjective approach leads to an expansion of ICSID jurisdiction, thus imposing additional increased financial and enforcement obligations on all ICSID contracting States.[152]

B. Limited support for the absence of independent requirements under Art 25 ICSID Convention

3.71 There is very limited scholarly support for the view that the term 'investment' under Art 25 ICSID Convention does not have an independent meaning. Only Ho appears to entirely reject the notion that Art 25 sets forth implied requirements for the existence of an investment. There are other authors who consider that the concept of 'investment' under Art 25 is very broad and that it only minimally limits the freedom of ICSID contracting States to determine the meaning of 'investment' in international investment agreements or domestic investment laws. Those authors do not, however (at least not openly), deny that the concept of 'investment' under Art 25 ICSID Convention has an independent meaning.

3.72 Ho rejects not only the *Salini* test (and the objective criteria applying under this test), but also the more moderate view according to which the term 'investment' under Art 25 ICSID Convention merely establishes the outer limits or boundaries of ICSID

(a) any subsequent agreement between the parties regarding the interpretation of the treaty or the application of its provisions;
(b) any subsequent practice in the application of the treaty which establishes the agreement of the parties regarding its interpretation;
(c) any relevant rules of international law applicable in the relations between the parties.'
[149] Pahis, 'Investment Misconceived' (n 7) 80, n 58 (arguing that BITs are neither subsequent agreements, nor subsequent treaty practice under art 31(3) VCLT).
[150] VCLT (n 57) Art 41(1) ('Two or more parties to a multilateral treaty may conclude an agreement to modify the treaty as between themselves alone ...').
[151] ibid Art 41(1)(b)(i).
[152] Roberto Castro de Figueiredo, 'The Investment Requirement of the ICSID Convention and the Role of Investment Treaties' (2015) 26 Am Rev Int'l Arb 453, 479–80.

jurisdiction. In both cases, her opposition seems to stem from her—entirely accurate—perception that ICSID tribunals have not been able reach consensus on either the objective criteria applying under the *Salini* test,[153] or the specific outer limits established in Art 25 ICSID Convention.[154] Ho also notes that a binding definition of the concept of 'investment' under Art 25 ICSID Convention requires an agreement between all ICSID contracting States, pointing out that arbitral case law is not an acceptable substitute for multilateral consensus.[155]

According to Ho, the absence of such consensus among ICSID contracting States 'strongly suggests that the opinions of individual contracting states should prevail'.[156] When these opinions are expressed in instruments of consent such as BITs, one should interpret the meaning of 'investment' under Art 25 ICSID Convention 'using the definition found in the relevant BIT'.[157] Although Ho does not substantiate this claim, she argues that this solution 'corresponds most closely to the object and purpose of the ICSID Convention'.[158] 3.73

Ho not only provides justifications for the subjective approach, but also rebuts two objections commonly raised against it. The first such objection highlights that, under this approach, ICSID jurisdiction would frequently extend to disputes arising from ordinary commercial transactions such as sales contracts, an outcome which Ho acknowledges to be undesirable.[159] In fact, as Ho rightly observes, many investment treaties contain broad definitions of investment under which virtually any contractual rights qualify as investments.[160] Also, some investment treaties do not define the term 'investment' at all.[161] Ho claims that, in such scenarios, it is not necessary to resort to Art 25 ICSID Convention in order to contain the scope of ICSID jurisdiction within reasonable limits. She argues that, in line with the decision of the Tribunal in *Romak v Uzbekistan*,[162] objective criteria can or should be derived from the applicable BIT,[163] rather than from the ICSID Convention. 3.74

---

[153] Ho, 'The Meaning of "Investment"' (n 14) at 641 ('Even tribunals that have accepted that "investment" in Article 25(1) of the ICSID Convention has an objective meaning are unable to agree on the content of this objective meaning. The divisions on this point cast serious doubt on the defensibility and existence of objective criteria.')
[154] ibid 643–44 (' "Outer limits" or a "core meaning" that defy articulation cannot assist a tribunal when it needs to ascertain if an "investment" exists. This state of affairs may change if there is an emerging consensus on the definition of "investment". Until such a consensus presents itself, no tangible control can be exerted by "outer limits" on the meaning of "investment" in the ICSID Convention') (internal footnotes omitted).
[155] ibid 641 ('Ultimately, the decision of the members of a tribunal to adopt a "test" for "investment" is not a replacement for the kind of consensus that is required to redraft the ICSID Convention in order for it to accommodate a common definition of "investment" ') (internal footnote omitted).
[156] ibid 644.
[157] ibid.
[158] ibid.
[159] ibid ('Broad definitions of "investment" in BITs give rise to the concern that any commercial transaction can benefit from the ICSID dispute settlement mechanism') (internal footnote omitted).
[160] ibid.
[161] ibid n 69 (acknowledging that 'BITs that do not contain any definition of "investment" do exist').
[162] *Romak S.A. (Switzerland) v The Republic of Uzbekistan*, PCA Case No AA280, Award (26 November 2009).
[163] Ho, 'The Meaning of "Investment"' (n 14) 645.

3.75 In reality, however, the *Romak* approach is largely identical to the *Salini* test, given that both entail the application of a set of independent or objective criteria which are not expressly mentioned in the relevant provisions (Art 25 ICSID Convention and treaty clauses defining the term 'investment'). Ho's rebuttal of this objection is thus unconvincing because the alternative approach she advocates involves—at least potentially—the same defects as the application of objective criteria or an outer limits test under Art 25 ICSID Convention, ie a risk of inconsistent decisions and questionable legitimacy.

3.76 The second objection that Ho seeks to rebut pertains to the distinction between consent and subject matter jurisdiction, ie to the idea that the jurisdictional requirement that the dispute be related to an investment is separate from the jurisdictional requirement of consent. Acknowledging that such an objection may in principle be valid, Ho nonetheless claims that in the absence of a clear definition of the term 'investment', it is not sensible to dissociate these two jurisdictional requirements.[164]

V. Assessment

A. Objective approach

3.77 As has been explained, the arguments relied upon in support of the objective approach include, or pertain to, (1) the principle of effectiveness of treaty interpretation (*effet utile*); (2) the Convention's negotiating history, including the drafters' emphasis of the fact that the requirement of the existence of an investment has to be distinguished from the requirement of consent; (3) the need to ensure certainty and uniformity of the Convention's scope of application; and (4) various interpretive flaws of the rival subjective approach.

3.78 Although compelling at first sight, the argument based on the principle of *effet utile* is, in reality, not convincing. This is because the subjective approach does not imply that the term 'investment' under Art 25 ICSID Convention does not have any meaning at all. It merely entails that, instead of laying down an *independent* notion of investment, the Convention implicitly refers to, or endorses, the definitions contained in the applicable consent instruments. Such a referral or 'incorporation' mechanism, which constitutes the central premise of the subjective approach, in no way deprives the term investment in Art 25 ICSID Convention of its meaning or usefulness.

3.79 The drafting history, on the other hand, does indeed provide substantial backing for the objective approach. The various attempts to agree a definition of the term 'investment' (and corresponding proposals) clearly show that the Convention's drafters considered

---

[164] ibid 646 ('This argument would be persuasive if there were firm and fixed criteria for "investment" in the ICSID Convention that can be analysed independently of the definition contained in the BIT') (internal footnote omitted).

the term 'investment' in Art 25 to have a specific meaning. There is nothing in the negotiating history that would indicate that the drafters considered it unnecessary to define the term 'investment' because they assumed that the meaning of this concept would be determined in the applicable consent instruments. The drafting history also unambiguously suggests that the parties' consent was considered a necessary, but not sufficient condition for the jurisdiction of the Centre and that the requirement of the existence of a dispute arising out of an investment was regarded as a separate requirement, beyond the reach of agreements between individual contracting States or disputing parties.

The argument based on the alleged necessity to ensure the uniform interpretation of the Convention's scope of application is not compelling. In fact, there is no reason to assume that the drafters of the Convention valued the achievement of such uniformity any more than the flexibility inherent in the subjective approach. Also, the objective approach does not actually ensure (a high level of) uniformity, given that, in most cases, the requirements under Art 25 ICSID Convention constitute only one of two applicable thresholds. Even if there is full consensus on the meaning of investment under the Convention, differences between the various treaty and statutory definitions necessarily entail that the scope of jurisdiction of ICSID tribunals varies depending on the applicable consent instrument. **3.80**

The arguments alleging that the subjective approach suffers from various interpretive deficiencies carry little, if any, weight. One argument, as has been seen, is that the subjective approach is flawed because it heavily relies on the Convention's drafting history, despite such history only being a subsidiary means of interpretation, ie a tool to which recourse can only be had if the meaning of the relevant provision is 'ambiguous or obscure' or if the application of the general rule of interpretation leads to a result that is 'manifestly absurd or unreasonable'.[165] This argument is not wrong per se, but it is rather formalistic and overlooks that the supporters of the objective approach similarly focus on the Convention's negotiating history and that, in practice, many arbitral tribunals consider that a treaty's drafting history can always be taken into account. **3.81**

Another argument, as has been mentioned, consists of denying the interpretive relevance of treaty definitions for the purposes of determining the meaning of 'investment' under Art 25 ICSID Convention on the grounds that such definitions do not constitute subsequent agreements or treaty practice between ICSID contracting States. This argument misunderstands the central claim of the subjective approach: The subjective approach does not consider that the term 'investment' in Art 25 ICSID Convention has a specific meaning and that such meaning can or should be determined using interpretive tools; it posits that the definitions contained in the relevant consent instruments are incorporated into Art 25, with no need for any further interpretive determination. **3.82**

---

[165] VCLT (n 57) Art 32.

3.83 The third argument, which is based on the premise that treaty definitions of 'investment' modify Art 25 ICSID Convention, is equally weak because it similarly misconstrues the meaning of the subjective approach. This approach is not based on the idea that definitions of 'investment' contained in investment treaties modify, or derogate from, the meaning that the term 'investment' has under the Convention. Instead, as has been explained, it postulates that the notion of investment in Art 25 ICSID Convention *incorporates* those treaty definitions.

B. Subjective approach

3.84 For the reasons discussed above, the argument that the Convention's drafting history provides support for the subjective approach is not compelling. In fact, this viewpoint fails to acknowledge that the repeated attempts to define the term 'investment' reflect the drafters' understanding that this concept had a specific meaning, independent of the definitions that may be contained in consent instruments. It also distorts and exaggerates the role that the drafters attributed to the parties' consent to submit a dispute to the Centre, elevating it to a criterion absorbing all other jurisdictional requirements, including the requirement that the dispute must arise out of an investment.

3.85 As has been explained, several tribunals adopting the subjective approach have held that the absence of a definition of 'investment' in Art 25 ICSID Convention indicates that this provision does not set forth any definitional requirements and that it does not, therefore, limit the freedom of individual contracting States to determine what constitutes an investment. This analysis is obviously flawed. The fact that a particular concept is not defined does evidently not mean that it is devoid of any substance. Many, if not most, terms used in international conventions are not defined, and it would obviously be unreasonable to claim that they are all meaningless.

3.86 As far as Ho's arguments in support of the subjective approach are concerned, they are also largely unconvincing. Her argument that the objective approach is flawed because arbitral tribunals have failed to agree on the applicable objective criteria does not call into question the appropriateness of the objective approach as such; it merely highlights practical difficulties in its application. The same can be said about her claim that it is preferable to apply implied criteria based on treaty definitions of 'investment', rather than Art 25 ICSID Convention. This argument does not, in fact, reject the objective approach; it simply provides an alternative legal basis for it. Finally, her claim that the uncertainty surrounding the meaning of 'investment' renders the distinction between the requirement of consent and the requirement of the existence of an investment unworkable is largely identical to her first argument and does not affect the appropriateness of the objective approach per se.

3.87 In addition, the subjective approach suffers from an even more fundamental flaw. As has already been explained, it is based on the erroneous assumption that instruments of consent always define the term 'investment'. Where this is not the case (eg where the parties' consent to refer disputes to ICSID is contained in an investment contract), the subjective approach can simply not operate, ie there is no 'subjective' definition that can be applied under Art 25 ICSID Convention.

It would of course be possible to follow the subjective approach only where the term 'investment' is defined in the applicable instrument of consent and to fall back on the objective approach in all other cases. This would, however, involve a major contradiction. In fact, in some cases, one would consider that the term 'investment' in Art 25 ICSID Convention does not have an independent meaning, while in other cases one would consider that it does have such a meaning. Since it would cause an unreasonable degree of non-uniformity in the Convention's application, such an interpretation of Art 25 must be rejected. **3.88**

4

The Meaning of Investment Under Art 25 ICSID Convention

I. Introduction	4.01	A. Meaning and recognition	4.65
II. The *Salini* Test	4.02	B. Assessment	4.72
A. History, evolution, and nature of the *Salini* test	4.02	IV. The Commercial-Transaction Test	4.78
		A. Meaning and recognition	4.78
B. The three core *Salini* criteria: contribution, duration, and risk	4.14	B. Assessment	4.88
		V. Principal Scholarly Debates and Viewpoints	4.93
C. The controversial criterion of a contribution to the economic development of the host State	4.39	A. Nature of the *Salini* test	4.93
		B. Core *Salini* criteria	4.96
D. Other criteria	4.50	C. Requirement of a contribution to the host State's economic development	4.102
E. Critical assessment	4.59		
III. The Permissibility Test	4.65		

I. Introduction

4.01 As has been explained in Chapter 3, most tribunals and scholars consider that the term 'investment' in Art 25 ICSID Convention has an 'independent' or 'objective' meaning. This chapter explores what that meaning is. Section II discusses the prevailing arbitral approach, the so-called '*Salini* test'. It examines (a) the history, evolution, and nature of this test; (b) the three core *Salini* requirements (contribution, duration, and risk); (c) the controversial criterion of a contribution to the economic development of the host State; and (d) other criteria occasionally applied in arbitral practice. It also offers a critical assessment of the *Salini* test, highlighting its various flaws and inconsistencies. Sections III and IV examine two alternative, less widely followed, approaches, namely, the permissibility test and the commercial-transaction test. Section V provides an overview of the principal scholarly debates and viewpoints.

II. The *Salini* Test

A. History, evolution, and nature of the *Salini* test

1. History

The *Salini* test (and the *Salini* criteria or requirements) owes its name to the decision of the Tribunal in *Salini v. Morocco*.[1] The *Salini* case was not, however, the first ruling to have established a set of objective characteristics of an investment. Almost exactly four years earlier, the Tribunal in *Fedax v Venezuela* handed down a very similar decision,[2] which was duly cited by the *Salini* tribunal.[3] It is not clear—but also not necessary to resolve—why the relevant legal requirements became known as the *Salini*, and not as the *Fedax*, test. **4.02**

In *Fedax*, the Republic of Venezuela obtained a loan from a Venezuelan company for which it issued promissory notes.[4] Those notes were subsequently acquired by Fedax, the Claimant in the ICSID proceedings.[5] The main issue before the Tribunal was whether the promissory notes constituted an investment under the applicable bilateral investment treaty (BIT) (the BIT between the Netherlands and Venezuela) and the ICSID Convention. Objecting to the Tribunal's jurisdiction, Venezuela argued that the relevant debt instruments were neither a foreign direct investment, nor a portfolio investment, nor an investment in the ordinary sense of the term.[6] **4.03**

Without clearly distinguishing between the requirements of the treaty and those of the Convention, the Tribunal held that the promissory notes qualified as an investment.[7] It placed particular emphasis on the fact that the issuance of those notes involved 'a fundamental public interest',[8] given that, under Venezuelan law, the borrowed funds had to be used to 'undertake productive works, attend to the needs of the national interest and cover transitory needs of the treasury'.[9] The Tribunal appears to have considered that the presence of this public interest distinguished the issuance of the promissory notes from 'ordinary commercial transactions' (although, on a literal reading, it distinguished not the loan itself, but rather the purchases facilitated by the loan, from such transactions).[10] **4.04**

---

[1] *Salini Costruttori S.P.A. and Italstrade S.P.A. v Kingdom of Morocco*, ICSID Case No ARB/00/4, Decision on Jurisdiction (23 July 2001) (hereafter *Salini v Morocco*). For a general overview of the *Salini* decision and its impact, see Emmanuel Gaillard and Yas Banifatemi, 'The Long March towards a *Jurisprudence Constante* on the Notion of Investment: *Salini v. Morocco*, ICSID Case No ARB/00/4' in Meg Kinnear, Geraldine Fischer, Jara Mínguez Almeida, Luisa Fernanda Torres and Mairée Uran Bidegain (eds), *Building International Investment Law: The First 50 Years of ICSID* (Wolters Kluwer 2015) 97.
[2] *Fedax N.V. v The Republic of Venezuela*, ICSID Case No ARB/96/3, Decision of the Tribunal on Objections to Jurisdiction (11 July 1997) (hereafter *Fedax v Venezuela*).
[3] *Salini v Morocco* (n 1) para 52.
[4] *Fedax v Venezuela* (n 2) para 13.
[5] ibid.
[6] ibid para 19. Venezuela considered that an investment in the ordinary sense consisted of 'the laying out of money or property in business ventures, so that it may produce a revenue or income'.
[7] ibid para 43.
[8] ibid para 42.
[9] ibid.
[10] ibid.

4.05 Somewhat curiously, it is only in the last paragraph of its analysis that the Tribunal actually proposed a definition of the concept of 'investment', stating that '[t]he basic features of an investment have been described as involving a certain duration, a certain regularity of profit and return, assumption of risk, a substantial commitment and a significance for the host State's development'.[11] In the same paragraph, the Tribunal also (superficially) examined whether these five requirements were met in the case at hand, answering this question in the affirmative.[12]

4.06 It is important to stress that the Tribunal derived the five basic features of an investment from the 1996 version of Schreuer's Commentary on Art 25 ICSID Convention.[13] Schreuer appears to have deduced the relevant characteristics from ICSID's 'experience' (ie ICSID caselaw).[14] According to Schreuer, the relevant characteristics do not, strictly speaking, constitute a definition of 'investment'; rather, they should be viewed as 'features that are typical to most of the operations in question'.[15]

4.07 *Salini* involved a contract concluded between two Italian companies (Salini Costruttori and Italstrade) and the Société Nationale des Autoroutes du Maroc, a state-owned enterprise tasked with building, maintaining, and operating highways and other roadworks, under which the Italian entities undertook to build a portion of the highway linking Rabat to Fès.[16] Faced with the question of whether Salini and Italstrade had made an investment in Morocco, the Tribunal stated that the existence of an investment inferred 'contributions, a certain duration of performance of the contract and a participation in the risks of the transaction', as well as a 'contribution to the economic development of the host State'.[17] It held that those characteristics were present in the case before it.[18]

4.08 The test adopted by the *Salini* tribunal differs in several respects from the one established in *Fedax*. Most noticeably, the *Salini* tribunal did not consider 'regularity of profit and return' (or any other profit-related feature) as a relevant criterion. In addition, there are two minor linguistic changes. Instead of using the term 'commitment' (the *Fedax* tribunal referred to a 'substantial commitment'), the *Salini* decision speaks of 'contributions'. As far as the criterion pertaining to the economic development of the host State is concerned, the *Salini* tribunal held that the investment had to make a 'contribution' to such development, while the *Fedax* tribunal considered that the investment had to have 'significance' for the host State's development.

---

[11] ibid para 43.
[12] ibid.
[13] ibid n 63.
[14] Christoph Schreuer, 'Commentary on the ICSID Convention' (1996) 11 ICSID Rev/FILJ 318, 372 (hereafter Schreuer, 'Commentary on the ICSID Convention').
[15] ibid.
[16] *Salini v Morocco* (n 1) para 2.
[17] ibid para 52.
[18] ibid paras 53–57.

As for the legal basis of the relevant criteria, the *Salini* tribunal noted that the first three requirements (commitment, duration, and risk) were recognized by scholarly writers.[19] It further considered that the fourth criterion (a contribution to the economic development of the host State) could be derived from the Convention's Preamble, relying on the reference to 'the need for international cooperation for economic development, and the role of private international investment therein'.[20]

4.09

2. Evolution

In subsequent decisions, the *Salini* test has evolved in three principal ways. First, the requirement of a contribution to the economic development of the host State has been rejected by numerous tribunals and can thus no longer be considered as a widely recognized criterion. Second, regularity of profit and returns, a feature mentioned in *Fedax* but abandoned by the *Salini* tribunal, has occasionally resurfaced in post-*Salini* rulings. Finally, a few tribunals have added further criteria and, more specifically, the requirements of legality and good faith. These three evolutions are examined in more detail in Sections II.C and II.D below.

4.10

3. Nature

A central question concerning the nature of the *Salini* test is whether the *Salini* criteria constitute jurisdictional requirements or merely typical characteristics of an investment. As has been explained in Chapter 3,[21] the latter approach is eminently questionable, given that a legal test whose requirements are not binding is of very limited use. However, as has been shown, there is substantial support for this approach in arbitral case law and the issue of the mandatory or optional nature of the *Salini* criteria is thus largely unresolved.

4.11

A rather uncontroversial feature of the *Salini* test consists of the interdependence of the various *Salini* requirements.[22] Interdependence means that the presence of one criterion, or the extent to which it is present, will often have an impact on whether, or to what extent, other requirements are met.[23] The magnitude of the financial risk involved in a particular investment, for instance, is arguably a reflection of both the size of the investor's commitment or contribution and of the duration of the investment project.[24] Similarly, the size of the investor's commitment/contribution is likely to affect the contribution that the investment makes to the economic development of the host State.

4.12

A number of tribunals have stressed that the *Salini* criteria must be examined globally[25] or

4.13

---

[19] ibid para 52.
[20] Convention on the Settlement of Investment Disputes between States and Nationals of Other States (adopted 18 March 1965, entered into force 14 October 1966) Preamble (hereafter ICSID Convention).
[21] See Chapter 3 Section III.D.
[22] *Salini v Morocco* (n 1) para 52 (noting that 'these various elements may be interdependent').
[23] ibid.
[24] ibid (observing that 'the risks of the transaction may depend on the contributions and the duration of performance of the contract').
[25] ibid para 52 (stating that 'these various criteria should be assessed globally').

(w)holistically,[26] rather than in isolation. This notably means that the absence, or limited presence, of one particular criterion can be compensated by the strength of other criteria.[27] If, for example, the duration of a given project or operation is limited, the substantial size of the investor's contributions and/or of the contribution to the economic development of the host State may justify the conclusion that the operation at stake qualifies as an investment.

B. The three core *Salini* criteria: contribution, duration, and risk

1. Contribution

4.14 Most ICSID tribunals employ to term 'contribution' to describe the first *Salini* criterion. However, it should not be forgotten that in *Fedax*, one of the founding cases of the *Salini* test, the Tribunal referred to this criterion as the requirement of a (substantial) 'commitment', an expression that can still occasionally be found in jurisdictional rulings.[28] Interestingly, the term 'commitment' has been preferred in BITs that have incorporated *Salini*-like requirements into their definitions of investment. Under the US Model BIT, for example, one of the three 'characteristics' of an investment consists of the 'commitment of capital or other resources'.[29]

4.15 The term 'contribution' is evidently very broad. In fact, it is possible to contribute to an almost infinite number of 'things'. One can, for instance, contribute to a present, to a book, to the escalation of an armed conflict, to a friendly work climate, to peace in the world, or to the economic development of a State. The different ways in which one can make a contribution are also nearly limitless. A contribution can take the form of money, of a book chapter, of a statement or attitude, of various types of efforts, or a broad range of economic and other activities or projects. In order for the *Salini* criterion of a 'contribution' to have any meaning, it is therefore necessary to clarify (1) *what* must be contributed to and (2) what the contribution must *consist of*.

4.16 As far as the first question (what must be contributed to?) is concerned, most earlier decisions lack clarifications. The *Salini* tribunal, for example, merely stated that an investment inferred 'contributions', without offering any further explanations.[30] The Tribunal in *Fakes v Turkey* considered that a contribution was a criterion 'within the framework of the ICSID Convention', but similarly refrained from specifying what it was that had

---

[26] *Malaysian Historical Salvors Sdn, Bhd v Malaysia*, ICSID Case No ARB/05/10, Award on Jurisdiction (17 May 2007) para 106 (hereafter *Malaysian Historical Salvors v Malaysia*).
[27] ibid ('Where there is some marginal evidence in support of one of the relevant hallmarks of "investment", but more conclusive evidence in support [of] the presence of the other relevant hallmarks of "investment", the tribunal may choose to discount the weakness of the claimant's case in one of the relevant hallmarks of "investment" by stating that the issue of "investment" should be approached on a holistic basis').
[28] See, for example, *Deutsche Bank AG v Democratic Socialist Republic of Sri Lanka*, ICSID Case No 09/02, Award (31 October 2012) para 294 (hereafter *Deutsche Bank v Sri Lanka*).
[29] United States Model BIT 2012 Art 1 (providing that the 'characteristics of an investment' include 'the commitment of capital or other resources, the expectation of gain or profit, or the assumption of risk').
[30] *Salini v Morocco* (n 1) para 52.

to be contributed to.[31] The decision of the Tribunal in *Deutsche Bank* likewise remained silent with regard to this issue.[32]

Yet, despite the silence of these and other decisions on the 'to what' issue, the very use of the term 'contribution' appears to suggest that the *Salini* test views investments as activities, operations, or projects, ie as having the fourth possible meaning of 'investment' identified in Chapter 2.[33] Indeed, it makes sense to speak of a contribution to a particular investment activity, operation, or project (such as the exploration of natural resources or an infrastructure project). By contrast, the term 'contribution' does not seem to be compatible with an asset-based notion of 'investment'. In fact, it means very little to say that one 'contributes' to an asset.

4.17

The decision of the Tribunal in *Poštová banka v Greece* supports this understanding of the contribution requirement. In this case, the question arose whether the Greek sovereign bonds acquired by the Claimant constituted investments. The Tribunal held that, if an objective test applied (an issue which the Tribunal refused to rule upon), this should be the three-prong *Salini* test requiring a contribution, a certain duration, and risk.[34] As far as the first criterion was concerned, the Tribunal considered that a contribution had to be made to an 'economic venture'.[35] It decided that this requirement was not met in the case before it because the Claimant had failed to establish that the funds used to purchase the sovereign bonds had been 'used in economically productive activities'.[36]

4.18

Several tribunals have emulated the approach adopted in *Poštová banka*. In *MNSS v Montenegro*, for example, the Tribunal expressly endorsed the *Poštová banka* definition of 'investment' as 'a contribution to an economic venture ...'.[37] It held that the company shares acquired by the Claimant constituted a (financial) contribution,[38] presumably to the economic activities of that company. The tribunal in *Eyre v Sri Lanka* followed the same approach,[39] again referring to the holding of the *Poštová banka* tribunal.[40] It decided that no contribution had been made because there was no evidence that the Claimant had actually acquired the alleged investment, a plot of land known as the 'Montrose land'.[41]

4.19

---

[31] *Mr. Saba Fakes v Republic of Turkey*, ICSID Case No ARB/07/20, Award (14 July 2010) para 110 (hereafter *Fakes v Turkey*).
[32] *Deutsche Bank v Sri Lanka* (n 28) para 295.
[33] See Chapter 2 Section VIII.
[34] *Poštová banka, a.s. v The Hellenic Republic*, ICSID Case No ARB/13/8, Award (9 April 2015) para 360 (hereafter *Poštová banka v Greece*).
[35] ibid para 361.
[36] ibid para 363 (adding that 'it appears that the funds were used for Greece's budgetary needs, and particularly for repaying its debts').
[37] *MNSS B.V. and Recupero Credito Acciaio N.V. v Montenegro*, ICSID Case No ARB(AF)/12/8, Award (4 May 2016) para 189 (holding that 'it can be said that an investment is "a contribution to an economic venture of a certain duration implying an operational risk"') (hereafter *MNSS v Montenegro*).
[38] ibid para 202.
[39] *Raymond Charles Eyre and others v Democratic Socialist Republic of Sri Lanka*, ICSID Case No ARB/16/25, Award (5 March 2020) para 294 (hereafter *Eyre v Sri Lanka*).
[40] ibid para 293.
[41] ibid para 300.

4.20 As regards the second question (the question of what contributions may consist of), most tribunals have largely refrained from imposing any limitations on possible forms of contributions. The *Salini* tribunal, for instance, listed the Claimants' know-how, equipment, and personnel, as well as the loans they had obtained to finance the works and the bank guarantees they had furnished to the client as qualifying contributions.[42] It concluded that the Claimants had made contributions 'in money, in kind, and in industry'.[43]

4.21 Another example is the decision of the Tribunal in *LESI v Algeria*,[44] which involved the construction of a dam by the Claimant. In this case, the Tribunal held that the notion of 'contribution' ('apport' in the French original version) was not limited to financial contributions, but also encompassed any other expenses incurred in the pursuit of an economic objective, expressly mentioning loans, materials, works, and services.[45] The Tribunal held that, *prima facie*, the Claimant had deployed important means in connection with the construction of the dam, and that the contribution requirement was therefore satisfied.[46]

4.22 In addition to the 'to what' and 'in what form' issues, the contribution criterion also (at least potentially) raises the question of whether any particular minimum threshold must be met. On this issue, it can be observed that most tribunals do not require that the investor's contribution be of any particular size or amount. The tribunals in *Salini*, *Fakes*, *Deutsche Bank*, *Poštová banka*, *MNSS*, *Eyre*, and *LESI*, for instance, do not seem to have applied any minimum threshold.

4.23 Other tribunals have taken a different approach. As has already been seen, the Tribunal in *Fedax* considered that the contribution criterion required a 'substantial' commitment on the part of the investor. In *Bayindir v Pakistan*,[47] which involved the construction of a motorway by the Claimant,[48] the Tribunal reasoned along the same lines, holding that, in order to qualify as an investment, 'the project in question must constitute a substantial commitment'.[49] The Tribunal decided that this requirement was met since 'it [could not] seriously be doubted that Bayindir made a significant contribution'.[50] In *Malaysian Historical Salvors*, which involved the salvage of a shipwreck in Malaysian territorial waters, the insufficiency of the contribution made by the Claimant appears to have been one of the reasons for denying the existence of an investment under Art 25 ICSID Convention. In fact, though acknowledging that the Claimant had made

---

[42] *Salini v Morocco* (n 1) para 53.
[43] ibid.
[44] *L.E.S.I.—DIPENTA v Democratic and Popular Republic of Algeria*, ICSID Case No ARB/03/08, Award (10 January 2005) (hereafter *LESI v Algeria*).
[45] ibid para 14(i).
[46] ibid.
[47] *Bayindir Insaat Turizm Ticaret Ve Sanayi A.Ş. v Islamic Republic of Pakistan*, ICSID Case No ARB/03/29, Decision on Jurisdiction (14 November 2005) (hereafter *Bayindir v Pakistan*).
[48] ibid paras 10–20.
[49] ibid para 131.
[50] ibid.

contributions in money, in kind, and in industry, the Tribunal emphasized that 'the size of the contributions [was] in no way comparable to those found in *Salini*, *Bayindir* and *Jan de Nul*'[51] and that they were ultimately not different from the contributions present in commercial salvage contracts.[52]

2. Duration

The rationale underlying the duration requirement is very rarely spelled out and remains somewhat obscure. The main idea seems to be that short-term 'investments' do not generate a lasting benefit for the host State and that they are therefore not deserving of protection under the ICSID Convention. A reference to this justification can be found in *Fedax*, where the Tribunal appears to have attached importance to the fact that the acquisition by the Claimant of promissory notes issued by Venezuela '[was] not merely a short-term, occasional financial arrangement, such as could happen with investments that come in for quick gains and leave immediately thereafter'.[53] **4.24**

Even more so than the contribution criterion, the requirement of a minimum duration implies that, under the *Salini* test, an investment is viewed as an operation, activity, or project. Arbitral decisions that have clarified the object of the duration requirement confirm this viewpoint. In *Salini*, for example, the relevant duration was considered to be the 'duration of performance of the contract'.[54] In *Poštová banka*, *MNSS*, and *Eyre*, where 'investment' was defined as a 'contribution to an economic venture of a certain duration implying an operational risk', the tribunals focused on the duration of the Claimants' economic activities.[55] **4.25**

Since most investment treaties and many investment laws define 'investments' as assets,[56] and since the *Salini* test does not expressly state that it views investments as activities, operations, or projects, it is inevitable that some tribunals apply the duration requirement to assets owned or controlled by the presumed investor. This is, however, rather awkward. In fact, what—if anything—does it mean to say that company shares or a plot of land have a certain duration? When applied to assets, the duration criterion thus needs some twisting and tweaking. One possible solution is to hold that the criterion of a certain duration refers to the duration of the investor's ownership of the relevant asset(s). This was, for instance, the approach followed by the Tribunal in *Phoenix v Czech Republic*. In this case, which involved the acquisition by the Claimant of two Czech companies,[57] the Tribunal held that these companies could in principle qualify as an investment, given that the Claimant had purchased them in 2002 and only sold its **4.26**

---

[51] *Malaysian Historical Salvors v Malaysia* (n 26) para 109.
[52] ibid.
[53] *Fedax v Venezuela* (n 2) para 43.
[54] *Salini v Morocco* (n 1) para 52.
[55] *Poštová banka v Greece* (n 34) para 366; *MNSS v Montenegro* (n 37) para 202; *Eyre v Sri Lanka* (n 39) paras 295–306.
[56] See Chapter 5 Section II.A.2 and Chapter 7 Section II.
[57] *Phoenix Action, Ltd. v The Czech Republic*, ICSID Case No ARB/06/5, Award (15 April 2009) para 22 (hereafter *Phoenix v Czech Republic*).

shares in these companies in January 2008, several years after initiating ICSID arbitration proceedings.[58] In *MNSS*, the Tribunal similarly held that the duration requirement was met because the Claimant's ownership of the company shares it had acquired was not 'limited in time'.[59]

4.27 This approach is evidently highly problematic. It implies that the acquisition of an asset does not per se constitute an investment, but that such acquisition (or the asset itself) morphs into an investment once a certain amount of time has passed. Not only does this approach require a determination of the point in time in which this transformation occurs, but, more fundamentally, it is difficult to provide a compelling explanation for the delay with which the asset (or its acquisition) turns into an investment. Contrary to investments that take the form of activities (such as the construction of a highway, for example), the passing of time is not, in principle, accompanied by any increase in the benefits accrued to the host State.

4.28 The application of the duration requirement inevitably raises the question of the relevant threshold. A number of tribunals appear to have required a specific minimum duration. The *Salini* tribunal, for instance, held that the minimum duration was between two and five years.[60] It considered that this requirement was met given that the planned and actual duration of performance of the contract were thirty-two and thirty-six months, respectively. In *Malaysian Historical Salvors*, the sole Arbitrator endorsed the minimum threshold established in *Salini* and found that this threshold was met because it 'took almost four years to complete' the contract.[61]

4.29 *Malaysian Historical Salvors* highlights how problematic (and arbitrary) the application of a minimum threshold can be. As has already been explained, this case involved a contract under which the Claimant undertook to locate and salvage a shipwreck in the Malaysian territorial waters. The duration requirement was found to be met because the salvage operations extended over a period of four years, thus arguably meeting the minimum duration established in *Salini*. The perverse effect of applying such a threshold is that, had the Claimant been more efficient and managed to salvage the shipwreck in twelve or eighteen months, the operation would not have qualified as an investment. Thus, instead of being rewarded for a speedy completion of its contractual task, the Claimant would have been penalized by having its investor status denied. More generally, delays in performance, whether attributable to the contractor or to events beyond his control, would have the rather absurd effect of transforming non-investments into investments. It is difficult to justify such outcomes, at least from the angle of the

---

[58] ibid para 124.
[59] *MNSS v Montenegro* (n 37) para 202.
[60] *Salini v Morocco* (n 1) para 54 (noting that the 'transaction ... complie[d] with the minimal length upheld by the doctrine, which is from 2 to 5 years'). The Tribunal's holding is rather problematic since it does not provide any clarification as to how the specific minimum threshold should be determined in individual cases.
[61] *Malaysian Historical Salvors v Malaysia* (n 26) paras 110–11. It should be pointed out, however, that the sole Arbitrator ultimately concluded that the duration requirement was only met 'in the quantitative sense', but not 'in the qualitative sense' since the contract as such did not meaningfully contribute to the economic development of Malaysia.

rationale underlying the duration requirement (the assumption that the benefits for the host State are proportionate to the investment's duration).

The undesirable effect of the application of a minimum threshold and the more general unsuitability of the duration requirement as a criterion determining the investment status of assets (rather than operations) are likely to have contributed to the current trend towards more flexible approaches. An example of such an approach can be found in *Romak v Uzbekistan* where the Tribunal rejected the view that, 'as a matter of principle, there [was] some fixed minimum duration that determines whether assets qualify as investments'.[62] In *Deutsche Bank*, the Tribunal approvingly cited Schreuer's view that duration was 'a very flexible term' and that the duration of an investment under the Convention 'could be anything from a couple of months to many years'.[63] Based on this understanding, it decided that the hedging agreement between the Claimant and Sri Lanka, which was concluded for a period of twelve months, satisfied the duration criterion.[64]

3. Risk

Like the notion of contribution, the concept of risk is undoubtedly very broad. The future being inherently unpredictable, it is always possible for certain undesirable or unpleasant events to occur and the risk of such events occurring characterizes virtually all forms of human activity, whether it is a walk in the park (one notably risks being bitten by a dog), an application for a job (one risks rejection), a romantic date (one again risks rejection, or simply disappointment), or a skiing trip (one risks injury). It is thus indispensable to define the *Salini* test's risk requirement with more precision.

Interestingly, not all tribunals have made an attempt at such a definition. The Tribunal in *Phoenix*, for example, remained silent with regard to the type of risk that the *Salini* test contemplates. Instead, it simply affirmed that, as a general rule, the acquisition of a company (even, or especially, of a bankrupt company) always 'carries a risk: namely that the investor loses the amount he has paid'.[65] Quoting Schreuer, the *Deutsche Bank* Tribunal observed, in general and rather ambiguous terms, that 'the very existence of the dispute [was] an indication of risk'.[66] Without any further analysis or explanation, it concluded that 'it [could not] seriously be doubted that Deutsche Bank's investment involved a risk'.[67]

Most tribunals, however, have sought to limit the scope of the *Salini* test's risk criterion. Some of these tribunals have required that the risk faced by the investor be of a certain

---

[62] *Romak S.A. v The Republic of Uzbekistan*, PCA Case No AA280, Award (26 November 2009) para 225 (observing that '[s]hort-term projects are not deprived of "investment" status solely by virtue of their limited duration' and that '[d]uration is to be analyzed in light of all the circumstances, and of the investor's overall commitment') (hereafter *Romak v Uzbekistan*).
[63] *Deutsche Bank v Sri Lanka* (n 28) para 303.
[64] ibid para 304.
[65] *Phoenix v Czech Republic* (n 57) para 127.
[66] *Deutsche Bank v Sri Lanka* (n 28) para 301.
[67] ibid para 302 (adding that the bank 'faced a substantial risk that it would pay up to USD 2.5 million to CPC').

magnitude. In *LESI*, for example, the Tribunal acknowledged that any transaction could in principle involve a risk under the *Salini* test, provided that it entailed 'increased risks' for the obligor.[68] The Tribunal did not elaborate any further on this notion of 'heightened' risk and the exact meaning of this concept (including the relevant object of comparison) therefore remains somewhat ambiguous.

4.34 In *Malaysian Historical Salvors*, the sole Arbitrator recognized that the salvage operations conducted by the Claimant involved certain risks and that those risks were substantial, given that the salvage contract had been concluded on a 'no-finds-no-pay' basis.[69] However, he noted that such clauses were common features of these types of contracts and that the risks assumed by the Claimant were thus not 'anything other than normal commercial risks'.[70] Relying on a distinction it had already drawn in connection with the duration criterion, sole Arbitrator concluded that the risk criterion was only met in a quantitative, not in a qualitative sense.[71]

4.35 The idea that commercial risks do not satisfy the *Salini* risk requirement ultimately led to the formal recognition of the notion of 'investment risk' as the relevant parameter. The first ruling to have expressly distinguished between these two categories of risk is the decision of the Tribunal in *Romak*. According to this Tribunal, a 'commercial risk' can be defined as 'the risk of non-performance [by the other party of its obligations]' or 'counterparty risk',[72] while an investment risk refers to the fact that 'the investor cannot be sure of a return on his investment . . . even if all relevant counterparties discharge their contractual obligations'.[73] Noting that the only risk assumed by Romak consisted of 'the possible non-payment of the wheat delivery',[74] the Tribunal concluded that 'Romak's economic activity did not involve the risk normally associated with an investment'.[75]

4.36 It should be noted that, although it appears to be compelling, the distinction adopted by the *Romak* tribunal does not withstand closer scrutiny. In fact, it is not correct that risks which go beyond the risk of non-performance by the other party of its contractual obligations are specific to investments. In reality, such risks may, and frequently do, arise in connection with 'ordinary' commercial transactions such as sale of goods contracts. A buyer (who is paying in a foreign currency), for example, bears the risk of a currency exchange fluctuation. A seller may have to bear the risk of an increase in the price of the raw materials needed to manufacture the goods. In both scenarios, the relevant events

---

[68] *LESI v Algeria* (n 44) para 14(iii) (stating that '[t]he relevant risk can in reality affect any contract that implies increased risks for the party assuming an obligation') (translation by the author).
[69] *Malaysian Historical Salvors v Malaysia* (n 26) para 112.
[70] ibid.
[71] ibid ('While the Claimant may have satisfied the risk characteristic or criterion in a quantitative sense . . ., the quality of the assumed risk was not something which established ICSID practice and jurisprudence would recognize').
[72] *Romak v Uzbekistan* (n 62) para 229.
[73] ibid para 230.
[74] ibid para 231.
[75] ibid.

may result in financial losses for the affected party. However, neither is related to a possible failure of the other party to perform its obligations.

The *Romak* approach has been followed by several other tribunals.[76] In *Poštová banka*, for example, the Tribunal referred to the *Romak* decision, expressly endorsing the distinction between commercial and investment risk (it qualified the latter as 'operational' risk[77]).[78] Further developing the rule established in *Romak*, the *Poštová banka* tribunal took the view that the investment risk had to be distinguished not only from commercial risks, but also from sovereign risk, ie from 'the risk of interference of the Government in a contract or any other relationship'.[79] For reasons which are not clearly stated in the decision, the Tribunal found that no such operational or investment risk was present in the case at hand.[80]

4.37

Not all tribunals have followed the *Romak/Poštová banka* example, however. In *Cortec v Kenya*,[81] for instance—a case which involved a mining project for which the Claimants had obtained a prospecting licence—the Tribunal did not draw any distinction between commercial and investment risk, nor otherwise define the meaning of the *Salini* test's risk criterion. Yet, it decided that the risk requirement was satisfied insofar as 'the Claimants' investments involved acceptance of the commercial risks that are inherent in a long-term mining project'.[82] The Tribunal thus implicitly acknowledged that the presence of commercial risks was sufficient for the purposes of the *Salini* test.

4.38

C. The controversial criterion of a contribution to the economic development of the host State

1. Recognition and meaning of the criterion

The criterion of a contribution to the economic development of the host State was expressly recognized in the two founding cases of the *Salini* test, ie *Fedax* and *Salini*. In *Fedax*, the Tribunal held that one of the 'basic features of an investment' consisted of its 'significance for the host State's development'.[83] In *Salini*, the Tribunal noted that an investment notably 'infer[red]' a 'contribution to the economic development of the host State of the investment', thus clarifying that this criterion was specifically concerned with the host State's *economic* development.[84] Most tribunals—including those that have rejected this particular requirement—have employed the *Salini* terminology.

4.39

---

[76] See, for example, *Poštová banka v Greece* (n 34) paras 367–70; *Eyre v Sri Lanka* (n 39) para 293.
[77] *Poštová banka v Greece* (n 34) para 369 (holding that, 'under an "objective" approach, an investment risk would be an operational risk').
[78] ibid para 368.
[79] ibid.
[80] ibid para 371.
[81] *Cortec Mining Kenya Limited and others v Republic of Kenya*, ICSID Case No ARB/15/29, Award (22 October 2018) (hereafter *Cortec v Kenya*).
[82] ibid para 300.
[83] *Fedax v Venezuela* (n 2) para 43.
[84] *Salini v Morocco* (n 1) para 52.

4.40 The requirement of a contribution to the host State's economic development has been applied in a number of post-*Salini* decisions. In *Mitchell v Congo*, for example, the ad hoc Committee observed that 'the economic development of the host State [had] always been taken into account ... by ICSID arbitral tribunals'.[85] Although it applied a slightly modified version of it, the *Phoenix* tribunal similarly acknowledged the relevance of this factor.[86] The need for an investment to contribute to the host State's economic development (or, at least, the possible relevance of this criterion) was also affirmed in the recent *Cortec* case.[87]

4.41 As has already been mentioned, the primary justification for the requirement that an investment must contribute to the host State's economic development is that the ICSID Convention's Preamble refers to 'the need for international cooperation for economic development, and the role of private international investment therein'.[88] To use the words of the *Salini* tribunal, it is this reference in the Preamble that justifies 'add[ing] the contribution to the economic development of the host State ... as an additional condition'.[89] A similar view has been expressed by other tribunals and committees.[90]

4.42 The *Mitchell* ad hoc Committee placed particular emphasis on a statement found in the 2001 version of Schreuer's Commentary on the ICSID Convention according to which the Preamble's reference to economic development constitutes the 'only possible indication of an objective meaning [of investment] that can be gleaned from the Convention'.[91] However, the authors of the Commentary themselves acknowledge that 'it does not necessarily follow that an activity that does not contribute to the host State's development cannot be an investment in the sense of Art. 25'.[92] Contrary to the assertion of the *Mitchell* ad hoc Committee, the Commentary (at least, in its current form) does not therefore provide support for the application of such a requirement.

4.43 A variation of the contribution to the economic development of the host State requirement is that the contribution should be made not to the State's economic development, but, more generally, to its economy. According to the *Phoenix* tribunal, for instance, it is difficult, if not impossible, to determine whether a particular 'investment' contributes to the economic development of the host State, given the inherent ambiguity of the term 'development'.[93] This Tribunal therefore advocated a simpler and less 'ambitious'

---

[85] *Mr. Patrick Mitchell v The Democratic Republic of Congo*, ICSID Case No ARB/99/7, Decision on the Application for Annulment of the Award (1 November 2006) para 29 (hereafter *Mitchell v Congo*).
[86] *Phoenix v Czech Republic* (n 57) paras 83–85.
[87] *Cortec v Kenya* (n 81) para 291 (noting that the 'contribution to the economic development of the host State' was one of the 'four Salini indicators' and that 'it [was] usual to take into account some or all of [these] indicators').
[88] ICSID Convention (n 20) Preamble.
[89] *Salini v Morocco* (n 1) para 52.
[90] See, for example, *Mitchell v Congo* (n 85) para 29 (noting that 'it [was] thus quite natural' that such a parameter should be taken into account).
[91] ibid para 31.
[92] Stephan W Schill, Christoph W Schreuer and Anthony Sinclair, 'Article 25' in Loretta Malintoppi, August Reinisch, Christoph W Schreuer and Anthony Sinclair (eds), *Schreuer's Commentary on the ICSID Convention: A Commentary on the Convention on the Settlement of Investment Disputes between States and Nationals of Other States* (3rd edn, Cambridge University Press 2022) para 228 (hereafter Schill, Schreuer and Sinclair, 'Article 25')
[93] *Phoenix v Czech Republic* (n 57) para 85.

criterion requiring not a contribution to the economic development, but merely to the economy, of the host State.[94] This approach has notably been endorsed by the *MNSS* tribunal.[95]

Like other *Salini* criteria, the contribution to the host State's economic development potentially raises a threshold question. In *Mitchell*, the ad hoc Committee rejected the application of any such requirement, observing that an investment's contribution did not have to be 'sizable' and that ICSID tribunals did not have to 'evaluate' the contribution made.[96] A majority of tribunals, however, have required that the contribution to the host State's (economic) development be 'significant'.[97] According to the sole Arbitrator in *Malaysian Historical Salvors*, the application of such a minimum threshold is necessary to avoid that 'any contract which enhances the Gross Domestic Product of an economy by any amount, however small' qualifies as an investment,[98] arguably an undesirable outcome.

4.44

2. Rejection of the criterion

In recent years, most tribunals have rejected the requirement of a contribution to the host State's economic development.[99] In a number of decisions, such rejection was implicit in the way in which the relevant tribunals formulated the *Salini* test. The *Romak* tribunal, for instance, considered that the inherent meaning of the term 'investment' (under the applicable BIT) entailed a contribution, duration, and risk, omitting any reference to the need to contribute to the host State's economic development.[100] The Tribunal in *Eyre* similarly considered that only the three 'core' *Salini* criteria (ie contribution, duration, and risk) were relevant for the purposes of determining the existence of an investment.[101]

4.45

Many tribunals have expressly rejected the requirement of a contribution to the host State's economic development.[102] The central reason for this rejection has been

4.46

---

[94] ibid.
[95] *MNSS v Montenegro* (n 37) para 189.
[96] *Mitchell v Congo* (n 85) para 33.
[97] See, for example, *Fedax v Venezuela* (n 2) para 43 (referring to the investment's 'significance for the host State's development'); *Joy Mining Machinery Limited v The Arab Republic of Egypt*, ICSID Case No ARB/03/11, Award on Jurisdiction (6 August 2004) para 53 (stating that in order to qualify as an investment under Art 25 ICSID Convention, an activity 'should constitute a significant contribution to the host State's development') (hereafter *Joy Mining v Egypt*); *Bayindir v Pakistan* (n 47) para 137 (noting that, 'to qualify as an investment, the project must represent a significant contribution to the host State's development'); *Malaysian Historical Salvors v Malaysia* (n 26) para 123 (holding that 'the weight of the authorities ... swings in favour of requiring a significant contribution to be made to the host State's economy').
[98] *Malaysian Historical Salvors v Malaysia* (n 26) para 123.
[99] See *Deutsche Bank v Sri Lanka* (n 28) para 306 (observing that 'the criterion of a contribution to the economic development has been discredited and has not been adopted recently by any tribunal').
[100] *Romak v Uzbekistan* (n 62) para 207. Although *Romak* is not an ICSID decision, the Tribunal's award is nevertheless relevant given that it applies the objective *Salini* approach under the applicable BIT. For a more detailed discussion of this ruling, see Chapter 6 Section IV.
[101] *Eyre v Sri Lanka* (n 39) paras 293–94.
[102] See, for example, *LESI v Algeria* (n 44) para 13; *Victor Pey Casado and Foundation 'Presidente Allende' v Republic of Chile*, ICSID Case No ARB/98/2, Award (8 May 2008) para 232 (hereafter *Pey Casado v Chile*); *Fakes v Turkey* (n 31) para 111; *Quiborax S.A. v Plurinational State of Bolivia*, ICSID Case No ARB/06/2, Decision on Jurisdiction (27 September 2012) para 225 (hereafter *Quiborax v Bolivia*); *Deutsche Bank v Sri Lanka* (n 28) para 306.

disagreement with the idea that such a requirement can be deduced from the Preamble's reference to 'economic development'. The *Pey Casado* tribunal, for example, acknowledged that economic development was a (possible) 'consequence' of foreign investment, but denied that it should be regarded as a definitional feature of investment.[103] The *Fakes* and *Quiborax* tribunals similarly held that the 'objective' or 'aspiration' of economic development mentioned in the Preamble was just that, ie a statement of the Convention's principal purpose, but not a criterion determining the existence of an investment.[104]

4.47 Another ground that has been relied upon in decisions rejecting the requirement of a contribution to the host State's development is that certain well-established and uncontroversial forms of investment do not typically involve any such contribution. One scenario that has been mentioned in this context is the case of 'unsuccessful'[105] or 'failed'[106] investments such as the unsuccessful exploration of natural resources. Another example of such investments would be mergers and acquisitions. Allegedly, such operations are and should be considered as investments under Art 25 ICSID Convention, even though they do not entail any evident or immediate economic benefits for the host State.[107]

4.48 A number of tribunals have taken the view that the requirement of a contribution to the host State's development is difficult to apply in practice. The *LESI* tribunal, for example, remarked that it was 'difficult to establish' whether this criterion was present in a given case.[108] In *Deutsche Bank*, the Tribunal considered that this requirement was 'unworkable', pointing out that the existence of a contribution to the host State's economic development 'can often be a matter of appreciation and ... generate a wide spectrum of reasonable opinions'.[109] It also emphasized the highly 'subjective' nature of this criterion.[110]

4.49 Lastly, it has also been observed that the criterion of a contribution to the development of the host State is in any case unnecessary given that such a contribution will necessarily exist if the other three *Salini* criteria (contribution, duration, and risk) are met. The Tribunal in *LESI*, for instance, noted that the contribution to the development of the host State requirement was 'implicitly covered by the three retained elements

---

[103] *Pey Casado v Chile* (n 102) para 232 (noting that 'this reference [the reference to "economic development"] is, however, presented as a consequence, and not as a requirement, of the investment') (translation by the author).

[104] *Fakes v Turkey* (n 31) para 111 (holding that 'it would be excessive to attribute to this reference [the reference to economic development] a meaning and function that is not obviously apparent from its wording'); *Quiborax v Bolivia* (n 102) para 235 (ruling that a contribution to the host State's economic development was 'not part of the definition of "investment" under Article 25(1), but rather an aspiration informing the system of international investment protection').

[105] *Fakes v Turkey* (n 31) para 111 ('Certain investments expected to be fruitful may turn out to be economic disasters. They do not fall, for that reason alone, outside the ambit of the concept of investment').

[106] *Deutsche Bank v Sri Lanka* (n 28) para 306 (referring to the example of 'failed construction projects').

[107] ibid.

[108] *LESI v Algeria* (n 44) para 13.

[109] *Deutsche Bank v Sri Lanka* (n 28) para 306.

[110] ibid.

[contribution, duration, risk]'.[111] A similar reasoning was adopted by the Tribunal in *Pey Casado*.[112]

D. Other criteria

1. Regularity of profits and return

The requirement of regularity of profit and return was recognized in *Fedax*, one of the two founding decisions of the *Salini* case law. In that case, the Tribunal considered that 'a certain regularity of profit and return' was a basic feature of an investment,[113] and held that this requirement was met in the case before it.[114] The Tribunal in *Joy Mining* also referred to this criterion, holding that one of the 'elements that an activity must have in order to qualify as an investment' was 'a regularity of profit and return'.[115] A similar reference can also be found in the decision of the sole Arbitrator in *Malaysian Historical Salvors*.[116] **4.50**

As the *Fedax* decision suggests, the regularity of profit and return criterion formally originated from the 1996 version of Schreuer's Commentary on the ICSID Convention. In this work, the author observed that one typical feature of an investment was 'a certain *regularity of profit and return*',[117] adding that a 'one-time lump sum agreement, while not impossible, would be untypical'. However, Schreuer expressly acknowledged that in connection with certain investments, 'no profits are ever made' and that, at least in those cases, the characteristic feature of an investment consisted not of regularity of profit and return, but of the simple 'expectation of return'.[118] **4.51**

There are other, more troubling, issues with the requirement of regularity of profit and return. This criterion is, in fact, irrationally demanding. While it makes sense to say that an investment implies the pursuit of profit,[119] it is unreasonable to require actual profitability. Not only does such a requirement neglect the existence of unsuccessful investments (or investments that have not *yet* generated any income), but it is also fundamentally incompatible with the generally accepted risk criterion. Indeed, the existence of risk necessarily implies the possibility that the investment will not be profitable and it is thus inherently contradictory to require both risk and profitability. As far as the additional feature of 'regularity' is concerned, it overlooks that profits are sometimes made **4.52**

---

[111] *LESI v Algeria* (n 44) para 13(iv) (translation by the author).
[112] *Pey Casado v Chile* (n 102) para 232 (noting that 'this fourth condition is in reality included in the first three') (translation by the author).
[113] *Fedax v Venezuela* (n 2) para 43.
[114] ibid (affirming that '[t]he regularity of profit and return [criterion] is ... met by the scheduling of interest payments through a period of several years').
[115] *Joy Mining v Egypt* (n 97) para 53.
[116] *Malaysian Historical Salvors v Malaysia* (n 26) para 108 (noting, however, that 'this criterion may not always be decisive').
[117] Schreuer, 'Commentary on the ICSID Convention' (n 14) 372 (original emphasis).
[118] ibid.
[119] See Chapter 2 Section VI. See also *Romak v Uzbekistan* (n 62) para 206 (noting that the ordinary meaning of the concept of investment 'entails ... the purpose of obtaining an economic benefit').

at one single point in time and not at regular intervals (eg where the investment consists of the purchase and resale of an asset or the provision of services which are remunerated after completion of the work).

4.53 Currently, the requirement of regularity of profit and return seems to have been largely abandoned. Many tribunals have implicitly rejected its application by omitting any reference to this criterion in their statements of the *Salini* test. The *Fakes* tribunal expressly denied its relevance when it held that '[a]n investment can be large or small, or it can be profitable or unprofitable',[120] adding that 'neither the size nor the profitability or usefulness of investments are included in the meaning of the word [investment]'.[121] Relying in part on the ruling in *Fakes*, the *Deutsche Bank* tribunal also expressly rejected the requirement of regularity of profit and return, holding that the only relevant criteria were contribution, risk and duration.[122]

4.54 At present, there is little support in arbitral practice for the proposition that the (less demanding requirement of) pursuit of profit constitutes a *Salini* criterion. However, as has been seen, it has been recognized as being inherent in the ordinary meaning of the term 'investment'.[123] As will be shown in Chapter 6, it has also been accepted as a 'characteristic' of investment in investment treaties that have adopted definitions based on, or reminiscent of, the *Salini* test.

2. Legality and good faith

4.55 According to a widely held view, the *Phoenix* tribunal decided that the concept of investment under Art 25 ICSID Convention required, in addition to the presence of the three core *Salini* criteria, that the investment be made (1) in compliance with host State law and (2) in good faith. It must be noted that the Tribunal established these requirements by interpreting the ICSID Convention and the applicable BIT (the BIT between Israel and the Czech Republic) in light of 'general principles of international law'.[124] It could thus be said that the Tribunal viewed these criteria as applying under Art 25 ICSID Convention. However, this conclusion is by no means inevitable. In fact, the Tribunal seems to have considered that legality and good faith were requirements for 'protection' under the BIT and the Convention, rather than definitional features of an investment.[125] The exact meaning of the Tribunal's ruling is therefore open to debate.

4.56 Assuming that the *Phoenix* tribunal did indeed hold that legality and good faith were *Salini* criteria, this decision would in any case have to be regarded as isolated. In fact, there does not seem to be any other ruling in which an ICSID tribunal adopted the

---

[120] *Fakes v Turkey* (n 31) n 73.
[121] ibid.
[122] *Deutsche Bank v Sri Lanka* (n 28) para 295.
[123] *Romak v Uzbekistan* (n 62) para 206.
[124] *Phoenix v Czech Republic* (n 57) paras 99–113.
[125] ibid para 114 (concluding that legality and good faith were 'requirements for an investment to benefit from international protection of ICSID'). The Tribunal's analysis thus seems to be based on a distinction between investment and protected investment, and it is likely—or at least possible—that the notion of protected investment used by the Tribunal is narrower than the concept of investment under Art 25 ICSID Convention.

same line of reasoning. At least one tribunal, namely, the Tribunal in *Fakes*, expressly rejected the relevance of these criteria under the ICSID Convention, observing that 'the principles of good faith and legality [could not] be incorporated into the definition of Article 25(1) of the ICSID Convention without doing violence to the language of the ... Convention'.[126]

4.57 The lack of recognition of the legality and good faith criteria under Art 25 ICSID Convention is hardly surprising. To begin with, the text of Art 25 itself does evidently not provide any basis for the application of such requirements. The drafters of the Convention do not seem to have considered that these issues bore any relevance in connection with the determination of the Centre's scope of jurisdiction. There are no scholarly contributions advocating the application of these criteria under Art 25 ICSID Convention. More generally, an investment's legality and its good faith character are not comprised within the ordinary meaning of the term 'investment'.

4.58 In any case, it is largely unnecessary to rely on Art 25's notion of investment as a legal basis for the application of the legality and good faith criteria. In fact, the former requirement is contained in the vast majority of investment treaties, either as part of the definition of 'investment' or as a separate requirement contained in the treaty's 'admission' clause or a/the provision determining the treaty's scope of application.[127] Where the relevant consent instrument does not contain an express legality requirement, such a requirement can be derived from general principles of law which deny legal protection to persons who have engaged in unlawful conduct. The application of a good faith requirement (and the resulting denial of protection to investments made in bad faith) can similarly be based on such general principles.

E. Critical assessment

4.59 The *Salini* test rests on very shaky foundations. The three core *Salini* criteria (contribution, duration, risk) find little to no support in either the text of the Convention, its drafting history, or the ordinary meaning of the term 'investment'. As their historical development suggests, the application of these requirements rests almost exclusively on two scholarly articles—written by Schreuer and Gaillard, respectively—in which the authors 'extracted' typical features of investment from ICSID case law, without however claiming that such features were always present or that they had to be viewed as definitional elements of investment under Art 25 ICSID Convention. These articles do not, therefore, support the application of jurisdictional requirements such as those established by the *Salini* test.

---

[126] *Fakes v Turkey* (n 31) para 112 (adding that 'an investment might be "legal" or "illegal", made in "good faith" or not, it nonetheless remains an investment'.)
[127] See Chapter 5 Section V.A.

4.60 The requirements of a contribution to the economic development of the host State and of regularity of profits and return are even more questionable. As has rightly been pointed out by a number of tribunals and writers, the textual argument in support of the former criterion is unconvincing. It is simply not sensible to derive a definitional requirement of investment from a very general reference in the Convention's Preamble to the 'need for international cooperation for economic development, and the role of private international investment therein'. The logical flaw of this approach becomes even more apparent when one transposes it to a different context. If, for example, two countries conclude a trade agreement with the declared aim of promoting 'peace and prosperity', it would be nonsensical to argue that a transaction can only be considered as 'trade' if it is established that it contributes to the achievement of these objectives. As regards the requirement of regularity of profits and return, it suffers from the same absence of formal support that characterizes the three core *Salini* criteria. In addition, as has been explained, it is unreasonably demanding since it denies investment status to unsuccessful investments (ie activities that turn out to be unprofitable) and investments that do not involve regular or repeated financial gains.

4.61 The *Salini* test is also inherently vague. As has been shown, the meaning of most of the *Salini* criteria is ambiguous and thus susceptible of diverging approaches and interpretations. For example, it is not clear what form of contribution or what type of risk the *Salini* test contemplates. Also, the application of several criteria (eg duration, contribution to the economic development of the host State) requires that specific thresholds be established. However, as is well-known, the *Salini* test does not lay down any such thresholds and it therefore falls upon arbitral tribunals to make the necessary determinations on a case-by-case basis.

4.62 Even though a significant majority of tribunals apply some variation of the *Salini* test, it is probable that a number of these tribunals are aware of its flaws and deficiencies and only apply it reluctantly and for the sake of not departing from established case law. It can be assumed that it is this dissatisfaction with the *Salini* approach that accounts, at least in part, for the rather broad acceptance of the typical-characteristics approach under which the *Salini* criteria are viewed not as jurisdictional requirements, but—as the terminology suggests—as typical features of an investment. As has been explained, the problem with this approach is that it does not represent any improvement of the 'traditional' *Salini* test—none of the *Salini* criteria are per se rejected as inappropriate, no attempt at greater precision is made. Instead, the typical-characteristics approach rejects the very idea of a (binding) definition of 'investment' and mandatory definitional elements. This entails broad, if not unfettered, arbitral discretion in the determination of whether a particular asset or activity constitutes an investment, which undermines the attainment of legal uniformity and certainty.

4.63 As has been shown, the *Salini* test reflects a certain approach to, or vision of, the nature of investment. Most, if not all, *Salini* criteria imply that an investment is perceived as a project, activity, or operation, rather than as an asset having a financial value. This 'orientation' of the *Salini* test is, however, highly debatable. First of all, it is not supported by the text or drafting history of the Convention. Second, and more importantly, it represents a departure from the ordinary meaning of the term 'investment' of questionable merit. In some cases, the *Salini* notion of investment may be broader than an investment in the ordinary sense. The performance of services, for instance, may (and generally does) qualify as an investment under the *Salini* test, even though it does not (at least not per se) constitute an investment in the ordinary sense.[128] In other contexts, the *Salini* approach may turn out to be more restrictive. Portfolio investments (which undeniably constitute investments in the ordinary sense), for example, do technically not meet the *Salini* requirements because they do not involve any economic activities or operations on the part of the presumed investor. It is questionable whether and/or to what extent these deviations from the ordinary meaning of 'investment' are justified.

Lastly, and perhaps most significantly, the *Salini* test does not actually *define* the term 'investment' (and the *Salini* criteria cannot therefore be regarded as definitional elements or criteria). In fact, the *Salini* test does not provide that an investment under Art 25 ICSID Convention *is* a particular thing or process, and it actually makes no attempt at defining that thing or process. Instead, the *Salini* approach considers that an investment 'requires', 'infers', or 'supposes' certain attributes or features. Those attributes or features, however, are very general in nature and fail to capture the essence of the concept of investment. In fact, the three core *Salini* criteria could be said to 'define' a broad range of transactions (or even activities), some of which may have very little do to with an investment. For instance, it could be said that the characteristic features of a commercial lease agreement (generally not regarded as an investment) consist of a contribution, duration, and risk. In fact, not only will such an agreement typically be concluded for a period of several years, but one could also consider that it involves contributions (the lessor makes premises available, the lessee contributes funds) and risks (for the lessor, the risk of not being paid and, for the lessee, the risk inherent in the commercial activity performed in the rented premises). Though contribution, duration, and risk may be present in one form or another, these attributes do evidently not *define* the commercial lease agreement, ie they do not constitute the characteristic features that distinguish such agreements from other types of contracts.[129]   **4.64**

---

[128] In fact, an investment in the ordinary sense requires the purchase of an asset (with the aim of generating a profit). See Chapter 2 Section VI.
[129] In fact, commercial lease agreements—like other categories of contract—are defined by reference to the specific obligations undertaken by each of the parties.

III. The Permissibility Test

A. Meaning and recognition

4.65 The permissibility test can be described as follows: Arbitral tribunals should examine, first of all, whether the relevant operation or asset constitutes an investment in the sense of the applicable consent instrument. If the answer is to the negative, they must evidently decline jurisdiction. If the answer is an affirmative one, tribunals have to verify whether the definition of 'investment' found in the consent instrument is 'permissible' under Art 25 ICSID Convention. Only if this is the case will Art 25's requirement of the existence of an investment be met.

4.66 The first ruling featuring a reference to the permissibility test is the decision of the ad hoc Committee in *Mitchell*. In this case, one of the issues was whether the Tribunal's holding that Mitchell had made an investment in the Congo was tainted by a failure to state reasons. Endorsing the *Salini* test, the ad hoc Committee considered that the existence of an investment under Art 25 ICSID Convention required a contribution, duration, risk, and a contribution to the host State's economic development.[130] The Committee noted that the Tribunal had not explained how Mitchell's activities—which consisted of the provision of legal consulting services—had contributed to the Congo's economic development.[131] It concluded that the Tribunal's reasoning was incoherent and inadequate, thus amounting to a failure to state reasons.[132]

4.67 While the ad hoc Committee's decision was based on the *Salini* test, its analysis of the meaning of 'investment' under Art 25 ICSID Convention also contained a reference to the permissibility issue. In fact, the Committee observed that, absent a definition of the term 'investment' in the Convention, 'it is in the parties' agreement or in the applicable investment treaty that one should look for such definition.'[133] While it thus acknowledged the crucial importance of definitions contained in consent instruments, the Committee clarified that the concept of investment in Art 25 ICSID Convention nevertheless 'prevail[ed]', and placed limits upon them.[134] According to the Committee, tribunals must therefore perform a permissibility analysis, ie they should 'verify the conformity of the concept of investment as set out in the parties' agreement or in the BIT with the concept of investment in the Washington Convention'.[135] However, for reasons which are not explained in its decision, the Committee failed to apply this test when examining the annulment grounds invoked by the Congo.

---

[130] *Mitchell v Congo* (n 85) para 27.
[131] ibid para 39 (noting that the award was 'mute on this issue').
[132] ibid para 41.
[133] ibid para 25.
[134] ibid.
[135] ibid.

The first tribunal to have *based* its decision on the permissibility test is the Tribunal **4.68**
in *Bureau Veritas v Paraguay*.[136] In this case, the question arose whether a 'contract for the provision of technical services for pre-shipment inspection of imports into Paraguay'[137] (and/or the rights arising under such contract) qualified as an investment under the BIT between the Netherlands and Paraguay and the ICSID Convention. Having concluded that the requirements of the BIT were met,[138] the Tribunal turned its focus to Art 25 ICSID Convention, noting that, under this provision, one had to examine whether 'the definition in the BIT exceed[ed] what is permissible under the Convention'.[139] The Tribunal held that, in the case at hand, the answer to this question was 'self-evidently negative',[140] emphasizing that the definition contained in the BIT 'follow[ed] the approach adopted in many other BITs concluded around the world' and that it would be unreasonable or inappropriate for Paraguay 'to argue that its own BIT [was] inconsistent with the requirements of the ICSID Convention'.[141]

Another decision applying the permissibility test is the decision of the Tribunal in *SGS* **4.69**
v Paraguay,[142] which involved an almost identical contract for the provision of pre-shipment inspection services.[143] Like the *Bureau Veritas* tribunal, the *SGS* tribunal first examined whether the Claimant had made an investment in the sense of the applicable BIT, the treaty between Switzerland and Paraguay.[144] Having answered this question in the affirmative,[145] the Tribunal then analysed whether the requirements of Art 25 ICSID Convention were met. It held that, in this context, the permissibility test formulated by the *Bureau Veritas* Tribunal was 'compelling'[146] and that '[n]othing in the Switzerland–Paraguay BIT's definition of investment would support characterizing it as an aberration that risks capturing economic activity clearly outside the ICSID Convention's intended reach'.[147] Like the Tribunal in *Bureau Veritas*, the *SGS* tribunal emphasized that it would in any case be contradictory for Paraguay to agree a specific

---

[136] *Bureau Veritas, Inspection, Valuation, Assessment and Control, BIVAC B.V. v The Republic of Paraguay*, ICSID Case No ARB/07/9, Decision of the Tribunal on Objections to Jurisdiction (29 May 2009) (hereafter *Bureau Veritas v Paraguay*). For commentary on this decision, see School of International Arbitration, Queen Mary, University of London, *International Arbitration Case Law*, Bureau Veritas, Inspection, Valuation, Assessment and Control, BIVAC B.V. v. The Republic of Paraguay, Case Report by Christina Beharry, edited by Ignacio Torterola < https://www.transnational-dispute-management.com/downloads/9535_case_report_bivac_v_paraguay_decision_on_objections_to_jurisdiction_2009.pdf> accessed 7 June 2023.
[137] ibid para 7.
[138] ibid para 91. The Tribunal decided that, under the contract, the Claimant possessed 'rights under public law' in the sense of Art 1(a)(v) of the BIT.
[139] ibid para 94.
[140] ibid.
[141] ibid.
[142] *SGS Société Générale de Surveillance S.A. v The Republic of Paraguay*, ICSID Case No ARB/07/29, Decision on Jurisdiction (12 February 2010) (hereafter *SGS v Paraguay*).
[143] ibid para 26.
[144] ibid paras 78–90.
[145] ibid paras 84, 86 (holding that the contract between the parties had given rise to 'claims to money or to any performance having an economic value' in conformity with Art 1(2)(c) of the BIT and that SGS's contractual rights constituted 'concessions under public law … as well as other rights given by law, by contract or by decision of the authority in accordance with the law' within the meaning of Art 1(2)(e) of the BIT).
[146] ibid para 95.
[147] ibid para 96.

definition of 'investment' in a treaty providing for ICSID arbitration and subsequently deny that such definition complies with the Convention.[148]

4.70 A further ruling following the permissibility approach is the decision of the Tribunal in *Garanti Koza v Turkmenistan*.[149] In this case, the Claimant entered into a contract with a Turkmen state entity under which it undertook to plan and construct twenty-eight highway bridges in Turkmenistan.[150] In its Art 25 decision, the Tribunal rejected the *Salini* test, apparently taking issue with the fact that it elevates typical features of an investment to strict legal requirements.[151] The Tribunal also refused to endorse the subjective approach, agreeing with the *SGS* tribunal that '[i]t would go too far to suggest that any definition of investment agreed by states in a BIT ... must constitute an "investment" for purposes of Article 25(1)'.[152] It considered that the permissibility test followed by the *Bureau Veritas* tribunal constituted a sensible approach,[153] given that it duly recognized the pivotal role of definitions contained in investment treaties and other consent instruments, without however depriving the term 'investment' under the Convention of its meaning.[154] The Tribunal decided that, in the case before it, '[n]either the nature of the Claimant's investment itself nor the definition of "investment" in the BIT' exceeded what is permissible under the Convention.[155]

4.71 The permissibility test has also been applied in the recent ruling in *CMC v Mozambique*,[156] a case involving a contract under which the Claimants undertook to reconstruct a portion of the principal north-south highway in Mozambique.[157] Like the *Garanti Koza* tribunal, the Tribunal in *CMC* rejected—at least implicitly—both the *Salini* test and the subjective approach,[158] expressing a preference for the permissibility test, which it considered a 'middle ground between these two approaches'. On the facts, the Tribunal concluded that the definition in the BIT did not exceed what is permissible under the Convention, stating rather ambiguously that '[t]he Claimants' claims "for sums of money or any performance having an economic value" within the meaning of Article 1(c) of the BIT arise directly out of their investment in the [reconstruction project]'.[159]

---

[148] ibid para 95.
[149] *Garanti Koza LLP v Turkmenistan* ICSID Case No ARB/11/20, Award (19 December 2016) (hereafter *Garanti Koza v Turkmenistan*).
[150] ibid para 4.
[151] ibid para 238.
[152] ibid para 240.
[153] ibid.
[154] ibid para 239.
[155] ibid para 241.
[156] *CMC Muratori Cementisti CMC Di Ravenna SOC. Coop. and others v Mozambique*, ICSID Case No ARB/17/23, Award (24 October 2019) (hereafter *CMC v Mozambique*).
[157] ibid para 4.
[158] ibid paras 190–95. The Tribunal discussed the *Salini* test, the subjective approach, and the permissibility test. It then applied the latter, implicitly rejecting the first two approaches. Although it ultimately also examined whether the *Salini* criteria were present, it did not condone this test and seems to have applied it for the sake of completeness.
[159] ibid para 194.

B. Assessment

Tribunals applying (or recognizing) the permissibility test have primarily justified their decisions by pointing out the perceived defects of alternative approaches. They consider the *Salini* test as too rigid and, more generally, as inappropriate or unfounded. They oppose the subjective approach on the grounds that it deprives the term 'investment' in Art 25 ICSID Convention of its usefulness. According to these tribunals, the permissibility test represents a reasonable compromise which, inasmuch as it recognizes the primary relevance of definitions contained in investment treaties and laws, arguably finds support in the Convention's drafting history. 4.72

In reality, however, the permissibility test is highly problematic. To begin with, tribunals have applied it with such caution that it is doubtful whether it can be regarded as a self-standing test. In fact, only the *Garanti Koza* Tribunal based its Art 25 conclusion exclusively on the permissibility of the definition contained in the applicable BIT. The *Bureau Veritas* tribunal applied the permissibility test, but also addressed (and succinctly dismissed) the Respondent's objection based on the *Salini* criteria.[160] Similarly, the *SGS* tribunal, though critical of the *Salini* test,[161] applied it on the grounds that the parties had 'dedicated considerable argument to the question [of whether the *Salini* requirements were met]'.[162] The *CMC* tribunal applied the *Salini* test 'to the extent to which it may be necessary or useful to apply [it]'.[163] None of these three tribunals have expressly rejected the relevance of the *Salini* criteria, and it is thus not clear whether they view the permissibility test as entirely independent of other inquiries. 4.73

Second, it is far from clear what it means to say that a particular definition is 'permissible' under another definition or, to use the language adopted by the *Mitchell* tribunal, that it is in 'conformity with'[164] such definition. The perhaps most sensible construction of this test is that it requires treaty and statutory definitions of investment to be narrower, or at least not wider, than the concept of investment contained in the ICSID Convention. The permissibility test would thus involve a comparison between the scope of the definition found in the applicable consent instrument and the scope of the term 'investment' under Art 25 ICSID Convention. Regrettably, none of the tribunals adopting this approach have carried out such an analysis or explained how it can or should be performed. 4.74

In addition, arbitral tribunals applying the permissibility test have failed to offer any definition of the meaning of 'investment' under the ICSID Convention. However, in order to perform a permissibility analysis, it is obviously necessary to determine the meaning of this concept since it is by reference to the Convention's notion of investment 4.75

---

[160] *Bureau Veritas v Paraguay* (n 136) paras 95–96.
[161] *SGS v Paraguay* (n 142) para 97.
[162] ibid para 99.
[163] *CMC v Mozambique* (n 156) para 195.
[164] *Mitchell v Congo* (n 85) para 25.

that the permissibility of a treaty or statutory definition of 'investment' is ascertained. Tribunals affirming the permissibility of treaty definitions have either not provided any explanation at all or have offered justifications that are unconvincing or impossible to understand.

4.76 Another, particularly serious, flaw of the permissibility test is its focus on the definition of 'investment' contained in the applicable consent instrument. In fact, what should matter for jurisdictional purposes is not whether a particular *definition* is permissible under Art 25 ICSID Convention, but whether the specific *operation* or *asset* is a permissible investment, ie whether it is covered by the Convention. As such, the fact that a particular definition is unduly broad is entirely irrelevant, given that it says nothing about whether the investment itself exceeds what is 'permitted' under Art 25 ICSID Convention. The *Garanti Koza* tribunal seems to have perceived this logical defect. While it did not openly criticize the permissibility test's focus on definitions of investment, it did extend the scope of its inquiry to the permissibility of the actual investment,[165] suggesting that the latter was primarily (or exclusively) relevant.

4.77 Lastly, the permissibility test is also defective because, like the subjective approach, it is based on the mistaken assumption that all consent instruments necessarily define the term 'investment'. As has already been explained, there are a number of investment treaties that are silent on the meaning of this term. Also, and more importantly, investment agreements virtually never contain a definition of the concept of 'investment'. In these scenarios, the permissibility test is thus simply not workable.

IV. The Commercial-Transaction Test

A. Meaning and recognition

4.78 Under the commercial-transaction test, an operation or activity will not be considered as an investment if it constitutes a commercial transaction. Like the permissibility (but unlike the *Salini*) test, the commercial-transaction test does not actually (seek to) define the concept of 'investment'. Rather, it denies investment status to a specific category of transactions, namely, commercial transactions. According to the relevant case law, the commercial-transaction test only operates to *exclude* commercial transactions from the scope of Art 25's notion of investment. It does not, however, imply that a transaction that is not 'commercial' necessarily qualifies as an investment.

4.79 The exact formulation of the commercial-transaction test is subject to some variation. In a number of decisions, tribunals have referred not to 'commercial' transactions,

---

[165] *Garanti Koza v Turkmenistan* (n 149) para 241. The Tribunal considered not only the permissibility of 'the definition of "investment" in the BIT', but also the permissibility of '(the nature of) the Claimant's investment itself'.

but to the arguably somewhat narrower concept of sales contracts (or sales transactions).[166] A majority of tribunals have qualified the notion of commercial transaction, holding that only 'ordinary',[167] 'one-off',[168] or 'pure'[169] commercial transactions are by definition excluded from the scope of the ICSID Convention's concept of investment. These decisions would seem to imply that, under certain circumstances, commercial transactions—or a set of related commercial transactions—may constitute investments.

Arbitral tribunals have provided two main justifications for the commercial-transaction test. The first such justification, based on the ICSID Convention's drafting history, was notably put forward by the ad hoc Committee in *Malaysian Historical Salvors*.[170] In this case, the Committee criticized the sole Arbitrator's recourse to the *Salini* test, finding that neither the Convention's travaux, nor the Report of the Executive Directors supported the application of the *Salini* criteria. In the Committee's opinion, the only requirement (or 'outer limit') imposed by Art 25's notion of investment related to the drafters' assumption that '[the] use of the term "investment" excluded a simple sale and like transient commercial transactions from the jurisdiction of the Centre'.[171]

4.80

Unlike the first justification, the second justification does not reject, but actually endorses the *Salini* test. In fact, a number of tribunals relying on the commercial-transaction test have also applied, or at least recognized the appropriateness of, the *Salini* test. The reasoning adopted by some of these tribunals suggests that they view the commercial-transaction test as a logical implication or consequence of the *Salini* test. These decisions are therefore based on the implicit assumption that commercial transactions do not—and cannot—satisfy the core *Salini* requirements of a contribution, a minimum duration, and (investment) risk.

4.81

One can distinguish three types of cases applying the commercial-transaction test. First of all, there are—as has already been mentioned—rulings that have applied both the commercial-transaction and the *Salini* test. This approach has notably been followed by the Tribunal in *Joy Mining*. In this case, Joy Mining delivered and installed mining systems and supporting equipment in connection with a phosphate mining project in Egypt,[172] and provided several bank guarantees for the performance of its

4.82

---

[166] See, for example, *Joy Mining v Egypt* (n 97) para 58 (noting that, 'if a distinction is not drawn between ordinary sales contracts, even if complex, and an investment, the result would be that any sales or procurement contract involving a State agency would qualify as an investment'); *Alps Finance and Trade AG v The Slovak Republic*, Investment Ad Hoc Arbitration, Award (5 March 2011) para 245 ('The constant jurisprudential trend has led the most prominent doctrine to exclude in categorical terms that a mere one-off sale transaction might qualify as an investment') (hereafter *Alps Finance v Slovakia*).
[167] *Joy Mining v Egypt* (n 97) para 58; *Malaysian Historical Salvors v Malaysia* (n 26) para 112; *Romak v Uzbekistan* (n 62) para 189.
[168] *Alps Finance v Slovakia* (n 166) para 245.
[169] *Global Trading Resource Corp and others v Ukraine*, ICSID Case No ARB/09/11, Award (1 December 2010) para 56 (holding that 'the purchase and sale contracts entered into by the Claimants were pure commercial transactions and therefore cannot qualify as an investment for the purposes of Article 25 of the Convention') (hereafter *Global Trading v Ukraine*).
[170] *Malaysian Historical Salvors Sdn Bhd v The Government of Malaysia*, ICSID Case No ARB/05/10, Decision on the Application for Annulment (16 April 2009).
[171] ibid para 69.
[172] *Joy Mining v Egypt* (n 97) para 15.

obligations.[173] A dispute arose between the parties concerning the quality of the equipment installed by Joy Mining, with Egypt refusing to release the bank guarantees.[174] Joy Mining initiated ICSID arbitration proceedings, primarily requesting the release of those guarantees.[175]

4.83 Examining the Respondent's objection that Joy Mining had not made any investment in Egypt, the Tribunal—somewhat oddly—considered that the relevant question was whether the bank guarantees provided by the Claimant—rather than the contract itself—constituted an investment under Art 25 ICSID Convention.[176] It considered the five-prong *Salini* test to be the pertinent threshold,[177] and found that the relevant requirements were not met.[178] In addition, it also relied on the commercial-transaction test, emphasizing the need to distinguish between investments and 'ordinary sales contracts'.[179] The Tribunal acknowledged that the contract concluded between the parties involved a number of 'additional activities' (engineering and design, production and stocking of spare parts, etc.), but held that those did not 'transform [it] ... into an investment'.[180]

4.84 Another decision relying on both the *Salini* and the commercial-transaction test is the ruling of the Tribunal in *Romak*. Though not an ICSID case, this decision nevertheless illuminates the meaning of 'investment' under Art 25 ICSID Convention, given that the Tribunal considered the term 'investment' under the applicable BIT to have an 'intrinsic meaning',[181] which it primarily derived from Art 25 case law.[182] The central issue in *Romak* was whether contracts for the supply of wheat to various Uzbek State entities (or the rights arising under such contracts) constituted investments under the BIT between Switzerland and Uzbekistan. The Tribunal held that the three-prong *Salini* test (contributions, duration, risk) was applicable,[183] and found that the relevant criteria were not present in the case before it. The Tribunal also referred to the distinction between investments and commercial transactions, holding that 'the object and purpose of the BIT ... suggests an intent to protect a particular kind of assets, distinguishing them from mere ordinary commercial transactions'.[184]

4.85 The *Alps Finance* tribunal, which had to decide whether receivables acquired by the Claimant constituted an investment, also applied both the *Salini* and the

---

[173] ibid para 17.
[174] ibid paras 18–19.
[175] ibid paras 22–24.
[176] ibid para 42.
[177] ibid para 53 (stating that, in order to qualify as an investment under Art 25 ICSID Convention, a project 'should have a certain duration, a regularity of profit and return, an element of risk, a substantial commitment and ... should constitute a significant contribution to the host State's development') (footnote omitted).
[178] ibid para 57.
[179] ibid para 58.
[180] ibid para 55.
[181] *Romak v Uzbekistan* (n 62) para 188.
[182] ibid paras 196–205.
[183] ibid para 207.
[184] ibid para 189.

commercial-transaction test. Being an ad hoc and not an ICSID tribunal, it did not apply the *Salini* test under Art 25 ICSID Convention, but because it considered this test to reflect customary international law.[185] The Tribunal held that the relevant requirements were not met, emphasizing the insufficient contribution and duration of the operation at stake.[186] It then referred to the need to distinguish one-off sales transactions from investments[187] and appears to have based its final conclusion that the Claimant had not made any investment in Slovakia on both the *Salini* and the commercial-transaction test.[188]

The second category of cases consists of decisions applying exclusively the commercial-transaction test, without reliance on the *Salini* criteria or any other alternative test. An example of such a decision is the ruling of the Tribunal in *Global Trading*. This case involved several contracts under which the Claimant sold poultry to a private company nominated by a Ukrainian State enterprise.[189] Citing the decisions of the Tribunal in *Joy Mining* and of the ad hoc Committee in *Malaysian Historical Salvors*,[190] the Tribunal concluded that 'the purchase and sale contracts entered into by the Claimants were pure commercial transactions and therefore [could not] qualify as an investment for the purposes of Article 25 of the Convention'.[191]

4.86

Finally, there are also decisions in which the tribunals primarily applied the *Salini* test but considered that the distinction between investments and commercial transactions informed the interpretation of (some of) the *Salini* criteria. In other words, they construed the *Salini* requirements against the background of the commercial-transaction test. In *Poštová banka*, for example, the Tribunal decided that the Greek government bonds purchased by the Claimant did not constitute an investment in the sense of the applicable BIT.[192] It further ruled that, in the event that an objective test (requiring a contribution, duration, and risk) applied under Art 25 ICSID Convention, the application of such a test would lead to the same conclusion.[193] In this context, the Tribunal placed particular emphasis on the risk criterion, holding that it was necessary to distinguish between investment risks, which are specific to investments, and commercial and sovereign risks, which arise in connection with any commercial transaction. According to the Tribunal, the *Salini* test's risk criterion requires the presence of an investment risk; a commercial or sovereign risk is not sufficient.[194]

4.87

---

[185] *Alps Finance v Slovakia* (n 166) para 241 ('A more than abundant number of cases have contributed to elucidate the notion of investment under the ICSID Convention and, more in general, international customary law').
[186] ibid paras 242–44.
[187] ibid para 245.
[188] ibid para 246.
[189] *Global Trading v Ukraine* (n 169) para 3.
[190] ibid para 55.
[191] ibid para 56.
[192] *Poštová banka v Greece* (n 34) para 350.
[193] ibid 360–71.
[194] ibid 367–70.

B. Assessment

4.88 At first sight, the commercial-transaction test appears to rest on solid foundations. It is, in fact, rather uncontroversial that the drafters of the ICSID Convention did not intend to make the Centre's services available for the resolution of disputes arising in connection with 'ordinary' commercial transactions. The *Salini* test itself (if it is correct) also provides a measure of support for the commercial-transaction test, given that commercial transactions such as contracts for the sale of goods will generally not meet the *Salini* requirements.[195] More generally, the commercial-transaction test arguably reflects the generally accepted distinction between the two main types of international business activity, namely, international trade (or commerce) and foreign investment.

4.89 Despite these apparently firm foundations, the commercial-transaction test suffers from several flaws.[196] First of all, as has already been mentioned, it does not actually define the term 'investment' but merely denies investment status to a defined category of transactions (commercial transactions). As a result, no inference can be drawn from the fact that a transaction does not qualify as a commercial transaction, ie the non-commercial nature of a transaction (whatever this may mean) does not imply that it necessarily qualifies as an investment.[197] The commercial-transaction test can therefore only apply where the alleged investment consists of such a transaction. In all other cases (especially in cases involving more complex operations), the commercial-transaction test will be of no assistance.

4.90 Another defect of the commercial-transaction test pertains to the uncertainty of its precise scope of application. This uncertainty derives, in the first place, from the inherent ambiguity of the term 'commercial transaction'. Absent a generally accepted definition of this term (or of the adjective 'commercial'), it is not entirely clear which categories of operations qualify as 'commercial' and which ones do not. It is noteworthy in this respect that tribunals applying the commercial-transaction test have not attempted to define the concept of 'commercial transaction'.

4.91 Additional uncertainty is caused by the common arbitral practice of *qualifying* the notion of commercial transaction or sales contract by terms such as 'ordinary', 'pure', or 'one-off'. The first two formulations suggest that certain types of commercial or sales contracts, ie those that are 'extraordinary' (rather than ordinary) or 'mixed' (rather

---

[195] This is so because the act of selling goods to a foreign buyer does not involve any activity on the part of the seller in the buyer's country. However, as has been explained, such an activity is implicitly required under the *Salini* test.

[196] For a critical assessment of the commercial-transaction test, see Stratos Pahis, 'Investment Misconceived: The Investment-Commerce Distinction in International Investment Law' (2020) 45 Yale J Int'l L 69.

[197] For a decision adopting a different understanding of the commercial-transaction test, see *Pawlowski AG and Projekt Sever s.r.o. v Czech Republic*, ICSID Case No ARB/17/11, Award (1 November 2021) paras 257–59. In this case, the alleged investment consisted of the purchase of land and other expenditures made in connection with the design and planning of a real estate development project. The Tribunal held that the land and expenditures constituted investments under the applicable BIT (it did not examine whether these items also qualified as investments under the ICSID Convention). The Tribunal appears to have based its decision to a significant extent on its observation that the relevant purchase and expenditures were not merely 'one-off commercial transactions'.

than pure) may very well constitute investments. The use of the latter term implies that a series of (connected) commercial transactions may qualify as an investment, even though individual transactions do not. The relevant case law is unfortunately silent with regard to the specific circumstances under which commercial or sales contracts may be, or involve, investments.

Lastly, it is also unclear whether the commercial-transaction test at all constitutes an independent, self-standing, legal threshold. It is true that several tribunals have applied the distinction between investments and commercial transactions without reference to any other test. However, a larger number of tribunals have applied the commercial-transaction test along with the *Salini* criteria, arguably viewing the former as a necessary implication of the latter. These decisions can be viewed as meaning that the commercial-transaction test only exists within the framework of the broader *Salini* test, whether or not this is expressly acknowledged. **4.92**

V. Principal Scholarly Debates and Viewpoints

A. Nature of the *Salini* test

Despite its practical significance, the question of the mandatory or optional nature of the *Salini* test has received surprisingly little attention from scholarly writers. Indeed, most authors appear to assume that the *Salini* criteria constitute actual *requirements* for the existence of an investment, rather than mere *typical characteristics* of an investment. In fact, the vast majority of the contributions discussing the *Salini* test (and the meaning of investment under Art 25 ICSID Convention more generally) focus on the determination of the applicable criteria and/or questions pertaining to the scope and meaning of these criteria. This analysis is, evidently, only meaningful if one considers that the *Salini* criteria are mandatory definitional elements. **4.93**

Several authors, however, seem to have expressed the opposite view. Rubins, for instance, has qualified the *Salini* criteria as 'general characteristics of investment'.[198] Waibel has similarly labelled them as 'typical characteristics',[199] specifying that the term 'typical' must be understood as entailing that 'a large majority of "investments" display these characteristics'.[200] Schill, Schreuer, and Sinclair have also considered that the *Salini* test merely establishes a set of such 'typical characteristics'.[201] Yet, the weight of **4.94**

---

[198] Noah Rubins, 'The Notion of "Investment" in International Investment Arbitration' in Norbert Horn and Stefan Michael Kröll (eds), *Arbitrating Foreign Investment Disputes: Procedural and Substantive Legal Aspects*, Studies in Transnational Economic Law, vol 19 (Kluwer Law International 2004) 283, 297 (hereafter Rubins, 'The Notion of "Investment"').

[199] Michael Waibel, 'Opening Pandora's Box: Sovereign Bonds in International Arbitration' (2007) 101 AJIL 711, 723.

[200] ibid.

[201] Schill, Schreuer and Sinclair, 'Article 25' (n 92) para 231 (quoting a statement from Schreuer's 1996 Commentary according to which '[t]hese features should not necessarily be understood as jurisdictional requirements but merely as typical characteristics of investments under the Convention').

these statements should not be exaggerated, given that they have been made in passing, without any analysis of the implications of this approach, or discussion of the rival view according to which the *Salini* criteria constitute legal requirements.

4.95 This gap in the scholarly literature has, at least to some extent, been filled in Chapter 3.[202] As has been explained, the approach that regards the *Salini* criteria as mere typical characteristics or features is highly problematic.[203] In fact, it ultimately denies the existence of any legal test under Art 25 ICSID Convention, thus implicitly—and contradictorily—rejecting the idea that the term 'investment' in the sense of this provision possesses an independent meaning.

B. Core *Salini* criteria

4.96 Scholars have not infrequently challenged the appropriateness of some of the three core *Salini* criteria (contribution, duration, and risk). As far as the duration requirement is concerned, it has notably been criticized by Manciaux.[204] He has argued that this criterion is unjustified because (1) it is not supported by the Convention's drafting history,[205] (2) duration frequently depends on external circumstances (eg adverse weather conditions delaying a construction project) which it would be unreasonable to take into account,[206] and (3) duration is not specific to investments and therefore not helpful to distinguish the latter from other long-term transactions.[207]

4.97 The first two arguments are rather persuasive. In fact, an early proposal to define the term 'investment' included a requirement that the investment be made 'for an indefinite period or, if the period be defined, for not less than five years'.[208] However, such a prerequisite was absent from subsequent proposals, indicating that the Convention drafters did not consider duration as a suitable definitional element. Also, as has been explained above, the application of a minimum threshold of duration has the unjustifiable effect of denying investor status to efficient contracting parties ('fast performers'), while at the same time conferring investor status on contracting parties whose performance has been delayed, notably due to unforeseen external events. Manciaux's third argument, however, is not convincing. The fact that a particular criterion also characterizes other types of transactions does not mean that it cannot be characteristic

---

[202] Chapter 3 Section III.D.
[203] ibid.
[204] Sebastien Manciaux, 'The Notion of Investment: New Controversies' (2008) 9 JWIT 443 (hereafter Manciaux, 'The Notion of Investment').
[205] ibid 453.
[206] ibid 454 (asking the rhetorical question of whether one can 'seriously submit the investment qualification to external events that might occur, such as local protests against what has been planned, bad weather or natural disasters').
[207] ibid 455 (citing loans and long-term supply and sale agreements as examples of transactions that present a certain duration without constituting investments).
[208] International Centre for Settlement of Investment Disputes, *History of the ICSID Convention: Documents Concerning the Origin and the Formulation of the Convention on the Settlement of Investment Disputes between States and Nationals of Other States* (1970), Vol I, 116.

of investments. This type of reasoning would indeed lead to absurd results. For instance, it would imply that the seller's obligation to pay for the goods is not a characteristic feature (or obligation) of a sales contract because payment obligations also arise under other types of transactions.

Other writers who have rejected the duration requirement notably include Rubins and Exelbert. While Rubins notes that, in principle, 'investment projects *tend* to have an extended duration' (emphasis added), he nonetheless appears to deny the appropriateness of this criterion when citing a US Senate report according to which '[i]t is entirely clear from [the] negotiating history that the term "investment" in article 25(1) of the [Washington] [C]onvention does not exclude from its scope an investment simply because it is a short-term investment'.[209] Exelbert advocates a rather extreme approach under which the only relevant factors are the existence of a contribution to the host State's economic development and value creation,[210] thus implicitly rejecting all three core *Salini* criteria, including the duration requirement.

4.98

The risk requirement has similarly been dismissed by several authors. Manciaux, for example, has argued that it suffers from three major defects: the lack of clarity of the concept of risk,[211] the fact that all transactions involve some type of risk and that this criterion is not therefore a distinguishing feature of investments,[212] and the idea that risk is simply an implication of the contribution made by the investor and should thus not be regarded as an independent criterion.[213]

4.99

The first observation is rather convincing. In fact, the term 'risk' is of considerable breadth and it is not clear what particular category or type of risk the *Salini* test contemplates. In an attempt to apply a clearer and narrower concept of risk, arbitral tribunals have elaborated the more specific notion of 'investment risk'.[214] However, for reasons which have already been explained, the distinction between investment and commercial risk is flawed and not particularly helpful.[215] The third observation also has merit. Indeed, it is sensible to argue that the existence of risk is a necessary implication of the contribution made by the investor (ie the risk that the contribution will be lost or that it will not generate any profits). In that sense, the risk criterion is arguably redundant and unnecessary. The second observation, however, is not persuasive. As has already been noted in connection with the duration requirement, the fact that a specific feature (such as duration or risk) characterizes a particular type of transaction does not mean

4.100

---

[209] Rubins, 'The Notion of "Investment"' (n 198) 297.
[210] Jeremy Marc Exelbert, 'Consistently Inconsistent: What Is a Qualifying Investment Under Article 25 of the ICSID Convention and Why the Debate Must End' (2016) 85 Fordham L Rev 1243, 1276–78 (hereafter Exelbert, 'Consistently Inconsistent').
[211] Manciaux, 'The Notion of Investment' (n 204) 455 (arguing that 'this criterion gives way to very diverse interpretations that show that there is no agreement on the appropriate meaning to attribute to this term').
[212] ibid.
[213] ibid 457 (observing that 'it clearly appears that the risk run by a foreign investor is only a version of the requirement of contribution').
[214] See Section II.B.3.
[215] ibid.

that such feature cannot be shared with other categories of transactions. It is not per se contradictory or illogical to state that the existence of risk is a characteristic feature of more than one type of transaction.

4.101 The only core *Salini* criterion that is not generally challenged by commentators is the requirement of a contribution. Manciaux has noted that this criterion is 'unquestioned and seems to be consensual' and that it is 'unanimously adopted' in arbitral case law and scholarship.[216] In his opinion, the general consensus on the relevance of this criterion is due, at least in part, to the substantial breadth and vagueness of the concept of contribution and its resulting ability to accommodate a wide range of approaches.[217] Only Exelbert, who considers the investment's contribution to the host State's economic development and the associated value creation as the sole relevant factor, (implicitly) rejects the contribution requirement.

C. Requirement of a contribution to the host State's economic development

4.102 Several authors have objected to the application of this criterion. Manciaux, for example, has claimed that this requirement is uncalled for because certain recognized forms of investment such as mergers and acquisitions and 'unsuccessful' investment projects do not contribute to the host State's economic development.[218] While this argument appears to make sense at first glance, it is not certain whether it withstands closer scrutiny. For instance, as far as Manciaux's second example is concerned, a particular project may 'fail' in the sense that it does not achieve its ultimate objective (eg the cost of the extraction of crude oil may turn out to be prohibitive), but to the extent that the investor hires and remunerates local workers and/or purchases machinery from local suppliers, the relevant operations nonetheless benefit the host State's economy. The question is simply whether this benefit satisfies the applicable threshold.

4.103 Gaillard has criticized decisions (such as the award of the sole Arbitrator in *Malaysian Historical Salvors*) that have applied the demanding threshold of a 'significant' contribution to the host State's economic development, arguing that such an approach 'ignores the intention of the drafters of the ICSID Convention'.[219] However, unlike Manciaux, he does not seem to be opposed to the criterion per se. In particular, he does not believe that the phenomenon of failed investments calls into question the reasonableness of

---

[216] Manciaux, 'The Notion of Investment' (n 204) 450.
[217] ibid (pointing out that 'the harmonious unanimity on their issue [the issue of contributions] is only possible thanks to the vagueness that reigns around this criterion').
[218] ibid 459.
[219] Emmanuel Gaillard, 'Identify or Define? Reflections on the Evolution of the Concept of Investment in ICSID Practice' in Christina Binder, Ursula Kriebaum, August Reinisch and Stephan Wittich (eds), *International Investment Law for the 21st Century: Essays in Honour of Christoph Schreuer* (Oxford University Press 2009) 403, 416.

this criterion, pointing out that even unsuccessful projects typically contribute to the host State's economic development.[220]

4.104 Despite, or perhaps because of, its abandonment in the majority of recent arbitral rulings, several scholars have vigorously defended this criterion. Grabowski, for example, has contended that there is strong textual support for this requirement, not only in the ICSID Convention's Preamble, but also in the UN Charter.[221] His rather questionable argument in this respect is that the UN Charter proclaims the principle of sovereign equality of States, which arguably justifies interpreting the scope of ICSID jurisdiction restrictively and, thus, as requiring a contribution to the host State's economic development. According to this author, a further reason for applying (and not abandoning) this criterion is the desirability of ensuring the stability of ICSID case law.[222]

4.105 Another writer advocating the application of the requirement of a contribution to the host State's economic development is Exelbert. As has already been mentioned, Exelbert supports a rather radical approach focusing exclusively on this particular criterion and the resulting creation of value, thus rejecting all three core *Salini* criteria.[223] His arguments in support of this approach are essentially defensive in nature, ie he seeks to demonstrate that the criticism of the contribution to the economic development criterion is not justified or exaggerated. In particular, he asserts that the criterion is not too difficult to apply in practice[224] and that its recognition does not have the effect of discouraging investment.[225]

4.106 It remains to be seen what impact scholarly writings in defence of this criterion will have on arbitral case law and whether they can halt, or even reverse, its progressive abandonment by arbitral tribunals. Judging from the strength of the relevant arguments, it appears rather unlikely that ICSID tribunals will be persuaded to (continue to) apply this requirement. However, a variety of non-legal factors, such as ideologies or policy considerations, might prompt tribunals to require such a contribution.

---

[220] ibid (noting that '[i]f an oil company dedicates human and financial resources to the exploration of an oil field pursuant to a production-sharing contract with the host State, and if that activity does not lead to any discoveries, the company's contribution to the venture would still constitute an investment'). The language used by Gaillard is, however, ambiguous. While he made this observation in the context of his discussion of the requirement of a contribution to the host State's economic development, the expression 'contribution to the venture' might in reality be a reference to the core *Salini* criterion of a contribution, and not to the more controversial criterion pertaining to the host State's economic development. As has already been mentioned, the coexistence of two distinct contribution criteria is undoubtedly a source of possible confusion.
[221] Alex Grabowski, 'The Definition of Investment under the ICSID Convention: A Defense of Salini' (2014) 15 Chi J Int'l L 287, 304–05.
[222] ibid 305–08.
[223] Exelbert, 'Consistently Inconsistent' (n 210) 1276–78.
[224] ibid 1273–75.
[225] ibid 1275.

5

The Concept of Investment in Investment Treaties

Traditional Definitions and Typical Requirements

I.	Introduction	5.01	B. Localization of different categories of assets	5.45
II.	The Traditional Model: Broad, Asset-Based Definitions	5.03	C. Case law	5.50
	A. Asset-based definitions	5.03	V. Legality of the Investment	5.67
	B. Broad definitions	5.12	A. Legality provisions in investment treaties	5.67
III.	Ownership or Control of the Investment	5.18	B. Meaning of legality	5.72
	A. Overview	5.18	C. Legality beyond investment treaties	5.82
	B. Direct ownership	5.22	VI. Requirement that the Investment be 'Actively' Made by the Investor	5.86
	C. Indirect ownership	5.29	A. Overview	5.86
	D. Control	5.34	B. Textual foundations of the requirement	5.88
IV.	Localization of the Investment in the Territory of the Host State (Territoriality)	5.38	C. Recognition and meaning of the requirement	5.92
	A. Treaty practice	5.38	D. Assessment of the requirement	5.96
			E. Requirement of an active investment under Art 25 ICSID Convention?	5.100

I. Introduction

5.01 This chapter has a twofold object. Section II presents 'traditional' treaty definitions of the term 'investment', ie the approach followed in the vast majority of investment treaties concluded in the 1990s and 2000s. Those traditional definitions are characterized by two principal features: first, they are 'asset-based' (they define 'investments' as assets) and, second, they are broad. As will be shown in Chapter 6, a growing number of recent investment treaties depart from this traditional model, introducing various exclusions and restrictions and adopting (occasionally) 'enterprise-based' definitions of 'investment'.

5.02 Sections III–VI explore four common definitional requirements found in investment treaties. These are not specific to the traditional model, ie they generally also apply under the more restrictive and/or enterprise-based definitions contained in recently concluded treaties. These requirements include (a) ownership or control by the presumed investor, (b) localization of the investment in the territory of the host State ('territoriality'), (c) legality (or lawfulness) of the investment, and (d) the requirement of an 'active' investment. The first three requirements are almost universally accepted; the fourth one enjoys only limited recognition.

II. The Traditional Model: Broad, Asset-Based Definitions

A. Asset-based definitions

1. Types of definitions

Any definition of the term 'investment', including definitions contained in investment treaties, must (or should) specify the 'nature' of the concept of investment. The answer to this question is by no means self-evident. In fact, as has been explained in Chapter 2, an 'investment' in the ordinary sense of the term may be viewed as referring to three distinct realities: (a) an asset purchased in order to make a profit, (b) the funds used to purchase such asset, and (c) the process of investing, ie the act of purchasing the asset concerned.[1]

Under Art 25 ICSID Convention, the term 'investment' as construed by arbitral tribunals arguably has neither of these ordinary meanings. Instead, an investment is viewed as an economic activity, operation, or project. As has been explained in Chapter 4, such a view is implicit in the *Salini* approach and the different criteria applied under the *Salini* test.[2] To the extent that the commercial-transaction test can be regarded as a specific manifestation or implication of the *Salini* approach,[3] it can be considered to encapsulate the same view of the nature of investment.

Investment treaty practice reflects this hesitation concerning the nature of investment. In fact, two types of definitions (are said to) coexist. There are, on the one hand, asset-based definitions, ie definitions under which investments consist of (specified) assets. Under the bilateral investment treaty (BIT) between Japan and Georgia, for example, 'investment' is defined as 'every kind of asset owned or controlled, directly or indirectly, by an investor of a Contracting Party, that is made in the territory of the other Contracting Party ...'.[4] On the other hand, there are also enterprise-based definitions, ie definitions that view investments as enterprises.[5] The BIT between Nigeria and Morocco, for example, defines investment as 'an enterprise within the territory of one

---

[1] See Chapter 2 Sections VI and VIII.
[2] See Chapter 4 Section II.E.
[3] See Chapter 4 Section IV.
[4] Agreement between Japan and Georgia for the Liberalisation, Promotion and Protection of Investment (adopted 29 January 2021, entered into force 23 July 2021) Art 1(a).
[5] See Stephan W Schill, Christoph Schreuer and Anthony Sinclair, 'Article 25' in Loretta Malintoppi, August Reinisch, Christoph H Schreuer and Anthony Sinclair (eds), *Schreuer's Commentary on the ICSID Convention: A Commentary on the Convention on the Settlement of Investment Disputes between States and Nationals of Other States* (3rd edn, Cambridge University Press 2022) para 222 (hereafter Schill, Schreuer and Sinclair, 'Article 25').

State established, acquired, expanded or operated, in good faith, by an investor of the other State ...'.[6]

5.06 It is important to highlight that asset-based and enterprise-based definitions of 'investment' are not diametrically opposed. In fact, an enterprise, at least when it is viewed as a legal entity, can be considered as representing a particular type of asset. This understanding is notably confirmed by the definition contained in the BIT between Austria and Kyrgyzstan.[7] This treaty features an asset-based definition, providing that the term 'investment' means 'every kind of asset'.[8] It lists several categories of qualifying assets, including 'an enterprise'[9] and 'shares, stocks and other forms of equity participation in an enterprise'.[10]

5.07 It may not always be easy to distinguish between asset-based and enterprise-based definitions. A treaty may, for example, define 'investment' as 'every kind of asset', ie seemingly adopt an asset-based definition. However, it may also require that, in order to qualify as investments, the relevant assets have to be owned or controlled by, or otherwise connected with, an enterprise established in the territory of the host State. In such a case, the existence of an investment requires the presence of an enterprise, and one could thus argue that, in substance, the relevant definition is enterprise-based, rather than asset-based.

5.08 Although the distinction between asset-based and enterprise-based definitions is widely recognized (and notably adopted in the United Nations Conference on Trade and Development's (UNCTAD) investment treaty database[11]), other classifications would in principle be conceivable. For instance, as will be seen in Chapter 6, there are a number of definitions that are formally asset-based, but require the assets concerned to be used in conjunction with economic activities conducted by the investor. Given the central role played by the existence of these activities (there can be no investment absent such activities), those definitions could be considered as activity-based, rather than asset-based. Accordingly, one could distinguish not just between two, but between three different types of definitions of the term 'investment'.

---

[6] See Reciprocal Investment Promotion and Protection Agreement Between the Government of the Kingdom of Morocco and the Government of the Federal Republic of Nigeria (adopted 3 December 2016, not in force) Art 1.
[7] Agreement for the Promotion and Protection of Investment Between the Government of the Republic of Austria and the Government of the Kyrgyz Republic (adopted 22 April 2016, entered into force 1 October 2017) Art 1(2).
[8] ibid.
[9] ibid Art 1(2)(a).
[10] ibid Art 1(2)(b).
[11] The UNCTAD database maps international investment agreements. It contains a rubric entitled 'scope and definitions' which includes a sub-rubric pertaining to the 'definition of investment'. Within this sub-rubric, a further distinction is made between the 'type of definition' and 'limitations to the definition of investment'. As far as the former is concerned, two options are referenced: asset-based definitions and enterprise-based definitions. See UNCTAD, 'International Investment Agreements Navigator' <https://investmentpolicy.unctad.org/international-investment-agreements/iia-mapping> accessed 13 February 2023 (hereafter UNCTAD, 'International Investment Agreements Navigator').

2. Prevalence of asset-based definitions

5.09 The data available on UNCTAD's investment treaty database clearly establishes the traditional prevalence of asset-based definitions of 'investment'. In fact, according this data, 2,059 out of 2,069 investment treaties concluded between 1990 and 2009 (99.51 per cent) featured asset-based definitions.[12] Only six treaties (0.28 per cent of all mapped treaties) used enterprise-based definitions; four treaties (0.21 per cent) did not contain any definition of 'investment'.[13]

5.10 Scientific publications from the relevant time period confirm the quasi-monopoly of asset-based definitions. The authors of a 2007 UNCTAD study on BITs, for instance, pointed out that '[m]ost BITs of the last 10 years have continued to adopt a broad "asset-based" definition of "investment".'[14] Writing in 2009, Malik similarly observed that '[t]he definition of investment in most IIAs [international investment agreements] follows a broad, asset-based formulation'.[15]

5.11 As will be seen in Chapter 6, the number of enterprise-based definitions has increased in recent years. However, the overall proportion of such definitions has remained rather limited, prompting distinguished commentators to conclude that this approach 'has found little resonance so far in actual treaty practice'.[16] It is thus not surprising that recent scholarship continues to refer to asset-based definitions as the generally accepted, or prevailing, approach.[17]

B. Broad definitions

1. Broad coverage of definitions

5.12 Traditional treaty definitions of investment are very broad, ie they cover all (or virtually all) forms of assets. An example of such a definition is the one contained in the UK Model BIT which defines 'investment' as 'every kind of asset, owned or controlled directly or indirectly' by an investor.[18] The German Model BIT defines the term 'investment' in similarly expansive terms as 'every kind of asset which is directly or indirectly invested by investors of one Contracting State in the territory of the other Contracting State'.[19]

---

[12] ibid.
[13] ibid.
[14] UNCTAD, *Bilateral Investment Treaties 1995–2006: Trends in Investment Rulemaking* (2007) 8 (hereafter UNCTAD, *Bilateral Investment Treaties 1995–2006*).
[15] Mahnaz Malik, 'Definition of Investment in International Investment Agreements' (2009) International Institute for Sustainable Development, Best Practices Series 1.
[16] See Schill, Schreuer and Sinclair, 'Article 25' (n 5) para 222.
[17] See, for example, Michael Waibel, 'Subject Matter Jurisdiction: The Notion of Investment' (2021) 19 ICSID Reports 25, para 10 (noting that 'many investment treaties ... adopt a broad, asset-backed definition of investment'); Jeswald W Salacuse, *The Law of Investment Treaties* (3rd edn, Oxford University Press 2021) 209 (remarking that '[m]ost modern investment treaties provide for a very broad asset-based definition of investment') (hereafter Salacuse, *The Law of Investment Treaties*).
[18] UK Model BIT 2008 Art 1(a).
[19] German Model BIT 2008 Art 1(1).

5.13 These broad definitions are typically followed by equally comprehensive catalogues of covered assets. The UK Model BIT, for example, lists '(i) movable and immovable property and any other property rights such as mortgages, liens or pledges; (ii) shares in and stock and debentures of a company and any other form of participation in a company; (iii) claims to money or to any performance under contract having a financial value; (iv) intellectual property rights, goodwill, technical processes and know-how; [and] (v) business concessions conferred by law or under contract' as (examples of) assets qualifying as investments.[20]

5.14 Under most treaties, these lists of qualifying assets are merely illustrative (or non-exhaustive),[21] ie categories of assets that are not expressly mentioned nonetheless qualify as investments under the applicable definitions. Less frequently, treaty definitions provide that only the expressly stated classes of assets qualify as investments for the purposes of the relevant treaty (these treaties follow the so-called 'closed-list approach').[22] Given that exhaustive lists generally cover all main forms of assets,[23] the difference between the two approaches has only limited practical ramifications.

5.15 Arbitral case law confirms that traditional treaty definitions of investment cover virtually all possible categories of assets. In fact, while a number of tribunals have denied investment status to certain assets on the grounds that (1) they were neither owned, nor controlled by the presumed investor,[24] (2) they were not located in the territory of the host State,[25] (3) they were made in violation of host State law,[26] and (4) they were not 'actively' made by the alleged investor,[27] there does not appear to be a single decision holding that certain assets were per se of a type not covered by the applicable treaty definition.

2. Absence of exclusions or additional requirements

5.16 Definitions contained in recent investment treaties often exclude certain categories of assets, ie they provide that the relevant types of assets do not constitute investments. Examples of such exclusions notably comprise portfolio investments, assets that are not connected to any economic activity, sovereign bonds, and rights arising under commercial contracts.[28] Exclusions of this type are absent from traditional investment

---

[20] UK Model BIT 2008 Art 1(a).
[21] See, for example, UK Model BIT 2008 Art 1(a) which provides that the term 'investment' comprises 'in particular, though not exclusively' the listed categories of assets.
[22] See, for example, Agreement Between Canada and the Republic of Peru for the Promotion and Protection of Investments (adopted 14 November 2006, entered into force 20 June 2007) Art 1; Agreement Between the Government of the United Mexican States and the Government of the State of Kuwait on the Promotion and Reciprocal Protection of Investments (adopted 22 February 2013, entered into force 28 April 2016) Art 1(5).
[23] Salacuse, *The Law of Investment Treaties* (n 17) 219 (observing that '[a]lthough such definitions limit the investments covered to only the listed forms, usually they are still broad enough to include all the major investment forms currently employed by investors').
[24] See Section III.
[25] See Section IV.
[26] See Section V.
[27] See Section VI.
[28] See Chapter 6 Section IV.

treaty definitions such as, for instance, those contained in the UK and German Model BITs.

In addition to providing for various exclusions, modern investment treaty definitions of 'investment' frequently incorporate additional requirements. In particular, many treaties require that in order to qualify as an investment, an asset must possess certain typical characteristics of an investment such as 'the commitment of capital or other resources, the expectation of gain or profit, or the assumption of risk'.[29] Such characteristics-requirements are absent from traditional treaty definitions of 'investment'. **5.17**

III. Ownership or Control of the Investment

A. Overview

In order to benefit from treaty protection, qualifying assets must bear a specific relationship with a covered investor. While this relationship may be couched in varying terms and while more than one type of relationship may be required under a given treaty, the most basic such relationship is that the assets at stake must be 'owned' by a protected investor. In fact, investment treaties do not protect investments of all foreign investors, but only those that have been made by investors having the nationality of a contracting State. For reasons which will be explained below, the majority of treaties contain broadly framed provisions requiring assets to be 'owned or controlled' by a qualifying investor. **5.18**

The requirement of ownership or control is most frequently set forth in the definition of the term 'investment'. The BIT between the United Kingdom and Colombia, for example, defines investment as 'every kind of economic asset, *owned or controlled* directly or indirectly, by investors of a Contracting Party in the territory of the other Contracting Party'.[30] Similar definitions can notably be found in the UK Model BIT[31] and the BIT between the United States and Argentina.[32] **5.19**

In some treaties, the requirement of ownership or control is not contained in the definition of 'investment', but in a/the provision specifying the treaty's scope of application. Under the BIT between the Netherlands and Turkey, for **5.20**

---

[29] US Model BIT 2012 Art 1. For a discussion of this requirement, see Chapter 6 Section III.
[30] Bilateral Agreement for the Promotion and Protection of Investments Between the Government of the United Kingdom of Great Britain and Northern Ireland and [the] Republic of Colombia (adopted 17 March 2010, entered into force 10 October 2014) Art I(2)(a) (emphasis added) (hereafter United Kingdom–Colombia BIT).
[31] UK Model BIT 2008 Art 1(a).
[32] Treaty Between [the] United States of America and the Argentine Republic Concerning the Reciprocal Encouragement and Protection of Investment (adopted 14 November 1991, entered into force 20 October 1994) Art I(1)(a) (hereafter United States–Argentina BIT).

example, the definition of 'investment' does not refer to any ownership or control criterion.[33] Instead, it specifies elsewhere that 'the present Agreement shall apply to investments *owned or controlled* by investors of one Contracting Party in the territory of the other Contracting Party'.[34]

5.21 A few investment treaties do not contain any express reference to the requirement that investments must be owned or controlled by covered investors. The BIT between Kazakhstan and Uzbekistan, for instance, defines investments as assets 'invested', rather than owned or controlled, by protected investors.[35] Under the BIT between Germany and Argentina, treaty protection is enjoyed by investments 'of' nationals or companies of a contracting State.[36] The effect of such provisions is arguably similar to the impact of express requirements of ownership or control, although it may be debatable whether the latter (ie control) would be sufficient to bring an asset within the scope of protection of either of these treaties.

B. Direct ownership

5.22 Direct ownership means that the investor him- or herself owns the assets concerned, without any ownership of an intermediary. Such direct ownership exists in many cases and is often uncontroversial. In *Salini*, for example, the investors had entered into a contract with a host State authority, and it was not contested by the Respondent that the investors' rights under such contract constituted assets *owned* by them.[37] In *Fedax*, it was similarly undisputed that Fedax had acquired and *owned* promissory notes issued by the Venezuelan government.[38] In the more recent *Dan Cake* case, it was also beyond dispute that the investor *owned* a majority shareholding in the Hungarian company Danesita.[39]

---

[33] Agreement on Reciprocal Encouragement and Protection of Investments between the Kingdom of the Netherlands and the Republic of Turkey (adopted 27 March 1986, entered into force 1 November 1989) Art 1(b) (hereafter Netherlands–Turkey BIT).

[34] ibid Art 2(2) (emphasis added).

[35] Agreement between the Government of the Republic of Kazakhstan and the Government of the Republic of Uzbekistan on the promotion and protection of investments (adopted 2 June 1997, entered into force 8 September 1997) Art 1(2) (defining investments as 'any kind of property and the rights thereto, and also intellectual property rights invested by the investors of one Contracting Party in the territory of the other Contracting Party for the purposes of obtaining a profit (return)') (hereafter Kazakhstan–Uzbekistan BIT).

[36] Agreement between the Federal Republic of Germany and the Argentine Republic Concerning the Promotion and Reciprocal Protection of Investments (adopted 9 April 1991, entered into force 8 November 1993) Art 2(2).

[37] *Salini Costruttori S.P.A. and Italstrade S.P.A. v Kingdom of Morocco*, ICSID Case No ARB/00/4, Decision on Jurisdiction (23 July 2001) paras 37–40. The Respondent did not argue that the Italian Claimants did not 'own' rights under the contract entered into with the host State authority; it merely contended that those rights had not arisen under a contract that had been approved by the competent authority, as required under the applicable BIT.

[38] *Fedax N.V. v The Republic of Venezuela*, ICSID Case No ARB/96/3, Decision of the Tribunal on Objections to Jurisdiction (11 July 1997) para 19 (hereafter *Fedax v Venezuela*). Venezuela did not challenge Fedax's ownership of the relevant promissory notes. It claimed that those notes did not qualify as an investment under Art 25 ICSID Convention because they allegedly constituted neither a foreign direct investment, nor a portfolio investment.

[39] *Dan Cake (Portugal) S.A. v Hungary*, ICSID Case No ARB/12/9, Decision on Jurisdiction and Liability (24 August 2015) paras 31, 67. In this case, the Respondent did not raise any jurisdictional objections.

In some cases, tribunals have held that the respective Claimants did not own the claimed assets.[40] In *Fakes*, for example, the Claimant argued that it had received an offer to purchase 67 per cent of the shares of Telsim, a Turkish Telecommunications company, and that it had accepted this offer.[41] The Tribunal, however, considered that the parties to the agreements relied upon by the Claimant 'never had any intention to transfer any rights to the Claimant in relation to Telsim's shares' and that no such transfer ever took place.[42] It concluded that 'the Claimant [did] not hold legal title over the share certificates in Telsim'.[43]

5.23

The question of whether a claimant possesses qualifying ownership is more complex when ownership is split between a nominal and a beneficial owner. In such cases, the nominal owner is the legal or formal owner of the asset, but all (or most) benefits associated with such right are enjoyed by the beneficial owner. In *Occidental v Ecuador*, for example, Occidental Exploration and Production Company (OEPC) entered into a farmout agreement with City Investing Company Limited (City) under which the latter purchased a 40 per cent share of OEPC's farmout property.[44] During a first (and, for the purposes of the ICSID proceedings, the only relevant) phase, City would be the beneficial owner of this share, while OEPC would act as the nominee, appearing as the formal owner vis-à-vis third parties.[45] As beneficial owner, City would have control over its share and bear 'the costs, profits, risks and rewards of ownership'.[46]

5.24

Tribunals have—apparently without exception—recognized that beneficial owners are protected under investment treaties.[47] The relevant decisions were, however, not based on treaty provisions laying down 'ownership or control' requirements, but on other treaty norms or more general principles of international law.[48] It is, therefore,

5.25

---

[40] See, for example, *Mr. Saba Fakes v Republic of Turkey*, ICSID Case No ARB/07/20, Award (14 July 2010) paras 130–47 (hereafter *Fakes v Turkey*); *Anglo-Adriatic Group Limited v Republic of Albania*, ICSID Case No ARB/17/6, Award (7 February 2019) paras 230–47; *Italba Corporation v Oriental Republic of Uruguay*, ICSID Case No ARB/16/9, Award (22 March 2019) paras 266–88 (hereafter *Italba v Uruguay*).
[41] *Fakes v Turkey* (n 40) para 130.
[42] ibid para 136.
[43] ibid para 135.
[44] *Occidental Petroleum Corporation and Occidental Exploration and Production Company v The Republic of Ecuador*, ICSID Case No ARB/06/11, Decision on Annulment of the Award (2 November 2015) para 202 (hereafter *Occidental v Ecuador*).
[45] ibid.
[46] ibid para 203.
[47] See, for example, *Occidental v Ecuador* (n 44) paras 259–64, 272; *Abaclat and others v The Argentine Republic*, ICSID Case No ARB/07/5, Decision on Jurisdiction and Admissibility (4 August 2011) paras 352–61 (hereafter *Abaclat v Argentina*); *Vladislav Kim and others v Republic of Uzbekistan*, ICSID Case No ARB/13/6, Decision on Jurisdiction (8 March 2017) paras 11, 320 (hereafter *Kim v Uzbekistan*); *Theodoros Adamakopoulos and others v Republic of Cyprus*, ICSID Case No ARB/15/49, Decision on Jurisdiction (7 February 2020) para 285 (hereafter *Adamakopoulos v Cyprus*).
[48] See *Occidental v Ecuador* (n 44) para 259 (holding that the protection of beneficial owners reflects 'the dominant position in international law'); *Abaclat v Argentina* (n 47) paras 352–61 (focusing on the question of whether the Claimants' security entitlements in bonds issued by the Respondent constituted 'obligations, private or public titles or any other right to performances or services having economic value, including capitalized revenues'); *Kim v Uzbekistan* (n 47) paras 11, 320 (holding, without providing any express legal basis or justification, that 'the fact that certain aspects of the ownership holding structure entail a beneficial, rather than a legal, ownership, [is not] material to the jurisdictional issue'); *Adamakopoulos v Cyprus* (n 47) para 285 (explaining the protection of beneficial owners on the basis of the fact that such ownership 'is a form of legal interest widely recognized by the principal legal systems of the world and by international law').

not entirely certain whether beneficial ownership would qualify as ownership under treaty provisions requiring ownership or control. However, since beneficial ownership often entails control over the relevant asset(s), it is likely that such requirements would be met.

5.26 As far as nominal ownership is concerned, case law seems somewhat divided.[49] A decision recognizing that nominally owned assets can constitute investments is the ruling in *Fakes*. In this case, the Tribunal observed that '[n]either the ICSID Convention, nor the BIT make any distinction which could be interpreted as an exclusion of a bare legal title from the scope of the ICSID Convention or from the protection of the BIT'.[50] By referring to the applicable treaty, the BIT between the Netherlands and Turkey, the Tribunal implicitly acknowledged that nominal ownership satisfied its requirement that investments must be 'owned or controlled' by covered investors in order to fall within the treaty's scope of application.

5.27 By contrast, the ad hoc Committee in *Occidental* considered that, '[i]n cases where legal title is split between a nominee and a beneficial owner[,] the dominant position in international law grants standing and relief to the owner of the beneficial interest—not to the nominee'.[51] Noting that the Tribunal had awarded compensation to OEPC in an amount corresponding to the full value of the farmout property, although it was only a nominal owner of 40 per cent of such property, the ad hoc Committee concluded that the Tribunal's decision amounted to an excess of powers.[52]

5.28 While nominal ownership is arguably covered by treaties requiring ownership or control by a qualifying investor,[53] it is questionable whether such an approach is reasonable. Indeed, it implies that both the beneficial and the nominal owner are considered as owners of one and the same investment and that both are thus entitled to claim investor status. This creates a risk of parallel proceedings and, from the perspective of the host State, the risk of having to compensate both investors for one and the same loss. At least from this perspective, it would be desirable to limit the benefit of treaty protection to one of the two owners.

C. Indirect ownership

5.29 Indirect ownership[54] means that the investor does not him- or herself own the relevant assets, but 'owns' them indirectly through ownership of one or several intermediary

---

[49] See Schill, Schreuer and Sinclair, 'Article 25' (n 5) paras 309–15.
[50] *Fakes v Turkey* (n 40) para 134.
[51] *Occidental v Ecuador* (n 44) para 259.
[52] ibid para 265.
[53] Nominal ownership is not expressly excluded under such provisions and one can, like the *Fakes* tribunal, take the view that there is no basis to read such an exclusion into the applicable treaty.
[54] In practice, the question of whether indirect ownership is protected under a given legal instrument often overlaps with the question of whether the shareholders of an entity that qualifies as an investor are protected under such instrument. For commentary on this issue, see Gabriel Bottini, *Admissibility of Shareholder Claims under*

entities. If, for example, company A (the investment) is wholly owned by company B which, in turn, is wholly owned by company C, then company C indirectly owns the investment. If, in addition, individuals D and E each own 50 per cent of company C, then they both indirectly own 50 per cent of the investment.

Treaty provisions requiring ownership or control by a covered investor almost always recognize indirect ownership. The BIT between the United States and Ecuador, for example, defines 'investment' as 'every kind of investment in the territory of one Party owned or controlled *directly or indirectly* by nationals or companies of the other Party'.[55] Similarly worded requirements can be found in many other treaties including, for instance, the BIT between the United Kingdom and Colombia and the BIT between the United States and Argentina.[56]   **5.30**

Provisions expressly referring to indirect ownership are of major practical significance because such ownership is traditionally not recognized under international law. In the well-known *Barcelona Traction* case,[57] Belgium sought to exercise diplomatic protection over the Belgian shareholders of the Canadian company Barcelona Traction for harm allegedly inflicted to the company's Spanish interests. The Court refused to recognize the existence of such right, holding that only the national country (ie the country of the place of incorporation) of the *Barcelona Traction*, namely, Canada, was entitled to seek compensation.[58] The Court thus refused to recognize the Belgian shareholders' indirect ownership of the Barcelona Traction's Spanish interests.   **5.31**

The recognition of indirect ownership is not unproblematic. In fact, it allows multiple shareholders to claim investor status and bring proceedings under one or several IIAs. Such parallel proceedings are generally not cost-effective and carry the risk that the different disputes will not be resolved in a uniform manner. In addition, where claims are brought by shareholders situated at different levels in the ownership chain, the aggregate compensation sought by the different Claimants may exceed the actual loss sustained. In the example above, both B and C can claim full ownership of company A, while D and E can each claim ownership of 50 per cent. If B, C, D, and E all bring claims under the applicable treaty or treaties, the total amounts claimed are likely to be three times higher than the actual loss sustained by company A.   **5.32**

Investment Treaties (Cambridge University Press 2020); Lukas Vanhonnaeker, *Shareholders' Claims for Reflective Loss in International Investment Law* (Cambridge University Press 2020).

[55] Treaty between the United States of America and the Republic of Ecuador concerning the Encouragement and Reciprocal Protection of Investment (adopted 27 August 1993, entered into force 11 May 1997) Art I(1)(a) (emphasis added).
[56] United Kingdom–Colombia BIT (n 30) Art I(2)(a); United States–Argentina BIT (n 32) Art I(1)(a).
[57] Case concerning the Barcelona Traction, Light and Power Company, Limited (*Belgium v Spain*) [1970] ICJ Rep 3.
[58] ibid para 88 (holding that, 'where it is a question of an unlawful act committed against a company representing foreign capital, the general rule of international law authorizes the national State of the company alone to make a claim').

5.33 The problematic nature of parallel proceedings initiated by multiple shareholders has not only been acknowledged by scholarly writers,[59] but also highlighted by arbitral tribunals. The tribunal in *Enron v Argentina*, in particular, advocated the establishment of a 'cut-off point beyond which claims would not be permissible as they would have only a remote connection to the affected company',[60] without however specifying where this cut-off point may be situated or how it can be determined. In any event, the application of such a cut-off point would not as such solve the problem of parallel proceedings, but simply limit the pool of shareholders benefiting from treaty protection.

D. Control

5.34 Under treaty provisions requiring 'ownership or control' of assets by a protected investor, control is expressly recognized as an alternative criterion to ownership. The concept of 'control' is frequently defined when it appears in treaty norms acknowledging the relevance of control for the purposes of establishing the nationality of a company or other juridical person.[61] In the context of rules addressing the relationship between a covered investor and qualifying assets, however, such definitions are rare. An example of such a provision—which also applies in connection with the nationality of investors—is Art 1(3) of the BIT between Australia and Pakistan under which control is equated with the rather vague notion of a 'substantial interest'.[62]

5.35 According to an UNCTAD study, the recognition of control as an additional criterion was intended to solve the problem of the absence of protection of indirect shareholders under international law. The authors of this study explain that '[t]he incorporation of the notion of control into BITs may be better understood in the light of the decision of the International Court of Justice (ICJ) in the Barcelona Traction, Light and Power Co., Ltd. Case'[63] in which, as has already been explained, the Court denied Belgium the right to exercise diplomatic protection over the Belgian shareholders of the Barcelona

---

[59] See, for example, Ursula Kriebaum, Christoph Schreuer and Rudolf Dolzer, *Principles of International Investment Law* (3rd edn, Oxford University Press 2022) 121 (hereafter Kriebaum, Schreuer and Dolzer, *Principles of International Investment Law*). The authors observe that '[p]ractical problems can arise where claims are pursued in parallel, especially by different shareholders or groups of shareholders'. They do not, however, expressly refer to the risks of inefficiency, lack of uniformity, or overcompensation, highlighting instead that 'shareholders and companies at different levels may pursue conflicting or competing litigation strategies that may be difficult to reconcile and coordinate').

[60] *Enron Corporation and Ponderosa Assets, L.P. v The Argentine Republic*, ICSID Case No ARB/01/3, Decision on Jurisdiction (14 January 2004) para 52.

[61] See, for example, Agreement Between the Government of Australia and the Government of the Republic of India on the Promotion and Protection of Investments (adopted 26 February 1999, entered into force 4 May 2000) Art 1(h) (defining control of a company as 'the ability to exercise decisive influence over the management and operation of the ... company, specifically demonstrated by way of: (i) ownership of 51% of the shares or voting rights of the ... company, or (ii) the ability to exercise decisive control over the selection of the majority of members of the board of directors of the ... company').

[62] See Agreement between Australia and the Islamic Republic of Pakistan on the Promotion and Protection of Investments (adopted 7 February 1998, entered into force 14 October 1998) Art 1(3) ('For the purposes of this Agreement, a natural person or company shall be regarded as controlling a company or an investment if the person or company has a substantial interest in the company or the investment.')

[63] UNCTAD, *Bilateral Investment Treaties 1995–2006* (n 14) 17.

Traction for damage sustained by the company's Spanish interests. The authors conclude that the effects of this decision were 'avoided by incorporating the notion of "control" into definitions of "investment" or "investor" '.[64]

One may wonder whether the use of the concept of control at all broadens the scope of covered assets, ie whether there are indeed situations where control can exist independently of any direct or indirect ownership rights. It may of course happen that control does not flow from a majority ownership, but from 'special voting rights and powers of operation and management, often conferred through contractual arrangements'[65] and that a minority shareholder can be considered as controlling a given company. However, since the minority shareholding will in any event qualify as an investment,[66] it is not necessary to resort to the notion of control to establish the investment status of the relevant shareholding and/or investor status of the minority shareholder.   **5.36**

While it is unlikely that control can exist absent any ownership rights, control of a company does evidently not require a 100 per cent shareholding. An individual or entity holding 51 per cent of the shares of a company generally exercises control over that company. The question is whether such control entitles the shareholder to claim the entire company as his or her investment and whether he or she can thus seek compensation for the entirety of the loss affecting, or sustained by, the company. Since control is treated as the equivalent of ownership in treaty requirements of ownership or control (ie an asset is an investment if it is either owned or controlled by a covered investor), it would be possible to answer this question in the affirmative. Such an answer would, however, entail that the investor is compensated in excess of the value of his or her shareholding, an outcome for which there is no valid justification.   **5.37**

IV. Localization of the Investment in the Territory of the Host State (Territoriality)

A. Treaty practice

It is hardly surprising that, as a general rule, an investor's assets will only enjoy treaty protection if those assets are situated in the territory of the host State. A BIT between countries A and B, for example, does not protect all investments made by nationals or companies of these two countries, but only those that investors of one contracting State make *in the other contracting State*. It would indeed be nonsensical for these two States to afford protection to investments that their respective investors make in third countries. Such an undertaking would be devoid of any rational justification since the   **5.38**

---

[64] ibid.
[65] Schill, Schreuer and Sinclair, 'Article 25' (n 5) para 322.
[66] This is because the vast majority of investment treaties recognize that company shares constitute investments, without requiring any minimum shareholding. See also *Hassan Awdi and others v Romania*, ICSID Case No ARB/10/13, Award (2 March 2015) para 165 (noting that 'even a minority shareholding amounts to an investment').

States concerned do not in any way benefit from investments made in third countries. In addition, it would also be impossible to comply with the obligation to protect such investments, given that States do not in principle have any control over the treatment of investments in foreign jurisdictions.[67]

5.39 Most frequently, territoriality requirements are set forth in a treaty's definition of the term 'investment'. The BIT between the United States and Argentina, for example, defines investment as 'every kind of investment *in the territory of one Party* owned or controlled directly or indirectly by nationals or companies of the other Party'.[68] Similar territoriality requirements can notably be found in the definitions contained in the German Model BIT,[69] the BIT between Kazakhstan and Uzbekistan,[70] and the BIT between the United Kingdom and Colombia.[71]

5.40 A slight variation of this model consists of territoriality requirements that are contained not in the definition of 'investment', but in the definition of the more specific notion of 'covered investment', employed in some treaties. The definition of 'investment' found in the US Model BIT, for example, does not refer to the location of the investment.[72] However, the Model BIT includes a separate provision which defines the term 'covered investment' as 'an investment in ... [the] territory [of a Party] of an investor of the other Party'.[73]

5.41 In some treaties, the requirement of territoriality is enshrined not in the definition of 'investment' or 'covered investment', but in a/the provision specifying the treaty's scope of application. Art 2(2) of the BIT between the Netherlands and Turkey, for example, provides that the treaty 'shall apply to investments owned or controlled by investors of one Contracting Party *in the territory of the other Contracting Party*'.[74] The ASEAN Comprehensive Investment Agreement similarly specifies that it applies to 'measures adopted or maintained by a Member State relating to: ... (b) investments, *in its territory*, of investors of any other Member State'.[75]

5.42 A few treaties do not lay down any express territoriality requirement. The BIT between Germany and Ukraine, for example, does not mention such a requirement in the definition of 'investment'[76] and, moreover, lacks a provision determining the treaty's scope of application in which such a requirement may have been set forth. However, (virtually)

---

[67] For commentary on the requirement of territoriality, see Christina Knahr, 'Investments "In the Territory" of the Host State' in Christina Binder, Ursula Kriebaum, August Reinisch and Stephan Wittich (eds), *International Investment Law for the 21st Century: Essays in Honour of Christoph Schreuer* (Oxford University Press 2009) 42.
[68] United States–Argentina BIT (n 32) Art I(1)(a).
[69] German Model BIT 2008 Art 1(1).
[70] Kazakhstan–Uzbekistan BIT (n 35) Art 1(2).
[71] United Kingdom–Colombia BIT (n 30) Art I(2)(a).
[72] US Model BIT 2012 Art 1.
[73] ibid.
[74] Netherlands–Turkey BIT (n 33) Art 2(2) (emphasis added).
[75] ASEAN Comprehensive Investment Agreement (adopted 26 February 2009, entered into force 24 February 2012) Art 3(1) (emphasis added).
[76] Treaty between the Federal Republic of Germany and Ukraine on the Promotion and Mutual Protection of Capital Investments (adopted 15 February 1993, entered into force 29 June 1996) Art 1(1).

all substantive standards of protection refer to an asset's localization in the territory of the host State as a prerequisite for protection. Full protection and security, for instance, is afforded to '[i]nvestments of nationals or companies of a Contracting Party ... *in the territory of the other Contracting Party*'.[77]

The question of whether these isolated references to territoriality contained in the BIT between Germany and Ukraine can be regarded as establishing a general territoriality requirement was raised, but not answered, in *Inmaris v Ukraine*.[78] In this case, the Claimants argued that these references merely specified the 'conditions under which various of the substantive BIT obligations will or will not apply' and that they did not limit the Tribunal's jurisdiction.[79] The Tribunal disagreed with this view, holding that territoriality was a jurisdictional matter.[80] However, it did not decide the issue of whether the 'the BIT [should be treated] as including a territoriality requirement as an overarching jurisdictional limit, or as including territorial limits among the elements of the substantive protections that underlie Claimants' claims'.[81] **5.43**

Since all standards of protection contained in the BIT between Germany and Ukraine require the investment to be located in the host State, the question of whether the treaty implicitly establishes a general requirement of territoriality is largely irrelevant. However, it is sensible to argue that such a general requirement should apply. In fact, as has already been explained, it would be irrational for States to agree to grant treaty protection to investments made in a third country. **5.44**

B. Localization of different categories of assets

Certain categories of assets can be located more easily than others. The localization of immovable property such as land or real estate is particularly straightforward. Not only can the location of such property be established without any difficulty, but any change of the relevant location is also *de facto* excluded. Thus, where an investor acquires a plot of land, a hotel, or a factory, there can be almost no doubt regarding the situation of the relevant asset. **5.45**

The determination of the location of *movable* tangible assets such as equipment or machinery is also rather uncomplicated. However, contrary to immovable property, the location of movable physical assets may, by definition, vary over time. This raises, at least in theory, the question of the point in time that is relevant to determine whether the applicable territoriality requirement is met. If, for example, an investor acquires a drilling machine in his or her home State, puts it to use in an oil exploration project in **5.46**

---

[77] ibid Art 4(1) (emphasis added).
[78] *Inmaris Perestroika Sailing Maritime Services GmbH and others v Ukraine*, ICSID Case No ARB/08/8, Decision on Jurisdiction (8 March 2010).
[79] ibid para 117.
[80] ibid para 121.
[81] ibid.

the host State, and ultimately repatriates it to the country of origin, can it be held that the machine is, for the purposes of the territoriality requirement, situated in the host State (assuming that it otherwise qualifies as an investment)?

5.47 Another category of assets whose localization is generally uncontroversial is company shares. In fact, it is almost universally accepted that such shares must be considered to be situated in the country in which the company concerned is incorporated. In cases in which the alleged investment consisted, in whole or in part, of shares of companies registered in the Respondent States, those States apparently never objected to the shares meeting the applicable territoriality requirement.[82]

5.48 The localization of various types of rights that investors may possess, in particular contractual ones, is more difficult. In fact, how does one determine the location of a right? A technical answer to this question would in principle take into account the place of performance of the corresponding obligation. If, for example, the investor's contractual entitlement consists of the right to be paid for services provided to the host State, one could determine the location of such right by reference to the place where the host State effects, or has to effect, payment for those services.

5.49 Clearly, such an approach would be unduly formalistic and, thus, inappropriate. In fact, whether an asset is situated in the host State and, by implication, whether the investor owns or controls a qualifying investment would depend on a factor that is entirely unrelated to the nature and characteristic features of the transaction, or the benefits that its performance entails for the host State. In a *Salini*-type scenario, for example, a company building a highway in the host State would own an investment (or be otherwise protected under the applicable treaty) if it is paid in the host State, but not if it is paid in its home State. This being a plainly unsatisfactory state of affairs, it is only natural that arbitral tribunals have, as will be explained below, adopted a radically different approach to this question.

C. Case law

5.50 Two categories of assets have given rise to repeated claims alleging a failure to meet the requirement of territoriality. One such category consists of (rights arising under) contracts for the provision of services concluded with the host State and, more particularly, contracts under which the presumed investor had to perform a substantial part of his or her obligations in a State other than the host State. The second category includes (rights arising under) debt-based financial instruments (eg promissory notes, bonds, or loans) that the presumed investor acquired without transferring any funds to the host State.

---

[82] See, for example, *Fakes v Turkey* (n 40); *ACP Axos Capital GmbH v Republic of Kosovo*, ICSID Case No ARB/15/22, Award (3 May 2018); *Italba v Uruguay* (n 40); *Raymond Charles Eyre and others v Democratic Socialist Republic of Sri Lanka*, ICSID Case No ARB/16/25, Award (5 March 2020).

1. Rights under service contracts

Under traditional asset-based definitions of investment, it is not the contract as such, but the presumed investor's rights under the contract that constitute an investment. In fact, such contractual rights are generally expressly recognized as one specific category of qualifying assets.[83] In order to determine whether such rights meet the requirement of territoriality, it would in principle be necessary to identify the location of the rights at stake. However, for the reasons indicated above, this is not the approach that tribunals have followed in practice.

5.51

In fact, most arbitral tribunals consider that it is the place of performance of the relevant services that is decisive for the purposes of locating the investment. In *SGS v Philippines*, for example, SGS and the Republic of the Philippines entered into a contract for the provision of 'pre-shipment inspection [of goods] in any country of export to the Philippines' covering 'quality, quantity and price comparisons'.[84] In the ICSID proceedings, the Respondent (the Republic of the Philippines) challenged the territoriality of the investment on two grounds: (1) the fact that the preponderant part of the Claimant's obligations was performed in countries other than the Philippines[85] and (2) the fact that the Claimant's claims allegedly all concerned services that were provided abroad.[86] Both arguments rely on the basic assumption that the place of performance of the services is relevant to establish whether the Claimant's investment can be regarded as being situated in the Philippines.

5.52

Addressing both objections raised by the Respondent, the Tribunal implicitly acknowledged the relevance of the place(s) where the services had to be rendered. As far as the Claimant's preponderance argument is concerned, the Tribunal rejected it on factual grounds, without however denying the legal relevance of the preponderance-test as such.[87] It emphasized the significance of the services SGS had provided in the Philippines, namely, 'the provision, in the Philippines, of a reliable inspection certificate ... on the basis of which import clearance could be expedited and the appropriate duty charged',[88] highlighting the role played by its Manila Liaison Office.[89] The Tribunal further held that it could 'not agree that SGS's services under the CISS Agreement [could] be subdivided in [the] way [suggested by the Respondent]',[90] seemingly

5.53

---

[83] See, for example, UK Model BIT 2008 Art 1(a)(iii) under which 'investment' notably includes 'claims to money or to any performance under contract having a financial value'.
[84] *SGS Société Générale de Surveillance S.A. v Republic of the Philippines*, ICSID Case No ARB/02/6, Decision of the Tribunal on Objections to Jurisdiction (29 January 2004) para 19 (hereafter *SGS v Philippines*).
[85] ibid para 100. The Respondent argued that '[t]hose aspects of SGS's performance which occurred in the Philippines ... were merely incidental or peripheral'.
[86] ibid. The Republic of the Philippines contended that 'the gist of the present case was a claim for money due for services performed in the country of export, not in the Philippines. No question arose, for example, as to the unfair treatment or wrongful expropriation of the Manila Liaison Office. The actual dispute revolved around non-payment for services provided, and necessarily provided, abroad'.
[87] It is not clear, however, whether the Tribunal's analysis constitutes an implicit acceptance of the correctness of the preponderance-test relied upon by the Respondent.
[88] *SGS v Philippines* (n 84) para 101.
[89] ibid.
[90] ibid.

rejecting the Respondent's argument that, for the purposes of the territoriality requirement, only the services that formed the basis of the claim (and not all services that had to be provided under the contract) had to be taken into account.

5.54 Given that the place of performance of the obligations of a service provider determines the location of the latter's rights under the contract, contracts that are entirely performed in a country other than the host State (or, more accurately, the rights arising under such contracts) do not meet the requirement of territoriality. Although *SGS v Philippines* involved a contract for services to be provided both abroad and locally, the Tribunal nevertheless clarified the legal status of such contracts, observing that 'the construction of an embassy in a third State, or the provision of security services to such an embassy, [for example,] would not involve investments in the territory of the State whose embassy it was, and would not be protected by the [applicable] BIT'.[91]

5.55 In *SGS v Paraguay*,[92] a case involving an almost identical fact pattern, the Tribunal rendered a very similar decision. Like the Tribunal in *SGS v Philippines*, the Tribunal implicitly acknowledged that the place of performance of the services was relevant to determine the location of SGS's presumed investment. It similarly held that it was not possible to distinguish between 'services provided abroad and services provided in Paraguay, and to then attribute Claimant's claims solely to the former category',[93] highlighting the interrelatedness of the different services.[94] The Tribunal also noted that SGS had 'injected funds and resources into the territory of Paraguay' where it maintained several offices.[95]

5.56 The two *SGS* decisions, as well as other similarly decided cases, raise a fundamental issue. In fact, the tribunals' focus on the place of performance of the services provided suggests that they viewed the relevant investments not as assets (ie as rights arising under the relevant contracts), but as activities or operations (ie as the services provided). This is, as has been explained, because asset-based notions of investment are not suitable for the purposes of locating certain categories of assets such as, for example, contractual rights. However, these decisions also raise the more general question of whether asset-based definitions of investment are at all appropriate or whether it is preferable to conceptualize investments as activities or operations, which is—as has been explained in Chapter 4— the approach implicitly endorsed by the *Salini* test.

2. Debt instruments

5.57 A foreign investor may acquire a debt instrument in two ways. First of all, he or she may him- or herself make funds available to the host State or to an entity established

---

[91] ibid para 99.
[92] *SGS Société Générale de Surveillance S.A. v The Republic of Paraguay*, ICSID Case No ARB/07/29, Decision on Jurisdiction (12 February 2010).
[93] ibid para 113.
[94] ibid (highlighting, in particular, that the inspections that were carried out abroad 'were indispensable operations for the issuance of the final certifications in Paraguay').
[95] ibid para 114.

in that State, for example by purchasing sovereign bonds directly from the State (ie on the 'primary market') or by lending money to a corporation registered in that State. Alternatively, the investor may acquire an existing debt instrument (sovereign bonds, promissory notes, etc.) from the initial or any subsequent holder of such instrument, without any direct contact with the borrower.

5.58 Where an investor holds a debt instrument, his or her investment consists of the rights arising under such instrument, ie the right to the agreed payments. Therefore, in order to determine whether the investor's assets are located in the territory of the host State, one would, in principle, have to locate the relevant rights. However, like in connection with rights arising under contracts for the provision of services, and presumably for very similar reasons, neither parties to investment disputes, nor arbitral tribunals have advocated or followed this approach.

5.59 In practice, objections to the territoriality of debt instruments have almost always been based on the (alleged) absence of any transfer of funds to the territory of the host State. The underlying argument is that rights under debt instruments must be considered as being located in the country to which the funds (or payment for the debt instrument) are (is) transferred. There are, in fact, various scenarios in which such a transfer to the host State does not occur. For example, where the presumed investor acquires an existing debt instrument from another foreign party (ie an entity that is not established in the host State), payment for this debt instrument is likely to be made in the country where the transferor is established. Even where the presumed investor provides direct financing to the host State or a host State entity, the parties' agreement may provide for the funds to be transferred to a different country, for example to pay a debt owed by the beneficiary to a third party.[96]

5.60 Arbitral tribunals have invariably rejected such objections, holding that a transfer of funds to the host State was not necessary for the purposes of the territoriality requirement. They have taken the view that the identity of the beneficiary and, to some extent, the place where the funds are ultimately used, were decisive. Thus, where the beneficiary is the host State or an entity established in the host State, the territoriality requirement will in principle be met. Applying the second criterion, the requirement will be met if the funds are used in connection with operations carried out in the host State.

5.61 An insightful decision is the jurisdictional ruling of the Tribunal in *Fedax*. In this case, the Republic of Venezuela issued promissory notes in connection with a contract entered into with a Venezuelan corporation,[97] presumably as payment for goods sold or services provided. Fedax subsequently acquired those promissory notes,[98] most

---

[96] See *Fedax v Venezuela* (n 38) para 41. The Tribunal observed that 'it [was] a standard feature of many international financial transactions that the funds involved are not physically transferred to the territory of the beneficiary, but put at its disposal elsewhere' and that 'many loans and credits do not leave the country of origin at all, but are made available to suppliers or other entities'.
[97] ibid para 18.
[98] ibid.

probably not from the initial holder, but from a transferee. In the ICSID proceedings, the Respondent argued that there had been no investment in Venezuela given that no funds or value had been transferred into the territory of the host country.[99] The Tribunal denied the relevance of such a transfer, stating that '[t]he important question [was] whether the funds made available were utilized by the beneficiary of the credit ... so as to finance its governmental needs'.[100] In the Tribunal's opinion, there was no doubt that Venezuela had '[received] an amount of credit that was put to work ... for its financial needs'.[101]

5.62 In *Abaclat*, the Claimants acquired, on the secondary market, a total of eighty-three sovereign bonds issued by Argentina.[102] The Republic of Argentina argued that the Claimant had not made any investment in Argentina, given that the 'purchase price paid by [the] Claimants for their security entitlements never ended up in Argentina'.[103] Like the *Fedax* tribunal, the Tribunal in *Abaclat* found that the place to which the funds had been transferred was irrelevant for the purposes of determining the investment's location[104] and that, in connection with financial investments, 'the relevant criteria should be where and/or for the benefit of whom the funds are ultimately used'.[105] Elsewhere, the Tribunal also seemed to attach importance to the question of whether the funds 'support[ed] the [host State's] economic development'.[106] On the facts, the Tribunal ruled that 'the funds generated through the bonds issuance process [had been] ... made available to Argentina, and served to finance Argentina's economic development', thus concluding that the investment was made in Argentina.[107]

5.63 In *Deutsche Bank*, the Claimant entered into a hedging agreement with Ceylon Petroleum Corporation (CPC), a 100 per cent state-owned Sri Lankan petroleum company established by legislative act.[108] The agreement, concluded for a duration of one year,[109] was intended to 'protect Sri Lanka against the impact of rising oil prices'.[110] Sri Lanka contended that, for a variety of reasons, the agreement (and, thus, the Claimant's investment) lacked a territorial nexus with Sri Lanka.[111] Those reasons did not, however, include any express allegation that Deutsche Bank had not transferred any funds to Sri Lanka, and it is not clear whether such a transfer took place. Addressing the Respondent's objection, the Tribunal expressly and unreservedly endorsed the *Abaclat* approach which focuses on the identity of the beneficiary and the place where the funds

---

[99] ibid para 41.
[100] ibid.
[101] ibid.
[102] *Abaclat v Argentina* (n 47) paras 51, 234.
[103] ibid para 373.
[104] ibid para 374 (denying the relevance of 'the place where the funds were paid out or transferred').
[105] ibid.
[106] ibid.
[107] ibid para 378.
[108] *Deutsche Bank AG v Democratic Socialist Republic of Sri Lanka*, ICSID Case No ARB/09/02, Award (31 October 2012) paras 12–13.
[109] ibid para 30.
[110] ibid para 14.
[111] ibid paras 221–29.

are used.[112] It held that 'the funds paid by Deutsche Bank in execution of the Hedging Agreement [had] been made available to Sri Lanka, were linked to an activity taking place in Sri Lanka [this activity presumably refers to the purchase of petroleum by CPC] and served to finance its economy'.[113] It concluded that the required territorial nexus was present.

While similar, the tests applied, respectively, by the *Fedax*, the *Abaclat*, and the *Deutsche Bank* tribunals are not identical. In *Fedax*, the Tribunal focused exclusively on the beneficiary, ie on whether the beneficiary was the host State or an entity established in the host State. The *Abaclat* and *Deutsche Bank* tribunals, by contrast, also took into consideration an additional factor, namely, the place where the funds were 'used'. From the decisions, it is not clear, however, whether the tribunals considered that these two criteria applied cumulatively or whether the presence of only one of them was sufficient. **5.64**

If the answer is that both criteria have to be satisfied, then the *Fedax* and the *Abaclat/Deutsche Bank* tests may lead to divergent outcomes. Under *Fedax*, for instance, a loan granted to the host State for the purposes of the construction of an embassy building in a foreign country would in principle meet the territoriality requirement because the territorial nexus would be established by the mere fact that the host State is the beneficiary of the loan. Under *Abaclat/Deutsche Bank*, however—if construed as requiring that the funds be used in connection with activities taking place in the host State, the requirement would not be met since the construction work takes place abroad, and not in the host State. **5.65**

It is noteworthy that the *Fedax* test contradicts the approach followed in connection with contracts for the provision of services. In fact, as has been explained, a loan to build a foreign embassy building would in principle be considered as an investment in the territory of the host State. The actual services (ie the contractor's rights under the construction contract), however, would not meet the territoriality requirement since the services are not performed in the host State.[114] **5.66**

V. Legality of the Investment

A. Legality provisions in investment treaties

Most investment treaties lay down a requirement of legality[115] (also 'lawfulness' or 'compliance with host State law'). This requirement can be found in three main types of **5.67**

---

[112] ibid para 288.
[113] ibid para 292.
[114] See *SGS v Philippines* (n 84) para 99 (observing that 'the construction of an embassy in a third State, or the provision of security services to such an embassy, would not involve investments in the territory of the State whose embassy it was, and would not be protected by the BIT').
[115] For commentary on this requirement, see Andrea Carlevaris, 'The Conformity of Investments with the Law of the Host State and the Jurisdiction of International Tribunals' (2008) 9 JWIT 35; Ursula Kriebaum, 'Investment Arbitration – Illegal Investments' in Christian Klausegger, Peter Klein and others (eds), *Austrian Arbitration*

treaty provisions. It may be contained, first of all, in the actual definition of the concept of 'investment'. The BIT between Ukraine and Lithuania, for example, defines 'investment' as 'every kind of asset invested by an investor of the (sic!) Contracting Party in the territory of the other Contracting Party *in accordance with the laws and regulations of the latter*'.[116] The BIT between Albania and Finland similarly defines the term 'investment' as 'any kind of asset, established or acquired by an investor ... *in accordance with the laws and regulations of the host Party*'.[117]

5.68 The legality requirement may also be set forth in a treaty's 'admission' clause. Under the BIT between Ethiopia and Russia, for instance, '[e]ach Contracting Party shall encourage and create favourable conditions for Investors of the other Contracting Party to invest in its territory and *admit* such investments *in accordance with its laws and regulations*'.[118] The BIT between the Netherlands and Argentina similarly prescribes that, '[s]ubject to its rights to exercise powers *conferred by its laws or regulations*, each Contracting Party shall admit ... investments [made by investors of the other Contracting Party]'.[119]

5.69 In some investment treaties, the lawfulness requirement is contained in a (or the) provision determining the treaty's scope of application. The BIT between the Netherlands and Turkey, for example, specifies that it 'shall apply to investments owned or controlled by investors of one Contracting Party in the territory of the other Contracting Party which are established *in accordance with the laws and regulations in force in the latter Contracting Party's territory* at the time the investment was made'.[120]

5.70 The effect of these different types of clauses is, by and large, the same. Unlawful investments do not enjoy treaty protection, whether because they do not constitute investments, because they are considered not to have been admitted by the host State, or because they do not fall within the scope of application of the relevant treaty. The only possible difference pertains to whether the lack of protection extends to the treaty's investor–state dispute settlement (ISDS) provision, ie whether the investor's claims will be rejected on jurisdictional grounds or on the merits. As regards legality requirements

---

Yearbook 2010 (C.H. Beck, Stämpfli & Manz 2010) 307; Stephan Schill, 'Illegal Investments in Investment Treaty Arbitration' (2012) 11 LPICT 281; Zachary Douglas, 'The Plea of Illegality in Investment Treaty Arbitration' (2014) 29 ICSID Rev/FILJ 155.

[116] Agreement between the Government of the Republic of Lithuania and the Government of Ukraine for the promotion and reciprocal protection of investments (adopted 8 February 1994, entered into force 6 March 1995) Art 1(1) (emphasis added) (hereafter Ukraine–Lithuania BIT).

[117] Agreement between the Government of the Republic of Finland and the Government of the Republic of Albania on the Promotion and Protection of Investments (adopted 24 June 1997, entered into force 20 February 1999) Art 1(1) (emphasis added) (hereafter Albania–Finland BIT).

[118] Agreement between the Government of the Federal Democratic Republic of Ethiopia and the Government of the Russian Federation on the Promotion and Reciprocal Protection of Investments (adopted 10 February 2000, not in force) Art 2(1) (emphasis added) (hereafter Ethiopia–Russia BIT).

[119] Agreement on encouragement and reciprocal protection of investments between the Kingdom of the Netherlands and the Argentine Republic (adopted 20 October 1992, entered into force 1 October 1994) Art 2 (emphasis added) (hereafter Netherlands–Argentina BIT).

[120] Netherlands–Turkey BIT (n 33) Art 2(2).

contained in definitions of 'investment' and provisions establishing a treaty's scope of application (including, by implication, the scope of application of the ISDS clause), the answer is rather straightforward: the investment's unlawfulness deprives the investor of the right to access an investor–state tribunal. As far as admission clauses are concerned, the answer is not entirely clear since it could be argued that non-admission only has the effect of depriving an investment of the substantive protections of the relevant treaty, without affecting the jurisdiction of investor–state tribunals.[121] While it ultimately makes little difference whether a claim is rejected on jurisdictional grounds or on the merits, considerations of procedural efficiency would in principle militate in favour of treating admission of an investment as a jurisdictional issue.

Where a treaty does not expressly provide for a legality requirement, it would be sensible to argue that such a requirement is implied. In fact, it would be unreasonable to consider that State parties to an investment treaty intend to grant protection to investments made in violation of their laws. It is thus not surprising that virtually all tribunals that were confronted with this issue have affirmed the existence of an implied legality requirement.[122] Some of these tribunals have considered the (potential) unlawfulness of the investment as a jurisdictional matter,[123] while others have viewed it as affecting the merits of the investor's claim.[124]

5.71

B. Meaning of legality

1. Applicable law

It is uncontroversial that the law determining an investment's legality is the law of the host State. In fact, whether an activity is lawful must necessarily be determined under the law of the place where the activity is conducted. Treaty clauses invariably provide that the relevant 'laws and regulations' are those of the State where the investment is

5.72

---

[121] See Anna Joubin-Bret, 'Admission and Establishment in the Context of Investment Protection' in August Reinisch (ed), *Standards of Investment Protection* (Oxford University Press 2008) 9, 27. Focusing on legality requirements contained in admission clauses, the author notes that there are several legal grey areas. One such grey area is the question of whether 'the consequences [of illegality] [are] to be drawn at the stage of jurisdiction or at the stage of merits of the case').

[122] See, for example, *Fraport AG Frankfurt Services Worldwide v Republic of the Philippines (II)*, ICSID Case No ARB/11/12, Award (10 December 2014) para 332 (noting that 'even absent the sort of explicit legality requirement that exists here, it would be still appropriate to consider the legality of the investment') (hereafter *Fraport v Philippines (II)*); *Álvarez y Marín Corporación S.A. v Republic of Panama*, ICSID Case No ARB/15/14, Award (12 October 2018) paras 132–37 (hereafter *Álvarez y Marín v Panama*); *Bear Creek Mining Corporation v Republic of Peru*, ICSID Case No ARB/14/21, Award (30 November 2017) 324, 335 (referring, somewhat cautiously, to the 'possible relevance' of the illegality of an investment and the idea that such illegality 'may become relevant') (hereafter *Bear Creek v Peru*).

[123] See *Fraport v Philippines (II)* (n 122) paras 332, 334 (holding that 'international legal remedies [are] unavailable with respect to illegal investments' and that the tribunal's jurisdiction is 'found[ed]' on 'the requirement of legality of investments'); *Álvarez y Marín v Panama* (n 122) para 401 (concluding that the acquisition of the Claimants' investment failed to comply with Panamanian law and that the Tribunal therefore lacked jurisdiction to hear the dispute).

[124] See *Bear Creek v Peru* (n 122) paras 323–24 (holding that the Tribunal's jurisdiction was not impacted by 'whether Claimant obtained the Concessions and made the investment in good faith and in accordance with Peruvian law' and that illegality or lack of good faith were possibly relevant 'with respect to the merits' of the case).

made.[125] The exclusive relevance of host State law is further confirmed by the fact that the legality requirement is also commonly referred to as the requirement of compliance with *host State law*.

5.73 In some cases, however, arbitral tribunals seem to have applied international law, rather than the law of the host State, to determine an investment's legality. In *Inceysa v El Salvador*, for example, the Tribunal applied general principles of law because they were a source of international law and because it considered international law to form part of the law of El Salvador.[126] It held that the Claimant's fraudulent conduct in the context of its successful bid to obtain a contract to provide mechanical inspection services in El Salvador[127] violated these principles.[128] It is not entirely clear why the Tribunal relied on such general principles, rather than more specific provisions of El Salvador law. One possible explanation is that it sought to 'strengthen' its ruling by demonstrating that it was based not only on domestic law, but also on principles recognized at the international level.

2. Relevant rules of domestic law

5.74 As has been shown, legality provisions contained in investment treaties require that investments be 'invested',[129] 'established',[130] 'acquired',[131] or 'admitted'[132] in conformity with the laws and regulations of the host State. These formulations suggest that the legality requirement applies to the actual 'making' of the investment, ie to the so-called 'entry' or 'establishment' of investments. Thus, an investment would be unlawful if the asset concerned was acquired in violation of host State law, for example where a foreign investor, using a middle-man, purchases agricultural land in circumvention of a prohibition under the law of the host State. An investment would also be illegal where the investor carries out business operations without having obtained the required permit or licence.

5.75 Where an investment consists of rights arising under a contract entered into with the host State, fraud in the conclusion of that contract would cause the investment to be unlawful. In *Inceysa*, for example, the Claimant participated in a bidding process organized to award a concession for the provision of mechanical inspection services of vehicles. The Tribunal found that the Claimant had acted fraudulently, providing false information regarding its financial situation,[133] its experience and capacity in the relevant sector,[134] and the relevant experience and capacity of the Claimant's sole

---

[125] See, for example, Ukraine–Lithuania BIT (n 116) Art 1(1); Albania–Finland BIT (n 117) Art 1(1); Ethiopia–Russia BIT (n 118) Art 2(1); Netherlands–Argentina BIT (n 119) Art 2; Netherlands–Turkey BIT (n 33) Art 2(2).
[126] *Inceysa Vallisoletana, S.L. v Republic of El Salvador*, ICSID Case No ARB/03/26, Award (2 August 2006) paras 218–29 (hereafter *Inceysa v El Salvador*).
[127] ibid paras 110, 118, 122.
[128] ibid paras 230–57.
[129] Ukraine–Lithuania BIT (n 116) Art 1(1).
[130] Albania–Finland BIT (n 117) Art 1(1); Netherlands–Turkey BIT (n 33) Art 2(2).
[131] Albania–Finland BIT (n 117) Art 1(1).
[132] Ethiopia–Russia BIT (n 118) Art 2(1); Netherlands–Argentina BIT (n 119) Art 2.
[133] *Inceysa v El Salvador* (n 126) para 110.
[134] ibid para 118.

administrator.[135] The Tribunal concluded that Inceysa's investment 'was made in a manner that was clearly illegal' and that the disputes arising from such investment '[we]re not [therefore] subject to the jurisdiction of the Centre'.[136]

5.76 Legal violations that occur after the investment is 'made' (ie at the post-entry or post-establishment stage), on the other hand, do not in principle affect the legality of the investment. For example, where the investor employs illegal immigrants in violation of the law of the host State or fails to comply with the host State's minimum-wage legislation, these infringements would not cause the investment to be unlawful. Similarly, where the investor declares only part of his or her income, such tax fraud would also not render the investment illegal.

5.77 A situation that has been assimilated to a breach of the host State's rules on establishment consists of the illegality of the activities performed by the investor. If, for example, the investor operates a gambling business, even though this type of activity is prohibited under the law of the host State, such an investment would be considered as unlawful. This was notably recognized by the Tribunal in *Tokios Tokelės v Ukraine*. In this case, the Tribunal rejected the Respondent's illegality-based defence, holding, *inter alia*, that the Respondent had not alleged that 'the Claimant's investment and business activity—advertising, printing, and publishing—[we]re illegal per se'.[137]

3. 'Seriousness' threshold

5.78 It would seem reasonable to hold that not all violations of host State law necessarily cause an investment to be unlawful and that minor infringements should be tolerated. For example, where host State law requires a contract to be registered and a certain number of copies to be provided to the authority in charge, submission of an insufficient number of copies should be considered as a 'minor' defect that does not warrant a denial of treaty protection.[138] Similarly, where the investor slightly 'embellishes' his or her credentials in the context of a bidding process, it would also seem excessive to deprive the investor of protection under the applicable treaty.

5.79 The applicability of a minimum threshold of 'seriousness' has notably been recognized by the Tribunal in *Tokios Tokelės*. In this case, the Respondent argued that the Claimant's investments had not been made in accordance with Ukrainian law.[139] It alleged that the Claimant had registered its company as a 'subsidiary private enterprise', although only 'subsidiary enterprise' was a recognized corporate form in Ukraine.[140] The Respondent also contended that there were 'errors in the documents provided by the Claimant related to asset procurement and transfer, including, in some cases, the

---

[135] ibid para 122.
[136] ibid para 257.
[137] *Tokios Tokelės v Ukraine*, ICSID Case No ARB/02/18, Decision on Jurisdiction (29 April 2004) para 86.
[138] Alternatively, one could take the view that the registration requirement does not relate to the establishment of the investment, but arises at the post-establishment stage.
[139] *Tokios Tokelės v Ukraine* (n 137) para 83.
[140] ibid.

absence of a necessary signature or notarization'.[141] The Tribunal rejected these objections, holding that 'to exclude an investment on the basis of such minor errors would be inconsistent with the object and purpose of the Treaty'.[142]

4. Relevance of State conduct

5.80 The host State's conduct may also be relevant to determine whether a given investment should be regarded as unlawful. In fact, in some cases, the host State may implicitly condone an investment made in violation of host State law. This could be the case, for example, where an investor is granted a construction permit even though he or she does not meet certain legal requirements. In other cases, the host State may have contributed to, or may be primarily responsible for, the investment's illegality. In both types of scenarios, it would be unreasonable to deny protection under the applicable treaty.

5.81 A useful example is *Kardassopoulos v Georgia*. In this case, the Claimant's investment took the form of a joint venture agreement entered into with the Georgian state-owned oil company SakNavtobi[143] and a concession agreement concluded between the joint venture company and Transneft, another Georgian state-owned entity (in charge of Georgia's oil pipelines).[144] In the ICSID proceedings, Georgia claimed that neither SakNavtobi nor Transneft were authorized to grant the rights purportedly conferred under the joint venture and concession agreements[145] and that, as a consequence, the Claimant's investment failed to comply with Georgian law,[146] as required under Art 12 of the BIT between Greece and Georgia.[147] The Tribunal rejected this argument, holding that Georgia could not escape its obligations under the treaty on the grounds of its own illegal conduct.[148] It also noted that the Respondent had not actually 'allege[d] that [the] Claimant committed any violation of Georgian law'.[149]

C. Legality beyond investment treaties

5.82 Legality requirements may apply not only under investment treaties, but also under other consent instruments, ie investment laws and investment contracts. In *Inceysa*, for example, the Claimant relied on two offers of consent: the one contained in the

---

[141] ibid.
[142] ibid para 86.
[143] *Ioannis Kardassopoulos v Georgia*, ICSID Case No ARB/05/18, Decision on Jurisdiction (6 July 2007) paras 20–23 (hereafter *Kardassopoulos v Georgia*).
[144] ibid paras 24–28.
[145] ibid para 50.
[146] ibid para 49.
[147] See Agreement between the Government of the Hellenic Republic and the Government of the Republic of Georgia on the Promotion and Reciprocal Protection of Investments (adopted 9 November 1994, entered into force 3 August 1996) Art 12: 'This Agreement shall also apply to investments made prior to its entry into force by investors of either Contracting Party in the territory of the other Contracting Party, consistent with the latter's legislation.'
[148] *Kardassopoulos v Georgia* (n 143) para 182.
[149] ibid para 183.

applicable BIT and the one found in El Salvador's investment law.[150] Contrary to the treaty, the investment law did not provide for an express legality requirement. However, the Tribunal decided that such a requirement was implicit and that only lawful investments benefited from protection under El Salvador's investment law, including the offer of consent to ICSID arbitration contained therein.[151]

5.83 A requirement of lawfulness may, in theory, also be considered to be implied in contracts concluded between the investor and the host State. In practice, however, it will generally not be necessary to rely on such an implied legality requirement, given that the investor's illegal conduct in principle entails the invalidity of the contract, thus depriving the investor of protection under the contract. In addition, the legality requirement can also be regarded as having an independent legal basis, ie it could be viewed as a general principle of law. This seems to have been the approach adopted by the Tribunal in *World Duty Free v Kenya*.[152] In this case, the Claimant had bribed the President of the Kenyan Republic[153] in order to be awarded a contract for the 'construction, maintenance and operation of duty-free complexes at Nairobi and Mombasa International Airports'.[154] The Tribunal held that such conduct was contrary to both international public policy[155] and English and Kenyan law (the laws governing the contract),[156] that the contract was legally void (or voidable), and that the Claimant was not therefore 'legally entitled to maintain any of its pleaded claims'.[157]

5.84 As has been explained in Chapter 4, the decision of the Tribunal in *Phoenix*[158] may be viewed as affirming the existence of a legality requirement under Art 25 ICSID Convention.[159] In this case, the Tribunal held that a requirement of compliance with host State law could be deduced from the ICSID Convention and the applicable BIT,[160] interpreted 'in light of the general principles of international law'.[161] However, since the Tribunal did not distinguish between the treaty and the ICSID Convention (it seems to have analysed them holistically), it is not clear to what extent it derived the legality requirement from each of these two instruments. Also, one may wonder whether the reference to 'general principles of international law' may suggest that the Tribunal viewed the requirement of lawfulness as such a general principle, ie as a rule that applies

---

[150] *Inceysa v El Salvador* (n 126) paras 130–31.
[151] ibid paras 263–64.
[152] *World Duty Free Company Limited v Republic of Kenya*, ICSID Case No ARB/00/7, Award (25 September 2006).
[153] ibid paras 130–36.
[154] ibid para 62.
[155] ibid paras 138–57.
[156] ibid paras 158–88.
[157] ibid para 188.
[158] *Phoenix Action, Ltd. v The Czech Republic*, ICSID Case No ARB/06/5, Award (15 April 2009) (hereafter *Phoenix v Czech Republic*).
[159] Schill, Schreuer and Sinclair, 'Article 25' (n 5) para 472 (noting that 'the *Phoenix* award is often viewed as lending support to the position that a legality ... requirement must be read into the notion of investment under Art 25(1) of the Convention').
[160] *Phoenix v Czech Republic* (n 158) paras 101–05.
[161] ibid para 99.

independently of the legal frameworks established by the Convention and the BIT. The exact meaning of the *Phoenix* ruling is impossible to ascertain.

5.85 Schill, Schreuer, and Sinclair reject the idea that Art 25 ICSID Convention lays down a requirement of compliance with host State law (they do not deny, however, that illegality issues may be relevant at the merits stage). Noting that Art 25 is 'silent' on this issue, they argue that '[r]eading such [a] requirement[...] into the notion of investment in Art. 25(1) of the ICSID Convention' would be incompatible with the Vienna Convention on the Law of Treaties' (VCLT) rules of treaty interpretation.[162] This argument is not entirely convincing. In fact, as has been seen, a number of tribunals have recognized the applicability of implied legality requirements under treaties that do not contain express provisions to this effect, an approach which the authors discuss, but do not object to. It is difficult to understand why it would be permissible to read a requirement of legality into investment treaties, but not into the ICSID Convention. More specifically, there is nothing unreasonable about considering that the drafters of the ICSID Convention only intended to make the Centre's services available to investors that have made lawful investments in the host State.

VI. Requirement that the Investment be 'Actively' Made by the Investor

A. Overview

5.86 As has already been explained, investments are in principle only protected under investment treaties if they are 'owned' or 'controlled' by a covered investor. Such ownership or control is not, however, the only nexus between investment and investor that arbitral tribunals have required. In fact, a few tribunals have held that, in addition to being owned or controlled by an investor, investments must be 'actively' made. In other words, only 'active' investments enjoy treaty protection; passive investments are not covered.[163]

5.87 The requirement of an 'active' investment is rather ambiguous. This is partly due to the fact that the criteria mentioned in the relevant decisions, if any, are not entirely clear. It is also due to the absence of a unanimous understanding of this requirement among the tribunals that have recognized its existence. More generally, as will be shown below, the conceptual distinction between active and passive investment is per se ambiguous.

---

[162] Article 25 (n 5) para 479.
[163] For commentary on this requirement, see Christoph Schreuer, 'The Active Investor' in Eric Bylander, Anna Jonsson Cornell and Jakob Ragnwaldh (eds), *Forward! Essays in Honour of Prof Dr Kaj Hobér* (Iustus Förlag 2019) 237; Jean Ho, 'Passive Investments' (2020) 35 ICSID Rev/FILJ 523.

B. Textual foundations of the requirement

The requirement of an active investment can be derived from three types of treaty provisions. It can, first of all, be based on clauses under which an investment must be 'made' by an investor. The BIT between Switzerland and the Philippines, for example, specifies that it applies to 'investments in the territory of one Contracting Party *made* ... by investors of the other Contracting Party'.[164] Similarly, the BIT between the United Arab Emirates and Israel defines 'investment' as 'every kind of asset, *made* in accordance with the legislation of the Party in whose territory the investment is *made* ...'.[165]

5.88

An active investment requirement can also be found to apply under provisions referring to the (somewhat tautological) idea that the investor must have 'invested' an investment. Such language can notably be found in the BIT between Spain and Venezuela which defines 'investment' as 'any type of asset *invested* by investors of one Contracting Party in the territory of the other Contracting Party'.[166] The BIT between Kazakhstan and Uzbekistan contains a similar provision, defining 'investments' as 'any kind of property and the rights thereto ... *invested* by the investors of one Contracting Party in the territory of the other Contracting Party'.[167]

5.89

Lastly, provisions defining the connection between investor and investment through expressions such as 'investment *of* an investor' or 'investment *by* an investor' can also be viewed as implying an active investment requirement. The BIT between the United Kingdom and Tanzania provides useful examples of these two types of norms. A reference to 'investment *of* an investor' can be found in the Treaty's definition of the scope of jurisdiction of investor–state arbitral tribunals.[168] The expression 'investment *by* an investor' is used in the provision specifying that the Treaty does not exclude the application of more favourable rules.[169]

5.90

These three types of provisions can all be considered to entail a requirement that an investment be 'actively' made by the investor. In fact, it is a priori sensible to construe the verbs 'make' and 'invest' as denoting some activity beyond mere ownership and control. In other words, an investor must not only 'have', but also 'do' something. It is similarly reasonable to hold that the preposition 'by' in the expression 'investment by

5.91

---

[164] See Agreement between the Republic of the Philippines and the Swiss Confederation on the Promotion and Reciprocal Protection of Investments (adopted 31 March 1997, entered into force 23 April 1999) Art II (emphasis added).
[165] See Agreement between the Government of the State of Israel and the Government of the United Arab Emirates on Promotion and Protection of Investments (adopted 20 October 2020, not in force) Sect. A (emphasis added).
[166] See Agreement between the Kingdom of Spain and the Republic of Venezuela on the Promotion and Reciprocal Protection of Investments (adopted 2 November 1995, entered into force 10 September 1997) Art 1(2) (emphasis added, translation by the author).
[167] Kazakhstan–Uzbekistan BIT (n 35) Art 1(2).
[168] See Agreement between the Government of the United Kingdom of Great Britain and Northern Ireland and the Government of the United Republic of Tanzania for the Promotion and Protection of Investments (adopted 7 January 1994, entered into force 2 August 1996) Art 8(1) (emphasis added).
[169] ibid Art 11 (emphasis added).

an investor' identifies the agent performing an action, thus also implying some active behaviour on the part of investor. A similar argument can be raised, though far less convincingly, in connection with the preposition 'of' in the expression 'investment of an investor'.

C. Recognition and meaning of the requirement

5.92 One decision having required an active investment is the ruling of the Tribunal in *Standard Chartered v Tanzania*.[170] In this case, a consortium of Malaysian lenders issued a loan to finance the construction of a power plant in Tanzania.[171] The consortium's rights under the loan were subsequently acquired by a subsidiary of the Claimant, Standard Chartered Bank (Hong Kong) Limited.[172] In the ICSID proceedings, brought under the BIT between the United Kingdom and Tanzania, the Respondent raised several jurisdictional objections, arguing *inter alia* that the only investor was the Hong Kong entity and that the Claimant itself had not 'made' any investment.[173]

5.93 As has already been explained, the BIT between the United Kingdom and Tanzania refers to investments 'of' and investments 'by' investors. Relying on this language, the *Standard Chartered* tribunal found that the treaty 'protect[ed] investments "made" by an investor in some active way, rather than simple passive ownership'.[174] It further observed that, in order to prove the existence of an active investment, a claimant had to establish that 'the investment was made at [its] direction, that [it] funded the investment or that [it] controlled the investment in an active and direct manner'.[175] The Tribunal held that this requirement was not met in the case before it.[176]

5.94 Another case in which a requirement of an active investment was found to exist is *Clorox v Venezuela*.[177] Although the award has apparently only been published in the original Spanish language, scholarly analysis is available in English.[178] In this case, the US corporation Clorox International established Clorox Spain and transferred all of its shares in Clorox Venezuela (the investment) to the Spanish entity, apparently for the sole purpose of benefiting from protection under the BIT between Spain and Venezuela.[179] This treaty, as has already been seen, defines investments as assets 'invested' by investors, and the Tribunal concluded that, therefore, an actual 'action of investing' was required. According to the Tribunal, the transfer of shares from Clorox International to Clorox

---

[170] *Standard Chartered Bank v United Republic of Tanzania*, ICSID Case No ARB/10/12, Award (2 November 2012).
[171] ibid para 28.
[172] ibid para 40.
[173] ibid paras 70–80.
[174] ibid para 225.
[175] ibid para 230.
[176] ibid paras 257–66.
[177] *Clorox Spain S.L. v Bolivarian Republic of Venezuela*, PCA Case No 2015-30, Award (20 May 2019).
[178] See, for example, Salacuse, *The Law of Investment Treaties* (n 17) 211–12.
[179] ibid 211.

Spain did not amount to any 'real act of investing or economic exchange' as required under the treaty.[180]

Overall, however, it appears that a majority of tribunals have considered that no requirement of an active investment can be inferred from references to investments 'made' or 'invested' by investors, or to investments 'of' or 'by' investors.[181] In *Orascom v Algeria*,[182] for instance, the Respondent argued that 'the mere holding of an indirect shareholding in [a locally incorporated company] [did] not constitute an investment ... pursuant to the [applicable] BIT',[183] the BIT between the Belgo-Luxembourg Economic Union and Algeria. The Tribunal rejected this assertion, ruling that '[n]o active involvement [was] required under the BIT'[184] and that treaty protection extended to indirect shareholding.[185] In *Kim v Uzbekistan*,[186] a case that also involved indirect shareholding,[187] the Respondent similarly contended that the applicable treaty (the BIT between Kazakhstan and Uzbekistan) required an 'active relationship' between investor and investment and, more particularly, a 'specific action [by the investor] involving substantial contribution and risk to make his or her investment'.[188] The Tribunal disagreed with this view, holding that it was not necessary for the investor to have 'an ongoing "active" role in the investment'.[189]

D. Assessment of the requirement

The requirement of an active investment suffers from several defects. First of all, it lacks a generally accepted meaning. In fact, according to the *Standard Chartered* tribunal, this requirement essentially consists of a direct ownership requirement, subject to limited exceptions. The *Clorox* tribunal, on the other hand, appears to have a different understanding of this concept. Denying investment status to shares assigned by the original investor, it seems to view the requirement of an active investment as excluding treaty protection of investments that the original investor assigns to third parties.

In light of the inherent ambiguity of the notion of active investment, it is not excluded that, in addition to the views held by the *Standard Chartered* and *Clorox* tribunals, other approaches may be followed in the future. Tribunals could, for example, hold that an investment is 'active' if the investor not only owns or controls the relevant assets, but also

---

[180] ibid 211–12.
[181] Schill, Schreuer and Sinclair, 'Article 25' (n 5) para 366 (noting that 'the majority of investment tribunals faced with arguments that the protection of an investment required an active contribution by the current owner rejected such an approach').
[182] *Orascom TMT Investments S.à r.l. v People's Democratic Republic of Algeria*, ICSID Case No ARB/12/35, Award (31 May 2017).
[183] ibid para 327.
[184] ibid para 384.
[185] ibid.
[186] *Kim v Uzbekistan* (n 47).
[187] ibid paras 126–41.
[188] ibid para 306.
[189] ibid para 310.

actively manages or uses those assets in connection with economic activities. The likely implication of such an approach is that FDI would in principle qualify as investment, while portfolios investments most probably would not.

5.98 Second, the recognition of an active investment requirement is incompatible with the well-established principle that indirect investments are protected under investment treaties. In fact, as has been seen, the Tribunal in *Standard Chartered* essentially equated the active investment requirement with direct ownership by the presumed investor. However, as has also been explained, most investment treaties expressly recognize the investment status of indirect (or indirectly owned) investments.[190] The requirement of an active investment thus conflicts with the predominant approach in investment treaty practice.

5.99 Third, under *Clorox*, the requirement of an active investment entails that only the initial investment and investor are protected, not the investments of subsequent owners who acquire the investment by way of transfer or assignment. Where, for example, a company of country A establishes a subsidiary in country B to manufacture goods, this operation (or the assets owned by the company) would qualify as an investment. However, if the company sells its business, the buyer would in principle not be protected because he or she would not him- or herself have made any investment in the host State. In other words, an investment would cease to be an investment when the investor sells it to a third party.

E. Requirement of an active investment under Art 25 ICSID Convention?

5.100 Art 25 ICSID Convention does not contain any language suggesting that the Convention only applies to 'active' investments.[191] Yet, according to distinguished writers, several tribunals have arguably applied such a requirement.[192] The relevant decisions do not, however, *expressly* refer to the concept of an active investment. Instead, they have relied on the *Salini* test's contribution criterion in order to deny investment status to company shares. In one case, the ruling seems to have been motivated by the suspiciously low amount paid to acquire those shares;[193] in the other, the fact that the share transfer occurred between two entities owned by the same individual appears to have played a central role.[194]

---

[190] See Section III.C.
[191] See Convention on the Settlement of Investment Disputes between States and Nationals of Other States (adopted 18 March 1965, entered into force 14 October 1966) Art 25(1). This provision defines the Centre's scope of jurisdiction as covering 'any legal dispute arising directly out of an investment, between a Contracting State ... and a national of another Contracting State'. It nowhere refers to the nature of the relationship that exists (or must exist) between an investor and his or her presumed investment.
[192] See Schill, Schreuer and Sinclair, 'Article 25' (n 5) paras 362, 365.
[193] See *Caratube International Oil Company LLP v Republic of Kazakhstan*, ICSID Case No ARB/08/12, Award (5 June 2012) paras 408, 437, 455.
[194] See *KT Asia Investment Group B.V. v Republic of Kazakhstan*, ICSID Case No ARB/09/8, Award (17 October 2013) paras 14, 206.

6
Recent Developments in Treaty and Arbitral Practice

I. Introduction	6.01	C. Assets not connected to any economic or business activity	6.36
II. Enterprise-Based Definitions of Investment	6.04	D. Sovereign debt instruments	6.39
III. Requirement that an Investment must Present Certain 'Characteristics'	6.12	V. Arbitral Recognition of an 'Objective' or 'Implied' Meaning of the Concept of Investment under Investment Treaties	6.42
A. Meaning and trend	6.12	A. Overview	6.42
B. Comparison with the *Salini* criteria	6.16	B. Decisions rendered by non-ICSID tribunals	6.44
C. Assessment	6.20	C. Decisions rendered by ICSID tribunals	6.54
IV. Exclusions	6.25	D. Assessment	6.66
A. Commercial transactions	6.25		
B. Portfolio investments	6.30		

I. Introduction

Over the past ten to fifteen years, a number of significant developments have occurred and/or gained momentum, both in the way in which 'investment' is defined in investment treaties and in the manner in which arbitral tribunals have construed such treaty definitions. The common feature of these developments is that they have led to the application of a more restrictive notion of investment. This evolution arguably reflects widespread concerns that traditional treaty definitions are unduly broad and/or ambiguous, leading to undesirable outcomes and unpredictable decisions.   **6.01**

Section II discusses the increasingly frequent adoption of enterprise-based, rather than asset-based, definitions of 'investment'. Section III examines the by now prevalent requirement that investments must possess certain 'characteristics'. Interestingly, those characteristics overlap to a large extent with the *Salini* criteria applied under Art 25 ICSID Convention, and this requirement can therefore be viewed as an incorporation of the *Salini* test into investment treaty definitions. Section IV explores common exclusions found in investment treaties, namely, the exclusion of (1) commercial contracts and/or the rights arising under such contracts, (2) portfolio investments, (3) assets that lack a connection with an economic activity in the host State, and (4) sovereign debt instruments.   **6.02**

6.03 Unlike Sections II–IV, Section V deals not with a development in treaty practice, but with a trend in arbitral interpretation. Specifically, it analyses case law that has considered that the notion of investment under investment treaties, like the term 'investment' under Art 25 ICSID Convention, has an 'objective' or 'implied' meaning. This trend leads to the application of the *Salini* criteria under investment treaties, thus producing an effect similar to the characteristics-requirements examined in Section III.

II. Enterprise-Based Definitions of Investment

6.04 As has been explained in Chapter 5,[1] definitions of 'investment' contained in investment treaties have traditionally been asset-based. Between 1990 and 2009, 2,059 out of 2,069 investment treaties mapped in the United Nations Conference on Trade and Development's (UNCTAD's) investment treaty database featured such definitions.[2] Only six treaties (0.28 per cent of all mapped treaties) used enterprise-based definitions; four treaties did not contain any definition of 'investment'.[3]

6.05 In recent years, however, enterprise-based definitions have become significantly more popular, with four out of fifty-three mapped treaties concluded between 2015 and 2019 (7.5 per cent of the relevant treaties) containing such definitions.[4] While enterprise-based definitions are thus no longer exceptional, they are also clearly far from being prevalent. Discussing this state of affairs, distinguished commentators have noted that enterprise-based definitions of 'investment' 'ha[ve] found little resonance so far in actual treaty practice'.[5]

6.06 An example of an enterprise-based definition is Art 1 of the bilateral investment treaty (BIT) between Morocco and Nigeria[6] which defines 'investment' as 'an enterprise within the territory of one State established, acquired, expanded or operated ... by an investor of the other State... taken together with the asset (sic!) of the enterprise....'[7] This definition is supplemented by a list of several categories of assets that enterprises are considered to 'possess'.[8] Under this definition, the notion of 'investment' thus covers enterprises and specified categories of assets owned by enterprises.

---

[1] See Chapter 5 Section II.
[2] UNCTAD, 'International Investment Agreements Navigator' <https://investmentpolicy.unctad.org/international-investment-agreements/iia-mapping> accessed 13 February 2023 (hereafter UNCTAD, 'International Investment Agreements Navigator').
[3] ibid.
[4] ibid.
[5] See Stephan W Schill, Christoph Schreuer and Anthony Sinclair, 'Article 25' in Loretta Malintoppi, August Reinisch, Christoph H Schreuer and Anthony Sinclair (eds), *Schreuer's Commentary on the ICSID Convention: A Commentary on the Convention on the Settlement of Investment Disputes between States and Nationals of Other States* (3rd edn, Cambridge University Press 2022) para 222.
[6] See Reciprocal Investment Promotion and Protection Agreement between the Government of the Kingdom of Morocco and the Government of the Federal Republic of Nigeria (adopted 3 December 2016, not in force) Art 1 (hereafter Morocco–Nigeria BIT).
[7] ibid.
[8] ibid.

In a number of treaties, the definitions of 'investment' are not 'pure' enterprise-based definitions, but rather 'mixed' enterprise- and asset-based ones. An example is the definition contained in the BIT between Austria and Kyrgyzstan,[9] somewhat inaccurately labelled as 'enterprise-based' in the UNCTAD investment treaty database.[10] In fact, although the investment status of enterprises and 'shares, stock and other forms of equity participation' in enterprises is expressly recognized,[11] the definition is formally asset-based[12] and extends to various categories of assets unrelated to enterprises.[13]

Most treaties containing enterprise-based definitions of 'investment' specify the meaning of 'enterprise'. The BIT between Austria and Kyrgyzstan, for example, defines 'enterprise' as 'any legal entity or other organisation constituted or organised under the national law of a Contracting Party',[14] citing a variety of legal forms (corporations, partnerships, joint ventures, trusts, sole proprietorships, and branches) as examples of such enterprises.[15] The BIT between Canada and Mongolia defines the concept of 'enterprise' in largely identical terms as: '1. any entity constituted or organized under applicable law ... including any corporation, trust, partnership, joint venture or other association; and 2. a branch of any such entity'.[16]

Some treaties adopting enterprise-based definitions, however, fail to define the concept of 'enterprise'. The BIT between Morocco and Nigeria, for instance, is silent with regard to the meaning of this term. It is thus not clear whether this notion should be given the meaning it has under definitions found in other treaties (which generally view enterprises as legal entities) or whether a different interpretation should be adopted. In fact, based on the ordinary meaning of 'enterprise', it would be possible to construe this term more broadly, ie not as a legal entity established in the host State, but as a project or undertaking.[17]

The specific implications of enterprise-based definitions depend on whether they are 'pure' or 'mixed' ones. The 'pure' enterprise-based definition contained in the Morocco–Nigeria BIT, for example, appears to require that the investor own an enterprise (assuming that the term 'enterprise' refers to a legal entity); partial ownership does not seem to be sufficient. This definition therefore excludes not only portfolio investments, but also those forms of foreign direct investment (FDI) in which the investor is not the

---

[9] See Agreement for the Promotion and Protection of Investment between the Government of the Republic of Austria and the Government of the Kyrgyz Republic (adopted 22 April 2016, entered into force 1 October 2017) Art 1(2) (hereafter Austria–Kyrgyzstan BIT).
[10] UNCTAD, 'International Investment Agreements Navigator' (n 2).
[11] Austria–Kyrgyzstan BIT (n 9) Art 1(2)(a) and (b).
[12] ibid Art 1(2) (providing that 'investment' means 'every kind of asset in the territory of one Contracting Party, owned or controlled, directly or indirectly, by an investor of the other Contracting Party').
[13] ibid Art 1(2)(c)–(f).
[14] ibid Art 1(3).
[15] ibid.
[16] See Agreement between Canada and Mongolia for the Promotion and Protection of Investments (adopted 8 September 2016, entered into force 24 February 2017) Art 1 (hereafter Canada–Mongolia BIT).
[17] See *Oxford English Dictionary* (3rd edn, 2018) defining 'enterprise' as an 'undertaking, task, or project; (usually) spec. one which is bold, difficult, or important; a venture, an endeavour'.

exclusive owner or shareholder of the enterprise concerned. This concept of investment is thus significantly narrower than the one established under traditional asset-based definitions.

6.11 Mixed enterprise- and asset-based definitions of investment are, in contrast, much less restrictive. In fact, since they recognize the investment status of both enterprises and assets (and since enterprises can be considered as a particular category of asset), these definitions are generally as broad as traditional asset-based definitions. Under the Canada–Mongolia BIT, for example, the concept of 'investment' is not actually defined; the treaty merely lists a catalogue of 'items' that constitute investments.[18] These items notably include 'an enterprise' and several enterprise-related assets such as equity participations in, and debt instruments of, an enterprise.[19] However, the treaty also lists various other types of assets, including a particularly broad category comprising 'any ... tangible or intangible, moveable or immovable, property and related property rights acquired in the expectation of or used for the purpose of economic benefit or other business purpose'.[20] This catch-all category arguably covers all types of assets.

III. Requirement that an Investment must Present Certain 'Characteristics'

A. Meaning and trend

6.12 While there may be occasional drafting variations, most investment treaties requiring that investments possess specific characteristics use almost identical language. A representative example is the US Model BIT which defines 'investment' as 'every asset that an investor owns or controls ... *that has the characteristics of an investment, including such characteristics as the commitment of capital or other resources, the expectation of gain or profit, or the assumption of risk*'.[21]

6.13 Largely identical characteristics-requirements can notably be found in treaties entered into by the United States in the 2000s, including, for example, the BITs concluded with Rwanda[22] and Uruguay.[23] Other treaties containing such definitions of investment include, for example, the BIT between Hungary and Oman,[24] the BIT between Japan

---

[18] Canada–Mongolia BIT (n 16) Art 1.
[19] ibid.
[20] ibid.
[21] US Model BIT 2012 Art 1 (emphasis added).
[22] Treaty between the Government of the United States and the Government of the Republic of Rwanda Concerning the Encouragement and Reciprocal Protection of Investment (adopted 19 February 2008, entered into force 1 January 2012) Art 1.
[23] Treaty between the United States of America and the Oriental Republic of Uruguay Concerning the Encouragement and Reciprocal Protection of Investment (adopted 4 November 2005, entered into force 31 October 2006) Art 1 (hereafter US–Uruguay BIT).
[24] Agreement between the Government of the Sultanate of Oman and the Government of Hungary for the Promotion and Reciprocal Protection of Investments (adopted 2 February 2022, not in force) Art 1(1) (hereafter Oman–Hungary BIT).

and Georgia,[25] and the Free Trade Agreement between the United Kingdom and New Zealand.[26]

Treaties providing for characteristics-requirements sometimes clarify under which circumstances certain operations and/or assets are likely to possess the relevant characteristics. The United States–Uruguay BIT, for instance, specifies that '[s]ome forms of debt, such as bonds, debentures, and long-term notes are more likely to have the characteristics of an investment' than others, such as 'a bank account that does not have a commercial purpose and is related neither to an investment ... nor to an attempt to make such an investment'.[27] The same treaty also contains a clarification regarding the investment status of licences, authorizations, permits, and similar instruments, stating that relevant factors notably include 'the nature and extent of the rights that the holder has under the law of the '[host State]'.[28]

6.14

Characteristics-requirements were largely absent from treaties concluded in the 1990s and 2000s, with only 24 out of 2,069 treaties mapped in UNCTAD investment treaty database (ie approximately 1 per cent) featuring such a requirement.[29] Today, however, it is a well-established feature of definitions of 'investment' found in the majority of investment treaties. In fact, between 2015 and 2019, twenty-nine out of fifty-three mapped treaties (ie approximately 55 per cent) provided for such a requirement.[30]

6.15

B. Comparison with the *Salini* criteria

As has been noted by some scholars, the characteristics mentioned in the relevant treaty definitions share a number of similarities with the *Salini* criteria elaborated under Art 25 ICSID Convention.[31] In fact, two of the three core *Salini* requirements are expressly referred to in such provisions, namely, the existence of a contribution and risk. As regards the former, it is true that treaty definitions do not usually employ the term 'contribution' but prefer the expression 'commitment of capital or other resources'.[32] However, there does not appear to be any substantial difference between such expressions and the *Salini* concept of a contribution, given that the *Salini* case law similarly considers that contributions may take the form of money and/or other 'resources'.[33] Also, it is worth

6.16

---

[25] Agreement between Japan and Georgia for the Liberalisation, Promotion and Protection of Investment (adopted 29 January 2021, entered into force 23 July 2021) Art 1(a).
[26] Free Trade Agreement between the United Kingdom of Great Britain and Northern Ireland and New Zealand (adopted 28 February 2022, not in force) Art 14(2).
[27] US–Uruguay BIT (n 23) n 1.
[28] ibid n 3.
[29] UNCTAD, 'International Investment Agreements Navigator' (n 2).
[30] ibid.
[31] See Jeswald W Salacuse, *The Law of Investment Treaties* (3rd edn, Oxford University Press 2021) 216 (noting that the language of characteristics-requirements is 'reminiscent' of the *Salini* test) (hereafter Salacuse, *The Law of Investment Treaties*).
[32] See, for example, US Model BIT Art 1.
[33] See Chapter 4 Section II.B.1.

recalling that the term 'commitment' was used in *Fedax*,[34] one of the two founding decisions of the *Salini* case law.[35]

6.17 There are, however, also differences between treaty-based characteristics-requirements and the *Salini* criteria. One such difference is that the relevant treaty definitions do not generally recognize—at least not expressly—the relevance of the duration requirement applied under the *Salini* test. In light of the various flaws of this requirement that have been highlighted in Chapter 4,[36] its rejection (or rather non-inclusion) as a characteristic feature of investment is understandable and should be welcomed.

6.18 The other difference is that the characteristics mentioned in the relevant treaty definitions include 'the expectation of gain or profit', a criterion that does not form part of the three core *Salini* criteria. It is true that one occasionally recognized *Salini* factor consists of the somewhat similar requirement of 'regularity of profit and return'.[37] However, this criterion differs significantly from the idea that an investment must be made in 'the expectation of gain or profit' since it requires not only the *pursuit* of profit, but the actual *realization* of such profit. Moreover, it also requires that profits be made at regular intervals. As has been explained in Chapter 4, this *Salini* criterion is unreasonably demanding,[38] and it is preferable to only require that an investment is made with the *objective* of making a profit. The inclusion of such a characteristic feature is appropriate because it reflects the ordinary meaning of the term 'investment'[39] and ensures that non-professional or non-commercial purchases (eg the acquisition of a vacation home) are not considered as investments.

6.19 Beyond the comparison of the specific criteria that apply under treaty-based characteristics-requirements and the *Salini* test, it is worth noting that the former appear to share the flexible nature of the typical-characteristics approach which—as has been explained in Chapters 3 and 4—rejects the idea that the *Salini* criteria constitute jurisdictional requirements.[40] This is suggested not only by the use of the term 'characteristics', but also by the fact that the three listed factors are typically linked by the conjunction 'or'. As authoritative writers have noted in connection with the US Model BIT of 2012, this implies that a particular asset or operation does not need to possess all mentioned characteristics in order to qualify as an investment.[41]

---

[34] *Fedax N.V. v The Republic of Venezuela*, ICSID Case No ARB/96/3, Decision of the Tribunal on Objections to Jurisdiction (11 July 1997) para 43.
[35] See Chapter 4 Section II.A.1.
[36] See Chapter 4 Section II.B.2.
[37] See Chapter 4 Section II.D.1.
[38] ibid.
[39] See Chapter 2 Section VI.
[40] See Chapter 3 Section III.D and Chapter 4 Section II.A.3.
[41] See Lee M Caplan and Jeremy K Sharpe, 'United States' in Chester Brown (ed), *Commentaries on Selected Model Investment Treaties* (Oxford University Press 2013) 755, 767 (observing that '[i]n practice, most "investments" will likely have at least two, if not all three, of these characteristics, though they need not in order to come within the scope of the definition') (hereafter Caplan and Sharpe, 'United States').

C. Assessment

6.20 The similarity between the characteristics required under (certain) treaty definitions of 'investment' and the *Salini* criteria raises the question of whether these definitions can be considered to have originated from the *Salini* case law, ie whether the treaty drafters have consciously chosen to incorporate (slightly amended versions of) the *Salini* test into treaty definitions. In addition to the evident similarity between the two sets of characteristics, the timeline suggests such a possibility. As far as the US Model BIT is concerned, for example, it is interesting to note that the pre-*Salini* version of 1994 does not contain any reference to the characteristics that an investment possesses or must possess,[42] while the first post-*Salini* version of the Model BIT—like the current one—does include such a reference.[43]

6.21 Treaty definitions requiring investments to have certain characteristics are very insightful because they reveal the contracting States' views on the strengths and weaknesses of the *Salini* test under Art 25 ICSID Convention. As has been seen, these treaties provide support for the appropriateness of the test's contribution and risk criteria. At the same time, they also seem to reject the *Salini* requirement of a minimum duration, as well as other less frequently recognized objective criteria, including the requirement of a contribution to the host State's economic development. Whether or not these criteria are in fact rejected is, however, uncertain, given that treaty-based lists of typical characteristics of an investment are generally not exhaustive, but merely illustrative.[44]

6.22 The similarity between treaty-based characteristics and the *Salini* criteria also raises the question of whether the *Salini* case law can be used to interpret the meaning of the different characteristics and/or to supplement those characteristics. One may ask, for example, whether the distinction between investment and commercial risk elaborated under Art 25 ICSID Convention[45] can be applied by analogy in connection with the risk-characteristic found in treaty definitions. Similarly, one may ask whether it is permissible or appropriate to add further characteristics such as, for example, the existence of a contribution to the economic development of the host State.

6.23 One may also wonder what impact the current proliferation of treaty definitions containing characteristics-requirements will have on the application of the *Salini* test under Art 25 ICSID Convention. If very similar criteria apply under the governing treaty, arbitral tribunals may be reluctant to apply a largely identical test under the Convention. Ultimately, there is a possibility that ICSID tribunals will start questioning

---

[42] See US Model BIT 1994 Art 1(d).
[43] See US Model BIT 2004 Art 1.
[44] Caplan and Sharpe, 'United States' (n 41) 767. Discussing the US Model BIT of 2012, the authors note that '[t]he phrase "including such characteristics as" [used in the definition of 'investment' contained in the Model BIT] indicates that the list is merely illustrative').
[45] See Chapter 4 Section II.B.3.

the soundness of the objective approach under Art 25 ICSID Convention and that treaty-based characteristics-requirements will replace the *Salini* test.

6.24 Lastly, it should be mentioned that treaty-based characteristics-requirements present a conceptual flaw. As has already been explained, the *Salini* test implicitly assumes that investments consist of operations or activities, not assets. The same observation can be made with respect to treaty lists of characteristics of an investment. However, since those lists typically form part of asset-based definitions of 'investment', it is therefore the different assets that must have the mentioned characteristics. The problem is that it means very little to say that a particular asset (such as, for example, a plot of land, shares in a company, industrial machinery, or contractual rights) is *characterized* by 'the commitment of capital or other resources, the expectation of gain or profit, or the assumption of risk'. In fact, those features do not appropriately characterize individual assets, but rather investment projects, activities, or operations. Regrettably, characteristics-requirements contained in investment treaties thus perpetuate the existing ambiguity affecting the question of the nature of investment.

IV. Exclusions

A. Commercial transactions

6.25 A number of recent investment treaties expressly provide that commercial agreements and/or the rights arising under such agreements do not qualify as investments. The BIT between Canada and Guinea, for example, clarifies that the term 'investment' does not cover 'a claim to money that arises solely from ... a commercial contract for the sale of a good or service'.[46] The BIT between the United Kingdom and Colombia contains an almost identical exclusion.[47]

6.26 Some treaties not only expressly deny investment status to rights arising under commercial contracts, but also provide guidance as to what types of contracts constitute, or may constitute, investments. Under the Canada–Guinea BIT, for example, contracts involving a 'commitment of capital or other resources ... to an economic activity in [the territory of the host State]' qualify as investments if they entail 'the presence of an investor's property in the territory [of the host State]' or if 'remuneration depends substantially on the production, revenues or profits of an enterprise'.[48] The treaty lists turnkey, construction, and concession contracts as examples of transactions meeting the former requirement.[49]

---

[46] Agreement for the Promotion and Reciprocal Protection of Investments between Canada and the Republic of Guinea (adopted 27 May 2015, entered into force 27 March 2017) Art 1 (hereafter Canada–Guinea BIT).
[47] Bilateral Agreement for the Promotion and Protection of Investments between the Government of the United Kingdom of Great Britain and Northern Ireland and Republic of Colombia (adopted 17 March 2010, entered into force 10 October 2014) Art I(2)(b)(ii) (hereafter UK–Colombia BIT).
[48] Canada–Guinea BIT (n 46) Art 1.
[49] ibid.

6.27 Express exclusions of rights arising under commercial contracts are arguably due to the fact that such rights would in principle be covered by traditional asset-based definitions of 'investment'. In fact, as has been seen,[50] those definitions do not impose any limits on the categories of assets that qualify as investments and often expressly recognize the investment status of contractual and similar rights.[51]

6.28 One may argue that such treaty exclusions are unnecessary given that rights arising under commercial agreements are, in any event, unlikely to satisfy the objective requirements of Art 25 ICSID Convention. It is indeed plausible that such rights do not meet the *Salini* requirements of a contribution, a minimum duration, and risk, especially if demanding and investment-specific thresholds are applied. Also, it almost goes without saying that rights under commercial contracts would be excluded from Art 25 under the commercial-transaction test occasionally applied by investment tribunals.

6.29 Such an argument would, however, be uncompelling. In fact, there is no certainty as to how individual tribunals will construe Art 25 ICSID Convention. In particular, it cannot be excluded that a given tribunal will either altogether deny the existence of objective requirements under this provision or adopt a broad and/or flexible interpretation (eg by applying the permissibility test discussed in Chapter 4). Also, Art 25 ICSID Convention obviously only applies in the context of ICSID proceedings, ie the *Salini* test does not in principle have to be complied with in non-ICSID cases.

B. Portfolio investments

6.30 An increasing number of investment treaties expressly exclude portfolio investments. Traditionally, such exclusions have been extremely rare. In fact, between 1990 and 2009, only 8 out of 2,069 treaties mapped in the UNCTAD investment treaty database, ie less than 0.4 per cent, contained such provisions.[52] This proportion has risen significantly in recent years. In fact, between 2015 and 2019, eleven out of fifty-three mapped treaties (ie more than 20 per cent) featured such exclusions.[53]

6.31 Portfolio investments are excluded, for example, under the Morocco–Nigeria BIT. Art 1 of this treaty specifies that, '[f]or greater certainty, Investment does not include ... b) Portfolio investments'.[54] The BIT between India and Brazil contains a very similar provision, excluding from its scope—somewhat ambiguously—'portfolio investments of the enterprise or in another enterprise'.[55] Another example is the BIT between Turkey

---

[50] See Chapter 5 Section II.
[51] See, for example, Agreement between the Government of the United Kingdom of Great Britain and Northern Ireland and the Government of Malaysia for the Promotion and Protection of Investments (adopted 21 May 1981, entered into force 21 October 1988) Art 1(1)(a)(iii) (listing 'claims to money or to any performance under contract having a financial value' as an example of an asset qualifying as an investment).
[52] UNCTAD, 'International Investment Agreements Navigator' (n 2).
[53] ibid.
[54] Morocco–Nigeria BIT (n 6) Art 1.
[55] Investment Cooperation and Facilitation Treaty between the Federative Republic of Brazil and the Republic of India (adopted 25 January 2020, not in force) Art 2(4)(1) (hereafter Brazil–India BIT).

and Cambodia. While it does not expressly refer to the notion of portfolio investment, the exclusion of 'the acquisition of shares or voting power amounting to, or representing of (sic!) less than ten (10) percent of a company'[56] most probably targets this form of investment.

6.32 Some treaties excluding portfolio investments fail to define this concept. The Morocco–Nigeria and Brazil–India BITs, for example, are silent with regard to the meaning of the term 'portfolio investment'.[57] Arbitral tribunals called upon to apply these exclusions are thus likely to refer to internationally accepted definitions (such as the OECD benchmark definition[58]) and the corresponding thresholds.

6.33 Other treaties, by contrast, provide definitions of the term 'portfolio investment'. As has been mentioned, the Turkey–Cambodia BIT specifies that 'shares or voting power' of less than 10 per cent of a company do not qualify as investments,[59] thus implicitly defining portfolio investment by reference to the generally accepted 10 per cent threshold. Other definitions do not refer to any precise numerical threshold. The BIT between Brazil and the United Arab Emirates, for example, defines portfolio investments as 'those that do not allow the investor to exert a significant degree of influence in the management of the enterprise or in another enterprise'.[60]

6.34 Like exclusions of rights arising under commercial agreements, exclusions of portfolio investments are intended to restrict the scope of the notion of investment. More specifically, such exclusions arguably reflect the perception that portfolio investments, unlike FDI, do not bring about any meaningful economic benefits for host States.[61] Whether such an assumption is correct is debatable. In fact, it is unlikely that a portfolio investment in an amount of, say, EUR 10 million benefits the host State's economy less than the purchase of a 20 per cent shareholding in a local company (which would not constitute a portfolio investment and would thus in principle be covered under the applicable treaty) worth EUR 1 million. There does not appear to be any obvious correlation between the investor's ability to exercise control over the management of a particular company and possible beneficial effects for the host State's economy.

6.35 To the extent that exclusions of portfolio investments are intended to limit the application of the treaty to FDI, it would in principle be necessary to use them in conjunction

---

[56] Agreement between the Government of the Republic of Turkey and the Government of the Kingdom of Cambodia on the Reciprocal Promotion and Protection of Investments (adopted 21 October 2018, not in force) Art 1(1) (hereafter Turkey–Cambodia BIT).
[57] Morocco–Nigeria BIT (n 6) Art 1; Brazil–India BIT (n 55) Art 2(4)(1).
[58] Organization for Economic Cooperation and Development, *OECD Benchmark Definition of Foreign Direct Investment* (4th edn, 2008).
[59] Turkey–Cambodia BIT (n 56) Art 1(1).
[60] Cooperation and Facilitation Investment Agreement between the Federative Republic of Brazil and the United Arab Emirates (adopted 15 March 2019, not in force) Art 3(1)(3).
[61] Salacuse, *The Law of Investment Treaties* (n 31) 244–45 (observing that 'in a few of the treaties concluded during the second decade of the twenty-first century, contracting states have chosen specifically to exclude "portfolio investment" from the definition of investment, apparently because such states have concluded that portfolio investments as a class do not contribute significantly to their economic development').

with enterprise-based definitions of investment.[62] In fact, if such exclusions are employed in combination with asset-based definitions,[63] they do not prevent various categories of assets not connected to a local enterprise (land, contractual rights, etc), ie investments other than FDI, from qualifying as investments. As the example of the BIT between Turkey and Cambodia shows, the exclusion of portfolio investments also contradicts the express and unqualified recognition of the investment status of 'shares, stocks or any other form of participation in companies' which is characteristic of asset-based definitions.[64]

C. Assets not connected to any economic or business activity

6.36 Some investment treaties require that, in order to qualify as investments, assets must be 'connected' to economic or business activities. The Oman–Hungary BIT, for example, defines 'investment' as every kind of asset an investor owns or controls in the territory of the host State 'in connection with economic activities'.[65] An almost identical definition is contained in another BIT concluded by Hungary, namely, the BIT between Hungary and the United Arab Emirates. Art 1(1) of this treaty defines 'investment' as assets owned or controlled by an investor which are 'invested' 'in connection with economic activities of one Contracting Party in the territory of the other Contracting Party ...'.[66]

6.37 The Turkey–Cambodia BIT provides for a similar, though slightly differently worded, requirement. Under Art 1(1) of this treaty, an asset will only constitute an investment if it is 'connected with business activities'.[67] This provision further requires that the asset must have been 'acquired for the purpose of establishing lasting economic relations in the territory of [the host State]'.[68]

6.38 Provisions requiring the existence of economic or business activities in the host State have comparable effects to enterprise-based definitions of investment and exclusions of portfolio investments. In fact, the latter also (implicitly) require that the investor conduct some form of economic activity in the host State. Indeed, an *enterprise* is, by definition, a legal entity that is engaged in some business activity. The exclusion of portfolio

---

[62] For examples of BITs following this approach, see Morocco–Nigeria BIT (n 6) Art 1; Brazil–India BIT (n 55) Art 2(4).
[63] See, for example, Turkey–Cambodia BIT (n 56) Art 1(1).
[64] ibid Art 1(1)(c).
[65] Oman–Hungary BIT (n 24) Art 1(1).
[66] Agreement between the Government of Hungary and the Government of the United Arab Emirates for the Promotion and Reciprocal Protection of Investments (adopted 15 July 2021, entered into force 10 April 2022) Art 1(1). The reference to economic activities 'of one Contracting Party' is most probably a drafting mistake since it would in principle require an activity performed by the investor's home State, rather than the investor himself or herself, a requirement for which there is no rational justification.
[67] Turkey–Cambodia BIT (n 56) Art 1(1).
[68] ibid.

investments similarly has the effect of requiring that the investor play, or at least be in a position to play, an active role in the management of an enterprise.

D. Sovereign debt instruments

6.39 Another rather common exclusion found in investment treaties is the exclusion of sovereign debt instruments such as sovereign bonds or loans extended to a State or State entity. An illustrative example is the Morocco–Nigeria BIT which specifies that the term 'investment' does not include '[d]ebt securities issued by a government or loans to a government'.[69] The UK–Colombia BIT features a similar provision, stating that 'investment' does not cover 'public debt operations'.[70]

6.40 The exclusion of sovereign debt instruments appears to be a necessary implication of enterprise-based definitions of 'investment', as well as of provisions excluding portfolio investments and assets that are not connected to any economic activity in the host State. In fact, this type of definition and these exclusions implicitly require that the investor conduct business operations in the host State. If an entity purchases sovereign bonds or lends money to a State, it does not pursue any business activities in that State. Where a treaty contains such provisions, it is therefore in principle not necessary to specify that sovereign debt instruments do not qualify as investments.

6.41 Treaty exclusions of sovereign debt instruments are not only valid clarifications or policy choices, but they also help to remedy the uncertainty resulting from conflicting decisions under Art 25 ICSID Convention. In fact, since investment treaties traditionally define the term 'investment' in broad, asset-based terms, sovereign debt instruments are likely to satisfy the relevant requirements. In ICSID proceedings, the issue of whether such instruments are protected will thus depend on whether they can be considered as investments under the Convention. While some tribunals have answered this question in the affirmative,[71] others have refused to recognize that sovereign debt instruments meet the objective requirements of Art 25 ICSID Convention.[72] Express treaty exclusions thus create greater certainty as to the legal status of such instruments.

---

[69] Morocco–Nigeria BIT (n 6) Art 1.
[70] UK–Colombia BIT (n 47) Art I(2)(b)(i).
[71] *Abaclat and others v The Argentine Republic*, ICSID Case No ARB/07/5, Decision on Jurisdiction and Admissibility (4 August 2011) para 367 (concluding that '[the] Claimants' purchase of security entitlements in Argentinean bonds constitutes a contribution which qualifies as "investment" under Article 25 ICSID Convention'); *Ambiente Ufficio S.P.A. and others v The Argentine Republic*, ICSID Case No ARB/08/9, Decision on Jurisdiction and Admissibility (8 February 2013) para 482 (holding that 'the bonds/security entitlements which are at stake in the present proceedings fulfill the criteria generally ascribed to the *Salini* test').
[72] *Poštová banka, a.s. and Istrokapital SE v The Hellenic Republic*, ICSID Case No ARB/13/8, Award (9 April 2015) para 371 (stating that 'under the objective approach of the definition of what constitutes an investment, i.e. a contribution to an economic venture of a certain duration implying an operational risk, the acquisition by Poštová banka of the interests in GGBs [Greek Government Bonds] would not constitute an investment').

V. Arbitral Recognition of an 'Objective' or 'Implied' Meaning of the Concept of Investment under Investment Treaties

A. Overview

Significant developments have occurred not only in treaty practice, but also in the manner in which arbitral tribunals have interpreted treaty definitions of 'investment'. In fact, a number of tribunals have recognized that the term 'investment' contained in investment treaties, like its counterpart in Art 25 ICSID Convention, has an 'implied' or 'objective' meaning. The existence of such an objective meaning has been acknowledged, in the first place, in the context of non-ICSID proceedings. This is understandable, given that non-ICSID tribunals cannot rely on the ICSID Convention in order to apply objective criteria. However, if a non-ICSID tribunal decides that the concept of investment in a given BIT has an implied meaning, there does not seem to be any reason why an ICSID tribunal could not (or should not) reach the same conclusion. On the contrary, it would be unreasonable for the interpretation of a particular treaty to vary depending on whether the proceedings are brought under the ICSID Convention or not. **6.42**

It is thus not surprising that the existence of an objective meaning of the term 'investment' in investment treaties has also been accepted by ICSID tribunals. The relevant case law is, however, more cautious. In fact, ICSID tribunals have not directly affirmed that objective criteria are applicable under investment treaty definitions of investment. Rather, they have held that the term 'investment' has, per se, an objective meaning, regardless of whether it is used in the ICSID Convention or an investment treaty (or elsewhere, for that matter). **6.43**

B. Decisions rendered by non-ICSID tribunals

The first decision in which a non-ICSID tribunal held that the term 'investment' in the applicable treaty had an objective meaning is *Romak v Uzbekistan*.[73] This case involved various contracts under which Romak agreed to deliver specified quantities of wheat to several Uzbek State entities.[74] When a dispute arose between the parties with regard to payment for some of the deliveries made,[75] Romak initiated Grain and Feed Trade Association (GAFTA) arbitration proceedings in accordance with the arbitration clause contained in the contracts.[76] It prevailed in those proceedings but was ultimately unable to enforce the award.[77] Romak therefore commenced United Nations **6.44**

---

[73] *Romak S.A. (Switzerland) v The Republic of Uzbekistan*, PCA Case No AA280, Award (26 November 2009) (hereafter *Romak v Uzbekistan*).
[74] ibid paras 24–37.
[75] ibid paras 41–47.
[76] ibid paras 52–61.
[77] ibid paras 62–70.

Commission on International Trade Law (UNCITRAL) arbitration proceedings under the BIT between Switzerland and Uzbekistan,[78] alleging various treaty violations.[79] The Republic of Uzbekistan raised several jurisdictional objections, including an objection to the investment status of Romak's rights under the contracts and the GAFTA award.[80]

6.45 In its ruling, the Tribunal first noted that the term 'investment', which the BIT between Switzerland and Uzbekistan defined in broad, asset-based terms, had an objective meaning beyond the one deriving from a literal reading of the treaty's definition. It based this interpretive finding on the object and purpose of the BIT and, more particularly, on its declared aim of 'foster[ing] economic prosperity' of the contracting States and 'intensify[ing] economic cooperation' between them.[81] It also relied on the treaty's context and, more particularly, the fact that the State parties had concluded a separate treaty on trade matters on the same day they signed the BIT, suggesting that they viewed trade (or commerce) and investment as two conceptually distinct forms of international business.[82]

6.46 The Tribunal further held that a literal interpretation of the treaty would lead to a manifestly absurd or unreasonable outcome, in violation of Art 32(b) of the Vienna Convention on the Law of Treaties.[83,84] Such an interpretation would, firstly, 'eliminate any practical limitation' to the term 'investment' and render the distinction between investment and commercial transactions meaningless.[85] Also, it would mean that every contract between a Swiss national and an Uzbek State entity would necessarily qualify as an investment and that dispute resolution provisions contained in such contracts would *ipso facto* be rendered ineffective.[86]

6.47 Based on arbitral case law[87] and the ordinary meaning of the term 'investment',[88] the Tribunal took the view that the inherent meaning of investment entailed 'a contribution that extends over a certain period of time and that involves some risk'.[89] It found that none of these three hallmarks were present in the case before it and that Romak's rights did not, therefore, constitute an investment in the sense of the BIT.[90]

---

[78] ibid para 71.
[79] ibid paras 7–8.
[80] ibid paras 97–100.
[81] ibid para 181.
[82] ibid para 182.
[83] Vienna Convention on the Law of Treaties (adopted 23 May 1969, entered into force 27 January 1980) Art 32(b). This rule provides that, under certain circumstances, recourse can be had to 'supplementary means of interpretation, including the preparatory work of the treaty and the circumstances of its conclusion'. This possibility notably exists when the general rule of interpretation of Art 31 'leads to a result which is manifestly absurd or unreasonable'.
[84] *Romak v Uzbekistan* (n 73) para 184.
[85] ibid para 185.
[86] ibid para 187.
[87] ibid paras 196–205.
[88] ibid para 206.
[89] ibid para 207.
[90] ibid paras 213–32.

6.48 A similar approach was adopted by the Tribunal in *Nova Scotia v Venezuela*.[91] This case involved a contract under which a company controlled by Venezuelan state-owned entities agreed to supply certain quantities of coal to Nova Scotia Power Incorporated (Nova Scotia), a Canadian corporation. A dispute arose between the parties when, apparently as a result of a government directive, the company ceased to supply coal.[92] Nova Scotia referred the dispute to ICSID's Additional Facility, claiming various violations of the BIT between Canada and Venezuela.[93] The Respondent objected to the Tribunal's jurisdiction on various grounds, arguing *inter alia* that Nova Scotia had not made any investment in the sense of the BIT.[94]

6.49 Like the *Romak* tribunal, the Tribunal in *Nova Scotia* found that the broad, asset-based definition of 'investment' contained in the applicable treaty was not 'self-sufficient'—it even doubted whether it could at all be considered a definition.[95] According to the Tribunal, investment status under the BIT required the presence of several 'inherent features'. In the Tribunal's opinion, recourse to such features was necessary because of the 'open-ended nature' of the definition and the need to restrict the possibility that non-listed assets qualify as investments.[96] The Tribunal also explained that the existence of inherent features derived from the relationship between investment and investor, and the implied requirement that an investment must have been 'made' (by an investor).[97] A further argument relied upon by the Tribunal was that the meaning of the term 'investment' should not vary depending on the forum in which a dispute is heard and, more particularly, according to whether or not it is submitted to ICSID.[98]

6.50 Relying primarily on arbitral case law, including decisions rendered under Art 25 ICSID Convention, the Tribunal identified the same inherent features as the *Romak* tribunal, ie contributions, duration, and risk.[99] While it left the question of whether the duration requirement was met unanswered, it decided that Nova Scotia's payment obligations under the contract were 'inadequate to be considered as the contribution which forms the basis of an investment'[100] and that the risk involved in the transaction was not 'of the sort that is inherent in the notion of investment'.[101] It concluded that Nova Scotia had not made any investment within the meaning of the BIT.

6.51 Another case in which a non-ICSID tribunal acknowledged the applicability of implied requirements for the existence of an investment under an investment treaty is

---

[91] *Nova Scotia Power Incorporated (Canada) v Bolivarian Republic of Venezuela*, ICSID Case No ARB(AF)/11/1, Award (30 April 2014).
[92] ibid para 1.
[93] ibid.
[94] ibid paras 51–62.
[95] ibid para 77.
[96] ibid para 78.
[97] ibid para 79.
[98] ibid para 80.
[99] ibid para 84.
[100] ibid para 97.
[101] ibid para 112.

Doutremepuich v Mauritius.[102] In this case, the Claimants undertook to establish a laboratory in Mauritius for genetic and DNA analysis, allegedly after being encouraged to do so by the local authorities.[103] Having obtained a preliminary approval of this project by the prime minister's office,[104] the Claimants set up three corporations in Mauritius.[105] Despite the initial support, the project was ultimately rejected,[106] and the Claimants brought UNCITRAL arbitration proceedings under the BIT between France and Mauritius.[107] The Respondent objected to the Tribunal's jurisdiction on two grounds, one of which was the alleged absence of an investment under the BIT.[108]

6.52 Pushing the analysis of the *Nova Scotia* tribunal one step further, the Tribunal took the view that the treaty's definition of 'investment' (which defined 'investment' in broad, asset-based terms) did not actually constitute a definition, but merely provided examples of different forms of investment, without specifying the relevant criteria or characteristics.[109] According to the Tribunal, this provision was therefore unable to 'play the gatekeeping role of establishing when a situation qualifies as an investment and when it does not'.[110] The Tribunal concluded that it was necessary to refer to the 'objective and ordinary' meaning of investment.[111]

6.53 The Tribunal held that this objective meaning consisted of the three core *Salini* criteria, namely, contributions, duration, and risk.[112] Interestingly, the Claimants did not challenge the applicability of the *Salini* test, despite the ICSID Convention not being applicable.[113] The Tribunal also discussed the possible relevance of another alleged *Salini* criterion, namely, the requirement of a contribution to the economic development of the host State. It refused to decide this issue, however, since it found that, in any event, the Claimants' activities failed to meet the other three criteria.[114]

C. Decisions rendered by ICSID tribunals

6.54 Less than two years after the *Romak* tribunal handed down its decision, an ICSID tribunal (namely, the Tribunal in *GEA v Ukraine*) also—implicitly—recognized that investment treaty definitions of 'investment' have an objective meaning, ie a meaning beyond the terms of the relevant definition. In this case, the German company

---

[102] *Professor Christian Doutremepuich and Antoine Doutremepuich v The Republic of Mauritius*, PCA Case No 2018-37, Award on Jurisdiction (23 August 2019).
[103] ibid para 10.
[104] ibid para 12.
[105] ibid para 13.
[106] ibid para 14.
[107] ibid para 22.
[108] ibid para 66.
[109] ibid para 117.
[110] ibid.
[111] ibid.
[112] ibid para 118.
[113] ibid.
[114] ibid para 119.

New Klöckner and its subsidiary Klöckner Chemiehandel GmbH (KCH) entered into a conversion contract[115] and several connected agreements[116] with Oriana, a Ukrainian entity. When a dispute arose between KCH and Oriana, the former initiated International Chamber of Commerce (ICC) arbitration proceedings in conformity with the contracts, obtaining a largely favourable decision.[117] Following the failure of various attempts at collecting under the award, KCH's parent company GEA Group Aktiengesellschaft initiated ICSID arbitration proceedings, alleging that Ukraine had promised KCH would be compensated under the contract and/or ICC award, and that Ukraine's failure to honour these promises constituted a violation of its obligations under the Germany–Ukraine BIT.[118] Ukraine raised a series of jurisdictional objections, alleging *inter alia* that KCH 'did not make an "investment" in Ukraine under either the BIT or the ICSID Convention'.[119]

6.55 Examining Ukraine's objection, the Tribunal observed that there were two approaches to the issue of the existence of an investment: an objective and a subjective one. Under the former, the existence of an investment requires that certain 'objective' criteria flowing from the ICSID Convention be met.[120] Under the latter, no such objective criteria apply—the 'subjective' definition contained in the relevant instrument of consent (investment treaty or law) constitutes the only relevant threshold.[121]

6.56 The Tribunal held that, in the case at hand, it was not necessary to decide which approach was the correct one.[122] In fact, having considered 'all potentially applicable criteria', the Tribunal noted that 'each [ie both the application of the BIT definition and the application of objective criteria] leads to the same conclusion with respect to each of the alleged "investments" in question'.[123] Specifically, the Tribunal found that the conversion contract constituted an investment under both the BIT and the ICSID Convention,[124] and that the other agreements[125] and the ICC arbitral[126] award did not meet the requirements of either.

6.57 Of particular interest for present purposes are the Tribunal's views on the objective approach. It first discussed legal authorities holding that objective definitional criteria derive from Art 25 ICSID Convention (*Mitchell v Congo*[127] and *Phoenix Action v Czech Republic*[128]).[129] Citing *Romak*, the Tribunal then observed that, in reality, 'it is not so

---

[115] *GEA Group Aktiengesellschaft v Ukraine*, ICSID Case No ARB/08/16, Award (31 March 2011) paras 44–50 (hereafter *GEA v Ukraine*).
[116] ibid paras 51–55.
[117] ibid paras 56–62.
[118] ibid paras 86–87.
[119] ibid para 91.
[120] ibid paras 139–41.
[121] ibid para 142.
[122] ibid para 143.
[123] ibid.
[124] ibid paras 150–53.
[125] ibid paras 154–57.
[126] ibid paras 158–64.
[127] *Patrick H. Mitchell v The Democratic Republic of the Congo*, ICSID Case No ARB/99/7, Award (9 February 2004).
[128] *Phoenix Action, Ltd. v The Czech Republic*, ICSID Case No ARB/06/5, Award (15 April 2009).
[129] *GEA v Ukraine* (n 115) paras 139–40.

much the term "investment" in the ICSID Convention than the term "investment" *per se* that is often considered as having an objective meaning in itself, whether it is mentioned in the ICSID Convention or a BIT'.[130] In other words, the Tribunal considered that the term 'investment' always has (or can have) an objective meaning, regardless of the instrument in which it appears.

6.58 *GEA v Ukraine* represents a significant development of the *Romak* case law because, for the first time, an ICSID—rather than non-ICSID—tribunal acknowledged that not only the term 'investment' in Art 25 ICSID Convention, but also treaty and statutory concepts of investment have (or may have) an objective meaning. *GEA v Ukraine* can therefore be considered to extend the reach of the *Romak* case law to ICSID arbitration.

6.59 The ruling of the Tribunal in *GEA v Ukraine* was at least partly confirmed by the decision in *Quiborax v Bolivia*.[131] In this case, the Claimants argued that they were shareholders of a Bolivian company holding concessions to mine boron deposits in the Salar de Uyuni, the largest dry salt lake in the world.[132] When Bolivia revoked those concessions and attempts to settle the matter amicably failed, the Claimants initiated ICSID arbitration proceedings,[133] arguing that Bolivia breached multiple provisions of the BIT between Chile and Bolivia.[134] Bolivia objected to the jurisdiction of the Tribunal, contending *inter alia* that the Claimants had not made any investment within the meaning of Art 25 ICSID Convention.[135]

6.60 Since the Respondent did apparently not dispute that the Claimants had made an investment in the sense of the BIT, the Tribunal focused on the question of whether Art 25 ICSID Convention 'contain[ed] a definition of "investment" that is independent from and thus additional to the definition of "investment" in the BIT'.[136] Relying on three factors,[137] the Tribunal answered this question in the affirmative.

6.61 Of particular significance for its ruling was the relevant arbitral case law which, according to the Tribunal, had 'given substance and content to an objective meaning of "investment"'.[138] The Tribunal first discussed *Global Trading v Ukraine*[139] which, as has

---

[130] ibid para 141.
[131] *Quiborax S.A. and others v Plurinational State of Bolivia*, ICSID Case No ARB/06/2, Decision on Jurisdiction (27 September 2012) (hereafter *Quiborax v Bolivia*).
[132] ibid paras 12–15.
[133] ibid para 17.
[134] ibid para 19.
[135] ibid para 39.
[136] ibid para 211.
[137] ibid paras 212–16. The first factor was that the ICSID Convention's silence on the meaning of 'investment' does not mean that this term does not have any meaning at all. Rather, it suggests that the Convention endorses the 'ordinary' meaning of investment, instead of establishing a 'special' meaning. The second factor was that the Claimants themselves acknowledged that Art 25 ICSID Convention placed certain limits on what could be considered as an investment and that those limits could only be determined on the basis of objective criteria. The third factor consisted of arbitral case law recognizing the objective meaning of the notion of investment under Art 25 ICSID Convention.
[138] ibid para 214.
[139] *Global Trading Resource Corp. and Globex International, Inc. v Ukraine*, ICSID Case No ARB/09/11, Award (1 December 2010).

been explained in Chapter 3,[140] supports the existence of objective requirements under Art 25 ICSID Convention. It also referred to *GEA v Ukraine* and *Romak v Uzbekistan* where the tribunals held that such an objective meaning was 'inherent to the term investment, irrespective of the application of the ICSID Convention'.[141]

6.62 The *Quiborax* Tribunal ultimately held that the objective defining criteria of an investment were 'contribution of money or assets, risk and duration'.[142] However, it failed to take a position on the controversy as to '[w]hether the objective test under the ICSID Convention is independent from and additional to the definition found in the BIT, or whether the same objective test is inherent to the term 'investment' used in the BIT'.[143] While it recognizes the relevance of objective criteria, the Tribunal's decision therefore fails to specify whether such criteria apply under the Convention, the BIT, or both. In other words, the *Quiborax* tribunal neither affirmed nor denied that the treaty concept of investment had an objective meaning; it merely acknowledged that this was a possibility.

6.63 A recent decision that provides unambiguous support for the existence of an objective notion of investment under investment treaties is *Eyre v Sri Lanka*.[144] In this case, the Claimants allegedly acquired a plot of land (the 'Montrose land') for the purposes of developing a hotel complex.[145] Following the adoption by Sri Lanka of measures restricting access to the land, the Claimants initiated ICSID arbitration proceedings, asserting that those measures constituted an expropriation in violation of the BIT between the United Kingdom and Sri Lanka.[146] Sri Lanka raised several jurisdictional objections, contending among others that absent a contribution and an investment risk, the Montrose land did not qualify as an investment under the BIT and Art 25 ICSID Convention.[147]

6.64 In support of this objection, Sri Lanka argued that the concept of 'investment' contained in Art 25 ICSID Convention reflected the ordinary meaning of this term and that such meaning consisted of the three core *Salini* criteria, namely, contribution, duration, and risk.[148] The Claimants objected to this approach, maintaining that the *Salini* test was an interpretive 'dead-end' and that Art 25 ICSID Convention should only be relied upon in order to 'exclude obviously absurd claims of investment'.[149]

---

[140] Chapter 3 Section III.B.
[141] *Quiborax v Bolivia* (n 131) para 215.
[142] ibid para 227.
[143] ibid para 217.
[144] *Raymond Charles Eyre and others v Democratic Socialist Republic of Sri Lanka*, ICSID Case No ARB/16/25, Award (5 March 2020).
[145] ibid para 5.
[146] ibid.
[147] ibid paras 154–63.
[148] ibid para 155.
[149] ibid para 165.

6.65 Like the *GEA* and *Quiborax* tribunals, the Tribunal in *Eyre* did not consider it necessary to decide the Art 25 controversy (although, in reality, it did[150]), given that there was substantial support for the proposition that the term 'investment' had an inherent meaning and 'implie[d] at least a contribution by the investor, a certain duration, and economic risk'.[151] Similarly to the *GEA* tribunal, the Tribunal in *Eyre* thus considered that under both the ICSID Convention and the applicable BIT, the term 'investment' had an objective meaning.

D. Assessment

6.66 The *Romak* and *GEA* case law suggest that there is growing support among arbitral tribunals for the idea that the term 'investment' has an objective meaning, regardless of the specific context in which it is used. The relevant decisions also indicate that the three core *Salini* criteria of a contribution, a minimum duration, and risk are considered as adequately capturing this meaning. The *Romak* and the *Doutremepuich* tribunals held that these three characteristics were inherent in the *ordinary* meaning of the concept of investment. However, as has been explained in Chapter 2, the risk requirement does not form part of the term's ordinary meaning and the time dimension only seems to play a secondary role.[152]

6.67 Unlike treaty-based characteristics-requirements, the *Romak* and *GEA* approaches remain largely faithful to the *Salini* test.[153] This is, at least in part, due to the fact that these decisions rely to a significant extent on Art 25 case law and that they do not subject the relevant rulings to any critical examination. The *Romak* and *GEA* decisions do not, therefore, develop, refine, or otherwise 'improve' the *Salini* test (unlike treaty definitions requiring investments to possess certain characteristics).

6.68 *Romak* and its offspring are based on understandable and seemingly valid policy considerations. In fact, traditional asset-based definitions of 'investment' can be considered as unreasonably broad, at least where they are construed literally. As a result, reliance on implied criteria is necessary to limit the scope of protection of investment treaties to operations and/or assets that it is 'sensible' to characterize as investments. Such a necessity does not arise in the context of ICSID proceedings, given that tribunals can rely on case law affirming the existence of objective requirements under Art 25 ICSID Convention.

---

[150] In fact, the Tribunal acknowledged that the term 'investment' as such had an objective meaning. The necessary implication is that 'investment' always has an objective meaning. Therefore, it has such a meaning under the ICSID Convention. Thus, the Tribunal resolved the controversy between the objective and subjective approach in favour of the former.

[151] ibid para 293.

[152] Chapter 2 Section VI.

[153] The only development is that the relevant decisions implicitly reject the controversial *Salini* features and, more particularly, the requirement of contribution to the host State's economic development.

6.69 While *Romak* and, to a lesser extent, *GEA* may be justified by legitimate policy considerations, they are questionable from an interpretive standpoint. To begin with, these decisions are arguably more objectionable than the equivalent Art 25 case law. In fact, it is one thing to give meaning to an undefined term; it is quite another thing to read additional requirements or criteria into an existing and, what is more, detailed definition. In the former scenario, the determination of implied or objective definitional features is a necessity (unless, of course, one considers that the subjective approach is appropriate). In the latter, the application of objective criteria may be seen as an amendment of the treaty definition, in disregard for the contracting States' intent.

6.70 Another interpretive issue affecting the *Romak* and *GEA* case law is that these decisions are based on the implicit assumption that the concept of investment has a single meaning, or core meaning, across all investment treaties. How else can one explain that the Tribunal in *Doutremepuich*, a case arising under the BIT between France and Mauritius, relied on a decision rendered by a tribunal interpreting the meaning of 'investment' in the BIT between Switzerland and Uzbekistan, which was applicable in *Romak*? Definitions of investment vary from treaty to treaty, and so may the intent of the relevant contracting States. It is of course correct that the application of a uniform notion of investment under all investment treaties may present certain advantages, but it is hardly defensible that the pursuit of such uniformity should trump the intent of the State parties to such agreements.

7
Definitions of Investment in Investment Laws

I. Introduction	7.01	B. Conclusions	7.29
II. Asset-Based Definitions	7.07	V. Requirement of a Capital Investment	7.32
III. Enterprise-Based Definitions	7.11		
A. Types of definitions	7.11	VI. Requirement of a Contribution to the Host State's Economic Development	7.36
B. Meaning of 'enterprise'	7.16		
C. Conclusions	7.21		
IV. Activity- and Project-Based Definitions	7.24	VII. Case Law	7.43
A. Definitions	7.24		

I. Introduction

7.01 Unlike investment treaty definitions of 'investment', definitions contained in investment laws are adopted unilaterally by the enacting State. They are not negotiated with another State or other States, and those definitions cannot, therefore, be imposed by a State or States having superior bargaining power. States adopting investment laws are, in other words, free to decide how they wish to define the notion of 'investment', ie the range of assets and/or operations that they consider worthy of protection under their laws. It is thus not surprising that, overall, definitions found in investment laws tend to be narrower than those contained in investment treaties.

7.02 Admittedly, States adopting investment laws seek to attract foreign investment[1] and one may argue that they are indirectly under pressure to define the term 'investment' in an investor-friendly manner, ie broadly. In reality, however, it is unlikely that the use of a restrictive concept of investment has, or would have, a deterrent effect on foreign investment. In fact, while the existence of an investment law and the nature and extent of the rights and privileges granted to foreign investors may have some impact on the decision to invest in a particular country, it would be unrealistic to assume that

---

[1] See, for example, Law of the Republic of Moldova on Investments in Entrepreneurial Activity (2004) Preamble (referring to 'the exclusive importance of attraction of... investments to the Republic of Moldova' and to 'the necessity of encouragement and protection through [the] creation of stable and equal legal, social and economical (sic!) conditions for investment activity') (hereafter Moldova Law on Investments); Vanuatu Foreign Investment Promotion Act No 15 of 1998 (1998) Art 1(a) and (c) (stating that the purposes of the Act notably include 'to promote and facilitate investment in Vanuatu by foreign investors' and 'to promote investments by foreign investors that will materially benefit Vanuatu and its people') (hereafter Vanuatu Foreign Investment Promotion Act).

the breadth or narrowness of the definition of 'investment' is likely to influence the decision-making process. Also, and more importantly, prospective foreign investors will frequently benefit from protection under a bi- or multilateral investment treaty, often making it unnecessary to rely on the host State's domestic investment law.

Despite their unilateral nature, definitions of investment contained in investment laws share a number of features with treaty definitions. Like the latter, definitions in investment laws are, in principle, either asset- or enterprise-based. The pursuit of an economic activity or project by the investor, a requirement found in a growing number of investment treaties,[2] is a regular feature of such definitions.[3] Another similarity is that both types of definitions sometimes provide for specific exceptions, such as the exclusion of portfolio investment.[4]

7.03

Generally speaking, however, the differences outweigh commonalities. The most notable such differences include (1) the more limited number of asset-based definitions and significantly higher proportion of enterprise-based definitions; (2) the more systematic requirement that an investment be associated with, or consist of, economic activities or projects; (3) the quasi-total absence of characteristics-requirements;[5] (4) the frequent references to a requirement to contribute 'capital';[6] and (5) the occasional requirement that an investment must contribute to the economic development of the host State.[7]

7.04

As has been explained in relation to treaty definitions, there is not only one possible way of classifying definitions of the concept of investment.[8] As has been seen, several asset-based treaty definitions require that in order to qualify as investments, assets must be used in connection with an economic activity or project. Given that the conduct or pursuit of an activity or project thus constitutes a central requirement of such definitions, these definitions could be characterized as 'activity/project-based', rather than asset-based. As will be shown in this chapter, some provisions define 'investments' 'purely' as activities or projects, rather than *assets used in connection with* such activities or projects.[9] In this particular context, it is thus appropriate to consider that activity/project-based definitions represent a third, separate category.

7.05

---

[2] See Chapter 6 Section IV.C.
[3] See Section IV.
[4] As far as investment treaty definitions are concerned, see Chapter 6 Section IV.B. For examples of investment laws that exclude portfolio investments, see, for example, Namibia Investment Promotion Act (2016) Sect 1 (requiring a minority ownership interest of 10 per cent on the part of the investor) (hereafter Namibia Investment Promotion Act); Mongolia Law on Investment (2013) Art 3(5) (providing that a 'business entity with foreign investment' requires that 'not less than 25 percent of [the entity's equity must be] invested by a foreign investor(s)') (hereafter Mongolia Law on Investment).
[5] See UNCTAD, *Investment Policy Monitor, Investment Laws—A Widespread Tool for the Promotion and Regulation of Foreign Investment* (2016) 4, n 4 (observing that, '[c]ontrary to certain international investment agreements (IIAs), national laws do not define the scope of "investment" by specifying that investment means every asset which has certain characteristics such as the commitment of capital or other resources, the expectation of gain or profit, or the assumption of risk') (hereafter UNCTAD, *Investment Laws*).
[6] See Section V.
[7] See Section VI.
[8] See Chapter 5 Section II.A.1.
[9] See Section IV.

7.06 This chapter provides a general overview and analysis of definitions of 'investment' found in investment laws, with particular focus on how those definitions differ from treaty definitions. Sections II, III, and IV discuss, respectively, asset-based, enterprise-based, and activity/project-based definitions of 'investment'. Section V explores the common requirement of a contribution of 'capital'. Section VI analyses the requirement of a contribution to the host State's economic development, a requirement that is almost entirely absent from treaty definitions but is contained in a number of investment laws. Section VII offers a few observations on the rather limited arbitral case law.

II. Asset-Based Definitions

7.07 Existing commentary on definitions of 'investment' in investment laws is slightly misleading when it comes to the significance of asset-based definitions. In fact, it is commonly assumed that all definitions are either asset-based or enterprise-based.[10] This overlooks not only the existence of activity- or project-based definitions,[11] but also the fact that many treaties only recognize the investment status of assets that are purchased, used, etc in connection with economic activities or enterprises, suggesting that the central element of the definition of 'investment' is the pursuit of such activities or the presence of an enterprise, rather than ownership or control of assets per se. It is thus misleading to state that a majority of investment treaties 'apply a broad asset-based approach'.[12]

7.08 'Pure' asset-based definitions, ie definitions that do not require a connection with economic activities (or projects) or enterprises, are relatively rare. An example of such a definition is the one contained in the Investment Promotion Act of Papua New Guinea which defines 'investment' as 'every kind of asset subject to the laws of Papua New Guinea',[13] thus following the broad, asset-based approach characteristic of investment treaties concluded in the 1990s and 2000s. Like those treaties, the definition of the Papua New Guinea law also features a non-exhaustive list of categories of qualifying assets.[14] Similar definitions can notably be found in the investment laws of Albania,[15] Cameroon,[16] Myanmar,[17] and Kyrgyzstan.[18]

---

[10] See, for example, UNCTAD, *Investment Laws* (n 5) 4 (noting that '[m]ore than half of the laws (60) [examined in the study] apply a broad asset-based approach and 38 a limited enterprise-based approach').
[11] See Section IV.
[12] UNCTAD, *Investment Laws* (n 5) 4.
[13] Papua New Guinea Investment Promotion Act 1992 Sect 3(1).
[14] ibid.
[15] Albania Foreign Investment Act (1990) Art 1 (defining the concept of 'foreign investment').
[16] Cameroon Investment Charter (2002) Art 4 (providing that '[a]n asset held by an investor shall be considered an investment under the present Law').
[17] Myanmar Investment Law (2016) Art 2(q) (defining 'investment' as 'any assets owned or controlled by the investor in accordance with this law', without however providing any illustrative or exhaustive list of qualifying assets).
[18] Kyrgyzstan Law on Investments (2003) Art 1(1) (defining 'investments' as 'tangible and intangible assets', listing various categories of covered assets).

Numerous asset-based definitions of 'investment' require some connection between **7.09** the assets concerned and economic activities or projects in the host State, thus assigning a central role to the pursuit of such activities or projects.[19] The El Salvador Investment Law, for example, defines 'investments' as '[t]angible and intangible assets or resources, the providing of services ... devoted to the execution of economic activities, or to the expansion or improving (sic!) of existing activities'.[20] Under the Investment Law of Madagascar, 'investment' is defined as 'a set of financial resources ... allocated to carry out an economic project...'.[21] The Uzbek Law on Investments and Investment Activity similarly contains a reference to the pursuit of specific activities, defining 'investments' as 'tangible and intangible assets ... invested by an investor ... in social facilities, entrepreneurial, scientific and other activities for profit...'.[22]

Several asset-based definitions of the term 'investment' require a connection with an **7.10** enterprise, thus indirectly requiring that the investor own or contribute to an enterprise. Under the Investment Code of Mali, for example, an 'investment' is defined as 'capital employed for the acquisition of [specified assets] in connection with the creation, expansion, or rehabilitation of an enterprise'.[23] The Law on Investment of Mongolia defines 'investment' as 'tangible and intangible assets attributed to the joint capital ... of ... business entities ... in the territory of Mongolia'.[24]

III. Enterprise-Based Definitions

A. Types of definitions

As has been explained, enterprise-based definitions are characterized by the central **7.11** role that the concept of enterprise plays in defining 'investment'. Provisions that define 'investment' as an enterprise or interest in an enterprise evidently fall into this category. But the concept of enterprise also plays a key role in other types of definitions, for example where an investment is considered to consist of a contribution of capital to an enterprise or of assets owned by an enterprise.

---

[19] See, for example, El Salvador Investment Law (1999) Art 2(a) (hereafter El Salvador Investment Law); Republic of Guinea-Bissau Investment Code, Law No 3/2011 (6 July 2011) Art 1; Haiti Investment Code (1989) Art 5(f); Kazakhstan Law on Investments (2003) Art 1(3); Kosovo Law No 04/L-220 on Foreign Investment (2014) Art 2(1)(4); Lao People's Democratic Republic Law on Investment Promotion (2016) Art 3; Madagascar Law No 2007-036 relating to investment law in Madagascar (2008) Art 1 (hereafter Madagascar Investment Law); Moldova Law on Investments (n 1) Art 3; Turkmenistan Law on Investment Activities (1992) Art 1 (hereafter Turkmenistan Investment Law); Law of the Republic of Uzbekistan on Investments and Investment Activity (2019) Art 3 (hereafter Uzbek Law on Investments); Bolivarian Republic of Venezuela Constitutional Law on Productive Foreign Investment (2017) Art 7(1).
[20] El Salvador Investment Law (n 19) Art 2(a).
[21] Madagascar Investment Law (n 19) Art 1.
[22] Uzbek Law on Investments (n 19) Art 3.
[23] Law No 2012-016 on an Investment Code (2012) Art 2 (hereafter Mali Investment Code).
[24] Mongolia Law on Investment (n 4) Art 3(1).

7.12 A number of investment laws define the concept of 'investment' as an enterprise or interest in an enterprise. Under the Namibian Investment Promotion Act, for example, 'investment' notably includes an 'enterprise', an 'enterprise ... that the investor is seeking to ... establish, acquire, merge with or expand', or 'the acquisition ... of a minority ownership interest' of more than 10 per cent in an enterprise.[25] The Philippines Foreign Investment Act defines 'investment' as an 'equity participation in any enterprise organized or existing under the laws of the Philippines'.[26] Under the South African Protection of Investment Act, the term 'investment' covers, among others, 'any lawful enterprise' or 'the holding or acquisition of shares ... or other ownership instruments of such an enterprise'.[27]

7.13 A slightly different approach consists of defining 'investment' not as an actual enterprise, but as the act of *establishing*, *acquiring*, or *investing in* an enterprise. Under the Investment Promotion Law of the Syrian Arab Republic, for example, 'investment' is defined as '[e]stablishing, expanding, developing or upgrading enterprises'.[28] The Nigerian Investment Promotion Commission Act defines 'investment' in similar terms as an 'investment made to acquire an interest in an enterprise'.[29]

7.14 Numerous domestic investment laws define the concept of 'investment' as a capital contribution to an enterprise. Under the Zambia Development Agency Act, for example, the term 'investment' is defined as a 'contribution of capital, in cash or in kind, by an investor to a new business enterprise, to the expansion or rehabilitation of an existing business enterprise or to the purchase of an existing business enterprise'.[30] Similar definitions can be found in the investment laws of various other countries.[31]

7.15 A few investment laws define the term 'investment' as assets owned by an enterprise. Under the Mongolian Law on Investment, for example, 'investment' means 'the tangible and intangible assets ... of the business entities which are for profit oriented (sic!)

---

[25] Namibia Investment Promotion Act (n 4) Sect 1.
[26] Philippines Foreign Investment Act (1991) Sect 3.b (hereafter Philippines Foreign Investment Act).
[27] South Africa Protection of Investment Act (2015) Sect 2(1).
[28] Syrian Arab Republic Investment Promotion Law (2007) Art 1(d) (hereafter Syrian Investment Promotion Law).
[29] Nigerian Investment Promotion Commission Act (1995) Sect 31 (hereafter Nigerian Investment Promotion Commission Act).
[30] Zambia Development Agency Act (2006) Art 3.
[31] See, for example, Swaziland Investment Promotion Act (1998) Sect 2 (defining investment as 'a contribution of capital, in cash or in kind, made by a person to a new enterprise or to the expansion or rehabilitation of an existing business enterprise or to the purchase of an existing business enterprise'); Ethiopia Proclamation No 1180/2020 (2020) Sect 2(1) (defining investment as 'expenditure of capital in cash or in kind or in both by an investor to establish a new enterprise, or to acquire, in whole or in part, or to expand or upgrade an existing enterprise'); Kenya Investment Promotion Act (2004) Sect 2 (defining investment as the 'contribution of local or foreign capital by an investor, including the creation or acquisition of business assets by or for a business enterprise and includes the expansion, restructuring, improvement or rehabilitation of a business enterprise'); Palau Foreign Investment Act (2014) Sect 102(j) (defining investment as 'cash or the value of tangible assets subscribed or contributed to the equity capital of or ownership interest in a business enterprise'); Sierra Leone Investment Promotion Act (2004) Sect 1 (defining investment as 'the direct investment of foreign or domestic capital into a business enterprise in Sierra Leone') (hereafter Sierra Leone Investment Promotion Act); State of Palestine Law on the Encouragement of Investment in Palestine (1998) Art 1 (defining investment as 'actual monetary investment of capital (fixed capital assets) by an Investor in an Enterprise, whether a newly-created or an existing enterprise') (hereafter Palestine Investment Law).

activities in the territory of Mongolia'.[32] Under such definitions, assets therefore only qualify as investments if they are owned by, or otherwise associated with, an enterprise. The existence of such an enterprise thus constitutes the central definitional prerequisite.

B. Meaning of 'enterprise'

As the term 'enterprise' is of crucial importance for enterprise-based definitions of investment, it is not surprising that a majority of investment laws adopting such definitions specify the meaning of this concept. Two approaches can be distinguished in legislative practice. Under the first approach, an 'enterprise' is defined as a legal entity established in the host State. Under the second approach, the concept of 'enterprise' is defined more broadly as an activity or project. **7.16**

Investment laws that define 'enterprise' as a legal entity notably include the Namibia Investment Promotion Act, the Law on the Encouragement of Investment in Palestine, and the Mongolian Law on Investment. Under the Namibian Act, for example, 'enterprise' means 'any organised business undertaking, legally established in Namibia'.[33] Under the Palestinian Law, an 'enterprise' is defined as 'any entity constituted and properly registered for profit, including any company, branch, partnership, sole proprietorship, joint venture, or other association'.[34] The Mongolian Law, which uses the largely synonymous term 'business entity' instead of the concept of enterprise, defines the former as 'a business entity incorporated according to the applicable legislations in Mongolia'.[35] **7.17**

A number of investment laws define the term 'investment' more broadly as activities or projects, without requiring the presence or establishment of a legal entity in the host State. The Syrian Investment Promotion Law, for example, defines 'enterprise' as '[a]ny economic activity operated by an investor'.[36] Similarly, under the Nigerian Investment Promotion Commission Act, the term 'enterprise' is defined not only by reference to the notions of 'undertaking' and 'business', but also more generally as an 'industry' or 'project'.[37] **7.18**

A few definitions contained in investment laws establish minimum capital and/or contribution thresholds. The Mongolian Law on Investment, for example, which requires the existence of a 'business entity' in Mongolia, defines the notion of 'business entity with foreign investment' as an entity having an 'overall equity of US$100,000 or more (or equivalent in Mongolian tugriks or MNT)',[38] further specifying that 'not less than 25 percent of [this equity must be] invested by a foreign investor(s)'.[39] **7.19**

---

[32] Mongolia Law on Investment (n 4) Art 3(1).
[33] Namibia Investment Promotion Act (n 4) Sect 1.
[34] Palestine Investment Law (n 31) Art 1.
[35] Mongolia Law on Investment (n 4) Art 3(5).
[36] Syrian Investment Promotion Law (n 28) Art 1(f).
[37] Nigerian Investment Promotion Commission Act (n 29) Sect 31.
[38] Mongolia Law on Investment (n 4) Art 3(5).
[39] ibid.

7.20 Some investment laws featuring enterprise-based definitions of investment do not specify the meaning of the term 'enterprise'. The Sierra Leone Investment Promotion Act, for example, is silent with regard to the meaning of 'enterprise'.[40] The Philippines Foreign Investment Act contains definitions of the specific notions of 'export enterprise' and 'domestic market enterprise', but not of the more general concept of enterprise.[41] Under such laws, the meaning of the term 'enterprise' is thus uncertain. More particularly, it is not clear whether this term should be understood as referring to a legal entity or, more broadly, to the conduct of certain activities or projects.

C. Conclusions

7.21 Several conclusions can be drawn from the above review of enterprise-based definitions. First, depending on the definition of the concept of 'enterprise', the existence of an investment may or may not require the establishment of a legal entity in the host State. Where no such requirement applies, the mere conduct of certain economic activities (eg the construction of a bridge or highway) will qualify as an investment even if the investor has not established any subsidiary or branch in the territory of the host State. In the opposite scenario, such activities only constitute an investment if they are undertaken by a separate legal entity.

7.22 Second, most enterprise-based definitions do not require that the investor own a specific minimum share in an enterprise. Under such definitions, any interest in an enterprise established in the host State, including a portfolio investment, will qualify. Only relatively few definitions impose a minimum ownership threshold, effectively requiring the existence of a foreign direct investment (FDI). As has been seen, such requirements can notably be found in the definitions contained in the Namibia Investment Promotion Act (requiring an ownership interest in excess of 10 per cent) and the Mongolia Law on Investment (requiring ownership of at least 25 per cent of the relevant business entity).[42]

7.23 Third, enterprise-based definitions follow varying approaches as to the nature of 'investment'. While some definitions treat investments as enterprises or interests in such enterprises, others formally consider that investments consist of capital contributions to, or assets owned by, enterprises. These differences have significant practical implications, in particular in relation to the determination of the value of investments. In fact, where an investment is regarded as the capital contributed to an enterprise, its value corresponds to the amount of capital invested. Where an 'investment' is defined as an interest in an enterprise, on the other hand, the value of the investment will reflect

---

[40] Sierra Leone Investment Promotion Act (n 31) Sect 1 (defining various terms used in the Act, but not the term 'enterprise').
[41] Philippines Foreign Investment Act (n 26) Sect 3(e) and 3(f).
[42] Namibia Investment Promotion Act (n 4) Sect 1; Mongolia Law on Investment (n 4) Art 3(5).

the value of the enterprise, which may differ significantly from the investor's capital contribution.

IV. Activity- and Project-Based Definitions

A. Definitions

Several investment laws define 'investment' by reference to the idea of an investment 'project'. Under the Egyptian Investment Law, for example, 'investment' is defined as 'us[ing] the money for the set up, expansion, development, funding, holding, or management of an Investment Project'.[43] An 'Investment Project' is defined as '[c]onducting an investment activity' in a broad range of specified industries and economic sectors.[44] The Private Investment Law of Angola similarly defines the concept of 'foreign investment' as 'carrying out investment projects',[45] without however specifying the meaning of the expression 'investment project'. **7.24**

A rather sizeable number of investment laws define 'investment' as consisting of, or requiring, investment activities. Several definitions fully equate investment with (the conduct of) such activities. The Foreign Investment Law of the People's Republic of China, for instance, defines the concept of 'foreign investment' as 'investment activities in mainland China conducted directly or indirectly by natural persons, enterprises, or other organizations of foreign countries'.[46] Under the Indonesian Law Concerning Investment, 'investment' is defined as 'any kinds of investing activity by both domestic and foreign investors for running business within the territory of the Republic of Indonesia'.[47] **7.25**

Other definitions consider investments as contributions of capital towards investment activities. The Investment Law of Cape Verde, for example, defines 'investment' as 'capital investment in the form of tangible or intangible assets, with a view to creating, modernizing or expanding an economic activity'.[48] The Federal Law on Foreign Investments of the Russian Federation defines 'foreign investment' as 'the investment of foreign capital in an object of entrepreneurial activity in the territory of the Russian Federation'.[49] **7.26**

A number of provisions define 'investments' as assets associated with investment activities. The Law of the Azerbaijan Republic on Investment Activity, for example, provides that '[i]nvestment is comprised of financial means, as well as material (actual) and **7.27**

---

[43] Egypt Investment Law (2017) Art 1 (hereafter Egypt Investment Law).
[44] ibid.
[45] Angola Private Investment Law (2018) Art 3.
[46] Foreign Investment Law of the People's Republic of China (2019) Art 2 (hereafter Chinese Foreign Investment Law).
[47] Indonesia Law Concerning Investment (2007) Art 1(1) (hereafter Indonesia Law Concerning Investment).
[48] Cape Verde Investment Law (2013) Art 4(c) (hereafter Cape Verde Investment Law).
[49] Russian Federation Federal Law on Foreign Investments (1999) Art 2 (hereafter Russian Law on Foreign Investments).

intellectual values, used in all kinds of business activity'.[50] Under the Moldovan Law on Investments, the concept of 'investment' is defined as the 'aggregate of values (assets), invested in any entrepreneurial activity on the territory of the Republic of Moldova'.[51] The Uzbek Law on Investments defines 'investments' as 'tangible and intangible assets and rights to them ... invested by an investor ... in social facilities, entrepreneurial, scientific and other activities'.[52]

7.28 Some investment laws require that the investor be engaged in a licensed activity. The Foreign Investment Law of Saudi Arabia, for example, defines 'foreign investment' as '[i]nvestment of foreign capital in an activity licensed by this Law'.[53] Under the Vanuatu Foreign Investment Promotion Act, 'investment' means 'to be engaged in an activity for the principal purpose of gain (pecuniary or otherwise) in conjunction with a business license'.[54]

B. Conclusions

7.29 Activity-based (or project-based) definitions and enterprise-based definitions of 'investment' overlap to a significant extent. In fact, the notions of enterprise and activity are closely linked, notably because the existence of an enterprise necessarily implies the pursuit of certain commercial activities. Therefore, where an investor owns an enterprise or an interest in an enterprise, he or she will generally be engaged in some kind of business activity or will have contributed capital, assets, etc to the conduct of such activity.

7.30 There is some variation in the way in which activity-based definitions describe qualifying activities. Some definitions are largely tautological, referring to 'investing'[55] or 'investment'[56] activities. Other definitions specify the nature of the relevant activities by reference to qualifiers such as 'entrepreneurial',[57] 'business',[58] or 'economic'.[59] The Uzbek Law on Investments expressly requires that the relevant activities must be 'for profit'.[60]

7.31 Like enterprise-based definitions, activity-based definitions reflect varying viewpoints as to the nature of 'investment'. As has been seen, some definitions assimilate investments to the actual activities conducted by the investor, while others consider that

---

[50] Law of the Azerbaijan Republic on Investment Activity (1995) Art 1 (hereafter Azerbaijan Law on Investment Activity).
[51] Moldova Law on Investments (n 1) Art 3.
[52] Uzbek Law on Investments (n 19) Art 3.
[53] Foreign Investment Law in the Kingdom of Saudi Arabia (2000) Art 1.
[54] Vanuatu Foreign Investment Promotion Act (n 1) Art 2(1).
[55] Indonesia Law Concerning Investment (n 47) Art 1(1).
[56] Chinese Foreign Investment Law (n 46) Art 2.
[57] Russian Law on Foreign Investments (n 49) Art 2.
[58] Azerbaijan Law on Investment Activity (n 50) Art 1.
[59] Cape Verde Investment Law (n 48) Art 4(c).
[60] Uzbek Law on Investments (n 19) Art 3.

investments consist of assets or capital contributions associated with such activities. As has been pointed out in connection with enterprise-based definitions, these differences have potentially far-reaching implications. In fact, where an investment is perceived as a set of assets or as capital invested in a given business activity, the value of the investment corresponds in principle to the value of the relevant assets, or the amount of capital injected. Where an investment is viewed as the activity itself, its value will take into account the profitability of the operations. As a result, the value of the investment may be either higher or lower than the value of the assets owned, or the capital contributed, by the investor.

V. Requirement of a Capital Investment

Definitions of 'investment' requiring a contribution of capital are rather common. As has been seen, such requirements can be found in a number of enterprise- and activity-based definitions of 'investment'. As the example of the Investment Code of Mali shows, a capital contribution may also be required under certain asset-based definitions. 7.32

Requirements of a capital contribution are not specific to definitions of 'investment' contained in investment laws. As has been seen in Chapter 4, a similar requirement is applied under the *Salini* test established under Art 25 ICSID Convention.[61] In fact, though larger in scope, the *Salini* criterion of a 'contribution' primarily refers to monetary or financial contributions to business activities or 'economic ventures'. Also, as has been shown in Chapter 6, many recent investment treaties require that investments possess the 'characteristics' of an investment, including 'the commitment of capital or other resources'.[62] 7.33

Although requirements of a capital contribution can be found in a number of definitions of 'investment', the exact meaning of such requirements is not entirely clear. There is, in fact, some ambiguity as to the types of capital contribution that are contemplated under such definitions. Does the notion of capital contribution refer to a contribution to the capital of a corporation, ie to a contribution whereby the investor acquires an equity interest in the relevant legal entity? Or should this concept be understood more broadly, ie as covering other types of contributions of capital such as, for example, a transfer of funds under a loan agreement? 7.34

Given that investment laws do generally not define the terms 'capital' or 'capital contribution', these questions are not easily answered. However, it will often be possible to glean the meaning of these expressions from the context and, more specifically, from the nature of the definition contained in the relevant investment law. In fact, where the applicable definition is enterprise-based, the contribution will generally have to be 7.35

---

[61] See Chapter 4 Section II.B.1.
[62] See Chapter 6 Section III.

made towards the capital of an enterprise. On the other hand, where the definition is activity-based, the meaning of 'capital contribution' may be broader. In fact, if a financial institution lends money to a corporation, one could consider that it has contributed capital to the commercial activities conducted by the corporation concerned. As a result, the loan granted to the corporation (and/or the rights arising under the loan agreement) would constitute an investment.

VI. Requirement of a Contribution to the Host State's Economic Development

7.36 As has been explained in Chapter 4, a contribution to the economic development of the host State is sometimes—though less and less frequently—considered a requirement under Art 25 ICSID Convention.[63] As has been seen, the questionable legal foundation of this requirement is the reference in the Convention's Preamble's to the role that 'private international investment' plays in the pursuit of 'economic development'. As far as investment treaty definitions of 'investment' are concerned, they virtually never require that investments must contribute to the host State's economic development. Tribunals have generally refrained from reading such a criterion into the applicable definitions.

7.37 In investment laws, by contrast, definitions requiring a contribution to the economic development of the host State are not uncommon. This is understandable given that States have a legitimate interest in confining legal protection to those operations that have a beneficial impact on their economy.

7.38 A number of investment laws expressly require that investments must contribute to the host State's 'development', 'economic development', or 'economy'. The Egyptian Investment Law, for instance, defines 'investment' as the 'use [of] ... money for the set up, expansion, development, funding, holding or management of an Investment Project thus *contributing in (sic!) the comprehensive and sustainable development of the State*'.[64] Under the Bolivian Investment Promotion Law, an investment must 'contribute to the *economic and social growth and development* of the country'.[65] The Investment Code of Benin similarly provides that an investment involves 'carrying out a project that *contributes to the development of the Beninese economy* ...'.[66]

7.39 Other investment laws define the required beneficial effects of an investment in broader or non-economic terms. Under the Investment Law of Iraq, for example, an investment consists of an 'investment of capital in any economic or service activity or project *that results in a legitimate benefit for the country*'.[67] The Turkmenistan Law on Investment

---

[63] See Chapter 4 Section II.C.
[64] Egypt Investment Law (n 43) Art 1 (emphasis added).
[65] Bolivia Investment Promotion Law (2014) Art 4 (translation by the author) (emphasis added).
[66] Law No 2020-02 on the Investment Code in the Republic of Benin (2020) Art 1 (emphasis added).
[67] Iraq Investment Law (2006) Art 1 (emphasis added).

Activities defines 'investments' as 'all kinds of property and intellectual values invested into the objects of entrepreneurial and other kinds of activities *resulting in generating profit or obtaining social benefit*'.[68]

The application of definitions requiring a contribution to the host State's economy (or economic development), or some other specified benefit raises a number of interpretive questions concerning the nature of the required contribution. What is meant, for example, by the requirement of 'social growth' set forth in the definition contained in the Bolivian Investment Promotion Law? What is the meaning of the requirement of a contribution to the host State's 'sustainable development' under the Egyptian Investment Law? Does it imply that an operation or project that has an adverse impact on the environment would not qualify as an investment? When is a benefit for the host State 'legitimate' in the sense of the Investment Law of Iraq? None of these questions receives an easy or obvious answer.

7.40

In addition to these interpretive issues, the relevant definitions raise a more general threshold question, ie the question of whether the benefit for the host State must be of a certain minimum significance or magnitude. What threshold (if any) applies depends, in the first place, on the language of the relevant definitions. The requirement of a contribution to 'the comprehensive and sustainable development' of the host State contained in the Egyptian Investment Law, for instance, may be viewed as establishing a rather high threshold. The more general requirement of a 'legitimate benefit' under the Investment Law of Iraq, on the other hand, appears to be less demanding.

7.41

Although the reasons for the adoption of contribution to the economic development and similar requirements are understandable, it is questionable whether such requirements are necessary or even desirable. In fact, as has been explained, the relevant provisions are frequently ambiguous, and it is difficult to foresee how investment tribunals will construe them in individual cases. If a State is keen on ensuring that investments protected under a particular domestic investment law bring about certain economic or other benefits, it can achieve this objective by defining the nature or characteristic features of an investment accordingly. For instance, it can require the existence of an economic project or activity, which necessarily entails a range of benefits for the host State economy such as, for example, employment and tax revenue. States wishing to limit legal protection to investments of a certain minimum size can establish monetary thresholds, for example with regard to the amount of capital invested in an enterprise or project.

7.42

---

[68] Turkmenistan Investment Law (n 19) Art 1 (emphasis added).

VII. Case Law

7.43 Arbitral case law addressing the meaning of 'investment' under domestic investment laws is limited. There are various reasons for this. First, as has already been explained, only a small proportion of investor–state disputes are brought under such laws, an overwhelming majority of claims being based on other types of consent instruments, in particular investment treaties.[69] Second, there are numerous cases in which the Respondents do not object to the existence of a qualifying investment.[70] Third, even where such objections are raised, they are sometimes only based on the ICSID Convention and/or another instrument of consent relied upon by the Claimant, rather than the applicable investment law.[71] Lastly, where objections alleging the absence of an investment are raised under the host State's investment law, tribunals sometimes fail to deal with them, chiefly because they decline jurisdiction on other grounds.[72]

7.44 One of the few noteworthy decisions is the ruling of the Tribunal in *Tradex v Albania*,[73] a case arising under the Albanian Law on Foreign Investments 1993.[74] In this case, the Claimant (Tradex) entered into a joint venture agreement with T.B. Torovitsa, an Albanian state-owned company, for the purposes of planning and overseeing the commercial and agricultural use of farmland owned by the latter.[75] In the ICSID proceedings, Tradex argued that several measures attributable to the Respondent had 'made the development of the joint venture impossible', thus amounting to an expropriation.[76]

---

[69] See Chapter 2 Section II.A.2.
[70] See, for example, *Pac Rim Cayman LLC v The Republic of El Salvador*, ICSID Case No ARB/09/12, Decision on the Respondent's Jurisdictional Objections (1 June 2012) para 5.3 (El Salvador raised several jurisdictional objections under its domestic investment law, none of which pertained to the existence—or absence—of an investment); *Société Resort Company Invest Abidjan and others v Republic of Côte d'Ivoire*, ICSID Case No ARB/16/11, Decision on the Respondent's Preliminary Objection to Jurisdiction (1 August 2017) para 57 (the Respondent only objected to the existence of consent to ICSID arbitration); *Oded Besserglik v Republic of Mozambique*, ICSID Case No ARB(AF)/14/2, Award (28 October 2019) para 212 (the Respondent alleged the absence of consent under its investment law, not the absence of an investment); *Interocean Oil Development Company and Interocean Oil Exploration Company v Federal Republic of Nigeria*, ICSID Case No ARB/13/20, Award (6 October 2020) para 107 (Nigeria raised various jurisdictional objections, but did not object to the existence of an investment).
[71] See, for example, *Vestey Group Limited v Bolivarian Republic of Venezuela*, ICSID Case No ARB/06/4, Award (15 April 2016) para 158 (the Respondent argued that the Claimant's alleged investment did not meet the legality requirement of the applicable bilateral investment treaty (BIT); it did not raise any investment-related objection under the Venezuelan Law on the Promotion and Protection of Investments); *MNSS B.V. and Recupero Credito Acciaio N.V. v Montenegro*, ICSID Case No ARB(AF)/12/8, Award (4 May 2016) (the Claimants challenged the existence of an investment only under the BIT between the Netherlands and Yugoslavia, not under the Montenegrin Foreign Investment Law).
[72] See, for example, *Menzies Middle East and Africa S.A. and Aviation Handling Services International Ltd. v Republic of Senegal*, ICSID Case No ARB/15/21, Award (5 August 2016); *Lighthouse Corporation Pty Ltd and Lighthouse Corporation Ltd, Ibc v Democratic Republic of Timor-Leste*, ICSID Case No ARB/15/2, Award (22 December 2017) paras 103, 335–36 (the Tribunal did not examine the existence of an investment under the ICSID Convention and the Timor-Leste Foreign Investment Law since 'it would [have] ma[de] no difference to the final assessment of the Tribunal's jurisdiction').
[73] *Tradex Hellas S.A. (Greece) v Republic of Albania*, ICSID Case No ARB/94/2, Award (29 April 1999) (hereafter *Tradex v Albania*).
[74] Albanian Law No 7764 on Foreign Investments (1993).
[75] *Tradex v Albania* (n 73) para 54.
[76] ibid para 57.

Albania raised a number of jurisdictional objections,[77] including an objection to the existence of an investment under the Foreign Investment Law.[78]

Distinguished commentators have highlighted two interpretive aspects of the Tribunal's decision.[79] The first one pertains to Albania's objection that Tradex did not own a qualifying investment because it used funds of foreign origin. The Tribunal rejected this argument, holding that 'the sources from which [Tradex] financed the foreign investment in Albania [we]re not relevant for the application of the [Foreign Investment Law]'.[80] It thus refused to apply a requirement that was not mentioned in the broad asset-based definition of 'investment' contained in the Law on Foreign Investments. 7.45

A second point of interest relates to the Tribunal's finding that under the Law on Foreign Investments, not only title to land, but also the right to use land constitutes an investment.[81] It based this finding on Art 1(3)(e) of the Law which expressly recognized the investment status of 'any right conferred by law or contract'.[82] The Tribunal concluded that, therefore, the joint venture company's right to use T.B. Torovitsa's land constituted an investment.[83] However, since such right belonged to the joint venture, it could not be regarded as an investment owned by the Claimant.[84] 7.46

Beyond these interpretive holdings, *Tradex* is of interest because it illustrates how tribunals sometimes struggle to identify which exact assets constitute the investment in a given case. In fact, the Tribunal apparently considered that the Claimant's investment consisted of its shares in the joint venture company.[85] Elsewhere, however, the Tribunal suggested that it was the various contributions of equipment that constituted Tradex' investment.[86] The Tribunal's hesitation was ultimately inconsequential, given that it held that no expropriation had occurred and that it was therefore not necessary to assess the value of the Claimant's investment. However, had it decided otherwise, it would have had to choose between one of the two conflicting viewpoints expressed in its decision. 7.47

---

[77] Most of these objections were dealt with in the Tribunal's Decision on Jurisdiction. See *Tradex Hellas S.A. (Greece) v Republic of Albania*, ICSID Case No ARB/94/2, Decision on Jurisdiction (24 December 1996). The question of the existence of an investment, however, was joined to the merits of the case.
[78] *Tradex v Albania* (n 73) para 90.
[79] See Stephan W Schill, Christoph Schreuer and Anthony Sinclair, 'Article 25' in Loretta Malintoppi, August Reinisch, Christoph H Schreuer and Anthony Sinclair (eds), *Schreuer's Commentary on the ICSID Convention: A Commentary on the Convention on the Settlement of Investment Disputes between States and Nationals of Other States* (3rd edn, Cambridge University Press 2022) para 203.
[80] *Tradex v Albania* (n 73) para 111.
[81] ibid para 127.
[82] ibid.
[83] ibid.
[84] ibid.
[85] ibid para 128 (observing that 'such an expropriation of a right of the Joint Venture [i.e., the joint venture's right to use T.B. Torovitsa's land] could affect the value of Tradex' share in the Joint Venture and such a share clearly is a "foreign investment" according to Art. 1 (3) b)').
[86] ibid para 113 (noting that Tradex had contributed to the joint venture company's capital by supplying equipment and that this equipment thus constituted an 'investment in kind').

7.48 Another decision rendered under a domestic investment law is *Zhinvali v Georgia*.[87] In this case, the Claimant, Zhinvali Development Ltd., negotiated various agreements with the Republic of Georgia in connection with the proposed rehabilitation of a hydroelectric power plant located near Tbilisi.[88] However, for various reasons, no contract was ever concluded between the parties.[89] Taking the view that this failure to conclude the contemplated agreements was due to 'culpable actions' on the part of Georgia, Zhinvali initiated ICSID arbitration proceedings, seeking compensation for development costs, lost profits, and moral damage.[90]

7.49 One of the issues before the Tribunal was whether Zhinvali had made an investment in Georgia within the meaning of the ICSID Convention and the Georgian Investment Law. Although neither the parties' argumentation, nor the Tribunal's analysis is always easy to follow, the Tribunal's central holding was that the various expenses incurred by the Claimant in connection with the negotiations with the Republic of Georgia, ie the Claimant's 'development costs', did not constitute an investment.[91]

7.50 From the award, the Tribunal's reasoning is not entirely clear considering that it did not explain which specific requirement(s) applicable under the definition of 'investment' contained in the Investment Law was (were) not met. However, this would arguably have been a rather straightforward task. In fact, under the Georgian Investment Law, the term 'investment' was defined as any asset 'used in the entrepreneurial activity carried out on (sic!) the territory of Georgia'.[92] Given that the contract negotiations between Zhinvali and the Republic failed, no such activity was ever carried out in Georgia, and the assets that Zhinvali allegedly contributed towards the rehabilitation project could not possibly have been used in connection with such an activity.

7.51 Another decision of interest is *Anglo-Adriatic v Albania*.[93] In this case, Anglo Adriatika Investment Fund S.H.A. (AAIF), a legal entity established under the laws of Albania which the Claimant alleged to partially own, collected privatization vouchers issued by the Republic of Albania entitling it to participate in a privatization process launched by the Respondent. In the ICSID proceedings, the Claimant argued that Albania intentionally prevented AAIF from acquiring participations in privatized companies,[94] thus violating its obligations under the Foreign Investment Law.

7.52 One of the questions before the Tribunal was whether the Claimant owned an investment in the territory of Albania. In this context, the Tribunal examined the existence of two presumed investments: the Claimant's alleged shareholding in AAIF and the loans which it claimed to have extended to AAIF. The Tribunal found that the evidence

---

[87] *Zhinvali Development Ltd. v Republic of Georgia*, ICSID Case No ARB/00/1, Award (24 January 2003).
[88] ibid para 2.
[89] ibid.
[90] ibid.
[91] ibid para 4.
[92] ibid para 377.
[93] *Anglo-Adriatic Group Limited v Republic of Albania*, ICSID Case No ARB/17/6, Award (7 February 2019).
[94] ibid para 106.

submitted by the Claimant to prove the existence of these investments was insufficient,[95] thus declining jurisdiction to hear Anglo-Adriatic's claims.[96]

7.53 Even though the Tribunal denied the existence of an investment on factual grounds, it nevertheless offered a clarification concerning the legal status of loans. In fact, it observed that, if the Claimant had indeed lent money to AAIF, such a loan would have qualified as an investment under the Law on Foreign Investments.[97] To reach this conclusion, it relied on Art 1(3)(c) of the Law which lists 'loans, monetary obligations or obligations in an activity of an economic value and related to an investment' as a category of assets that qualifies as an investment under the Law.

7.54 While decisions such as *Tradex*, *Zhinvali*, and *Anglo-Adriatic* provide useful illustrations of how investor–state tribunals interpret definitions of 'investment' contained in domestic investment laws, they do not tackle the more difficult or controversial issues that the application of such definitions may involve. As has been explained, complex issues may notably arise in connection with (a) the meaning of 'economic activities' in activity-based definitions, (b) the meaning of the term 'enterprise' in enterprise-based definitions, and (c) the question of whether the investment consists of the invested funds, rather than the assets acquired by the investor (a question that is likely to arise where the applicable definition requires a contribution of capital by the investor). Requirements of a contribution to the economic development of the host State may also give rise to intricate interpretive questions. It remains to be seen how investment tribunals will answer these and other complex questions that may be raised in future cases.

---

[95] ibid paras 247, 280.
[96] ibid para 311.
[97] ibid para 269.

8

Investment Status of Specific Categories of Assets and Operations

I.	Introduction	8.01		A. Preliminary observations	8.23
II.	Construction and Service Contracts			B. Sovereign bonds	8.27
	Concluded with the Host State or a			C. Loans	8.38
	Host State Entity	8.04	IV.	Arbitral Awards and Court	
	A. Overview	8.04		Judgments	8.50
	B. Construction contracts	8.07		A. The terms of the problem	8.50
	C. Contracts for the provision of services	8.13		B. Case law	8.56
	D. Critical assessment	8.16	V.	Funds 'Invested'	8.65
III.	Debt Instruments	8.23			

I. Introduction

8.01 This chapter examines the investment status of several specific categories of assets and operations. These include construction and service contracts concluded with the host State or a host State entity (Section II), debt instruments and, more particularly, sovereign bonds and loans (Section III), arbitral awards and court judgments obtained by the presumed investor (Section IV), and funds 'invested' (or expenses incurred) in connection with an alleged investment (Section V).

8.02 As the reference to 'assets and operations' in the title of this chapter suggests (and as has been explained throughout this book), there is no single generally accepted view as to the nature of investment. In particular, there is no unanimity as to whether an investment is (or should be considered as) an asset or an operation. In many cases, tribunals will scrutinize both of these dimensions. In fact, under traditional asset-based definitions of investment contained in investment treaties and laws,[1] tribunals have to (a) identify assets owned or controlled by the investor in the territory of the host State and (b) determine whether those assets qualify as investments (given the breadth of traditional definitions, this second issue is rarely problematic). Under the ICSID Convention, on the other hand, tribunals generally focus on the economic activities conducted by the presumed investor (if any) and examine whether those activities

---

[1] See Chapter 5 Section II.

meet the *Salini* criteria[2] or can otherwise be distinguished from 'ordinary' commercial transactions.[3]

8.03 The reasons for selecting the four chosen categories of assets and operations are as follows. Debt instruments and awards and judgments are discussed primarily because of the controversy surrounding their investment status, ie the existence of conflicting decisions and viewpoints. As far as construction and service contracts concluded between the presumed investor and the host State are concerned, there is no such controversy—on the contrary, there seems to be quasi-universal agreement among tribunals that such contracts generally qualify as investments. This conclusion is not, however, as self-evident as one may think, and it is thus appropriate to examine the relevant decisions more closely (and critically), as other writers have done.[4] Lastly, there appears to be latent ambiguity as to the relevance of funds 'invested', ie the money spent, by the alleged investor, for the existence of an investment, including the question of whether those funds may, in and of themselves, constitute an investment. It is thus useful to attempt to shed some light on these issues.

II. Construction and Service Contracts Concluded with the Host State or a Host State Entity

A. Overview

8.04 Evidently, not all contracts concluded with a foreign State constitute, or involve, investments. Sale of goods contracts, for instance (eg the sale of a military ship), do not in principle qualify as investments. It is of course true that the rights arising under such contracts (like any contractual rights) can be regarded as investments under broad, asset-based definitions (though their localization in the territory of the host State may be debatable). Under the ICSID Convention, however, tribunals applying the *Salini* or the commercial-transaction test would generally not hesitate to deny the investment status of such contracts.

8.05 There are two categories of contracts that ICSID tribunals have almost invariably characterized as investments: construction contracts and contracts for the provision of services. The former consist of contracts under which a contractor agrees to build (or repair) facilities or installations, such as roads, bridges, and power plants. The latter refer to the broader category of contracts whereby a party provides services (financial, technical, etc) to (or on behalf of) a foreign State.

---

[2] For a detailed examination of the *Salini* test and criteria, see Chapter 4 Section II.
[3] For discussion of the commercial-transaction test, one of the two alternatives to the *Salini* inquiry, see Chapter 4 Section IV.
[4] See, for example, Farouk Yala, 'The Notion of "Investment" in ICSID Case Law: A Drifting Jurisdictional Requirement?' (2005) 22 J Intl Arb 105 (hereafter Yala, 'The Notion of "Investment"'); Sebastien Manciaux, 'The Notion of Investment: New Controversies' (2008) 9 JWIT 443 (hereafter Manciaux, 'The Notion of Investment').

8.06 The investment status of at least some of these contracts is indirectly recognized in a number of investment treaties. The US Model bilateral investment treaty (BIT), for instance, defines not only the term 'investment', but also the related notion of 'investment agreement',[5] implying that such an agreement constitutes, or relates to, an investment. It distinguishes three types of such investment agreements, all of which involve either construction or the supply of certain services: (a) agreements pertaining to (the exploration and/or extraction of) natural resources, (b) agreements related to the supply of services to the public, and (c) agreements concerning infrastructure projects.[6]

B. Construction contracts

8.07 ICSID tribunals have consistently held that construction contracts (and/or the rights arising under such contracts) qualify as investments under both the ICSID Convention and definitions found in investment treaties and laws.[7] The existing case law should not, however, be (mis)understood as meaning that contrary outcomes are precluded. In fact, it is conceivable that certain construction contracts are held not to meet the requirements found to be applicable under Art 25 ICSID Convention. Also, and more importantly, it is probable that construction contracts do not per se qualify as investments under enterprise-based definitions requiring at a minimum partial ownership of an enterprise established in the host State.

8.08 ICSID tribunals have not generally had difficulty finding that construction contracts qualify as investments under traditional asset-based investment treaty definitions. In *Salini*, for example, the Tribunal did not hesitate to find that the builders' rights arising under a contract for the construction of a segment of a highway constituted 'a contractual benefit having an economic value' and a 'right of an economic nature' in the sense of Art 1(c) and 1(e) of the BIT between Italy and Morocco.[8] The Tribunals in *Bayindir*, which involved the construction of a six-lane motorway, and *Garanti Koza*, where the Claimant undertook to build a number of highway bridges, similarly had no trouble deciding that the relevant transactions gave rise to qualifying rights under the

---

[5] US Model BIT 2012 Art 1.
[6] ibid.
[7] See, for example, *Salini Costruttori S.P.A. and Italstrade S.P.A. v Kingdom of Morocco*, ICSID Case No ARB/00/4, Decision on Jurisdiction (23 July 2001) paras 43–58 (examining the existence of an investment under the applicable BIT and the ICSID Convention) (hereafter *Salini v Morocco*); *L.E.S.I.—DIPENTA v Democratic and Popular Republic of Algeria*, ICSID Case No ARB/03/08, Award (10 January 2005) para 14 (focusing on Art 25 ICSID Convention) (hereafter *LESI v Algeria*); *Bayindir Insaat Turizm Ticaret Ve Sanayi A.Ş. v Islamic Republic of Pakistan*, ICSID Case No ARB/03/29, Decision on Jurisdiction (14 November 2005) paras 104–38 (examining objections raised under the applicable BIT and Art 25 ICSID Convention) (hereafter *Bayindir v Pakistan*); *Garanti Koza LLP v Turkmenistan*, ICSID Case No ARB/11/20, Award (19 December 2016) paras 228–42 (examining the existence of an investment under the applicable BIT and Art 25 ICSID Convention) (hereafter *Garanti Koza v Turkmenistan*); *Standard Chartered Bank (Hong Kong) Limited v United Republic of Tanzania*, ICSID Case No ARB/15/41, Award (11 October 2019) 213 (holding that 'the construction and operation of an infrastructure project, such as the Facility [the electric generating facility to be built and operated by Independent Power Tanzania Limited] in Tanzania, is an investment') (internal footnote omitted).
[8] *Salini v Morocco* (n 7) para 45.

asset-based definitions of the applicable BITs (the BIT between Turkey and Pakistan and the BIT between the United Kingdom and Turkmenistan).[9]

Arbitral tribunals have also recognized that constructions contracts (or the rights arising under such contracts) constitute investments for the purposes of Art 25 ICSID Convention. Leaving aside rather exceptional rulings that have applied the permissibility rule,[10] tribunals have generally reached this conclusion on the basis of their understanding of the *Salini* test. The *LESI* tribunal, for instance, applied the three core *Salini* criteria (ie contributions, duration, and risk);[11] the Tribunals in *Salini* and *Bayindir* additionally took into account the controversial fourth *Salini* criterion, ie the existence of a contribution to the economic development of the host State.[12]

8.09

As the decisions in *Salini*, *LESI*, and *Bayindir* show, compliance with the requirements of a minimum duration and of a contribution to the economic development of the host State is rather unproblematic.[13] This is because construction projects are, by definition, long-term agreements which will in principle satisfy the *Salini* test's duration requirement, at least if the relevant threshold is construed flexibly. In addition, it is rather obvious that the construction of roads, dams, bridges, etc benefits the economic development (or economy) of the host State. The construction of a highway, for example, notably facilitates the carriage of goods and, therefore, domestic and international trade. In addition, building companies frequently purchase equipment from local suppliers and hire local workers, which further stimulates the host State's economy.

8.10

When examining compliance with the risk requirement, tribunals generally emphasize the risks associated with the long-term nature of the relevant projects. In *Salini*, for instance, the Tribunal highlighted the risk of an increase in the cost of labour and the risk of the occurrence of unforeseen events.[14] In *Bayindir*, the Tribunal similarly stressed the existence of an 'inherent risk in long-term contracts',[15] without however providing any further specifications. Both Tribunals also acknowledged that risks may flow from the applicable contractual framework. The *Salini* tribunal, for instance, noted that the owner's right to 'prematurely put an end to the contract' and to 'impose variations ... without changing the manner of fixing prices' constituted a qualifying risk.[16]

8.11

---

[9] *Bayindir v Pakistan* (n 7) paras 105–21; *Garanti Koza v Turkmenistan* (n 7) paras 228–34.
[10] See, for example, *Garanti Koza v Turkmenistan* (n 7) paras 235–42.
[11] *LESI v Algeria* (n 7) para 14.
[12] *Salini v Morocco* (n 7) paras 53–57; *Bayindir v Pakistan* (n 7) paras 122–38.
[13] *Salini v Morocco* (n 7) paras 54, 57 (holding that a performance duration of thirty-six months 'complies with the minimal length of time upheld by the doctrine' and that 'the contribution of the contract to the economic development of the Moroccan State cannot seriously be questioned'); *LESI v Algeria* (n 7) para 14(ii) (ruling that the duration requirement was met given that the contractual performance period was fifty months); *Bayindir v Pakistan* (n 7) paras 133, 137 (deciding that a three-year contractual duration was sufficient because '[c]ontracts over similar periods of time have been considered to satisfy the duration test for an investment' and that the existence of a contribution to the economic development of Pakistan was a necessary implication of the presence of the three core *Salini* criteria of contributions, duration, and risk).
[14] *Salini v Morocco* (n 7) para 55.
[15] *Bayindir v Pakistan* (n 7) para 136.
[16] *Salini v Morocco* (n 7) para 55.

In *Bayindir*, such a risk was held to result from the contractually agreed defect liability and maintenance periods.[17]

8.12 As far as the requirement of contributions is concerned, tribunals usually adopt a flexible approach, imposing very few, if any, limits on what qualifies as a 'contribution'. In *Salini*, for example, the Tribunal held that the Italian companies' contributions included (a) their know-how, (b) the equipment and personnel used to carry out the works, (c) the setting up of the production tool, (d) the loans that they had obtained to finance the works, and (e) the bank guarantees issued in relation to performance.[18] In *Bayindir*, the Tribunal similarly identified know-how and equipment as relevant contributions, adding that Bayindir had also made a contribution 'in financial terms'.[19] In *LESI*, the Tribunal somewhat ambiguously held that the Claimant had made contributions because it had incurred various expenses and performed services giving rise to a right to remuneration or indemnification.[20]

C. Contracts for the provision of services

8.13 Like construction contracts, contracts for the provision of services are generally considered to qualify as investments. In *SGS v Paraguay*,[21] for example, the Tribunal held that a contract for the provision of pre-shipment inspection services constituted an investment, both under the applicable BIT (the BIT between Switzerland and Paraguay)[22] and Art 25 ICSID Convention.[23] In *SGS v Pakistan*,[24] another case brought by SGS which involved a largely identical transaction, the Respondent did not even object to the existence of an investment, which arguably suggests that the investment status of service contracts is widely accepted.

8.14 *Deutsche Bank v Sri Lanka*[25] involved financial services and, more specifically, a hedging agreement under which the Claimant agreed to protect Ceylon Petroleum Corporation, Sri Lanka's national petroleum corporation, from the risk of an increase in oil prices. The Tribunal held that the Claimant's rights under this agreement qualified as an investment in the sense of the applicable BIT (the BIT between Germany and Sri Lanka), given that they constituted 'assets' with the meaning of this treaty.[26]

---

[17] *Bayindir v Pakistan* (n 7) para 136 (holding that 'the very existence of a defect liability period of one year and of a maintenance period of four years against payment, creates an obvious risk for Bayindir').
[18] *Salini v Morocco* (n 7) para 53.
[19] *Bayindir v Pakistan* (n 7) para 131.
[20] *LESI v Algeria* (n 7) para 14(i).
[21] *SGS Société Générale de Surveillance S.A. v The Republic of Paraguay*, ICSID Case No ARB/07/29, Decision on Jurisdiction (12 February 2010).
[22] ibid paras 78–90.
[23] ibid paras 91–108. The Tribunal applied both the permissibility and the *Salini* test, holding that the requirements of both were met in the case before it.
[24] *SGS Société Générale de Surveillance S.A. v Islamic Republic of Pakistan*, ICSID Case No ARB/01/13, Decision of the Tribunal on Objections to Jurisdiction (6 August 2003).
[25] *Deutsche Bank AG v Democratic Socialist Republic of Sri Lanka*, ICSID Case No ARB/09/02, Award (31 October 2012).
[26] ibid para 285.

It also ruled that the hedging agreement satisfied the *Salini* test under Art 25 ICSID Convention, finding that the requirements of contributions,[27] a minimum duration,[28] and risk[29] were met.

One of the few cases in which a tribunal found that services provided to a foreign State did not constitute an investment is the decision of the sole Arbitrator in *Malaysian Historical Salvors v Malaysia*.[30] As has been seen, this case involved a contract for the salvage of the cargo (porcelain) of the 'DIANA', a ship that had sunk in Malaysian territorial waters at the beginning of the nineteenth century.[31] Focusing exclusively on Art 25 ICSID Convention,[32] the sole Arbitrator acknowledged that the services provided involved certain contributions and risks,[33] and that performance took place over an extended period of time.[34] However, he decided that the different requirements were only met superficially, not in a 'qualitative' sense,[35] ultimately concluding that the Claimant had not made an investment within the meaning of the ICSID Convention. 8.15

D. Critical assessment

Although it is well-established that the provision of construction and other services qualifies as an investment, this characterization is nevertheless counter-intuitive. In fact, as such, neither of these services constitutes an investment in the ordinary sense of the term, which—as has been explained[36]—centres on the purchase of an asset with the aim of realizing a profit. It is also uncontroversial that the provision of construction or other types of services does not per se constitute an FDI or a portfolio investment in an economic sense, because both of these types of investment presume the acquisition of an equity interest in an enterprise established in the host State.[37] 8.16

---

[27] ibid paras 297–300. Like other tribunals, the *Deutsche Bank* tribunal construed the term 'contribution' in a broad and flexible manner. It considered that the Claimant had made contributions by (a) undertaking a commitment to pay a certain amount of money to the Ceylon Petroleum Company in the event that the cost of importing oil continues to exceed a contractually agreed threshold, (b) effecting payment of an amount of money in performance of the commitment undertaken, and (c) by attending meetings, conducting negotiations, and exchanging correspondence with the Ceylon Petroleum Company and the Sri Lankan Central Bank.

[28] ibid paras 303–04. The Tribunal took the view that duration was a flexible requirement and that it was met in the case before it, considering that the hedging agreement had been concluded for a period of twelve months and that the conclusion of this agreement had been preceded by lengthy negotiations conducted over another twenty-four months.

[29] ibid para 302. The Tribunal decided that the risk incurred by the Claimant consisted of the risk that it would have to make a payment to the Ceylon Petroleum Company under the hedging agreement.

[30] *Malaysian Historical Salvors Sdn, Bhd v Malaysia*, ICSID Case No ARB/05/10, Award on Jurisdiction (17 May 2007) (hereafter *Malaysian Historical Salvors v Malaysia*).

[31] ibid para 7.

[32] This focus, along with the sole Arbitrator's ensuing failure to examine the existence of an investment under the applicable BIT, was the principal reason for the annulment of his award. See *Malaysian Historical Salvors Sdn Bhd v The Government of Malaysia*, ICSID Case No ARB/05/10, Decision on the Application for Annulment (16 April 2009).

[33] *Malaysian Historical Salvors v Malaysia* (n 30) paras 109, 112.

[34] ibid paras 110–11 (noting that the contract was concluded for an initial period of eighteen months and that it ultimately 'took almost four years to complete').

[35] ibid paras 109, 111–12.

[36] See Chapter 2 Section VI.

[37] See Chapter 2 Section VII.

8.17 An example will be helpful to highlight this dilemma. If a medical doctor performs medical services abroad, very few people would argue that this doctor made (or owns) an investment in the country concerned. Yet, he or she certainly made various types of contributions that qualify as such under the *Salini* case law: a contribution of know-how (the doctor's medical expertise), a contribution of equipment (his or her medical instruments), and a contribution of personnel (if the doctor is accompanied by an assistant, for example), to mention only the most obvious ones. If the doctor happens to visit patients in the relevant country on a regular basis and over an extended period of time, one could further consider that the requirement of a minimum duration is met. And it would doubtlessly be possible to identify certain qualifying risks (eg the risk of non-payment, the risk that the travel expenses exceed the doctor's fees, etc). In sum, it would not be too far-fetched to argue that our doctor is an investor.

8.18 The question that this example raises is the following: Why do we consider that it is unreasonable to qualify the medical doctor's services as an investment, but sensible to characterize the construction of a road, or the provision of import-related inspections services (such as those involved in the three *SGS* cases) as an investment? One explanation may be that the construction of a road and the provision of import-related inspection services are services provided to the *State*, not to private parties. This explanation cannot be crucial, however, given that our analysis of the doctor's medical services would most probably not change if he or she was hired by a governmental agency to treat a group of civil servants. Another possible explanation may relate to the scale of the relevant services and the magnitude of their positive (economic or other) impact for the host State. But if this is indeed the decisive factor, then the difference is merely one of degree, and the medical services provided by the doctor would be more accurately described as a 'small' investment, rather than as activities that do not at all qualify as an investment.

8.19 Also, it is not clear why, or in what sense, a contract for the provision of services (including construction services) would be fundamentally different from a contract for the sale of goods. Admittedly, in one case, the private party agrees to *do* something, while in the other, it undertakes to *give* something. Beyond this difference, however, sale of goods contracts and contracts for the supply of services are quite similar. In particular, it can be argued that sale of goods contracts also meet the three core *Salini* criteria of contributions (eg in the form of funds used to purchase goods for resale or to purchase raw materials to manufacture the goods, or in the form of know-how or intellectual property rights), duration (this requirement would notably be met where the parties conclude a long-term supply agreement, but it may also be met when one takes into account the time needed to negotiate the contract and/or manufacture the goods), and risk (eg the risk of non-payment, the risk of loss or destruction of the goods before the passing of risk, or the risk of an increase in the price of the raw materials needed to manufacture the goods). The only major difference is that the service provider is physically present in the host State, while the foreign seller is not. Is this, ie physical presence in the host State, the distinguishing feature of an investment?

If one wanted to remain more faithful to the ordinary meaning of the term 'investment', one could focus on the question of whether the presumed investor purchased assets in the host State. As has already been mentioned, service providers (including builders) frequently purchase local machinery or equipment and hire local workers (the right to performance under such employment contracts could be viewed as assets purchased by the presumed investor). Under this approach—which does not seem to find any support in practice—it would not be the services themselves that constitute the investment (nor the contractual rights arising under the relevant contracts), but the individual assets that the investor purchases in order to supply those services.

Manciaux has made several interesting observations in relation to the investment status of construction and service contracts. Being critical of the broad interpretation of the term 'contributions' adopted by investment tribunals, he has underlined the need to distinguish such contributions from a mere 'allocation of resources'.[38] Although the specifics of the suggested distinction are not entirely clear, Manciaux firmly rejects the idea that 'contributions of industry', which is the literal translation of the French notion of *apports en industrie* and notably covers know-how and labour, qualify as contributions.[39]

Another point raised by Manciaux pertains to the impact of the manner in which the private party is remunerated. In fact, according to Manciaux, the uncertainty of the amount of such remuneration constitutes a key characteristic of an investment (it should be noted that Manciaux rejects the pertinence of the related, but more general, risk requirement[40]).[41] Specifically, Manciaux argues that construction and service contracts only constitute investments 'if the entrepreneur's remuneration depends at least in part on the operating of the constructed ensemble ... such as in BOT or concession contracts'.[42] Where this is not the case, for example in a *Salini*-type scenario, the relevant services do not qualify as an investment.

---

[38] Manciaux, 'The Notion of Investment' (n 4) paras 32–33.
[39] ibid para 33 (noting that, while 'the contribution in property and in possession is discriminatory [i.e., distinguishes investments from other types of transactions or operations], such is not the case for the contribution of industry that does not entail any appropriation').
[40] ibid para 25 (maintaining that 'the risk criterion does not constitute an autonomous criterion of an investment transaction').
[41] ibid para 34 (arguing that, '[o]ther than the existence of a contribution in a strict sense, it is the uncertain remuneration of this contribution that distinguishes an investment from other transactions of international economic relations').
[42] ibid para 39.

III. Debt Instruments

A. Preliminary observations

8.23 A *debt instrument* has been defined as 'a tool an entity can use to raise capital' and, more specifically, as 'a documented, binding obligation that provides funds to an entity in return for a promise from the entity to repay a lender or investor in accordance with terms of a contract'.[43] Debt instruments not only include negotiable instruments such as corporate and sovereign bonds or promissory notes, but also purely contractual arrangements in the form of loans and the like. As has been seen in Chapter 5, one complex legal issue raised by debt instruments relates to the criteria that are relevant to determine whether they meet the requirement of territoriality (ie of being situated in the host State).[44] This section examines the more general question of whether, and under what circumstances, debt instruments at all qualify as investments.[45]

8.24 There is sometimes confusion as to whether it is the act of lending or the act of borrowing that may potentially constitute an investment. In principle, the answer should be that it is the lenders (or, more generally, holders of debt instruments) that may be considered as owning or having made an investment. However, some decisions suggest that the act of borrowing funds may also amount to an investment or, at least, to a contribution in the sense of the *Salini* test. In fact, the *Salini* Tribunal itself recognized that one of the qualifying contributions made by the Italian Claimants consisted of the 'loans ... [they had obtained] to finance the purchases necessary to carry out the works and to pay the salaries of the workforce'.[46]

8.25 One can distinguish between debt instruments pertaining to sovereign debt (eg sovereign bonds, loans to a State or State entity, etc) and those that relate to private debt (eg corporate bonds, loans to private entities, etc). For various reasons, this distinction may be relevant for the purposes of determining the investment status of a given debt instrument. For instance, it could be argued that sovereign bonds, which represent funds made available to a State, are more likely to entail a contribution to the economic development of the State concerned (and, thus, to meet this particular *Salini* requirement) than corporate bonds. As will be shown below, there are also reasons to adopt the opposite approach, ie to consider that private debt instruments are more likely to qualify as investments than sovereign debt instruments.

8.26 This section focuses on the investment status of two specific types of debt instruments, namely, sovereign bonds and loans (without any restriction based on the legal status of

---

[43] James Chen, 'What Is a Debt Instrument? Definition, Structure, and Types' (*Investopedia*, 26 September 2022) <https://www.investopedia.com/terms/d/debtinstrument.asp> accessed 19 May 2023.
[44] See Chapter 5 Section IV.
[45] For commentary, see Michael Waibel, 'Opening Pandora's Box: Sovereign Bonds in International Arbitration' (2007) 101 AJIL 711; Michael Waibel, 'Subject Matter Jurisdiction: The Notion of Investment' (2021) 19 ICSID Reports 25 paras 111–20 (hereafter Waibel, 'Subject Matter Jurisdiction').
[46] *Salini v Morocco* (n 7) para 53.

the beneficiary of the loan). Corporate bonds are not examined per se, notably because there does not seem to be any case law dealing with the investment status of such instruments. However, given that the discussion of loans covers not only loans granted to States or State entities, but also those granted to private parties (it actually focuses on such loans), the relevant analysis is, at least in part, also relevant for the analysis of corporate bonds.

B. Sovereign bonds

1. Investment status under definitions contained in investment treaties and laws

Whether sovereign bonds qualify as an investment under a particular investment treaty or law depends, in the first place, on the type of definition that the relevant treaty or law adopts. Under traditional asset-based definitions of 'investment', there is no reason why sovereign bonds should not constitute an investment. Under enterprise-based definitions, on the other hand, sovereign bonds will in principle not qualify, given that they do not as such involve the acquisition of an equity interest in a local corporation. Whether sovereign bonds may constitute an investment under activity- or project-based definitions will depend on how the notions of activity and project are interpreted. If they are construed as referring to activities conducted, and projects undertaken, by the presumed investor himself or herself, sovereign bonds are unlikely to qualify as investments. However, if these concepts are understood as encompassing State activities and projects, sovereign bonds may be characterized as such.

8.27

The investment status of sovereign bonds may be expressly excluded under the applicable treaty or law. As has been shown in Chapter 6, a number of investment treaties exclude these instruments from their scope of application.[47] The BIT between Morocco and Nigeria, for example, specifies that the term 'investment' does not include '[d]ebt securities issued by a government or loans to a government'.[48] The BIT between the United Kingdom and Colombia contains a comparable exclusion, providing that the term 'investment' does not cover 'public debt operations'.[49] Similar provisions can presumably be found in at least a few domestic investment laws.

8.28

Given that sovereign bonds in principle qualify as investments under traditional asset-based definitions of 'investment', it is not surprising that tribunals have generally affirmed their investment status under such definitions. Illustrative rulings notably include the decisions in *Abaclat*,[50] *Ambiente*

8.29

---

[47] See Chapter 6 Section IV.D.
[48] Reciprocal Investment Promotion and Protection Agreement between the Government of the Kingdom of Morocco and the Government of the Federal Republic of Nigeria (adopted 3 December 2016, not in force) Art 1 (hereafter Morocco–Nigeria BIT).
[49] Bilateral Agreement for the Promotion and Protection of Investments between the Government of the United Kingdom of Great Britain and Northern Ireland and Republic of Colombia (adopted 17 March 2010, entered into force 10 October 2014) Art I(2)(b)(i) (hereafter UK–Colombia BIT).
[50] *Abaclat and others v The Argentine Republic*, ICSID Case No ARB/07/5, Decision on Jurisdiction and Admissibility (4 August 2011) (hereafter *Abaclat v Argentina*).

Ufficio,[51] and *Alemanni*,[52] three cases brought against Argentina under the BIT between Argentina and Italy. In these cases, the Tribunals recognized that sovereign bonds constituted assets under the broad, asset-based definition of 'investment' contained in the BIT, notably holding that those bonds fell within one or several specific categories of qualifying assets listed in the BIT.[53]

8.30 The Tribunal in *Poštová banka*,[54] a case arising under the BIT between Slovakia and Greece,[55] however, reached a different conclusion. This BIT also contained a broad asset-based definition of 'investment', defining it as 'every kind of asset'.[56] It included, as is customary, a non-exhaustive catalogue of qualifying assets. One of these categories consisted of 'loans, claims to money or to any performance under contract having a financial value'.[57] The central issue in this case was whether the bonds held by the Claimants could be regarded as 'loans' and/or 'claims to money' within the meaning of this provision or, alternatively, whether they could otherwise be considered as 'assets' in the sense of the BIT.

8.31 As regards the question of whether the bonds held by the Claimants could be regarded as loans, the Tribunal provided a negative answer, highlighting various basic differences between these two categories of debt instruments.[58] The Tribunal also refused to accept that the bonds constituted, or gave rise to, 'claims to money or to any performance under contract having a financial value'.[59] In this connection, it highlighted the need to interpret the relevant category narrowly[60] and emphasized the absence of a contractual relationship between the Claimants and the Respondent (the Claimants had acquired the bonds on the secondary market, rather than purchasing them directly from the State).[61] Lastly, the Tribunal also held that the expression 'every kind of asset'

---

[51] *Ambiente Ufficio S.P.A. and others v The Argentine Republic*, ICSID Case No ARB/08/9, Decision on Jurisdiction and Admissibility (8 February 2013) (hereafter *Ambiente Ufficio v Argentina*).

[52] *Giovanni Alemanni and others v The Argentine Republic*, ICSID Case No 07/8, Decision on Jurisdiction and Admissibility (17 November 2014) (hereafter *Alemanni v Argentina*).

[53] See *Abaclat v Argentina* (n 50) para 361 (holding that the bonds constituted 'obligations, private or public titles or any other right to performances or services having economic value' within the meaning of Art 1(1)(c) of the BIT); *Ambiente Ufficio v Argentina* (n 51) para 495 (deciding that the bonds held by the Claimants not only met the requirements of Art 1(1)(c) of the BIT, but also qualified as 'any right of economic nature conferred under law or contract' in the sense of Art 1(1)(f)); *Alemanni v Argentina* (n 52) para 296 (endorsing the decisions rendered in *Abaclat* and *Ambiente Ufficio*).

[54] *Poštová banka, a.s. and Istrokapital SE v The Hellenic Republic*, ICSID Case No ARB/13/8, Award (9 April 2015) (hereafter *Poštová banka v Greece*).

[55] Agreement between the Government of the Czech and Slovak Federal Republic and the Government of the Hellenic Republic for the Promotion and Reciprocal Protection of Investments (adopted 3 June 1991, entered into force 31 December 1992) (hereafter Slovakia–Greece BIT).

[56] ibid Art 1(1).

[57] ibid Art 1(1)(c).

[58] *Poštová banka v Greece* (n 54) paras 337–40 (concluding that 'the Parties to the treaty did not intend to treat government securities, such as the GGBs [Greek Government Bonds], as investments for [the] purposes of the BIT').

[59] ibid para 349.

[60] ibid para 342 (noting that 'a Tribunal should not lightly expand the language of a treaty so as to conclude that a general reference to "claims to money" includes bonds or other securities issued by a State').

[61] ibid paras 343–49.

did not cover all possible forms or types of assets[62] and that, in particular, it did not include sovereign bonds.

2. Investment status under Art 25 ICSID Convention

Whether sovereign bonds (and/or their acquisition) qualify as an investment under Art 25 ICSID Convention evidently depends on what test is applied. Under the prevailing approach, the *Salini* test, there is no obvious answer to this question. In fact, the duration requirement would most probably be met, given that it is frequently applied in a flexible manner.[63] However, it is doubtful whether the purchase of sovereign bonds can be considered to involve an 'investment risk', ie a risk that is unrelated to the risk of non-performance by the other party of its obligations.[64] Whether the contribution requirement is met will depend on how one answers the 'to what' question, ie the question of the nature of the activity or operation that must be contributed to.[65]

8.32

Despite these uncertainties, most tribunals have held that sovereign bonds do indeed constitute investments in the sense of Art 25 ICSID Convention. One such decision is *Abaclat*. In this case, the Tribunal rejected the application of the *Salini* test, finding that it lacked a basis in the text of the Convention.[66] Instead, it considered that an investment under the Convention consisted of a value-creating contribution.[67] It held that, in the case before it, both of these elements, ie a contribution and the creation of value, were present. According to the Tribunal, the Claimants' contribution took the form of the payment of money for the bonds (or, to be more precise, for the security entitlements in the bonds), while the value created consisted of the rights attached to those bonds.[68]

8.33

Another decision affirming the investment status of sovereign bonds under Art 25 ICSID Convention is *Ambiente Ufficio*. Contrary to the *Abaclat* tribunal, the Tribunal in *Ambiente Ufficio* followed the *Salini* approach, even though it seems to have rejected the idea that the *Salini* criteria constitute mandatory jurisdictional requirements.[69] Applying the *Salini* test to the facts of the case, the Tribunal notably held that the three core criteria of a contribution, a minimum duration, and risk were present in the case before it.[70] Of particular interest is its analysis of the risk assumed by the Claimants. In fact, the Tribunal held that the purchase of the bonds involved a 'sovereign' risk, ie 'the risk of the host State's sovereign intervention'.[71] It considered that such a risk exceeded 'an ordinary commercial risk' and that it was therefore characteristic of an investment.[72]

8.34

---

[62] ibid para 287. The Tribunal stated that it was 'not persuaded that a broad definition necessarily mean[t] that any and all categories, of any nature whatsoever, may qualify as an "investment"'.
[63] See Chapter 4 Section II.B.2.
[64] For a more detailed discussion of the notion of investment risk, see Chapter 4 Section II.B.3.
[65] See Chapter 4 Section II.B.1.
[66] *Abaclat v Argentina* (n 50) para 364.
[67] ibid para 365.
[68] ibid para 366.
[69] *Ambiente Ufficio v Argentina* (n 51) para 481.
[70] ibid paras 483–85.
[71] ibid para 485.
[72] ibid.

8.35 The Tribunal in *Alemanni* handed down a very similar ruling. Its decision seems to have been based, to a large extent, on its approval of the rulings in *Abaclat* and *Ambiente Ufficio*.[73] The language used in the Tribunal's decision also suggests an implicit endorsement of the permissibility test,[74] a test that—as has been seen—was first applied in *Bureau Veritas v Paraguay*.[75] Finally, the Tribunal also relied on the Convention's drafting history, noting that, during the negotiations, 'sovereign bonds [had] actually [been] used as an example of the potential breadth of the Convention's reach in terms of what sorts of future dispute could be put before an ICSID tribunal'.[76]

8.36 The *Poštová banka* tribunal, on the other hand, found that the sovereign bonds purchased by the Claimants did *not* constitute an investment under the Convention. One reason for this decision was its holding that the transaction at stake did not involve a qualifying contribution, which the Tribunal defined as 'a contribution to an economic venture'.[77] In fact, it considered that there was no evidence that the funds made available to Greece had been used in connection with 'economically productive activities' and that it appeared, on the contrary, that those funds had been used for Greece's budgetary needs, including for the repayment of its debts.[78]

8.37 Another ground relied upon by the Tribunal was the absence of a specific investment risk. As its analysis shows, the Tribunal implicitly rejected the approach followed in *Ambiente Ufficio* which centred on the distinction between sovereign and commercial risk. In fact, the Tribunal observed that sovereign risks were not specific to investments[79] and that the existence or absence of such risks was therefore not relevant. According to the Tribunal, the relevant risk was the operational risk, ie the 'risk inherent in the investment operation in its surrounding'.[80] The Tribunal held that no such risk was, or had been, present in the case before it.[81]

C. Loans

1. Loans as such

8.38 Analysed in isolation, ie without taking into account any possible connection with another investment made, or owned, by the lender, or the use of the funds loaned, can it be said that a loan qualifies as an investment? If, for instance, a financial institution

---

[73] *Alemanni v Argentina* (n 52) para 296. The Tribunal noted that it '[found] itself in agreement with the comprehensive treatment given to it [the question of whether sovereign bonds constitute an investment under Art 25 ICSID Convention] by the *Abaclat* and *Ambiente Ufficio* tribunals'.
[74] ibid (holding that '[n]othing in the ICSID Convention itself presents an obstacle to considering that bonds are capable of constituting investments').
[75] *Bureau Veritas, Inspection, Valuation, Assessment and Control, BIVAC B.V. v The Republic of Paraguay*, ICSID Case No ARB/07/9, Decision of the Tribunal on Objections to Jurisdiction (29 May 2009). For a more detailed discussion of the permissibility test, see Chapter 4 Section III.
[76] *Alemanni v Argentina* (n 52) para 296 (internal footnote omitted).
[77] *Poštová banka v Greece* (n 54) para 361.
[78] ibid para 363.
[79] ibid para 369.
[80] ibid para 370.
[81] ibid para 371.

established in country A grants a loan to a company incorporated in country B (eg to finance the acquisition of new technology or equipment), does this loan (or the financial institution's rights under the agreement) constitute an investment in country B?

Under definitions contained in investment treaties and laws, the answer to this question will generally be an affirmative one. In fact, the financial institution's contractual rights are likely to constitute 'assets' in the sense of traditional asset-based definitions of 'investment'. Also, as has been seen in connection with *Poštová banka*, some treaties (such as the BIT between Slovakia and Greece[82]) expressly mention 'loans' as a specific category of qualifying assets. Such an express recognition of the investment status of loans can also be found in a number of domestic investment laws.[83]

8.39

Under Art 25 ICSID Convention, however, the investment status of loans is more questionable, especially if the *Salini* test is applied. In fact, the risk incurred by the lender does not in principle constitute an 'investment risk' in the sense of the relevant case law,[84] ie it does not go beyond the risk that the borrower will not reimburse the loan. This is because the lender does not conduct any economic activities in the country of incorporation of the borrower that may or may not turn out to be profitable. Whether a loan involves a contribution in the sense of the *Salini* inquiry is similarly uncertain. The term 'contribution' can of course be construed broadly to cover any imaginable type or form of contribution. However, if it is understood as a contribution to an activity (an 'economic venture'[85]) conducted in the host State, and if one considers that such an activity must be conducted by the presumed investor himself or herself,[86] then a loan would not in principle involve any such contribution.

8.40

Interestingly, there do not seem to be any cases in which the question of the investment status of a loan has arisen independently of the question of whether other assets or operations constituted investments. In fact, in most cases, the issue of whether a loan qualified as an investment formed part of a series of issues pertaining to the existence of an investment. That is probably the reason why arbitral tribunals have generally not assessed the legal status of loans in isolation, but rather in their broader economic context, examining possible connections with other investments.

8.41

---

[82] Slovakia–Greece BIT (n 55) Art 1(1)(c).
[83] See, for example, Albanian Law No 7764 on Foreign Investments (1993) Art 1(3)(c) (providing that one category of qualifying assets consists of 'loans, cash obligations or liabilities in an activity that is economically viable and related to an investment').
[84] See Chapter 4 Section II.B.3.
[85] Several tribunals have held that a contribution under the *Salini* approach must be understood as a contribution to an 'economic venture'. See, for example, *Poštová banka v Greece* (n 54) para 361; *MNSS B.V. and Recupero Credito Acciaio N.V. v Montenegro*, ICSID Case No ARB(AF)/12/8, Award (4 May 2016) para 189 (hereafter *MNSS v Montenegro*); *Raymond Charles Eyre and others v Democratic Socialist Republic of Sri Lanka*, ICSID Case No ARB/16/25, Award (5 March 2020) para 294.
[86] It should be noted, however, that tribunals requiring a contribution to an 'economic venture' do not seem to restrict the notion of economic venture to activities conducted by the presumed investor himself or herself.

2. Loans that are 'connected' to other investments

8.42 Existing case law indicates that there are two possible types of connections between loans and (other) investments. The most obvious connection arises when a loan is granted to finance a given investment in the host State (eg the construction of a highway or of a power plant). In such a case, the question arises whether the investment status of the 'main' investment (ie the construction project) can or should be extended to the facilitating loan (or whether it should otherwise be taken into consideration when determining whether the loan constitutes an investment).

8.43 Some decisions suggest that this may indeed be the way in which investment tribunals (and parties to investment disputes) analyse such scenarios. In *Standard Chartered*, for example, a consortium of Malaysian lenders had extended a loan to Independent Power Tanzania Limited (IPTL) for the purposes of the construction of a power plant in Tanzania.[87] A subsidiary of the Claimant, Standard Chartered Bank, namely, Standard Chartered Bank (Hong Kong) Limited, subsequently acquired the Malaysian lenders' rights under the loan agreement.[88] Interestingly, in the ICSID proceedings, Tanzania did not object to the investment status of the loan as such, but focused on the narrower argument that, under the BIT between the United Kingdom and Tanzania, only 'active' (or direct) investments were protected.[89] This could be viewed as an implicit acknowledgement of the fact that, in principle, loans granted to finance investment projects qualify as investments.

8.44 A second type of connection arises where the lender has made, or owns, another investment (ie an investment other than the loan) in the host State and the issuance of the loan is related to that investment. In *MNSS*, for example, MNSS (one of the two Claimants) acquired a majority shareholding in Zeljezara Niksic AD Niksic (ZN), a company registered in Montenegro.[90] In addition, MNSS also granted a total of five loans to ZN.[91] The Tribunal held that the shares constituted investments under the applicable BIT (the BIT between the Netherlands and Yugoslavia) and the ICSID Convention, emphasizing the presence of the *Salini* criteria of contributions, a minimum duration, and risk.[92] It further ruled that the loans also qualified as investments, highlighting that they were 'intimately linked to the operation of ZN'[93] and, thus, to MNSS's other investment, ie its shareholding in ZN. In other words, the Tribunal deduced the loans' investment status from the existence of another (the main) investment.

8.45 Although the factual setting of this case is rather complex, *CSOB v Slovakia* also seems to have involved such a scenario.[94] In this case, the Claimant (CSOB) entered into a

---

[87] *Standard Chartered Bank v United Republic of Tanzania*, ICSID Case No ARB/10/12, Award (2 November 2012) para 28.
[88] ibid para 40.
[89] ibid paras 70–80.
[90] *MNSS v Montenegro* (n 85) para 48.
[91] ibid para 50.
[92] ibid para 202.
[93] ibid.
[94] *Ceskoslovenska Obchodni Banka, A.S. v The Slovak Republic*, ICSID Case No ARB/97/4, Decision of the Tribunal on Objections to Jurisdiction (24 May 1999).

consolidation agreement with the Czech and the Slovak Republics which aimed 'to facilitate the privatization of CSOB and its operation in the Czech and Slovak Republics after their separation'.[95] The agreement notably provided for the assignment by CSOB of certain non-performing receivables to two collection companies, one to be established by Slovakia and the other by the Czech Republic.[96] Those purchases were to be financed by means of loans granted by CSOB (the assignor).[97]

When examining whether the loan provided to the Slovak collection company qualified as an investment under the applicable BIT and the ICSID Convention, the Tribunal did not analyse the loan in isolation, but in its broader economic context. It held that the loan constituted an investment because it was 'closely connected to the development of CSOB's banking activity in the Slovak Republic'.[98] In other words, the Tribunal based its conclusion regarding the investment status of the loan on its finding that the broader economic operation which it formed part of, ie the 'development of CSOB's banking activity' in Slovakia (and presumably the consolidation agreement), constituted an activity that qualified as an investment.

8.46

3. Loans granted to a State or State entity

One question that arises (or may arise) is whether the fact that the borrower is the host State, rather than a private entity established in the host State, has any impact on whether a loan qualifies as an investment. In other words, is a loan extended to the host State any more or any less likely to constitute an investment under definitions of 'investment' contained in investment treaties and laws and the ICSID Convention?

8.47

As far as definitions found in instruments of consent are concerned, several factors suggest that the investment status of loans granted to the host State is more debatable. In fact, as has been seen, some treaty definitions of 'investment' expressly exclude such loans.[99] Also, while a number of treaties explicitly recognize that corporate debt instruments qualify as investments,[100] specific mention of sovereign debt instruments is extremely rare. This could be viewed as implying that such debt, including loans extended to the host government, are not considered as investments. Finally, the *Poštová banka* tribunal highlighted various fundamental differences between private and sovereign debt operations, taking the view that the political nature of, and public interest involved in, the latter strongly militates against qualifying such operations as investments.[101]

8.48

---

[95] ibid para 2.
[96] ibid.
[97] ibid.
[98] ibid para 91.
[99] See, for example, Morocco–Nigeria BIT (n 48) Art 1; UK–Colombia BIT (n 49) Art I(2)(b)(i).
[100] See, for example, UK Model BIT 2008 Art 1(a)(ii) (stating that 'investment' notably includes 'shares in and stock and debentures of a company and any other form of participation in a company').
[101] *Poštová banka v Greece* (n 54) paras 318–23 (listing a total of six fundamental differences between these two types of operations), 324 (concluding that 'sovereign debt is an instrument of government monetary and economic policy and its impact at the local and international levels makes it an important tool for the handling of social and economic policies of a State' and that 'it cannot, thus, be equated to private indebtedness or corporate debt').

8.49 Under Art 25 ICSID Convention, there do not seem to be any noteworthy differences between loans granted to private entities and loans provided to the host government. Admittedly, one could argue that the risk of default of a private debtor is higher, but such a risk would in any case only be a purely 'commercial' risk, in principle insufficient to meet the *Salini* test's risk requirement. To the extent that the existence of a contribution to the economic development of the host State is found to be a relevant factor, one may be inclined to think that such a contribution is more likely to be made by a loan granted to the State. However, the impact of the loan will ultimately depend on how the loaned funds are used. Since possible uses may vary greatly, it is not possible to make any generalizations based on the beneficiary's legal status.

IV. Arbitral Awards and Court Judgments

A. The terms of the problem

8.50 Can an arbitral award or court judgment be considered as an investment made, or owned, by the successful claimant?[102] If, for example, a Colombian buyer brings a claim against a French seller in a French court, can a favourable judgment obtained by the buyer be considered as an investment that the buyer made, or owns, in France? Most people would intuitively answer this question in the negative. In fact, such a judgment (or award) would seem to be very far removed from the ordinary meaning of the term 'investment', ie from the understanding that an investment involves the purchase of an asset with the aim of earning a profit.

8.51 In principle, it should therefore be uncontroversial that, per se (ie analysed in isolation), an arbitral award or court judgment does not qualify as an investment in the context of ICSID arbitration proceedings. Technically, however, a claimant's rights under an award or judgment may qualify as 'assets' in the sense of broad asset-based definitions of 'investment' contained in investment treaties and laws. And given the breadth and vagueness of the *Salini* criteria, it would at least be *possible* to argue that those criteria are present. Focusing on the three core *Salini* factors, it could indeed be said that the successful claimant made contributions by financing the legal or arbitral proceedings, that the duration requirement is met given that the proceedings extended over a period of sufficient length, and that the claimant faced various risks (most importantly, the risk of losing the case). Such an analysis is, however, inherently unreasonable and, thus, very unlikely to be adopted by investment tribunals.

8.52 As arbitral practice has shown,[103] investment tribunals are more likely to conclude that an award or judgment constitutes an investment if it is rendered in a dispute arising in

---

[102] See Loukas Mistelis, 'Award as an Investment: The Value of an Arbitral Award or the Cost of Non-Enforcement' (2013) 28 ICSID Rev/FILJ 64; Waibel, 'Subject Matter Jurisdiction' (n 43) paras 121–28.
[103] See Section IV.2.

connection with an investment (the 'main' or 'underlying' investment). If, for example, a company incorporated in country A agrees to build a power plant in, and for the benefit of, country B (an operation that will generally qualify as an investment), it could be held that an arbitral award deciding a dispute arising in connection with the parties' contract should also—because of the close connection with the transaction—be considered as an investment.

One interesting question that may arise in this context—and that investment tribunals have apparently not yet dealt with—is how the requirement of territoriality of the investment[104] should be applied. Under this requirement, it is in principle necessary for the award/judgment creditor's rights to be situated in the territory of the host State (at least, if one considers that any possible investment consists of those rights, rather than the award/judgment itself). How such rights should be 'localized' is not, however, a straightforward matter. Under one approach (which most tribunals have rejected in connection with contractual rights[105]), the place of performance of the corresponding obligation (ie the place where the award/judgment debtor must effect payment) would be decisive. Another approach would be to focus on the place where the court or arbitral tribunal is seated. Alternatively, one could take into account the place where the underlying investment is (considered to be) located. 8.53

On a more fundamental level, one may wonder to what extent it is at all relevant whether an award or judgment that is connected to a main investment can also be regarded as an investment. In fact, since the investor in any case owns or controls a main investment, the jurisdiction of an investment tribunal does not in principle depend on the investment status of the judgment or award. Also, if the investor's claim faces a jurisdictional obstacle, it is unlikely that reliance on the award or judgment would somehow help the investor overcome or remove that obstacle. It is also unlikely that an investment tribunal would consider itself bound by a damages award rendered by a domestic court or contract-based tribunal, or that it would otherwise consider this decision to be reflective of the value of the investor's investment. 8.54

As *Gavazzi v Romania*[106] shows, the issue of the investment status of awards/judgments has notably arisen in connection with claims alleging that the annulment of an arbitral award by the courts of the host State constitutes a denial of justice and, thus, a violation of the fair and equitable treatment standard. In this type of scenario, two separate claims coexist: a claim pertaining to the treatment of the investor's main investment (in *Gavazzi*, company shares) and a separate claim based on the treatment of the award or judgment obtained by the investor. However, contrary to what the parties to investor–state proceedings may assume, the success of such a denial-of-justice claim does not 8.55

---

[104] For a detailed examination of the meaning and application of this requirement, see Chapter 5 Section IV.
[105] See Chapter 5 Section IV.C.1.
[106] *Marco Gavazzi and Stefano Gavazzi v Romania*, ICSID Case No ARB/12/25, Decision on Jurisdiction, Admissibility and Liability (21 April 2015) (hereafter *Gavazzi v Romania*). For a more detailed discussion of this decision, see Section IV.2.

hinge on whether the award or judgment qualifies as an investment. All that is required is that the investor establish a denial of justice, as well as the existence of a loss caused by such denial of justice.

B. Case law

8.56 Arbitral case law on the investment status of judgments and awards is divided. At least one tribunal, namely, the Tribunal in *GEA v Ukraine*,[107] expressly rejected the idea that such decisions qualify as investments. In this case, Klöckner & Co Aktiengesellschaft (Klöckner), a wholly owned subsidiary of the Claimant, entered into a contract with OJSC Oriana (Oriana), a state-owned Ukrainian entity, under which it was to provide certain quantities of naphtha fuel oil to Oriana for conversion.[108] A dispute arose between the parties due to alleged discrepancies between the quantity of raw materials shipped to Oriana and the quantity of finished products.[109] The parties successfully settled their dispute, concluding a settlement and a repayment agreement in which Oriana undertook to pay a specified amount of money to Klöckner.[110] Alleging that Oriana failed to comply with this obligation, Klöckner initiated ICC arbitration proceedings in Vienna in conformity with the arbitration clause contained in the repayment agreement,[111] obtaining a largely favourable award.[112] Since it ultimately failed to collect on the award, its parent company GEA initiated ICSID proceedings under the BIT between Germany and Ukraine.[113]

8.57 One of the issues before the Tribunal was whether the Claimant owned any investment in Ukraine. As far as the conversion contract and the rights arising under this contract were concerned, the Tribunal held that they constituted a qualifying investment under the BIT and the ICSID Convention.[114] The Tribunal did not, however, accept that the settlement and repayment agreements constituted investments, pointing out that, '[a]s legal acts[,] they [we]re not the same as the investment in Ukraine itself'.[115] While the Tribunal did not further elaborate on why such 'legal acts' did not (or could not) constitute investments under the relevant instruments, it appears that it refused to attach any weight to the fact that these agreements were connected to the Claimant's (main) investment in Ukraine, ie that these agreements were concluded to resolve a dispute arising in connection with such investment.[116]

---

[107] *GEA Group Aktiengesellschaft v Ukraine*, ICSID Case No ARB/08/16, Award (31 March 2011).
[108] ibid para 44.
[109] ibid para 47.
[110] ibid paras 51–52.
[111] ibid para 57.
[112] ibid para 62.
[113] ibid para 85.
[114] ibid para 146–53.
[115] ibid para 157.
[116] ibid. The Tribunal held that 'neither the Settlement Agreement nor the Repayment Agreement—*in and of themselves*—constitute "investments" under Article 1 of the BIT or (if needed) Article 25 of the ICSID Convention' (original emphasis). The Tribunal thus analysed the investment status of these agreements in isolation, ie without

Finally, the Tribunal also denied the investment status of the ICC award. Interestingly, its decision relied at least in part on the observation that the settlement and repayment agreements (out of which the award arose) themselves did not constitute investments.[117] This is interesting because it suggests that the Tribunal recognized the possible relevance of a connection between the award and an underlying investment, in apparent contradiction to its earlier holding that the legal status of the settlement and repayment agreements had to be assessed independently of any such connection. However, the Tribunal ultimately clarified that even if the relevant agreements could be considered as investments, the award itself would still not be an investment because it remained 'analytically distinct' and because it did not involve any 'contribution to, or relevant economic activity within, Ukraine',[118] as required under the Convention and the BIT.[119] In other words, the Tribunal took the view that the investment status of the underlying operation did not extend to an award rendered in connection with such operation.

8.58

Other rulings have been more receptive towards the idea that arbitral awards deciding investment-related disputes constitute investments. One such decision is *Saipem v Bangladesh*.[120] In this case, Saipem concluded a contract for the construction of a gas pipeline with Petrobangla, the Bangladesh Oil, Gas & Mineral Corporation.[121] When a dispute arose in connection with Petrobangla's payment obligations, Saipem initiated ICC arbitration proceedings under the arbitration clause contained in the parties' contract,[122] obtaining a favourable decision.[123]

8.59

One of the issues before the ICSID Tribunal was whether Saipem had made any investment in Bangladesh. As far as the applicable BIT (the BIT between Italy and Bangladesh) was concerned, the Tribunal found that Saipem's rights under the contract with Petrobangla constituted an investment under the treaty's broad asset-based definition, notably holding that those rights qualified as a 'credit for sums of money' in the sense of Art 1(1)(c) of the BIT.[124] While it considered that Saipem's rights under the award in principle also constituted an investment, it acknowledged that 'the rights embodied in the ICC Award were not created by the Award, but ar[o]se out of the

8.60

---

regard to the close connection they presented with the conversion contract and the rights arising under that contract.

[117] ibid para 161 (emphasizing that neither the settlement agreement nor the repayment agreement were investments).
[118] ibid para 162.
[119] The 'contribution' requirement mentioned by the Tribunal presumably relates to the *Salini* test, even though it is not clear whether it refers to the core criterion of a contribution or to the more controversial criterion of a contribution to the economic development of the host State. As far as the 'economic activity' requirement is concerned, this derives from Art 1(1) of the applicable BIT under which one recognized category of qualifying assets consists of 'rights to the exercise of an economic activity'.
[120] *Saipem S.p.A. v The People's Republic of Bangladesh*, ICSID Case No ARB/05/07, Decision on Jurisdiction and Recommendation on Provisional Measures (21 March 2007) (hereafter *Saipem v Bangladesh*).
[121] ibid para 7.
[122] ibid para 18.
[123] ibid para 34.
[124] ibid paras 121–28.

Contract'.[125] Since it was established that Saipem's rights under the contract constituted an investment, the Tribunal concluded that '[i]t c[ould] thus be left open whether the Award itself qualifie[d] as an investment'.[126]

8.61 As regards the existence of an investment under Art 25 ICSID Convention, the Tribunal applied the four-prong *Salini* test requiring the presence of the three core *Salini* criteria[127] and a contribution to the economic development of Bangladesh[128]. Focusing on the parties' contract and their respective contractual obligations, the Tribunal found that the relevant requirements were satisfied.[129] While it did not directly address the issue of whether the ICC award constituted an investment (this had apparently not been argued by the Claimant), the Tribunal nevertheless observed that, for the purposes of the Art 25 analysis, it would 'consider the entire operation', ie 'the Contract, the construction itself, the Retention Money, the warranty and the related ICC Arbitration'.[130] By holding that this operation qualified as an investment, the Tribunal arguably recognized the investment status of the ICC award.

8.62 A more explicit affirmation of the investment status of arbitral awards can be found in *Gavazzi v Romania*. This case involved a share purchase agreement concluded between the Claimants and the State Ownership Fund (SOF), a Romanian governmental entity tasked with the negotiation of privatization agreements with investors, whereby the Claimants acquired a 70 per cent shareholding in S.C. Socomet S.A.[131] In the ICSID proceedings, the Tribunal ruled that the shares acquired by the Claimants constituted an investment under the BIT between Italy and Romania and the ICSID Convention.[132] It also held that the ICC arbitration award, which the Claimants obtained by initiating proceedings under the share purchase agreement concluded with SOF, similarly qualified as an investment because it represented a 'claim to money' in the sense of the BIT and because, for the purposes of Art 25 ICSID Convention, it 'form[ed] part of the Claimants' overall investment'.[133] The Tribunal thus acknowledged that the award's connection with the underlying investment (the share purchase agreement) supported the conclusion that it should also be considered as an investment.

8.63 The issue of whether an arbitral award obtained by an investor can be characterized as an investment also arose in *Romak v Uzbekistan*.[134] In this case, as has been seen in Chapter 6,[135] the Claimant entered into contracts with several Uzbek State

---

[125] ibid para 127.
[126] ibid.
[127] See Chapter 4 Section II.B.
[128] See Chapter 4 Section II.C.
[129] *Saipem v Bangladesh* (n 120) paras 98–111.
[130] ibid para 110.
[131] *Gavazzi v Romania* (n 106) para 43.
[132] ibid paras 98–114.
[133] ibid para 120.
[134] *Romak S.A. (Switzerland) v The Republic of Uzbekistan*, PCA Case No AA280, Award (26 November 2009) (hereafter *Romak v Uzbekistan*).
[135] See Chapter 6 Section V.B.

entities under which it undertook to deliver specified quantities of wheat.[136] When a dispute arose between the parties with regard to payment for some of the deliveries made,[137] Romak initiated Grain and Feed Trade Association (GAFTA) arbitration proceedings in accordance with the arbitration clause contained in the contracts.[138] It prevailed in those proceedings but was ultimately unable to enforce the award.[139]

8.64 One of the issues in the ISCID proceedings brought by Romak was whether the GAFTA award qualified as an investment. In its ruling on this issue, the Tribunal observed that the award 'merely constitute[d] the embodiment of Romak's contractual rights (as determined by the GAFTA Arbitral Tribunal) stemming from the wheat supply transaction' and that such 'embodiment or crystallization ... [could] not transform it [i.e., the award] into an investment' if 'the underlying transaction [itself] is not an investment within the meaning of the BIT'.[140] The Tribunal ultimately held that the wheat supply contracts did not qualify as an investment, logically entailing that the award did not either. However, the Tribunal's decision nonetheless suggests that, as a matter of principle, an award rendered in connection with an investment-related dispute would (or might) constitute an investment.

V. Funds 'Invested'

8.65 Whether funds 'invested' by an investor (or a presumed investor), ie money used to purchase assets or to finance economic activities in the host State, qualify as an investment is a question that is easily misunderstood. This is because the investment status of such funds (including their relevance in establishing the existence of an investment) is inherently dependent on the specific context in which the question arises.

8.66 As has been shown in Chapter 2, money used to purchase an asset with a view to realizing a profit undoubtedly constitutes an 'investment' in the ordinary sense of the term.[141] In fact, as has been explained, the ordinary meaning of 'investment' comprises three distinct dimensions. More specifically, an investment can be conceived of as (1) a profit-generating *asset* acquired by the investor, (2) the *funds* used for such acquisition, or (3) the *act* of purchasing the asset concerned. Funds 'invested' by an investor thus clearly constitute an investment.

8.67 Under the vast majority of definitions contained in investment treaties and laws, however, the funds 'invested' by an investor will not qualify as investments. Under traditional asset-based definitions, an investment consists of an asset purchased or otherwise established by the investor, not of the funds used for such purchase or

---

[136] *Romak v Uzbekistan* (n 134) paras 24–37.
[137] ibid paras 41–47.
[138] ibid paras 52–61.
[139] ibid paras 62–70.
[140] ibid para 211.
[141] See Chapter 2 Section VI.

establishment. Under enterprise-based definitions of 'investment', an investment similarly consists of an enterprise owned or controlled by the investor, not of the money used to purchase or establish the enterprise. The same observation applies to activity/project-based definitions under which it is the activity or project concerned that constitutes the investment, not the funds 'invested' in the relevant activity or project.

8.68 A possible exception consists of definitions that view investments as contributions of capital. As has been seen, such definitions can notably be found in a few domestic investment laws.[142] The Investment Law of Cape Verde, for example, defines 'investment' as 'capital investment in the form of tangible or intangible assets, with a view to creating, modernizing or expanding an economic activity'.[143] The Federal Law on Foreign Investments of the Russian Federation defines 'foreign investment' as 'the investment of foreign capital in an object of entrepreneurial activity in the territory of the Russian Federation'.[144] Under such definitions, funds 'invested' in specific economic activities in principle qualify as investments.

8.69 Under Art 25 ICSID Convention and, more specifically, the widely followed *Salini* test, the investment status of money spent by an investor is analysed very differently. In fact, funds do not as such qualify as investments. However, they represent 'contributions', ie one particular component or characteristic feature of an investment under the *Salini* case law. This does not mean, however, that the existence of an investment in the sense of the *Salini* test necessarily requires an investment in the form of funds. In fact, as has been explained in Chapter 4, the term 'contribution' is generally construed broadly and covers various forms of non-monetary contributions (eg labour, know-how, etc).[145]

8.70 Whether the funds 'invested' by an investor can be regarded as an (or the) investment is evidently of significant practical relevance. In fact, if one answers this question in the affirmative, this would in principle mean that the value of a given investment corresponds to the amount of money invested, for example the price the investor paid to acquire a corporation established in the host State. If, on the other hand, one considers that an investor's investment consists of the assets purchased or activities conducted by the investor, the value of the investment will reflect the value of the relevant assets or the profitability of the relevant activities, independently of the amount of money invested.

8.71 Arbitral case law suggests that tribunals sometimes wrongly characterize funds 'invested' by an investor as investments. In *Bayindir*, for example, the Tribunal examined whether the Claimant, who had undertaken to build a six-lane motorway in and for Pakistan, had made any investment in that country. As far as the existence of an investment under the BIT between Turkey and Pakistan was concerned, the Tribunal held that the financial contributions made by Bayindir—in particular, the substantial

---

[142] See Chapter 7 Sections III–V.
[143] Cape Verde Investment Law (2013) Art 4(c).
[144] Russian Federation Federal Law on Foreign Investments (1999) Art 2.
[145] See Chapter 4 Section II.B.1.

commission charges it incurred in providing bank guarantees—constituted assets in the sense of the BIT and thus qualified as investments.[146]

The Tribunal seems to have confused the notion of asset under the BIT with the *Salini* requirement of a 'contribution' under Art 25 ICSID Convention. In fact, the bank charges incurred by Bayindir do not constitute assets owned or controlled by the investor, but an amount of money the investor spent in connection with the performance of its obligations under the contract. Under the asset-based definition found in the applicable BIT, the investor's assets are the rights it enjoys under the contract (ie primarily the right to be paid the contractually agreed fee), not the funds it may have employed or needed to perform some of its contractual duties.

8.72

---

[146] *Bayindir v Pakistan* (n 7) paras 119–21.

9

Conclusion

I. Summary of Principal Findings 9.01 II. The Way Forward 9.12

I. Summary of Principal Findings

9.01 A significant majority of investment tribunals appear to adopt the 'objective approach', ie the view that the term 'investment' under Art 25 ICSID Convention has an 'objective'[1] meaning.[2] In fact, only very few tribunals have expressly rejected this approach, adopting the competing 'subjective' approach under which the definitions contained in the applicable instruments of consent constitute the sole relevant threshold.[3] In reality, however, this broad consensus is more apparent than real. Indeed, under the widely followed typical-characteristics approach (one of two rival understandings of the *Salini* test), the objective definitional elements of Art 25 ICSID Convention are not mandatory, but merely illustrative of typical features of an investment.[4] By effectively denying the existence of binding criteria, this approach implicitly calls into question the very concept of an independent legal test under Art 25.

9.02 The principal arguments relied upon in support of the objective approach comprise (a) the principle of effectiveness of treaty interpretation and (b) the ICSID Convention's negotiating history, including the drafters' emphasis of the need to distinguish between the requirement of consent and jurisdictional requirements (ie the idea that consent alone is not sufficient to establish jurisdiction).[5] While both of these arguments may have some merit, none of them is plainly convincing. Interestingly, the most compelling argument in favour of the objective approach is one that is rarely, if ever, mentioned: namely, that the alternative subjective approach is simply impracticable. In fact, the subjective approach is based on the idea that Art 25 ICSID Convention incorporates, or refers to, the definition contained in the applicable instrument of consent.[6]

---

[1] As has been explained in Chapter 3, this 'objective' meaning can also be referred to as an 'implied' or 'independent' meaning. These two expressions are preferable because they are far less ambiguous than the notion of an 'objective' meaning. See Chapter 3 Section II.
[2] See Chapter 3 Section III.B.
[3] See Chapter 3 Section III.C.
[4] See Chapter 3 Section III.D.
[5] See Chapter 3 Section III.B.2.
[6] See Chapter 3 Section V.A (discussing objections to the subjective approach).

The problem is that this approach wrongly assumes that instruments of consent *always* define the term 'investment'. As has been seen, this is not the case.[7] Not only are there some investment treaties and laws (few, admittedly) that do not contain such definitions, but also—and more importantly—definitions of 'investment' are entirely absent from investment contracts.

9.03 If one accepts the idea that the term 'investment' in Art 25 ICSID Convention has an independent meaning, one obviously needs to answer the question of what that meaning is. Most ICSID tribunals have considered that the test established in *Fedax v Venezuela* and *Salini v Morocco* (the *Salini* test),[8] or some variation thereof, adequately encapsulates this meaning. There is, however, only limited agreement as to the relevant requirements. While there are three rather uncontroversial 'core' criteria (contributions, duration, and risk),[9] tribunals have at times applied other, more controversial, requirements (contribution to the economic development of the host State, regularity of profits and return, legality and good faith).[10] In addition, there is no unanimous understanding of the meaning of these different criteria.[11] While case law suggests that there is a trend towards convergence in certain areas (eg flexible application of the duration requirement, distinction between commercial and investment risk, etc), substantial differences between the viewpoints taken by individual tribunals persist. Finally, and perhaps most worryingly, tribunals even fail to agree on the 'nature' of the *Salini* test, with some tribunals considering it to lay down jurisdictional requirements and others opposing its binding nature.[12]

9.04 Though the *Salini* test is widely followed, its legal foundations are rather shaky.[13] In fact, it is almost exclusively based on two scholarly papers, one authored by Schreuer and the other by Gaillard, that only superficially touch upon the meaning of the concept of investment in ICSID arbitration. Significantly, neither the ordinary meaning of the term 'investment' nor the ICSID Convention's *travaux* provide meaningful support for the *Salini* requirements, including the three core criteria. As has been shown, these three criteria are inherently vague and at least partly devoid of a rational justification.[14] More fundamentally, the *Salini* test does not genuinely *define* what an 'investment' is.[15] It holds that a contribution must be made to *something*, that this *something* must have a duration and be associated with certain risks, but it is entirely silent as to *what* that *something* is.

9.05 What can be inferred from the *Salini* criteria, however, is the view that the *Salini* test arguably adopts with regard to the nature of investment. In fact, the three core criteria

---

[7] See Chapter 3 Section II.A.2.
[8] For the historical development of the *Salini* test, see Chapter 4 Section II.A.1.
[9] See Chapter 4 Section II.B.
[10] See Chapter 4 Sections II.C and II.D.
[11] As far as the meaning of the three core *Salini* criteria is concerned, see Chapter 4 Section II.B.
[12] See Chapter 3 Section III.D and Chapter 4 Section II.A.3.
[13] See Chapter 4 Section II.E.
[14] ibid.
[15] ibid.

quite clearly suggest that the *Salini* test contemplates some form of operation, project, or activity such as the performance of an investment contract entered into with the host State.[16] Such operations, projects, or activities indeed have a certain duration, involve various risks, and their performance requires that the investor make various contributions, including a financial commitment. The *Salini* test therefore follows an approach that deviates from the traditional asset-based definitions found in the majority of investment treaties and a large number of investment laws. As has been shown, this is a source of various practical complications and difficulties.

9.06 Presumably because of their awareness of the defects of the *Salini* test, a few tribunals have opted for one of two alternative approaches. One of these is the permissibility test which asks whether the definition contained in the instrument of consent is permissible under, or compatible with, Art 25 ICSID Convention.[17] The other approach consists of the commercial-transaction test under which an operation that constitutes a commercial transaction is denied investment status.[18] While one may sympathize with tribunals attempting to avoid the application of the *Salini* test, both of these alternative pathways are, as has been shown, equally, if not more deeply, flawed.[19]

9.07 Investment treaties traditionally define the concept of 'investment' in broad, asset-based terms.[20] In the past ten to fifteen years, however, there has been a noticeable departure from this traditional approach. To begin with, an increasing (though still limited) number of treaties feature enterprise-based definitions which, as the term suggests, view investments as enterprises established in the host State, rather than assets.[21] Also, and more importantly, recent investment treaties often expressly exclude certain categories of assets (eg portfolio investments, sovereign debt instruments, rights arising under commercial contracts, assets not connected to economic activities, etc),[22] thus denying their investment status. Finally, a rather sizeable number of modern treaties have incorporated a slightly modified version of the *Salini* test, labelling those requirements as 'characteristics of an investment'.[23] The differences between those characteristics and the *Salini* criteria, which have been highlighted in Chapter 6,[24] provide useful insights into which factors States consider meaningful and which they reject.

9.08 Major transformations have occurred not only in treaty, but also in arbitral, practice. The most significant evolution in arbitral case law has been the transposition of the *Salini* test to the context of investment treaties and, arguably, investment laws. In fact, several non-ICSID and ICSID tribunals have held that the term 'investment' in investment treaties, like the notion of investment under Art 25 ICSID Convention, has an

---

[16] See Chapter 4 Sections II.B.1 and II.B.2.
[17] See Chapter 4 Section III.A.
[18] See Chapter 4 Section IV.A.
[19] See Chapter 4 Sections III.B and IV.B.
[20] See Chapter 5 Section II.
[21] See Chapter 6 Section II.
[22] See Chapter 6 Section IV.
[23] See Chapter 6 Section III.
[24] See Chapter 6 Section III.C.

CONCLUSION 185

objective or implied meaning beyond the meaning derived from a literal reading of the relevant definitions.[25] According to these tribunals, this objective meaning consists of the three core *Salini* criteria of a contribution, a minimum duration, and risk.[26] The effect of this case law is twofold. First, it means that the *Salini* test also applies (or can be applied) in non-ICSID arbitration proceedings. Second, it provides ICSID tribunals with an alternative legal basis for the application of objective criteria.

Virtually all (asset-based) investment treaty definitions share a number of common requirements. These include (a) the requirement of ownership or control by the investor, (b) the requirement that the investor's assets be located in the territory of the host State (territoriality), and (c) the requirement of legality of the investment (compliance with host State law).[27] The application of these criteria raises a number of interpretive questions, the most important of which have been examined in Chapter 5. Some tribunals have applied an additional requirement, namely, the requirement that the investment be 'actively' made by the presumed investor.[28] As has been shown, this requirement not only lacks a solid textual foundation in the relevant treaties,[29] but it is also inherently illogical and problematic, notably because it conflicts with the well-established principle that indirect ownership of assets qualifies as an investment.[30]

9.09

Although investment laws play a rather modest role in the context of ICSID arbitration, the relevant legislative practice is a useful indicator of host State concerns and preferences.[31] While there are evidently similarities between definitions contained in investment laws and treaty definitions, there are also substantial differences. The most fundamental such difference is that definitions found in investment laws are not predominantly asset-based, a significant number of them being either activity/project-based or enterprise-based.[32] These rather novel definitional approaches are bound to raise a host of interpretive issues. Arbitral tribunals have apparently not yet had to address those issues,[33] but they are likely to face them in the years to come.

9.10

There are several categories of assets and operations whose investment status is particularly controversial or otherwise of special interest.[34] These include (a) contracts concluded with the host State and, more particularly, construction contracts and contracts for the provision of (other) services, (b) private and sovereign debt instruments, (c) arbitral awards and court judgments, and (d) funds 'invested' by an investor. As has been shown, the controversies surrounding the investment status of the first three categories of assets/operations are complex and arise under both treaty definitions of investment

9.11

---

[25] See Chapter 6 Section V.
[26] ibid.
[27] See Chapter 5 Sections III, IV, and V.
[28] See Chapter 5 Section VI.
[29] See Chapter 5 Section VI.B.
[30] See Chapter 5 Section VI.D.
[31] See Chapter 7 Section I.
[32] See Chapter 7 Sections III and IV.
[33] See Chapter 7 Section VII.
[34] See Chapter 8.

and Art 25 ICSID Convention.[35] The question of whether funds 'invested' by an investor constitute an investment is sometimes misunderstood, presumably because of (a) the contrast between the ordinary meaning and legal definitions of the term 'investment' and (b) the overlap with the *Salini* test's contribution requirement.[36]

II. The Way Forward

9.12 How the meaning and interpretation of the notion of investment will evolve in the future depends, in the first place, on whether the relevant institutional and legal framework will undergo any change. If, for example, a permanent investment court with appellate jurisdiction were to be established, this would in principle enhance the uniform interpretation of Art 25 ICSID Convention and of definitions contained in investment treaties and laws. If a multilateral investment treaty were to be adopted, this would similarly improve uniformity at the international level. At present, it is difficult to predict whether and, if so, when such institutional and legal transformations might take place.

9.13 As far as Art 25 ICSID Convention is concerned, it is improbable that, within the current institutional and legal framework, a general consensus will emerge. In fact, in a system that (a) is largely based on arbitral 'precedents' and (b) lacks a supreme judicial (or arbitral) authority capable of ensuring the uniform application of the law, it can be expected that the existing divides will persist. It is thus likely that each of the existing approaches (subjective approach, 'mandatory' *Salini* test, 'optional' *Salini* test, permissibility test, commercial-transaction test) will, at least to some extent, continue to be followed.

9.14 It will be interesting to see how the incorporation of 'characteristics-requirements' into treaty definitions and the *Romak* case law will impact the analysis under Art 25 ICSID Convention. In fact, arbitral tribunals no longer need to resort to Art 25 to apply objective requirements for the existence of an investment. They can, instead, rely on the *Romak* idea that investment treaty definitions of 'investment', like the term 'investment' under Art 25 ICSID Convention, have an objective meaning. Conversely, it will be interesting to see what impact existing Art 25 case law will have on the interpretation of characteristics-requirements and treaty definitions more generally.

9.15 Another question is whether the use of enterprise-based and activity/project-based definitions of 'investment' will become more widespread in investment treaty practice. As has been seen, such definitions are arguably narrower than traditional asset-based definitions of 'investment' and can thus be considered to favour the interests of capital-importing countries over those of capital-exporting countries.[37] Future developments

---

[35] See Chapter 8 Sections II, III, and IV.
[36] See Chapter 8 Section V.
[37] See Chapter 2 Section IX.A.

may therefore depend on the respective bargaining powers of States concluding international investment agreements.

Finally, increased awareness of the issue of the 'nature' of investment will be crucial. It is important for all stakeholders (States, investors, arbitral tribunals) to understand that there are different ways of defining the nature of an investment and that the answer in an individual case will depend on the approach expressly or implicitly endorsed in the applicable instrument(s). As has been seen, the uncertainty surrounding the question of the nature of investment, in particular in the context of Art 25 ICSID Convention, is a source of misunderstandings and tensions that undermine the efficiency of the ICSID dispute settlement system.[38]

9.16

---

[38] See Chapter 2 Section VIII.

Index

active investments 5.02, 5.86–5.100
   Art 25 ICSID Convention 5.100
   assessment of the requirement 5.96–5.99
   overview 5.86–5.87
   recognition and meaning 5.92–5.95
   textual foundations 5.88–5.91
activity-based definitions 7.29–7.31, 7.54, 8.27, 9.10, 9.15
   conclusions 7.29–7.31
   definitions 7.24–7.28
Albania 7.08
   Finland, BIT with 5.67
   Law on Foreign Investments 3.18 n.24, 7.44–7.47, 7.51–7.52
Algeria
   Belgo-Luxembourg Economic Union, BIT with 5.95
Angola
   Private Investment Law 7.24
appellate mechanisms 2.62
arbitral approach *see* Salini test
Argentina 5.62
   Germany, BIT with 5.21
   Italy, BIT with 8.29
   Netherlands, BIT with 5.68
   US, BIT with 5.19, 5.30, 5.39
ASEAN Comprehensive Investment Agreement 5.41
asset-based definitions 5.03–5.11, 6.11, 6.24, 6.27, 7.32, 8.27, 8.29, 8.72
   see also assets
   broad approach 2.49 n.75, 2.56 n 82, 7.07, 8.31 n.62, 8.51, 9.07
   common requirements 9.09–9.10
   investment laws 7.07–7.10
   prevalence of 5.09–5.11
   'pure' 7.08
   types of definitions 5.03–5.08
assets
   see also asset-based definitions
   act or process of purchasing 2.45, 5.03
   asset-based definitions of investment 2.49
   categories of 5.14–5.16, 8.01–8.72, 9.07
   covered assets, scope of 5.36
   economic activity in host State 6.02
   funding 2.45, 5.03
   loans 8.30, 8.39
   not connected to any economic or business activity 6.36–6.38, 9.07
   permissibility test 4.76
   profit, pursuit of 3.56, 5.03, 6.18
   purchase of 2.45, 3.56
   qualifying as investments 5.13
   tangible/intangible assets 2.52, 5.46, 7.08–7.10, 7.15, 7.26–7.27, 8.68
   types of 8.30–8.31
   unrelated to enterprises 6.07
   used in connection with activities/projects 7.05, 7.07
Australia
   Pakistan, BIT with 3.18 n.22, 5.34
Austria
   Kyrgyzstan, BIT with 5.06, 6.08
Azerbaijan Republic
   Law on Investment Activity 7.27

bad faith 4.58
Bangladesh
   Italy, BIT with 8.60
Belgium
   Barcelona Traction case 5.31
Belgo-Luxembourg Economic Union
   Algeria, BIT with 5.95
   Malaysia, BIT with 3.54
Benin
   Investment Code 7.38
Bilateral Investment Treaties (BITs) 2.05, 2.23, 2.28–2.29, 3.45, 3.53, 3.65, 3.69, 3.73, 4.45, 4.67, 4.84, 5.84, 6.62, 7.01, 8.46, 8.64
   Albania-Finland 5.67
   Argentina-Italy 8.29
   Australia-Pakistan 3.18 n.22, 5.34
   Austria-Kyrgyzstan 5.06, 6.08
   Belgo-Luxembourg Economic Union-Algeria 5.95
   Bolivia 3.15
   Brazil-India 6.32
   Brazil-United Arab Emirates 6.33
   Canada-Guinea 6.25–6.26
   Canada-Mongolia 6.08, 6.11
   Canada-Venezuela 1.03 n.5, 6.48
   Chile-Bolivia 6.59
commitment 4.14
control, concept of 5.35

Bilateral Investment Treaties (BITs) (*cont.*)
El Salvador-Spain 2.06
Ethiopia-Russia 5.68
France-Mauritius 2.28 n.42, 6.51, 6.70
France-Saudi Arabia 3.18 n.25
Germany-Argentina 5.21
Germany-Sri Lanka 8.14
Germany-Ukraine 1.03 n.6, 5.42–5.44, 6.54, 8.56
Greece-Georgia 5.81
Hungary 2.17
Hungary-Oman 6.13
Hungary-United Arab Emirates 6.36
Israel-Czech Republic 4.55
Italy-Bangladesh 8.60
Italy-Morocco 2.25, 8.08
Japan-Georgia 5.05, 6.13
Kazakhstan-Uzbekistan 5.21, 5.39, 5.89, 5.95
Malaysia-Belgo-Luxemburg Economic Union 3.54
Morocco-Nigeria 6.06, 6.09, 6.31–6.32, 6.39, 8.28
Mozambique 4.70
Netherlands-Argentina 5.68
Netherlands-Paraguay 4.68
Netherlands-Turkey 5.20, 5.26, 5.41, 5.69
Netherlands-Venezuela 4.03–4.04
Netherlands-Yugoslavia 7.43 n.71, 8.44
Nigeria-Morocco 5.05
Oman-Hungary 6.36
Pakistan 3.46
Slovakia-Greece 3.19, 8.30, 8.39
Spain-Venezuela 1.03 n.7, 5.89, 5.94
Switzerland-Paraguay 4.69, 8.13
Switzerland-Philippines 3.45, 5.88
Switzerland-Uzbekistan 1.03 n.5, 6.44–6.47, 6.70
Turkey-Cambodia 6.31, 6.33, 6.35, 6.37
Turkey-Pakistan 8.08, 8.71
Turkmenistan 4.70
UK-Colombia 5.19, 5.30, 5.39, 6.25, 6.39, 8.28
UK-Egypt 1.03 n.5
UK-New Zealand 6.13
UK-Sri Lanka 1.03 n.5, 6.63
UK-Tanzania 1.03 n.7, 5.90, 5.92–5.93, 8.43
UK-Turkmenistan 8.08
UK-Venezuela 2.02
Ukraine-Lithuania 5.67
UNCTAD study 5.10
United Arab Emirates-Israel 5.88
US-Argentina 5.19, 5.30, 5.39
US-Congolese Republic 2.52
US-Ecuador 5.30
US-Republic of Zaire 1.03 n.5
US-Rwanda 6.13
US-Turkey 1.03 n.5, 3.18 n.20
US-Ukraine 2.16
US-Uruguay 6.13–6.14
Bolivia 3.15, 6.59
Chile, BIT with 6.59
Investment Promotion Law 7.38, 7.40
bonds *see* corporate bonds; sovereign bonds
BOT contracts 8.22
Brazil
India, BIT with 6.32
United Arab Emirates, BIT with 6.33
broad definitions 5.12–5.17
absence of exclusions 5.16–5.17
additional requirements 5.16–5.17
asset-based definitions 2.49 n.75, 2.56 n 82, 7.07, 8.31 n.62, 8.51, 9.07
broad coverage of definitions 5.12–5.15
Broches, Aron 3.49, 3.65

Cambodia
Turkey, BIT with 6.31, 6.33, 6.35, 6.37
Cameroon 7.08
Investment Charter 7.08 n.16
Canada
Barcelona Traction case 5.31
Guinea, BIT with 6.25–6.26
Mongolia, BIT with 6.08, 6.11
Nova Scotia Power case 6.48–6.50
Venezuela, BIT with 1.03 n.5, 6.48
Cape Verde
Investment Law 7.26, 8.68
capital
importing/capital-exporting countries 9.15
investment, requirement of 7.32–7.35
requirement to contribute 7.04
Castro de Figueiredo, Roberto 3.70
characteristics requirements 5.17, 6.03, 6.12–6.24, 6.67, 7.04, 9.07, 9.14
assessment 6.20–6.24
meaning and trend 6.12–6.15
Salini criteria, comparison with 6.16–6.19
Chile
Bolivia, BIT with 6.59
China
Foreign Investment Law 7.25
choice of law 2.21
Colombia
UK, BIT with 5.19, 5.30, 5.39, 6.25, 6.39, 8.28
commercial contracts 6.02, 9.07
rights arising under 5.16
commercial lease agreements 4.64
commercial transaction test 2.60, 4.01, 4.78–4.92, 6.28, 9.06, 9.13

INDEX

ambiguity of language 4.90
assessment 4.88–4.92
exclusions 6.25–6.29
meaning and recognition 4.78–4.87
qualifying practice 4.91
transient 3.34
commitment 4.08, 4.12, 4.14
of capital or other resources 6.16, 6.24, 6.26
company law 5.13
see also shareholders
voting shares 2.44
compensation
development costs 7.48
lost profits 7.48
moral damage 7.48
tax stabilization 2.11
concept of investment
applicable law 2.21–2.25
BITs, effect of 3.54
complexity of 1.04–1.09, 2.37
consent instruments 2.04–2.09
core meaning 3.72 n.154
damages, assessment of 2.10–2.12
economic concept. 39–2.44
ex officio examination of
jurisdiction 2.17–2.18
existing literature 1.10–1.15
express meaning 3.14
failure to define 3.54
host State interests 2.54–2.58
ICSID Convention 2.03
ICSID Secretary General 2.19–2.20
ICSID tribunals, jurisdiction
of 2.02–2.09
implied meaning 3.17
importance of 1.01–1.03
independent meaning 3.17
interests involved 2.01, 2.54–2.63
interpretive issue, as a 2.01, 2.26–2.32
investor interests 2.54–2.58
jurisdictional objections 2.14–2.16
jurisdictional relevance of 1.02–1.03
nature of investment 2.45–2.53
object and purpose 1.16–1.17
objective approach 1.08, 1.13
ordinary meaning 2.33–2.38
outer limits 3.72 n.154
practical relevance 2.01–2.12
procedural settings 2.13–2.20
scope 1.18–1.19
subjective approach 1.08
systemic interests 2.59–2.63
uniformity 2.63
concession contracts 8.22

Congo
Congolese Republic-US BIT 2.52
economic development 4.66–4.67
consent
absence of 7.43 n.70
Contracting Parties 3.49
instrument *see* consent instrument
objective approach 3.77
objective limitations of ICSID
jurisdiction 3.65
offers of 1.05, 2.04
parties to the dispute 3.33
consent instrument 3.80, 4.58, 4.65, 9.02
types of 1.05, 2.04, 3.13, 3.40–3.41
constitutional law 1.01
construction contracts 8.07–8.12, 9.11
critical assessment 8.16–8.22
host State/host State entities 8.04–8.22
overview 8.04–8.06
contract for services 2.25
contract law 1.01
contracts for the provision of services 9.11
contribution(s) 4.08, 4.12
broad and flexible interpretation 8.14
capital 7.34–7.35
definition of 8.12
economic venture, to a 8.36
in financial terms 8.12
of industry 8.21
requirement 8.58 n.119
Salini test 1.09, 2.28, 2.50, 2.60 n.86, 4.01,
5.100, 6.16, 6.66, 7.33, 8.14, 8.19, 8.44, 8.69,
8.72, 9.03, 9.08, 9.11
to the venture 4.103 n.220
value-creation 8.33
control 1.12, 5.02, 5.34–5.37, 9.09
see also ownership
corporate bonds 8.26
court judgments 8.50–8.64, 9.11
see also arbitral awards
covered investment
definition of 5.40
credits for sums of money 8.60
customary international law 2.27
Czech Republic 8.45
Israel, BIT with 4.55

debt instruments 6.11, 8.23–8.49
see also loans; sovereign bonds
definition of 8.23
preliminary observations 8.23–8.26
Democratic Republic of the Congo (DRC) 2.52
denial of justice 8.55
direct agreements 1.05

double-keyhole/double-barrelled test 1.08, 1.14, 2.51, 3.10–3.13, 3.22

economic activities
  definition of 7.54
  rights to the exercise of 8.58 n.119
economic development 4.01, 4.08–4.09, 4.12, 4.98, 6.67 n.153, 7.04, 9.03
  Congo 4.66
  host States:
    contribution requirement 4.102–4.106
    controversial criterion 4.39–4.49
    investment laws 7.36–7.42
    meaning of the criterion 4.39–4.44
    recognition of the criterion 4.39–4.44
    rejection of the criterion 4.45–4.49
    Malaysia 4.28 n.61
    objective of (Preamble to ICSID) 4.46
    private international investment 7.36
economics 2.01
  see also economic activities; economic development; macroeconomics
  economic concept of investment, meaning of 2.39–2.44
  economic nature, right of an 8.08
  economic value 8.08
  economic ventures 7.33, 8.40, 8.39 nn.85–6
Ecuador
  US, BIT with 5.30
effectiveness principle 2.31, 3.25–3.30, 3.77, 9.02
effet utile 2.31, 3.25, 3.28, 3.30, 3.36, 3.66, 3.77–3.78
Egypt
  Investment Law 7.24, 7.40–7.41
  phosphate mining projects 4.82–4.83
  UK, BIT with 1.03 n.5
El Salvador 5.73
  investment law 5.82, 7.09
  Spain, BIT with 2.06
enterprise
  concept of 6.08–6.09, 7.11, 7.21
  definition of 2.46, 6.08–6.10, 7.54
  lawful 7.12
enterprise-based definitions 5.01–5.02, 5.05–5.06, 5.09, 6.04–6.11, 6.38, 7.11–7.23, 7.29, 8.67, 9.10, 9.15
  conclusions 7.21–7.23
  meaning of enterprise 7.16–7.20
  pure vs mixed 6.07, 6.10
  types of definitions 7.11–7.15
equity
  entry modes 2.42
  participations 5.06, 6.07, 6.11, 7.12

Ethiopia
  Russia, BIT with 5.68
ex officio examination 2.13, 2.17–2.18, 3.45
Exelbert, Jeremy Marc 3.63, 4.98, 4.105
exports, direct and indirect 2.42
expropriation 7.44, 7.47 n.85
  compensation for 2.07 n.9

fair and equitable treatment (FET) 8.55
Fellenbaum, Joshua 3.22
finance 2.34, 2.39
Finland
  Albania, BIT with 5.67
foreign direct investment (FDI) 2.42, 4.03, 5.22 n.38, 5.97, 6.10, 6.34–6.35, 7.22, 8.16
  concept of 2.46
  definition 2.43
  hotel construction 2.46
  OECD benchmark definition 2.43
  shared vs full ownership of enterprises 2.44
foreign investment
  concept of 7.08 n.15
  definition of 7.26, 7.28
  direct *see* foreign direct investment (FDI)
France
  Mauritius, BIT with 2.28 n.42, 6.51, 6.70
  Model BIT 2.56
  Saudi Arabia, BIT with 3.18 n.25
franchising agreements 2.42
fraud 5.76
Free Trade Agreements (FTAs)
  US-Oman 3.46
funds 'invested' 8.65–8.72, 9.11

Gaillard, Emmanuel 3.22, 3.38, 4.59, 4.103, 9.04
gambling businesses 5.77
general principles of international law 4.55, 4.58, 5.25, 5.31 n.58, 5.84
Georgia 7.48–7.50
  Greece, BIT with 5.81
  Investment Law 7.50
  Japan, BIT with 5.05, 6.13
  state-owned entities 5.81
Germany
  Argentina, BIT with 5.21
  Model BIT 2.56, 5.12, 5.16, 5.39
  Sri Lanka, BIT with 8.14
  Ukraine, BIT with 1.03 n.6, 5.42–5.44, 6.54, 8.56
good faith 2.28, 4.10, 5.05, 9.03, 5.71 n.124
  principle of 4.55–4.58
Grabowski, Alex 3.63, 4.104
Greece 5.81
  Georgia, BIT with 5.81

INDEX

government bonds 3.19 n.30, 6.41 n.72
Slovakia, BIT with 3.19, 8.30, 8.39
sovereign debt crisis 8.36
greenfield investment 2.44
Gross Domestic Product (GDP) 4.44
Guinea
   Canada, BIT with 6.25–6.26

habitual characteristics 3.28
Ho, Jean 3.71, 3.73–3.74, 3.76
Hong Kong 5.92, 8.43
host State law 5.72
   see also economic development
Hungary
   farming businesses 2.17–2.18
   Oman, BIT with 6.13, 6.36
   UAE, BIT with 6.36
ICSID Convention
   absence of a definition 3.51–3.54
   Additional Facility 2.04 n.3, 6.48
   admission clause 4.58
   alternatives to ICSID 1.18
   arbitration proceedings 3.39, 6.54, 7.48
   automatic enforceability of awards 1.18 n.27
   drafting history 2.30, 3.31–3.34, 3.47–3.50, 3.64, 4.88, 4.103, 5.85, 9.02, 3.32 n.61
   efficiency of dispute settlement system 9.16
   ICSID Convention 2.03
   institutional and procedural framework 1.04
   jurisdiction, outer limits of 3.34
   language of 4.56
   legal bases of arbitration proceedings 1.04–1.05
   legislative history 2.30
   modifications of 3.70
   object and purpose 2.28
   Preamble 4.46, 4.60, 4.104, 7.36
   preparatory work 2.30
   scope of application 1.04, 4.58
   statistics 2.05–2.06
   travaux préparatoires 2.30, 3.32, 3.34 n.68, 9.04
ICSID Secretary General 2.19–2.20
ICSID tribunals
   consent instruments 2.04–2.09
   ICSID Convention 2.03
   ICSID tribunals, decisions rendered by 6.54–6.65
   jurisdiction of 2.02–2.09
   non-ICSID tribunals, decisions rendered by 6.44–6.53
illegal conduct 5.81
illegality-based defence 5.77
immigration, illegal 5.76

implied meaning 3.17, 3.58, 6.42, 9.01 n.1
   see also objective approach

incorporation mechanisms 3.78
independent requirements 3.01–3.88, 4.01, 9.01 n.1
   absence of a definition under ICSID 3.51–3.54
   arbitral case law 3.18–3.62
   assessment 3.77–3.88
   background to 3.01
   broad support 3.63–3.70
   case law and scholarship 3.35–3.38
   conceptual framework 3.02–3.17
   Convention's drafting history 3.47–3.50
   critical analysis 3.06–3.13
   double-keyhole approach 3.05, 3.10–3.13
   drafting history of ICSID Convention 3.31–3.34
   effectiveness principle 3.25–3.30
   ICSID Art 25 does not lay down requirements 3.44–3.54
   implications 3.39–3.43
   implied/independent meaning 3.14–3.15
   inconclusive decisions 3.18–3.20
   independent legal test, concept of 9.01
   justifications 3.25–3.38, 3.47–3.54
   limited support 3.71–3.76
   objective approach 3.06–3.09, 3.77–3.83
   objective meaning 3.02–3.04
   overview 3.21–3.24, 3.44–3.46
   prevailing conceptualization 3.02–3.05
   requirements for the existence of an investment 3.21–3.43
   scholarly opinions 3.63–3.76
   silent decisions 3.18–3.20
   subjective approach 3.06–3.09, 3.84–3.88
   terminology 3.16–3.17
   typical-characteristics approach 3.55–3.62
India
   Brazil, BIT with 6.32
indirect ownership
   recognition of 5.32
Indonesia
   Law Concerning Investment 7.25
instrument of consent *see* consent instrument
intellectual property (IP) rights 5.13, 8.19
intent of the parties 3.06
International Chamber of Commerce (ICC) 6.54, 6.56, 8.58–8.59, 8.61–8.62, 2.04 n.3
International Court of Justice (ICJ) 5.35
international investment agreements (IIAs) 5.10, 5.32, 7.04 n.5

internationalization 2.41–2.42
interpretive issues 2.22
　see also Vienna Convention on the Law of
　　Treaties (VCLT)
　investor-investment relationships 2.26
　supplementary means of interpretation 2.30
investment
　asset-based definitions of 2.49
　asset(s), purchase of 2.35–2.37
　bankers 2.39
　banking 2.39
　broad definitions 2.55–2.56, 3.41
　characteristics of 1.09, 1.13, 4.14
　commitment of capital or other resources 4.14
　concept of. 1.07–1.08
　contracts 2.04, 2.05, 9.02
　definitions of 1.03 n.8, 1.06–1.07, 1.11, 1.13–1.14,
　　1.19, 2.08 n.10, 2.16 n.21, 3.07, 3.11–3.13, 3.18
　　n.22, 3.56 n.115, 3.60 n.135, 3.72 n.155, 3.74
　　n.159, 3.74 n.161, 4.46 n.104, 7.14 n.31
　disputes, definition of 1.02 n.4, 2.07 n.7
　elements of 2.10
　existence of 2.02, 2.03, 2.10, 4.23
　failed/unsuccessful 4.47, 4.103
　financial value 5.51 n.83, 6.27 n.51
　habitual characteristics of 3.61
　hallmarks of 3.31 n.55, 3.57 n.121, 4.13 n.27
　'in kind' 7.47 n.46
　independent meaning 3.37 n.77
　laws 1.05, 2.04, 2.05, 7.01–7.54
　'meaning' of 1.10
　money or capital 2.35, 2.37
　nature of 1.15, 1.16, 9.16
　objective meaning 2.28 n.42, 3.03 n.2, 3.36 n.71,
　　3.37 n.76, 3.41–3.43, 3.72 n.153, 6.42–6.43,
　　6.52, 6.60 n.137, 6.65, 6.66, 9.01 n.1, 9.08, 9.14
　ordinary meaning 2.01, 2.33–2.38, 3.68, 4.52
　　n.119, 4.63, 6.18, 6.52, 6.66, 9.11
　Oxford English Dictionary
　　definitions 2.34–2.38
　profit, pursuit of 2.35–2.36
　project, definition of 7.24
　scope of 7.05 n.5
　senses, categories of 2.34
　'special' meaning 6.60 n.137
　test for 3.72 n.155
　trade-related transactions 2.28 n.43
　types of 2.28
　validity of 2.25
　value of 2.12, 2.39
investment treaties 1.05, 2.04, 2.05
　importance of 2.05–2.06
　joint interpretative declarations 2.62
　scope of application 2.23

Investor-State Dispute Settlement (ISDS) 5.70
　decisions, inconsistency of 2.62
　investment treaties 2.08
　offers of consent 2.04
　unpredictability 2.62
Iraq
　Investment Law 7.39–7.40
Israel
　Czech Republic, BIT with 4.55
　UAE, BIT with 5.88
Italy 2.25
　Argentina, BIT with 8.29
　Bangladesh, BIT with 8.60
　Morocco, BIT with 2.25, 8.08

Japan
　Georgia, BIT with 5.05, 6.13
joint ventures 2.44, 7.47 n.46
jurisdictional objection 2.14–2.16
　claims manifestly without legal merit 2.15
　ordinary 2.14
　right to file 2.15
jurisdictional requirements 9.02–9.03

Kazakhstan
　Uzbekistan, BIT with 5.21, 5.39, 5.89, 5.95
Kenyan Republic 5.83
Kyrgyzstan 7.08
　Austria, BIT with 5.06, 6.08
　Law on Investments 7.08 n.18

legality (lawfulness) of investment 1.12, 2.24–
　2.25, 4.10, 5.02, 5.67–5.85, 9.03, 9.09
　admissions clauses 5.71 n.121
　applicable law 5.72–5.73
　background to 5.01–5.02
　beyond investment treaties 5.82–5.85
　domestic law, relevant rules of 5.74–5.77
　investment treaty provisions 5.67–5.71
　meaning of 5.72–5.81
　principle of 4.55
　seriousness threshold 5.78–5.79
　State conduct, relevance of 5.80–5.81
licensing agreements 2.42
Lithuania
　Ukraine, BIT with 5.67
loans 5.50, 8.38–8.49
　see also debt instruments
　'as such' 8.38–8.41
　connected to other investments 8.42–8.46
　granted to a State or State entity 8.47–8.49
localization 5.45–5.49, 8.53
　see also territoriality
lump sum agreements 4.51

macroeconomics
  see also economics
  consumption 2.40
  principles 2.40–2.41
  trade-related transactions 2.40
Madagascar 7.09
Malaysia 8.43
  Belgo-Luxembourg Economic Union, BIT with 3.54
  economic development of 4.28 n.61
  territorial waters 4.23, 4.28–4.29, 8.15
Mali
  Investment Code 7.10, 7.32
Malik, Mahnaz 5.10
Manciaux, Sébastien 3.67, 4.96–4.97, 4.99, 4.102, 8.21–8.22
'manifestly outside the jurisdiction of the Centre' 2.19–2.20
'manifestly without legal merit' 2.15, 2.20
Mauritius 6.51
  France, BIT with 2.28 n.42, 6.51, 6.70
minimum wage legislation 5.76
Moldova
  Law on Investments 7.02 n.1, 7.03 n.4, 7.10, 7.15, 7.17, 7.19, 7.22, 7.27
Mongolia
  Canada, BIT with 6.08, 6.11
Montenegrin Foreign Investment Law 7.43 n.71
Morocco 2.25
  Italy, BIT with 2.25, 8.08
  Nigeria, BIT with 5.05, 6.06, 6.09, 6.31–6.32, 6.39, 8.28
  state-owned enterprises 4.07
Mozambique 4.70–4.71
multilateral investment courts 2.62
multilateral investment treaties 7.02
multinational enterprises (MNEs) 2.41
Myanmar 7.08
  Investment Law 7.08 n.17

Namibia
  Investment Promotion Act 7.03 n.4, 7.12, 7.17, 7.22
natural resources 4.47
Netherlands
  Argentina, BIT with 5.68
  Paraguay, BIT with 4.68
  Turkey, BIT with 5.20, 5.26, 5.41, 5.69
  Venezuela, BIT with 4.03–4.04
  Yugoslavia, BIT with 7.43 n.71, 8.44
New Zealand
  UK, BIT with 6.13

Nigeria
  Investment Promotion Commission Act 7.13, 7.18
  Morocco, BIT with 5.05, 6.06, 6.09, 6.31–6.32, 6.39, 8.28

objective approach 1.10 n.19, 3.77–3.83, 6.42–6.70, 9.01–9.02
  assessment 6.66–6.70
  decisions rendered by ICSID tribunals 6.54–6.65
  decisions rendered by non-ICSID tribunals 6.44–6.53
  independent requirements 3.01, 3.16, 3.19–3.20, 3.21–3.24, 3.38, 3.45, 3.49, 3.56, 3.62, 3.64, 3.86
  meaning of investment 4.01, 4.37 n.77
  overview 6.42–6.43
  subjective approach compared 3.06–3.09
  treaty practice 6.55, 6.65 n.150, 6.69
Occidental Exploration and Production Company (OEPC) 5.24, 5.27
OECD see Organisation for Economic Cooperation and Development (OECD)
Oman
  Hungary, BIT with 6.13, 6.36
ordinary commercial transactions 4.04, 4.88, 4.91
Organisation for Economic Cooperation and Development (OECD) 2.43
  benchmark definition 6.32
ownership 1.12, 5.02, 5.18–5.37, 9.09
  see also control
  beneficial vs legal 5.25 n.48
  direct 5.22–5.28
  indirect 5.29–5.33, 9.09
  nominal 5.28 n.53
  overview 5.18–5.21
  passive 5.93
  shared vs full 2.44

Pahis, Stratos 2.40, 3.66
Pakistan 8.10 n.13, 3.46
  Australia, BIT with 3.18 n.22, 5.34
  Turkey, BIT with 8.08, 8.71
Palestine 7.17
Papua New Guinea
  Investment Promotion Act 7.08
Paraguay
  imports, pre-shipment inspection of 4.68–4.69, 5.55
  Netherlands, BIT with 4.68
  Switzerland, BIT with 4.69, 8.13
Parra, Antonio R. 3.65

performance of services 4.63
permissibility test 2.60, 4.01, 4.65–4.77, 9.13
   assessment 4.72–4.77
   meaning and recognition 4.65–4.71
   unworkability of 4.77
Philippines 5.52–5.53
   Foreign Investment Act 7.12, 7.20
   Switzerland, BIT with 3.45, 5.88
portfolio investment 2.43, 4.63, 5.16, 6.02, 6.38, 7.03, 8.16, 9.07, 5.22 n.38
   exclusions 6.30–6.35
predictability 2.59–2.63
   see also uniformity
procedural settings 2.01, 2.13–2.20
   ex officio examination of jurisdiction 2.17–2.18
   jurisdictional objections 2.14–2.16
profit
   expectation of gain or 6.18, 6.24
   lost 7.48
   objective of making 6.18
   profitability 4.52
   pursuit of 2.35–2.36, 3.56, 5.03, 6.18
   realization of 6.18
   return and, regularity of 4.08, 4.10, 4.50–4.54, 4.60, 4.83 n.177, 6.18, 9.03
project-based definitions 7.24–7.31
   see also activity-based definitions
promissory notes 4.03–4.04, 4.24, 5.22, 5.50, 5.57, 5.61
property rights 5.13, 6.11
   see also intellectual property (IP) rights
   moveable and immoveable property 5.46, 6.11
protected investment, concept of 4.55 n.125
public debt operations 6.39, 8.28
   see also sovereign debt instruments
pure commercial transactions 2.16

referral mechanisms 3.78
Report of the Executive Directors 3.34, 3.49–3.50, 4.80
rights conferred by law or contract, definition of 2.26 n.37
risk
   commercial vs investment 9.03
   concept of 4.31
   existence of 3.56
   investment 4.100, 8.40
   long-term contracts 8.11
   loss or destruction of goods 8.19
   non-payment 8.19
   operational, definition of 4.19 n.37, 8.37
   passing of 8.19

raw materials, increase in price of 8.19
Salini test 1.09, 2.28, 2.50, 2.60 n.86, 4.01, 4.99–4.100, 6.16, 6.66, 8.11, 8.14, 8.19, 8.22 n.41, 8.44, 8.49, 9.03, 9.08
   sovereign 8.34
Rubins, Noah 2.48, 3.65, 4.98
Russian Federation
   Ethiopia, BIT with 5.68
   Federal Law on Foreign Investment 7.26, 8.68
Rwanda
   US, BIT with 6.13

sale of goods contracts 2.40, 4.36, 4.88, 8.04, 8.19
Salini test 1.10, 1.13, 1.15, 2.50, 2.60, 3.24, 3.55, 3.58–3.59, 3.63, 4.01, 4.02–4.38, 8.04, 9.03
   applicability of 2.60
   asset-based definitions 5.04
   commercial-transaction test compared 4.78, 4.84, 4.87, 4.88, 4.92
   contributions 1.09, 2.28, 2.50, 2.60 n.86, 4.01, 4.14–4.23, 5.100, 6.16, 6.66, 7.33, 8.14, 8.19, 8.44, 8.69, 8.72, 9.03, 9.08, 9.11
   criteria 3.72, 3.75–3.76, 4.01, 4.45, 4.96–4.101, 6.53, 6.66, 8.02, 8.09–8.10, 8.19, 8.51, 8.61, 9.04–9.08
   direct ownership 5.22
   evolution 4.10
   global examination of 4.13
   history 4.02–4.09
   indicators 4.40 n.87
   investment treaties, recent developments 6.02–6.03
   localization of assets 5.49
   mandatory 9.13
   minimum duration 1.09, 2.28, 2.50, 2.60 n.86, 4.01, 4.24–4.30, 6.21, 6.66, 8.10, 8.14, 8.17, 8.19, 8.44, 9.03, 9.08
   nature 4.11–4.13, 4.93–4.95, 9.03
   objective criteria 2.58, 2.60
   optional 9.13
   permissibility test compared 4.71–4.73
   rights under services contracts 5.56
   risk 1.09, 2.28, 2.50, 2.60 n.86, 4.01, 4.31–4.38, 4.99–4.100, 6.16, 6.66, 8.11, 8.14, 8.19, 8.22 n.41, 8.44, 8.49, 9.03, 9.08
   sovereign bonds 8.32
   treaty practice 6.20–6.22, 6.29
salvage operations 3.31, 4.23, 4.28–4.29
Saudi Arabia
   BITs 3.18 n.25
   Foreign Investment Law 7.28
   France, BIT with 3.18 n.25
Schill, Stephan W. 3.46, 3.64, 5.85

Schreuer, Christoph 2.19, 3.46, 3.64, 4.06, 4.42, 4.51, 4.59, 5.85, 9.04
Secretary General of ICSID 2.13
seriousness threshold 5.78–5.79
service contracts 8.13–8.15
  critical assessment 8.16–8.22
  host State/host State entities 8.04–8.22
  overview 8.04–8.06
shareholders 5.36–5.37
  minority shareholding 5.36
Sierra Leone
  Investment Promotion Act 7.20
Sinclair, Anthony 3.46, 3.64, 5.85
Slovakia 8.45–8.46
  economic development of 3.56, 4.85
  Greece, BIT with 3.19, 8.30, 8.39
social growth 7.40
South Africa
  Protection of Investment Act 7.12
sovereign bonds 4.18, 5.16, 5.50, 5.57, 6.40, 8.27–8.37
  see also debt instruments
  Art 25 ICSID 8.32–8.37
  contained in investment treaties and laws 8.27–8.31
sovereign debt instruments 6.02, 8.25, 8.48, 9.07, 9.11
  treaty exclusion of 6.39–6.41
sovereign equality of states 4.104
sovereign risk 8.34
Spain
  El Salvador, BIT with 2.06
  Venezuela, BIT with 1.03 n.7, 5.89, 5.94
Sri Lanka 4.30, 5.63, 6.63–6.64
  Germany, BIT with 8.14
  UK, BIT with 1.03 n.5, 6.63
subjective approach 1.10 n.19, 2.60, 3.84–3.88
  independent requirements 3.01, 3.03–3.04, 3.16, 3.19, 3.22–3.23, 3.44, 3.46, 3.49, 3.50, 3.51, 3.69–3.70, 3.80, 3.82–3.83
  objections to 9.02
  objective approach compared 3.06–3.09
  Salini test 4.48, 4.71
  treaty practice 6.55, 6.65 n.150
subsequent agreements 3.69
subsequent practice 2.29 n.47
substantial interest, concept of 5.34
summary dismissal procedures 2.20
Switzerland
  Paraguay, BIT with 4.69, 8.13
  Philippines, BIT with 3.45, 5.88
  Uzbekistan, Bit with 1.03 n.5, 6.44–6.47, 6.70
Syrian Arab Republic
  Investment Promotion Law 7.13, 7.18

Tanzania 5.92, 8.43, 8.07 n.7
  UK, BIT with 1.03 n.7, 5.90, 5.92–5.93, 8.43
taxation
  fraud 5.76
  stabilization clauses 2.11
telecommunications 5.23
territoriality 1.12, 3.45, 5.02, 5.38–5.66, 8.53, 9.09
  case law 5.50–5.66
  debt instruments 5.57–5.66
  localization of different categories of assets 5.45–5.49
  service contracts, rights under 5.51–5.56
  treaty practice 5.38–5.44
traditional model 5.03–5.17
  see also asset-based definitions; broad definitions
Turkey
  Cambodia, BIT with 6.31, 6.33, 6.35, 6.37
  Netherlands, BIT with 5.20, 5.26, 5.41, 5.69
  Pakistan, BIT with 8.08, 8.71
  US, BIT with 1.03 n.5, 3.18 n.20
Turkmenistan 4.70
  Law on Investment Activities 7.39
  UK, BIT with 8.08
typical-characteristics approach 2.60, 3.01, 3.24, 3.50, 3.55–3.62, 4.62, 4.93–4.94, 3.57 n.120
  hallmarks of investment 3.57
  problems with 3.62

Ukraine
  Germany, BIT with 1.03 n.6, 5.42–5.44, 6.54, 8.56
  Lithuania, BIT with 5.67
  seriousness threshold 5.79
  state-owned entities 2.16, 4.86, 6.54–6.55, 8.56–8.58
  US, BIT with 2.16
UNCITRAL see United Nations Commission on International Trade Law (UNCITRAL)
UNCTAD investment treaty database 2.08, 5.08, 5.09, 5.10, 5.35, 6.04, 6.07, 6.15, 6.30
uniformity 2.63, 3.88, 4.62
  see also predictability
United Arab Emirates (UAE)
  Brazil, BIT with 6.33
  Hungary, BIT with 6.36
  Israel, BIT with 5.88
United Kingdom (UK)
  Colombia, BIT with 5.19, 5.30, 5.39, 6.25, 6.39, 8.28
  Egypt, BIT with 1.03 n.5
  English law 5.83

United Kingdom (UK) (*cont.*)
  Model BIT 2.56, 5.12, 5.13, 5.16, 5.19, 5.51 n.83, 8.48 n.100
  New Zealand, BIT with 6.13
  Sri Lanka, BIT with 1.03 n.5, 6.63
  Tanzania, BIT with 1.03 n.7, 5.90, 5.92–5.93, 8.43
  Turkmenistan, BIT with 8.08
  Venezuela, BIT with 2.02
United Nations Charter 4.104
United Nations Commission on International Trade Law (UNCITRAL) 2.04 n.3, 2.62, 6.44, 6.51
United States (US)
  Argentina, BIT with 5.19, 5.30, 5.39
  Congolese Republic, BIT with 2.52
  Ecuador, BIT with 5.30
  Model BIT 1.02 n.4, 1.11 n.20, 2.56, 4.14, 5.40, 6.12, 6.19–6.21, 8.06
  Oman, FTA with 3.18 n.21
  Republic of Zaïre, BIT with 1.03 n.5
  Rwanda, BIT with 6.13
  Senate reports 4.98
  Turkey, BIT with 1.03 n.5, 3.18 n.20
  Ukraine, BIT with 2.16
  Uruguay, BIT with 6.13–6.14
unlawful acts 5.31 n.58
unlawful conduct 4.58, 5.76, 5.80
Uruguay
  US, BIT with 6.13–6.14
Uzbekistan 6.44–6.47
  Kazakhstan, BIT with 5.21, 5.39, 5.89, 5.95

Law on Investments and Investment Activity 1.02 n.4, 7.09, 7.27, 7.30
state entities 8.63
Switzerland, BIT with 1.03 n.5, 6.44–6.47, 6.70

Vanuatu
  Foreign Investment Promotions Act 7.02 n.1, 7.28
Venezuela
  Canada, BIT with 1.03 n.5, 6.48
  Netherlands, BIT with 4.03–4.04
  promissory notes 4.03–4.04, 4.24, 5.22, 5.61
  Spain, BIT with 1.03 n.7, 5.89, 5.94
  state-owned entities 6.48
  UK, BIT with 2.02
Vienna Convention on the Law of Treaties (VCLT) 2.22, 2.27–2.28, 3.32, 3.68, 3.90, 5.85, 6.46
  supplementary means of interpretation 2.30, 3.32, 3.68 n.146, 6.46 n.83

Waibel, Michael 3.23, 3.65
Washington Convention 4.67, 4.98

Yugoslavia
  Netherlands, BIT with 7.43 n.71, 8.44

Zaïre, Republic of
  US, BIT with 1.03 n.5
Zambia
  Development Agency Act 7.14